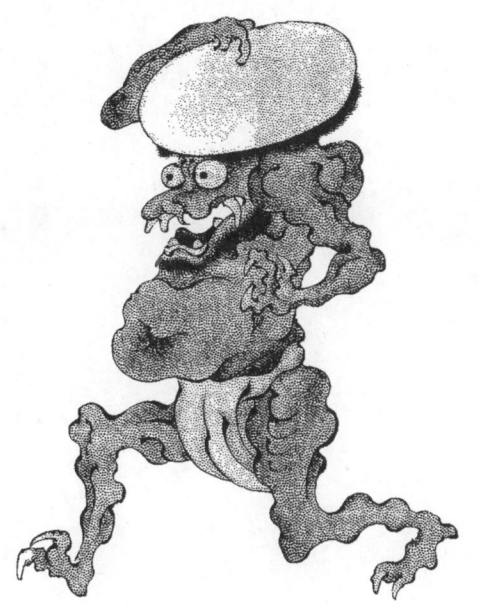

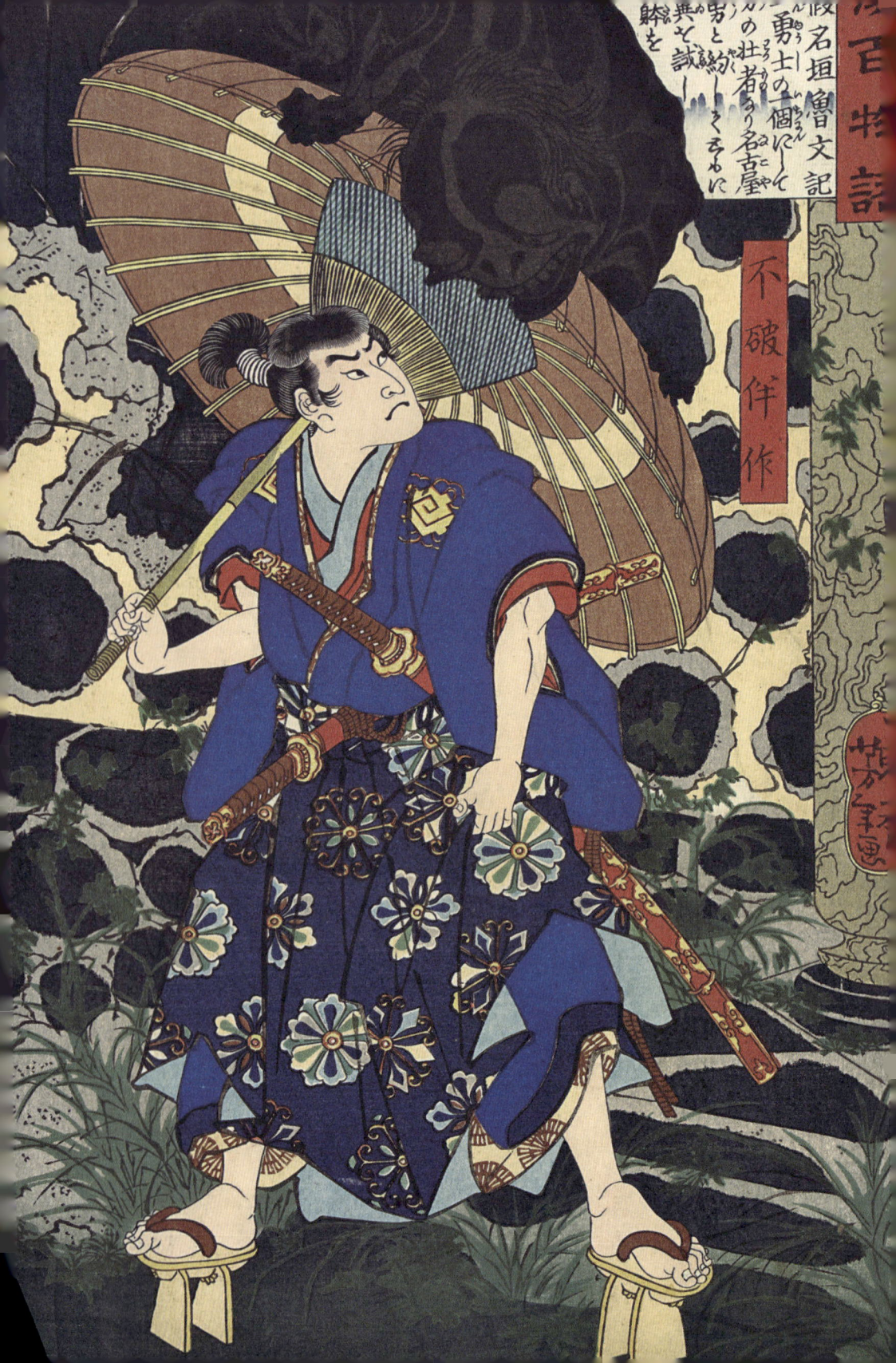

YŌKAI
MONSTERS

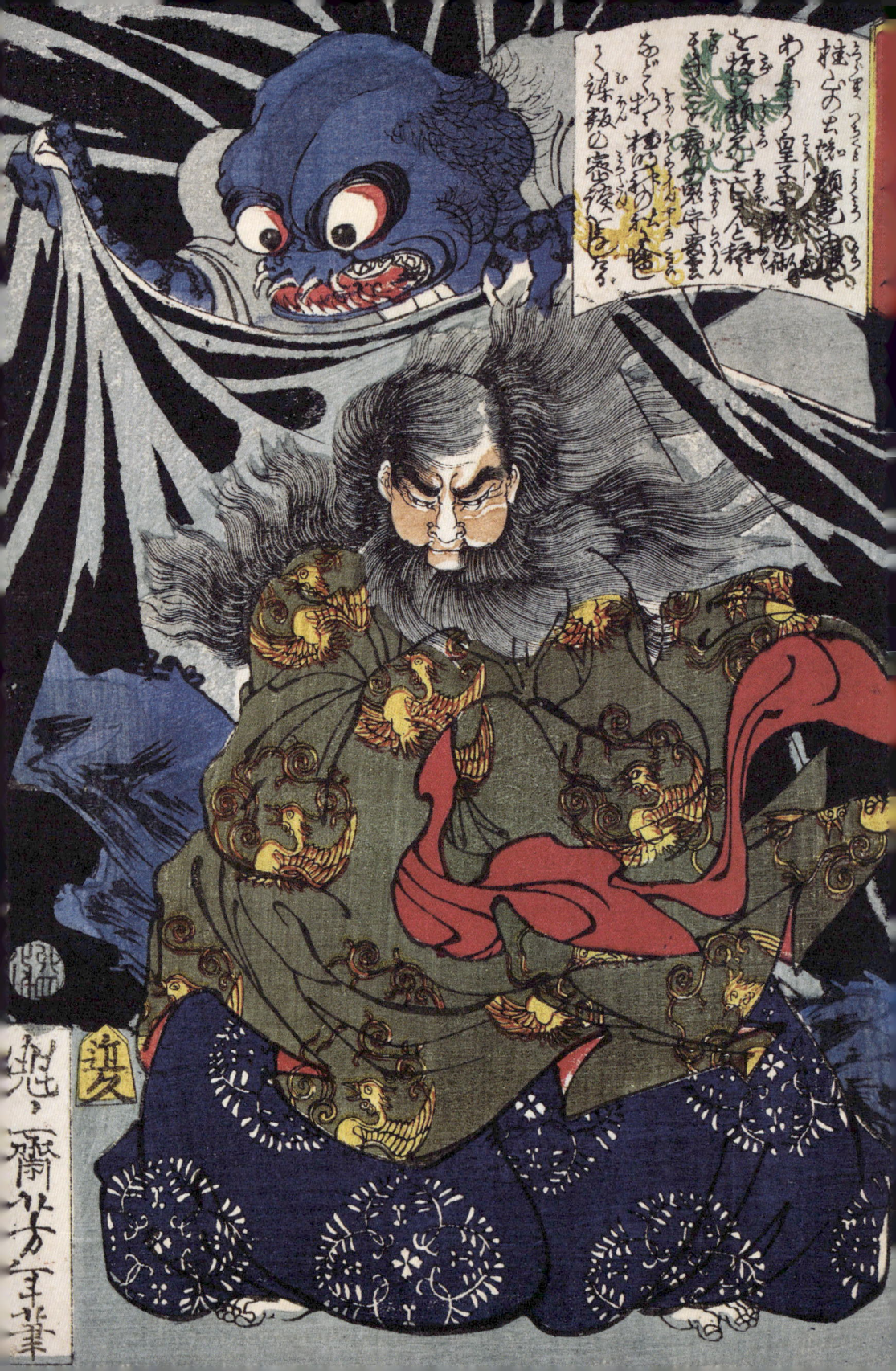

YŌKAI MONSTERS

By the Great Masters of Japanese

Woodblock Printing

PRESTEL

MUNICH · LONDON · NEW YORK

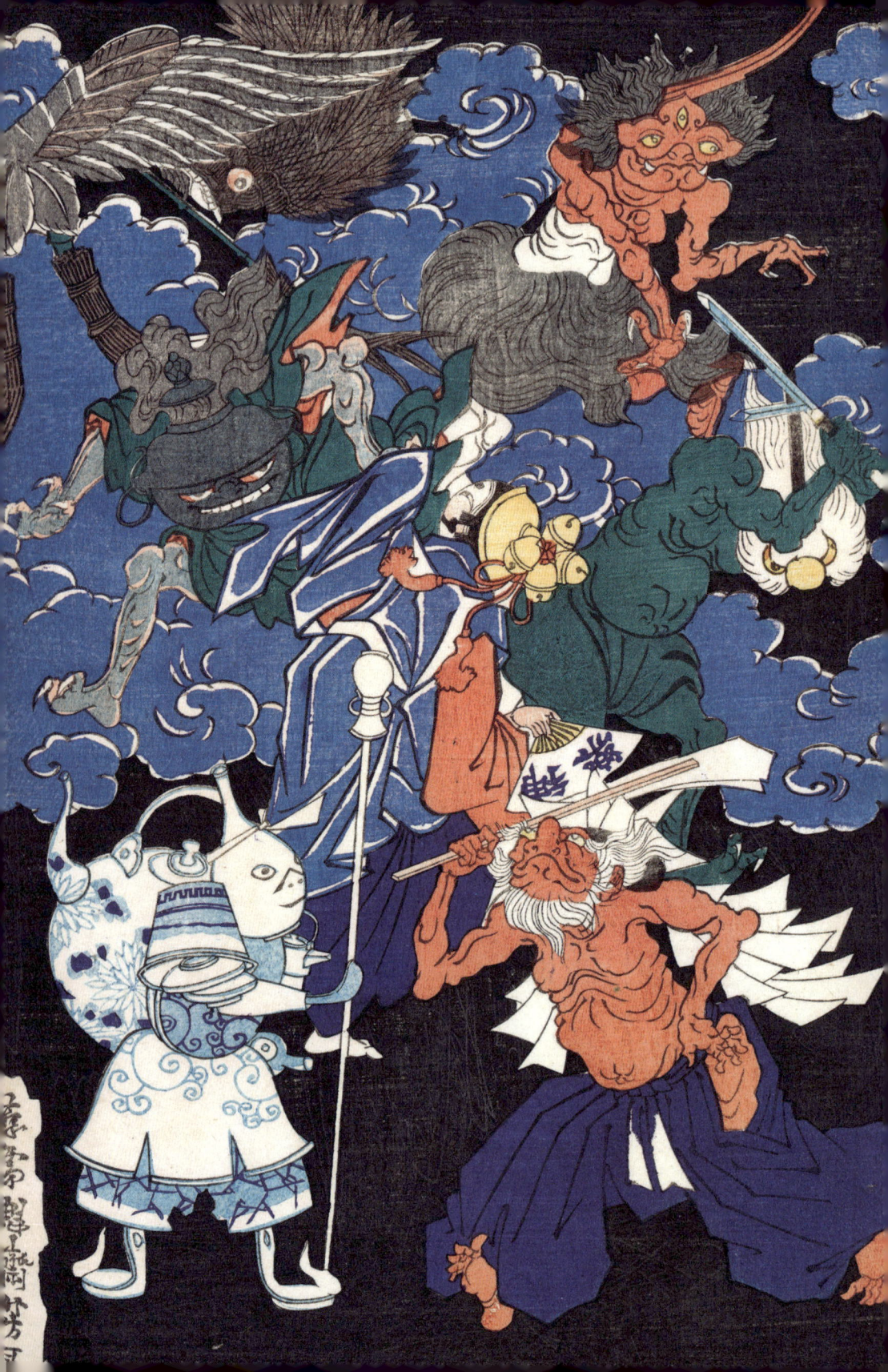

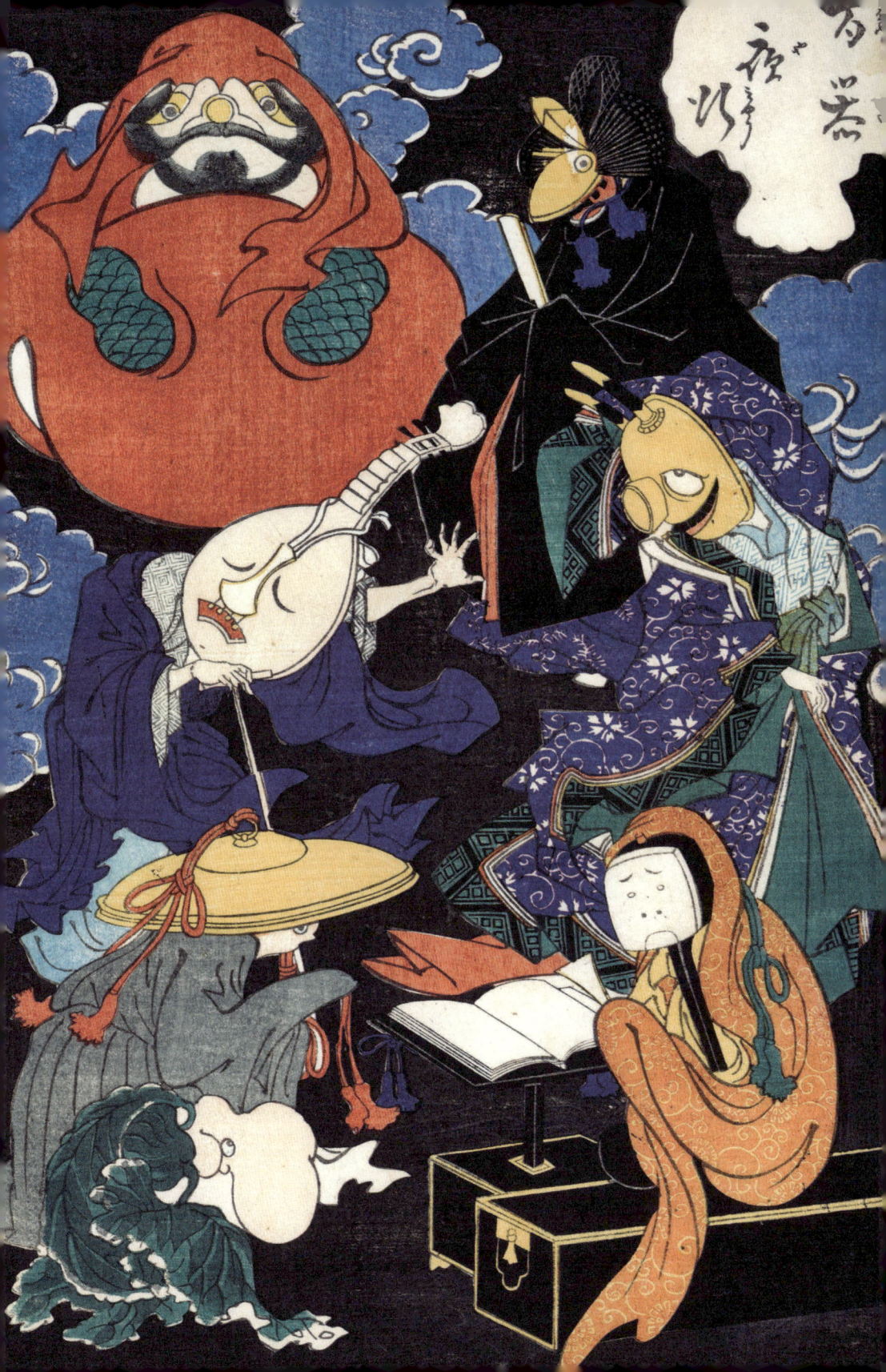

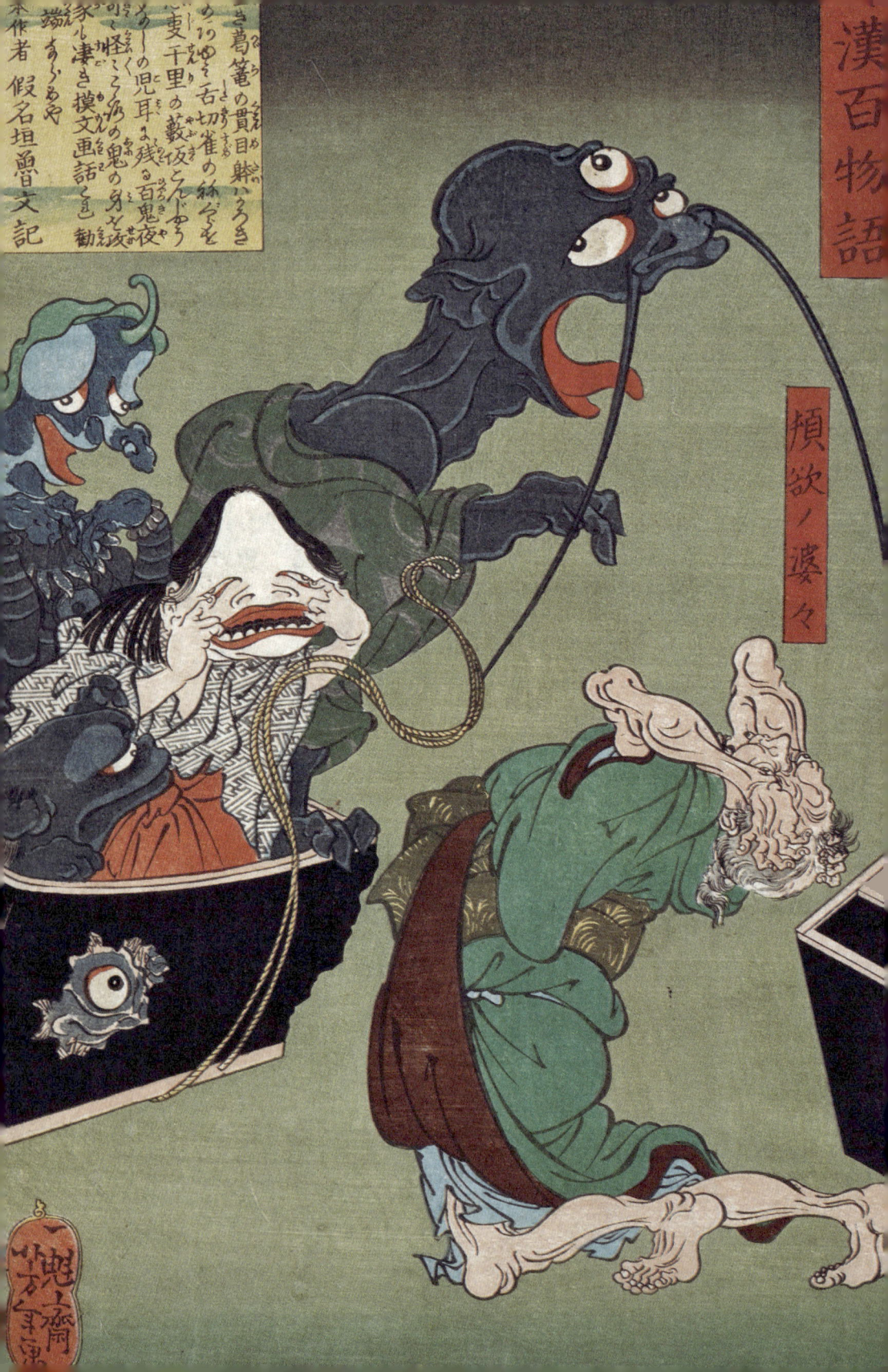

煩欲ノ婆々

き葛篭の貫目躰いろ〳〵
かりそめにも古切雀の縁ぐさを
せて千里の薮〳〵夜とんぢう
めーの児耳ヱ残る百鬼夜
明しふるの鬼の牙と夜
かせろうの鬼の牙と夜
緑ル凄き模文連語の
躰るすあらゆるや

本作者
假名垣魯文記

一蛙上飛開
小芳年畫

Inside cover: Tsukioka Yoshitoshi, *Kiyohime Changes into a Serpent at the Hidaka River*, detail, 1902
Philadelphia Museum of Art
p. 1: Unknown artist, *Nocturnal Procession of the Hundred Demons (Hyakki yagyō)*, detail
Tokyo, National Diet

Library Digital Collections
p. 2: Tsukioka Yoshitoshi, *Fuwa Bansaku*, detail, 1865
Amsterdam, Rijksmuseum
p. 4: Tsukioka Yoshitoshi, *Prince Kurokumo and the Earth Spider*, detail, 1867
Oxford, Ashmolean Museum
pp. 6–7: Tsukioka Yoshito-

shi, *Nocturnal Procession of the Hundred Demons (Hyakki yagyō)*, detail, 1865
United States, Egenolf Gallery
p. 8: Tsukioka Yoshitoshi, *The Story of the Tongue-Cut Sparrow*, detail, 1865
Minneapolis Institute of Art
pp. 10–11: Unknown artist,

The Four Retainers of Raikō and the Monster Candle, ca 1868
Boston, Museum of Fine Arts
p. 12: Unknown artist, *The God Susanoo no Mikoto Killing the Demons*, detail, ca 1868
Boston, Museum of Fine Arts

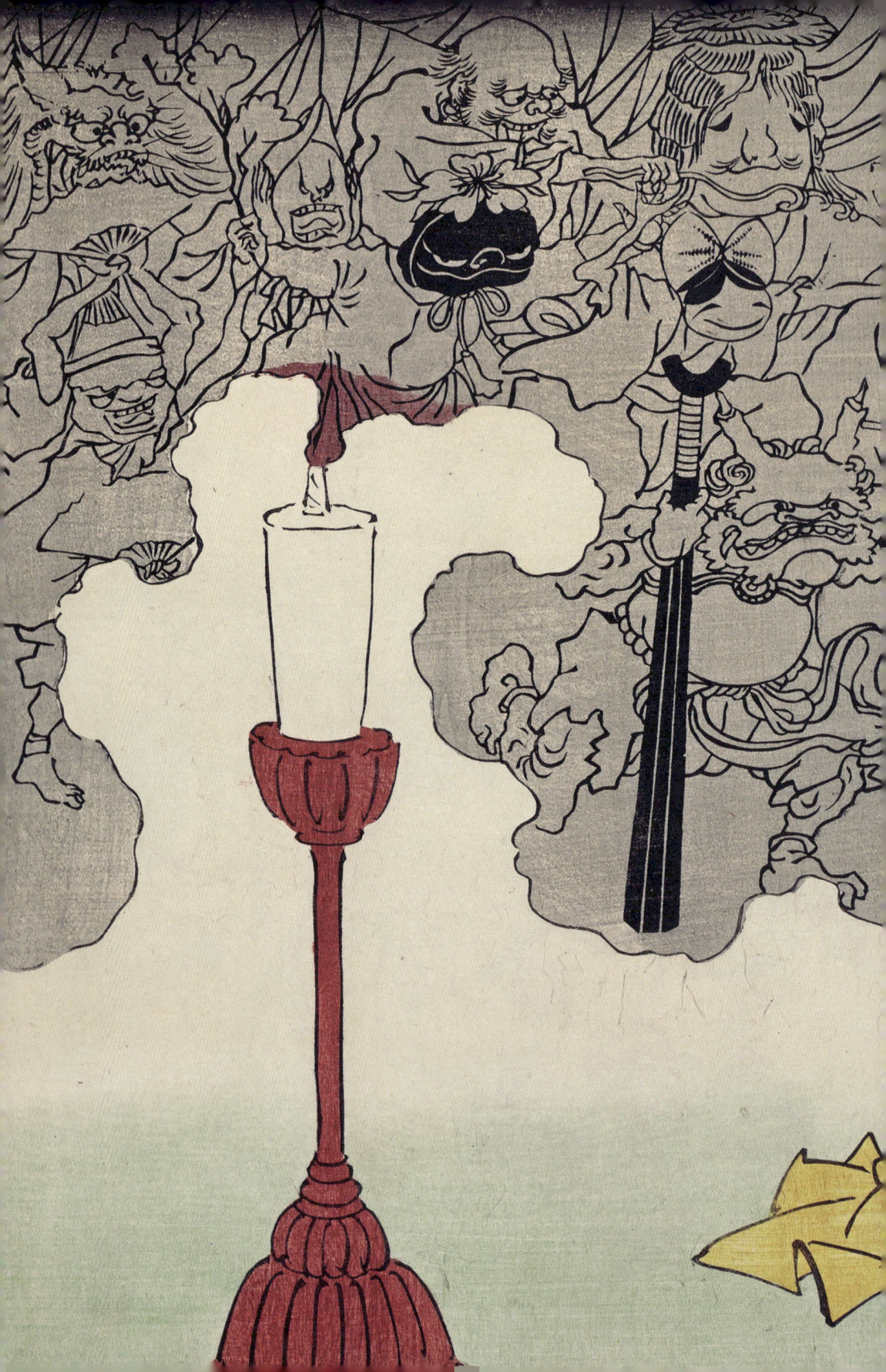

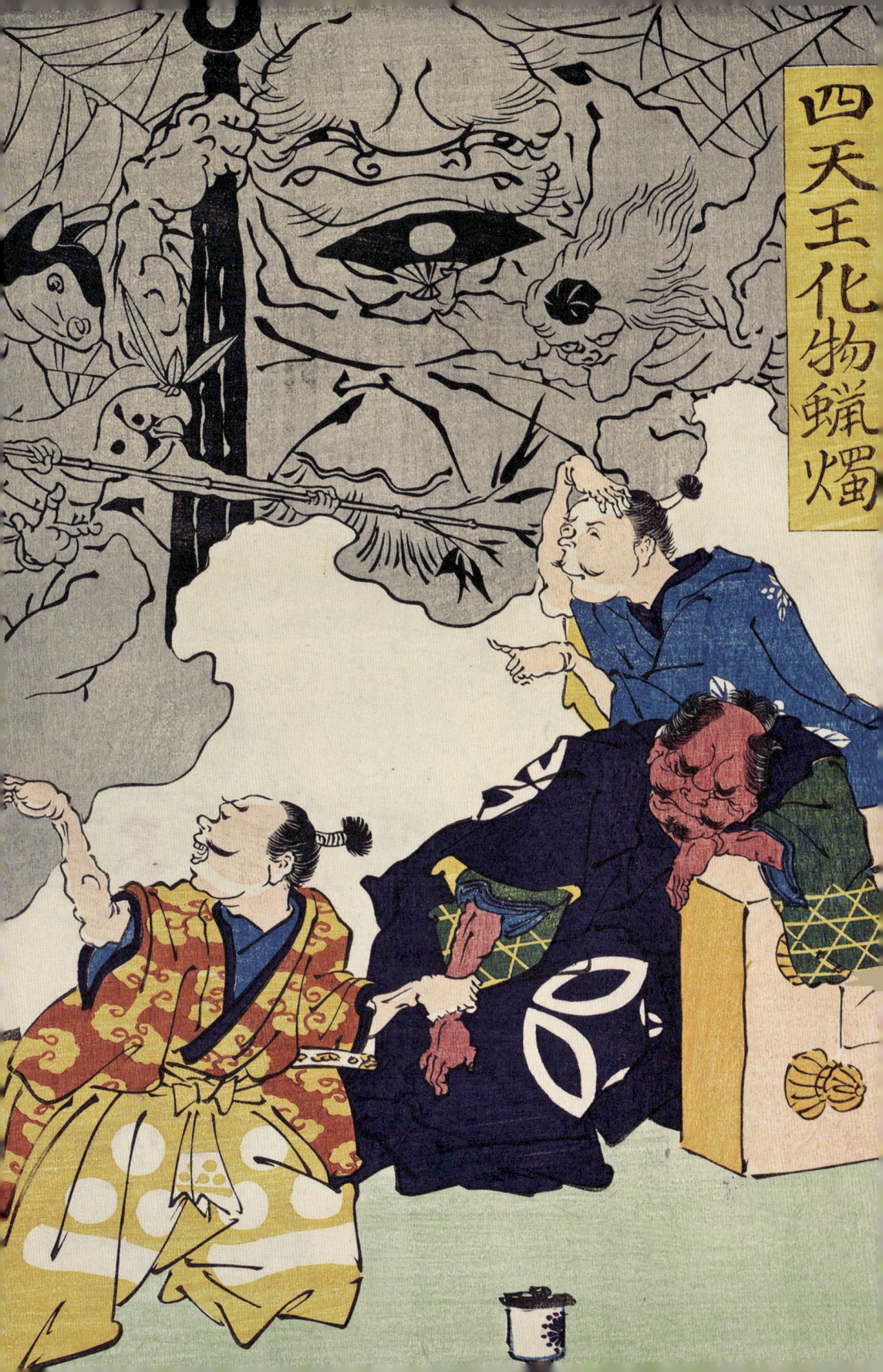

四天王化物蝋燭

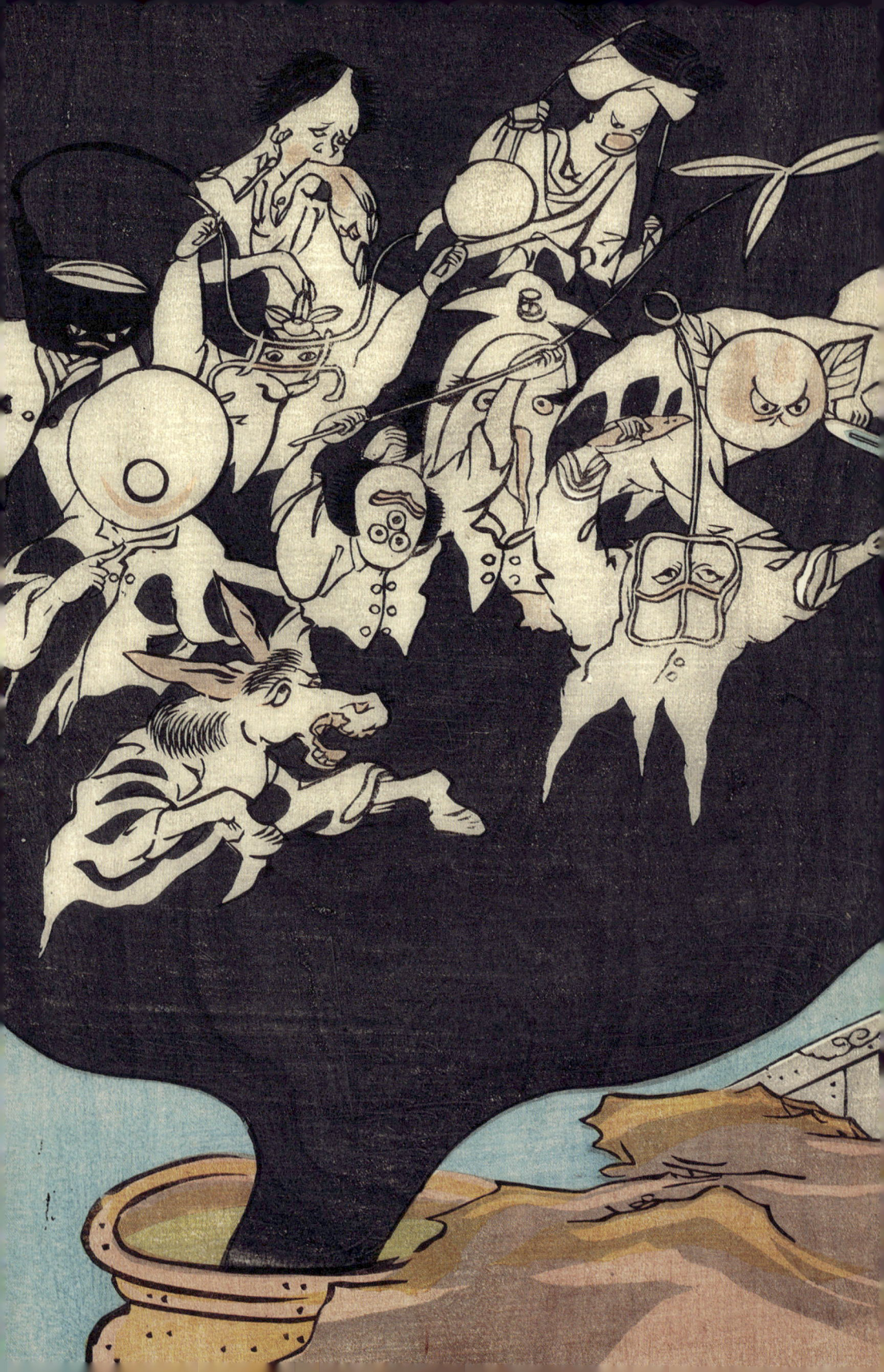

YŌKAI

PHILIPPE CHARLIER

•

Those that we call monsters are not so
to God, who sees in the immensity of His
work the infinite forms that He has com-
prehended therein.

Michel de Montaigne, 'Of a Monstrous Child', *Essays*,
translated by Charles Cotton

The special quality of hell is
to see everything clearly down to
the last detail. And to see all that in
the pitch darkness!

Yukio Mishima, *The Temple of the Golden Pavilion* (1956),
translated by Ivan Morris

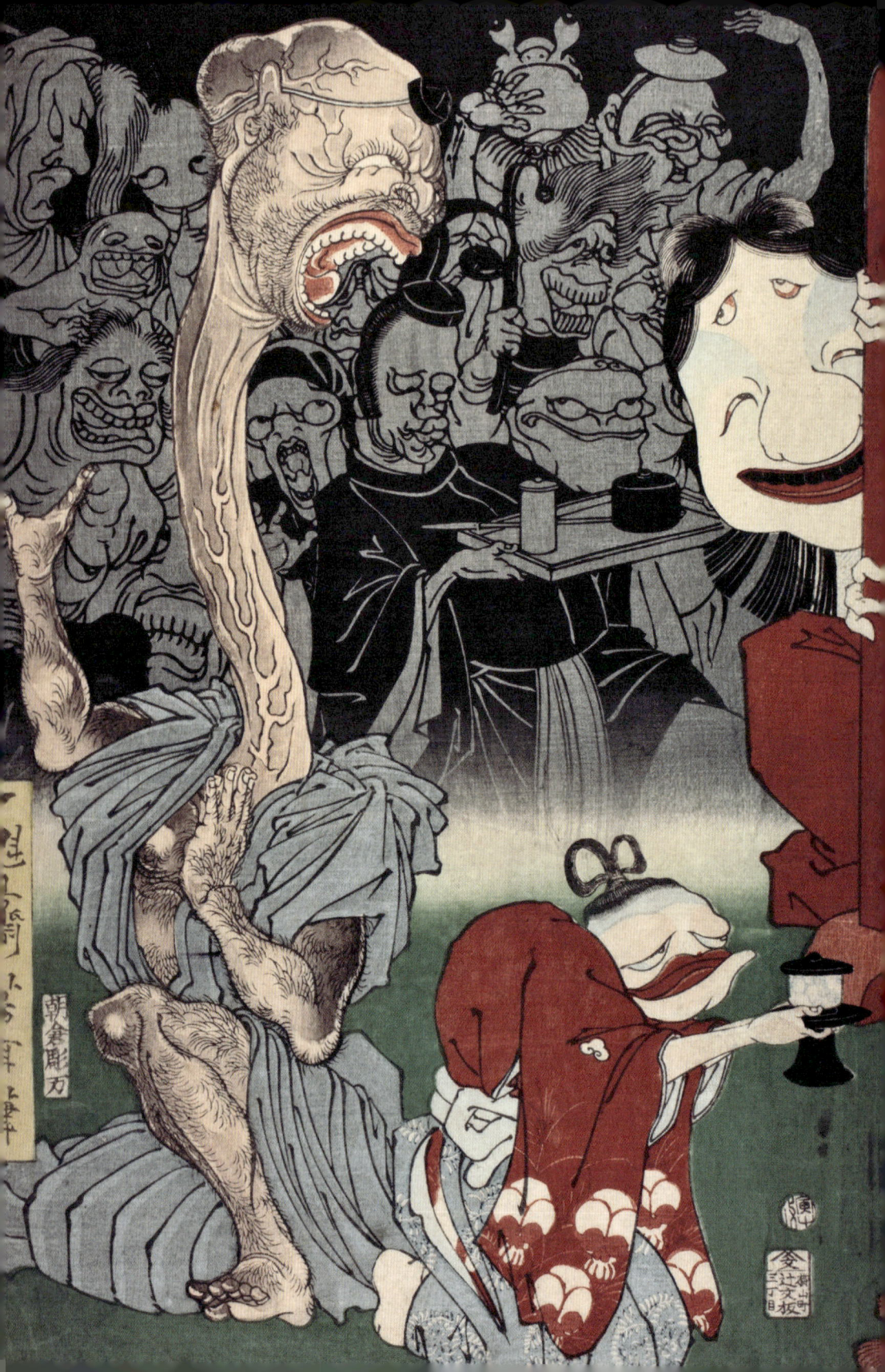

ORIGINS

•

They are cloaked in the colors of our dreams – or rather, our nightmares... It is said that *yōkai*, literally 'mysterious creatures', are materialisations of our fears, of our anxiety vis-à-vis nature, darkness and the unknown. They are anxiety made flesh, and as such can only be monstrous. So it is with the serpent bearing the human head of Bishu, a widow whose jealousy was so great that each night she transformed into a horned serpent with wild hair and a tail shaped like a metal sword, which she used to attack happily married women.

Yōkai are everywhere that fear grips us: forests, wells, dark rooms, castle cellars, temple sheds, isolated pavilions, cemeteries, ceilings, dens. Wherever there is cold sweat, there resides a *yōkai*. But whereas people very quickly move on, *yōkai* end up staying. Like an indelible stain, like a scar that never goes away, the *yōkai* remain in the place where fear was first felt and continue to arouse the same or even greater fear in newcomers, inhabitants or the merely curious who cross their path. The *yōkai* are contagious fear embodied, as fantastical as the human imagination can be – infinite, therefore.

In the beginning, all is blackness, a darkness that arouses fear and insecurity. Recall that in the Edo period (1603–1867), the streets everywhere (except in the pleasure districts) were plunged into complete darkness as soon as the sun set. Only a few beams of light shone from the lanterns of those who dared to venture into the night – an atmosphere conducive to the apparition of supernatural beings, or at least to dreams of their presence. And in the wake of the *yōkai* come epidemics, sudden deaths, crimes, rapes, disappearances, cataclysms and other inexplicable phenomena. Talismans and amulets (*ofuda*) may be used as protection against miasmas and curses, but it is also important not to

15

'tempt fate' by leaving home during the forbidden hours – especially around midnight – or on inauspicious days, of which there are said to be around thirty each year. If evil has already taken hold, only ritual intervention remains: rites of cleansing and purification performed by Shinto or Buddhist exorcists or masters of the Way of Yin and Yang (*onmyōji*).

It is to the proliferation of *ukiyo-e* prints or 'images of the floating world' during the Edo period that we owe the widespread distribution of *yōkai* imagery and perhaps also the exponential increase in their diversity. This period of political change was also a pivotal moment on a metaphysical level: 'In the nineteenth century, the surprising popularity of images celebrating the bizarre and ghostly suggests that the influence of traditional religions [Buddhism and Shinto] was declining in favour of popular beliefs and folk practices' (Guth, 1996, p. 34, translated by David Wharry). Other means of showing *yōkai* were provided by prints depicting warriors (*musha-e*), historic figures from the past battling with monsters springing from the depths of the earth or the night. The leading figure in the creation of these supernatural scenes is Utagawa Kuniyoshi (1797–1861), followed by his disciples Utagawa Yoshitsuya (1822–1866) and Tsukioka Yoshitoshi (1839–1892), to whom we owe some of the most beautiful and haunting masterpieces of this singular artistic genre.

At the same time, members of the cultural and literary elite organised *hyakumonogatari kaidankai* – literally 'gatherings of one hundred supernatural tales' – during which eerie stories were recounted one by one. After each tale, one of the hundred candles burning on the floor was extinguished, gradually plunging the room into darkness. As the light faded, it was believed that the *yōkai* slipped out from the scrolls on which they were painted or emerged from a mirror placed on the floor. In this charged atmosphere, ghosts (*yūrei*) and other supernatural beings could materialise at will – sometimes to the peril of those present. For summoning spirits has never been without risk.

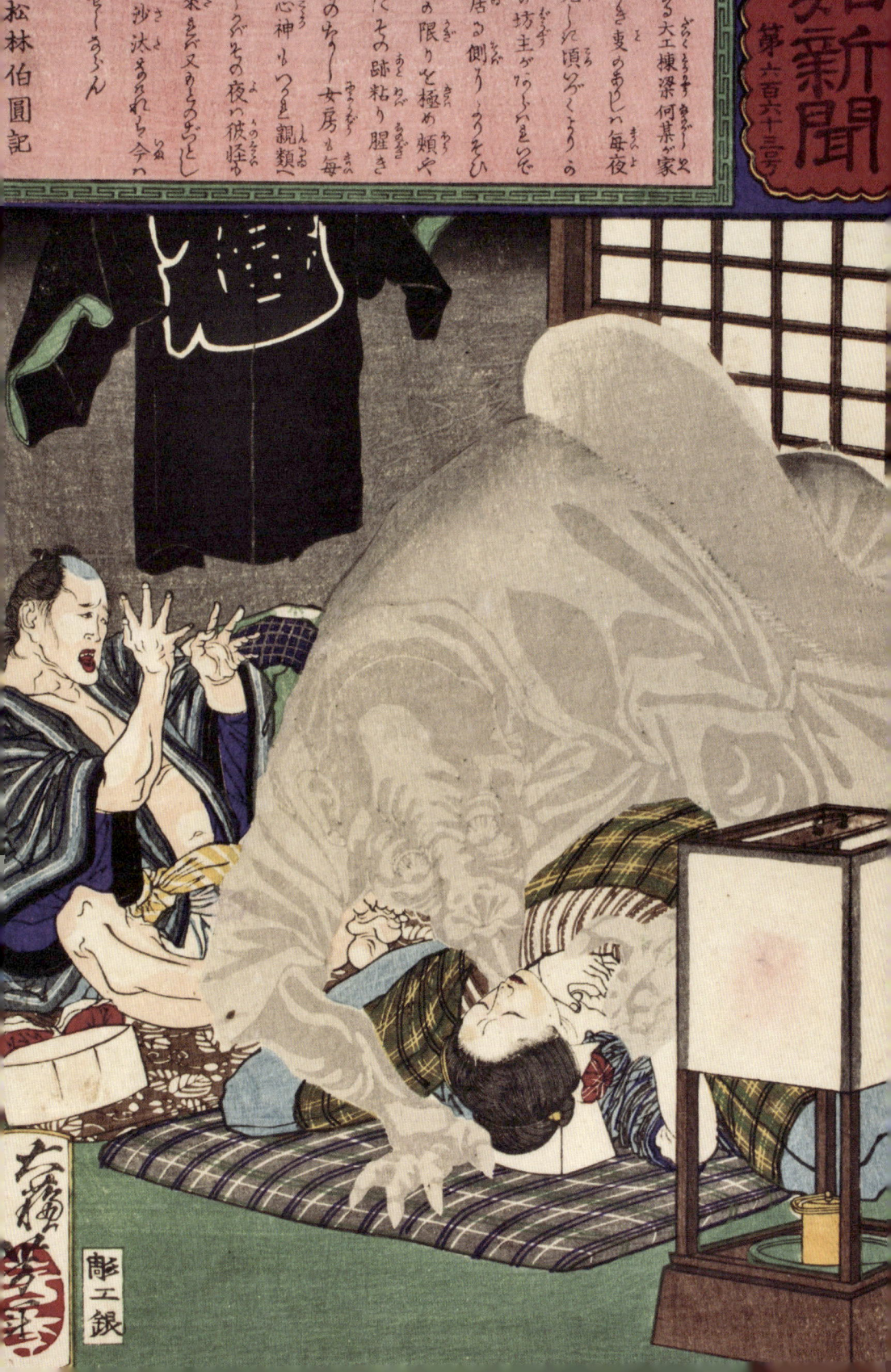

松林伯圓記

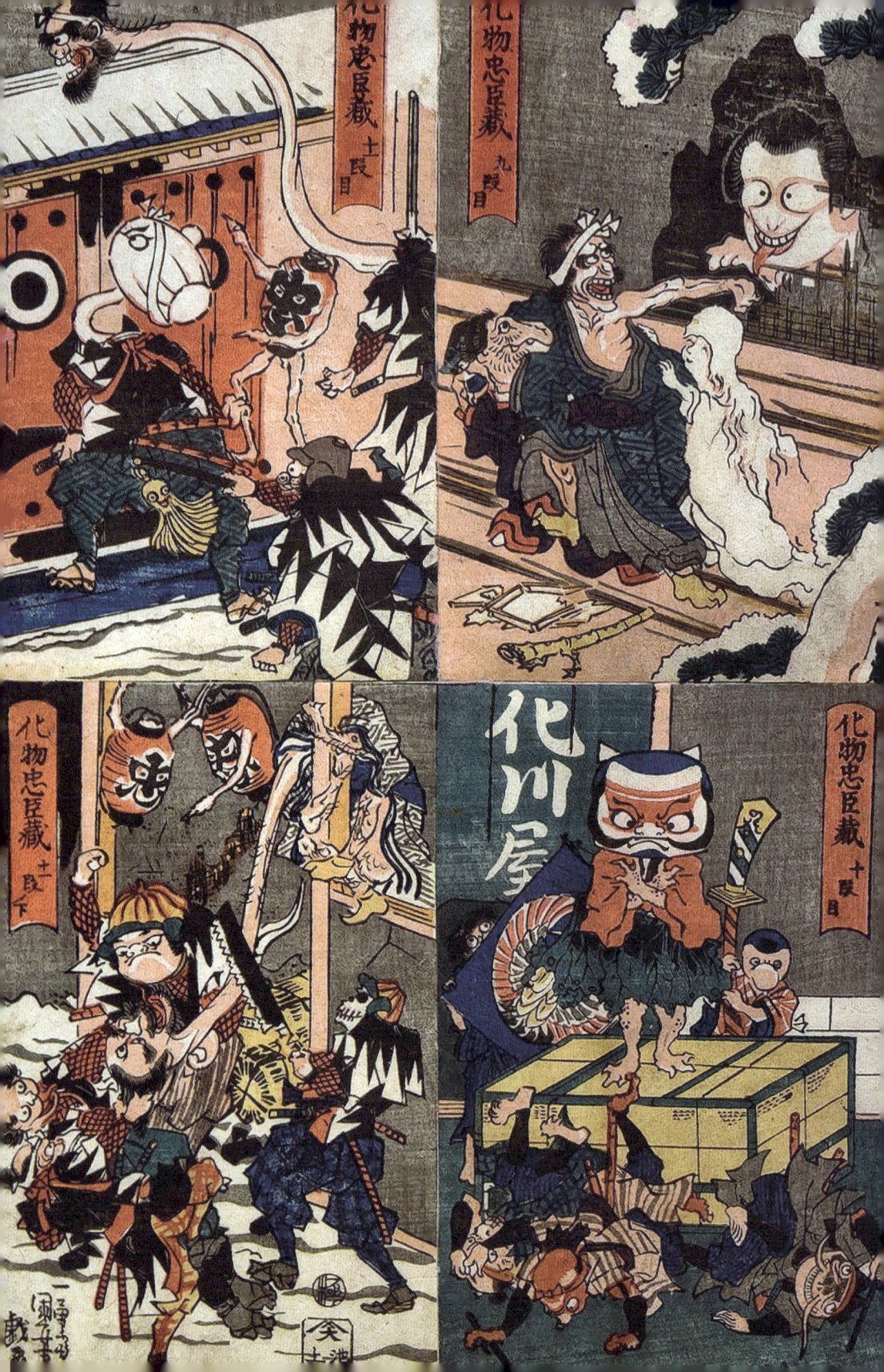

Certain poltergeist episodes implicating *yōkai* are described in Japanese literature, including *Ino mononoke roku*, a collection of scrolls, books and legends recounting the bizarre phenomena that occurred over a month in 1749 in the house of a certain Ino Heitaro at Miyoshi in the former province of Bingo (near present-day Hiroshima): apparitions of a monstrous giant head floating in the air, of enormous eyes materialising in the paper of a sliding partition (*shōji*), of a centipede floating on a tatami and attacking the house's occupants, of a ball of fire moving through the rooms and corridors, of poltergeists overturning furniture and wall hangings, of a bloody head flying from wall to wall, of flames surrounding a gravestone, of the ground metamorphosing into a raging sea, of a giant toad tearing down a mosquito net, of countless impaled children's heads dancing a jig in the air. All this, as we learn in the end, was the fault of the young warrior Heitaro himself. One evening, out of bravado, he had organised a 'gathering of one hundred candles' with his neighbour Mitsui Genpachi to prove that he was the stronger and more courageous of the two. Once the gathering was over, the *yōkai* that appeared at the summit of Mount Higuma did not return to hell but discreetly followed Ino Heitaro back to his residence and began haunting his days and nights.

But rest assured, not all *yōkai* are malevolent – on the contrary, as we can see in the tale of Emperor Go-Toba (1180–1239). Bedridden with a lengthy chronic illness, he dreamed of these supernatural beings and woke up in excellent health, as though invigorated to his very core. Other stories tell of similar creatures, who, though physically grotesque, harbour kind, even loving feelings towards humans.

These supernatural beings are everywhere, in woodblock prints, for example, or painted scrolls (*kakemono*), decorated lanterns, printed books, textiles, *netsuke*, *obi*, *kozuka*, *tsuba*, engraved snuffboxes, votive plaques (*ema*), film posters, portable *kamishibai* theatre boards, magic lantern slides, game boards (the first square being a

depiction of a gathering of one hundred candles and the last a rising sun repelling the *yōkai*), collectible cards, figurines, prayer labels, manhole covers, stickers and decals. They even make regular appearances from behind screens or spring up through trapdoors in shopping centres, much to the delight of children and their parents.

Regarding their appearance, the literary and aesthetic influence of China and Flanders probably began to be felt in Japan during the eighteenth century, despite the country's closed borders. *Yōkai* may have three eyes, unkempt hair, reptilian skin, cow's horns, claws, red eyes, gold teeth, cat whiskers, bald heads, two chins, nine red tails, four arms, three anuses, noses as long as an arm, pig ears, skeletal bodies, bat wings, elephant trunks, gigantic waists, magical powers, mortiferous breath, endlessly long necks, eyes in their backs, pestilential stench, voices from beyond the grave – the list goes on. Although many appear 'monstrous' – some could have come straight out of Hieronymus Bosch – they are not necessarily so in the European sense. That is, they do not necessarily represent a threat, nor are they malevolent. Some are merely materialisations of natural phenomena: echoes in the mountains, a tornado, a hailstorm, an epidemic, the flickering shadow of an object in the candlelight, a draft causing a lantern to sway or a sliding door to slam. Other *yōkai* are stranger – for example, the *akaname* that lick the scum off bathtubs; the *kamikiri*, which cut women's hair while they are on the toilet; or the *abura-akago* that suck the oil from traditional lamps in the dead of night.

In everyday life, any abnormal birth or apparition of a malformed animal is a materialisation of a *yōkai* or proof of the reality of their existence: a turtle with a woman's face, found on the shore by two fishermen; a rabbit with enormous eyes and giant ears ('the remarkable beast of Doshū'); or a sheep with five legs or two heads.

During the Covid-19 crisis, certain *yōkai* became extremely popular. One was Amabie, a spirit that appeared at sea for the first time in 1846, with long hair, a bird's beak instead of a mouth,

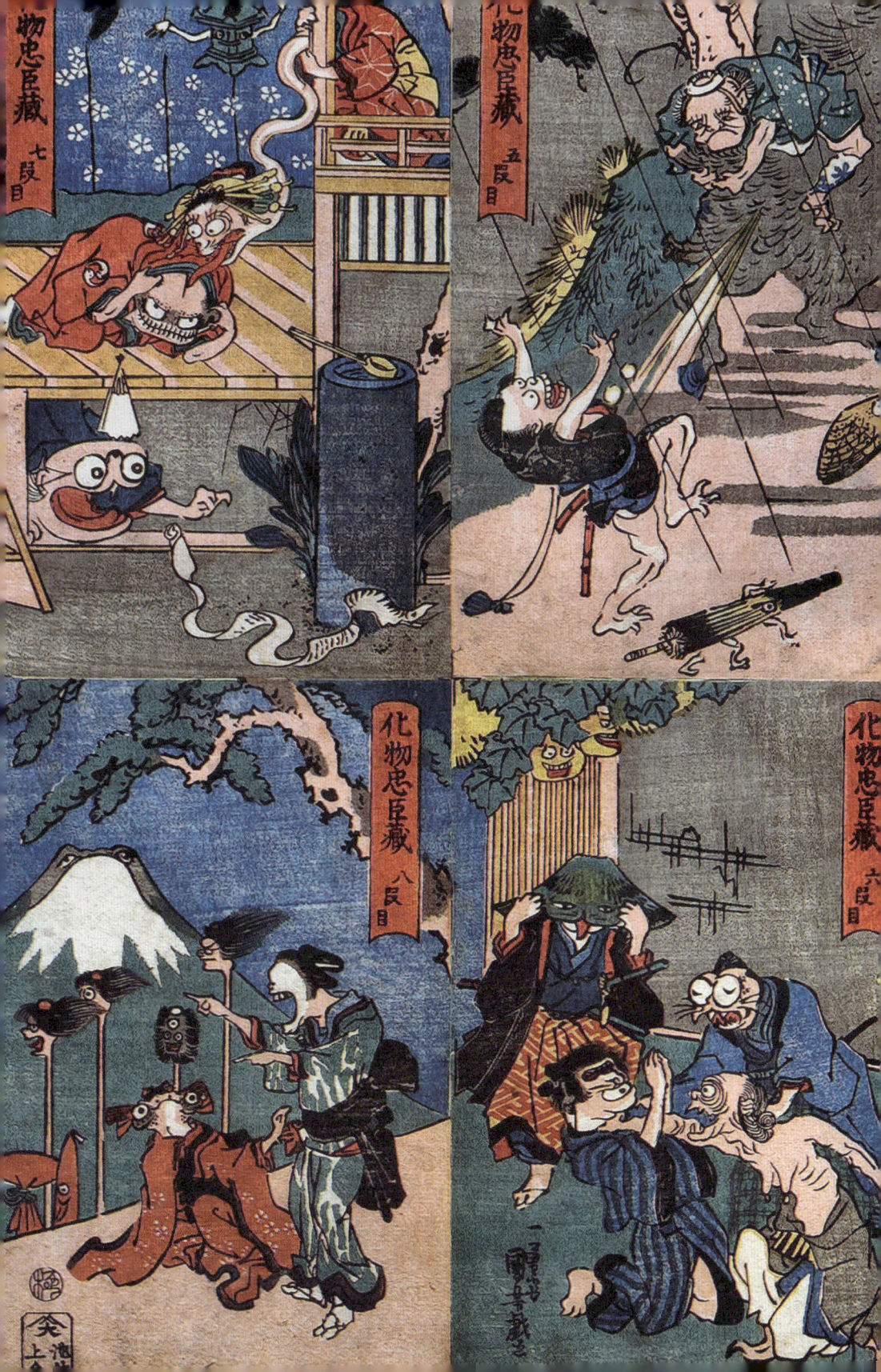

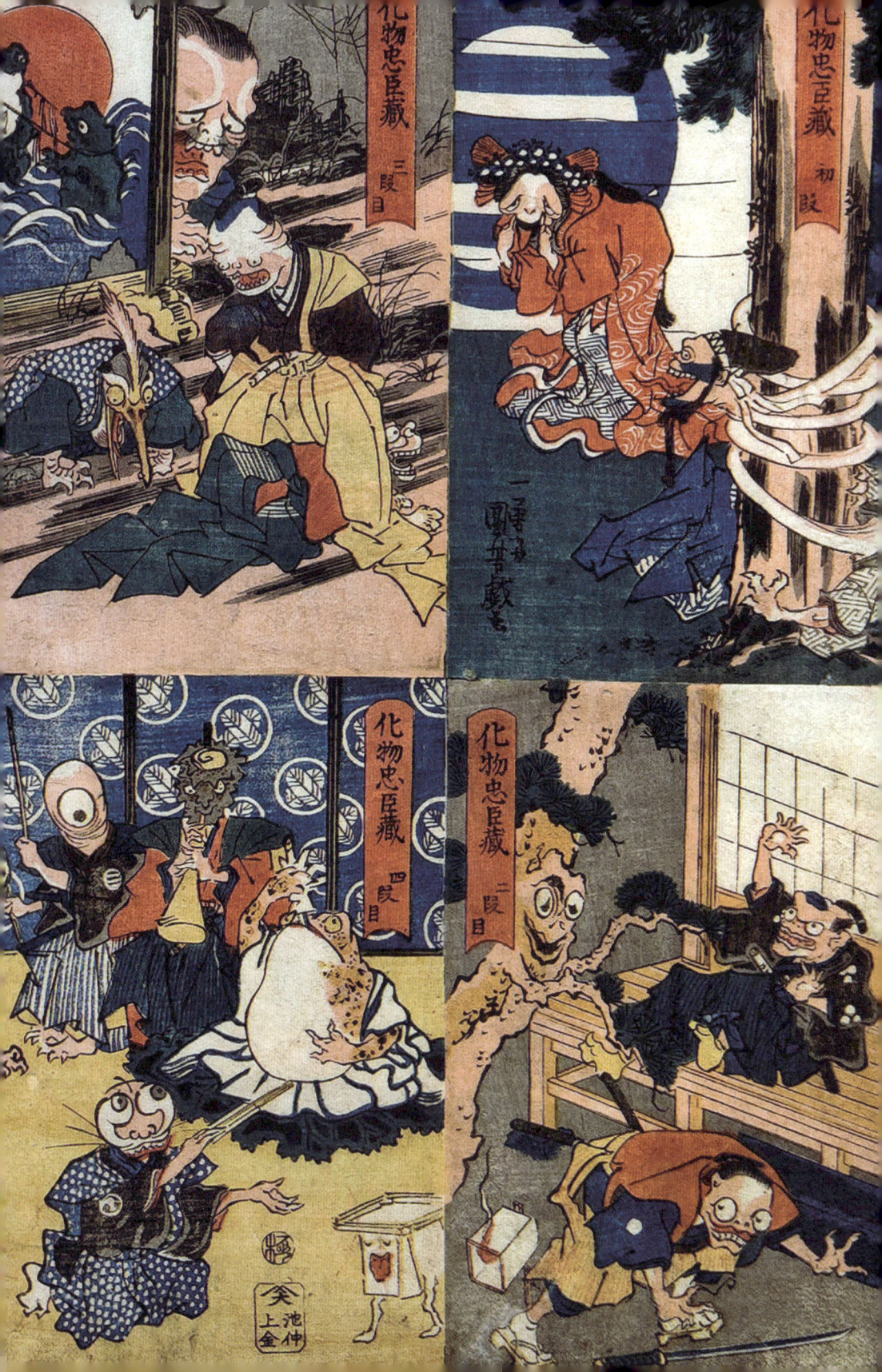

skin covered with scales, and three legs. Amabie vowed that 'if an illness spreads, show an image of me to those who fall ill, and they will be healed.' Countless drawings of Amabie were produced from 2019 to 2021 to ward off the illness and protect patients infected with the virus. Thousands of talismans – folded in four and kept in a pocket, stuck to the door of a house or fixed to the windows of hospital rooms – made Amabie one of the most famous *yōkai* in Japan and abroad. In reality, the mysterious, ethereal, supernatural world of the *yōkai* is even more 'floating' than that of Japanese prints. It is infinite.

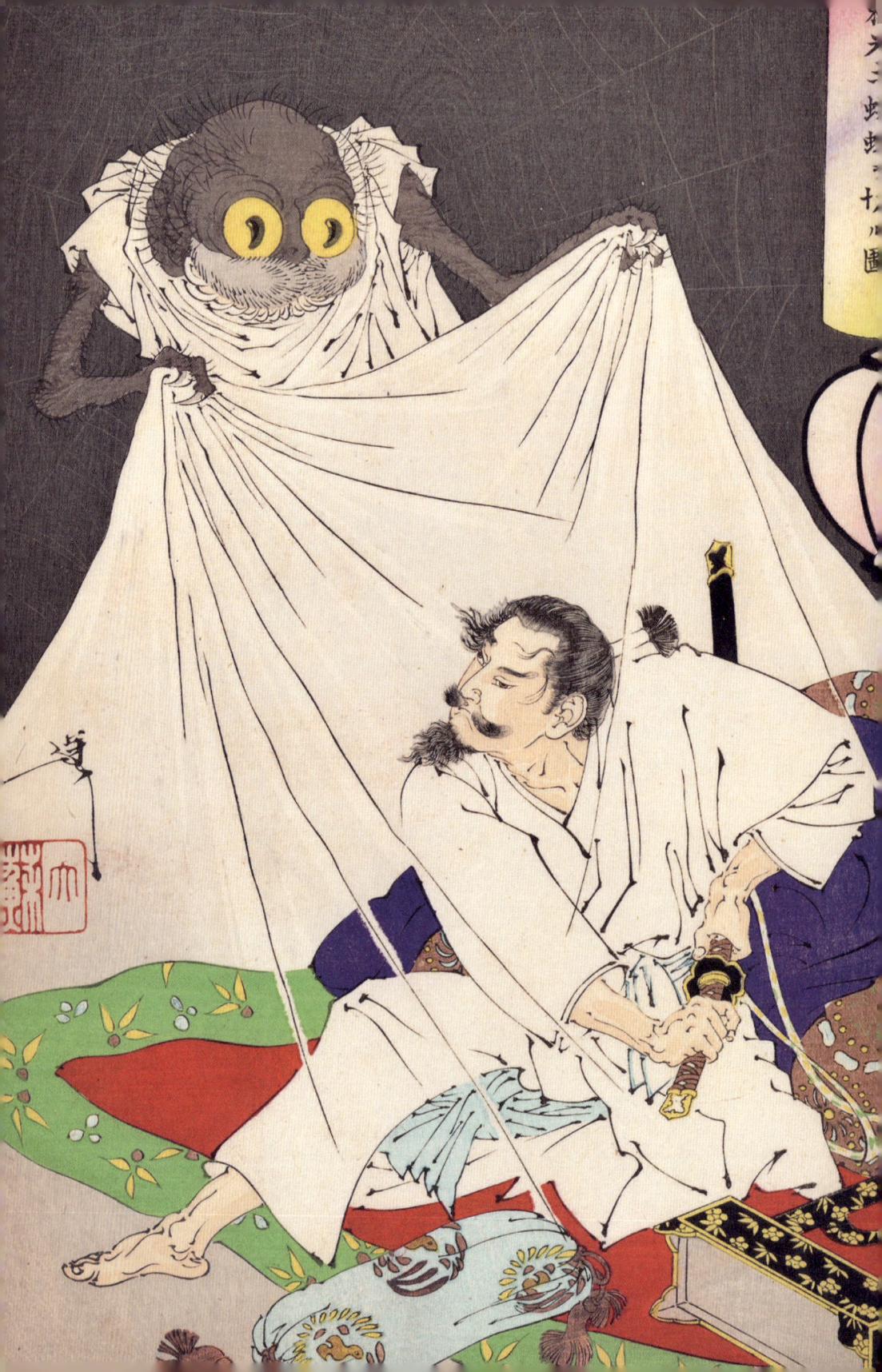

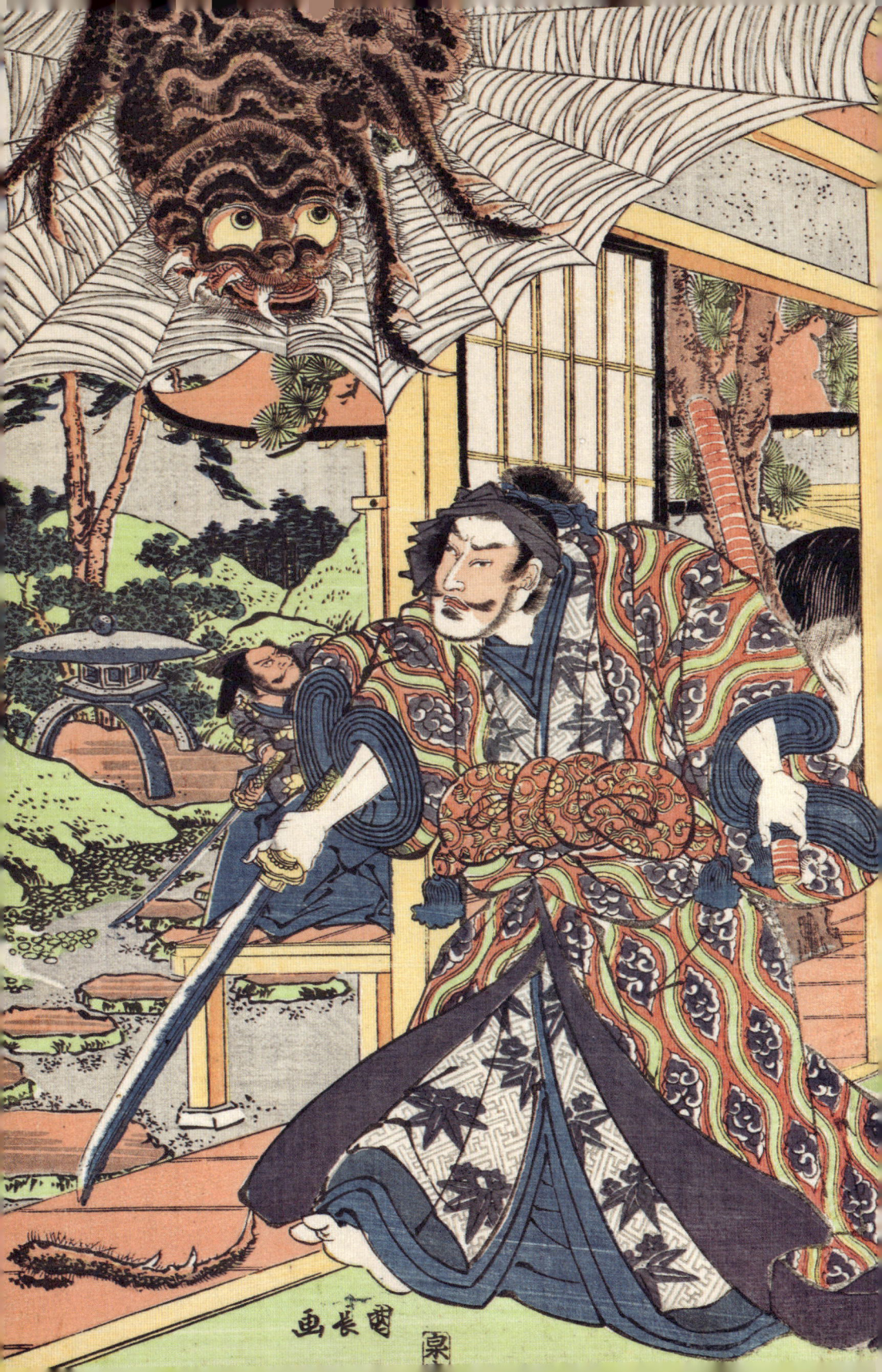

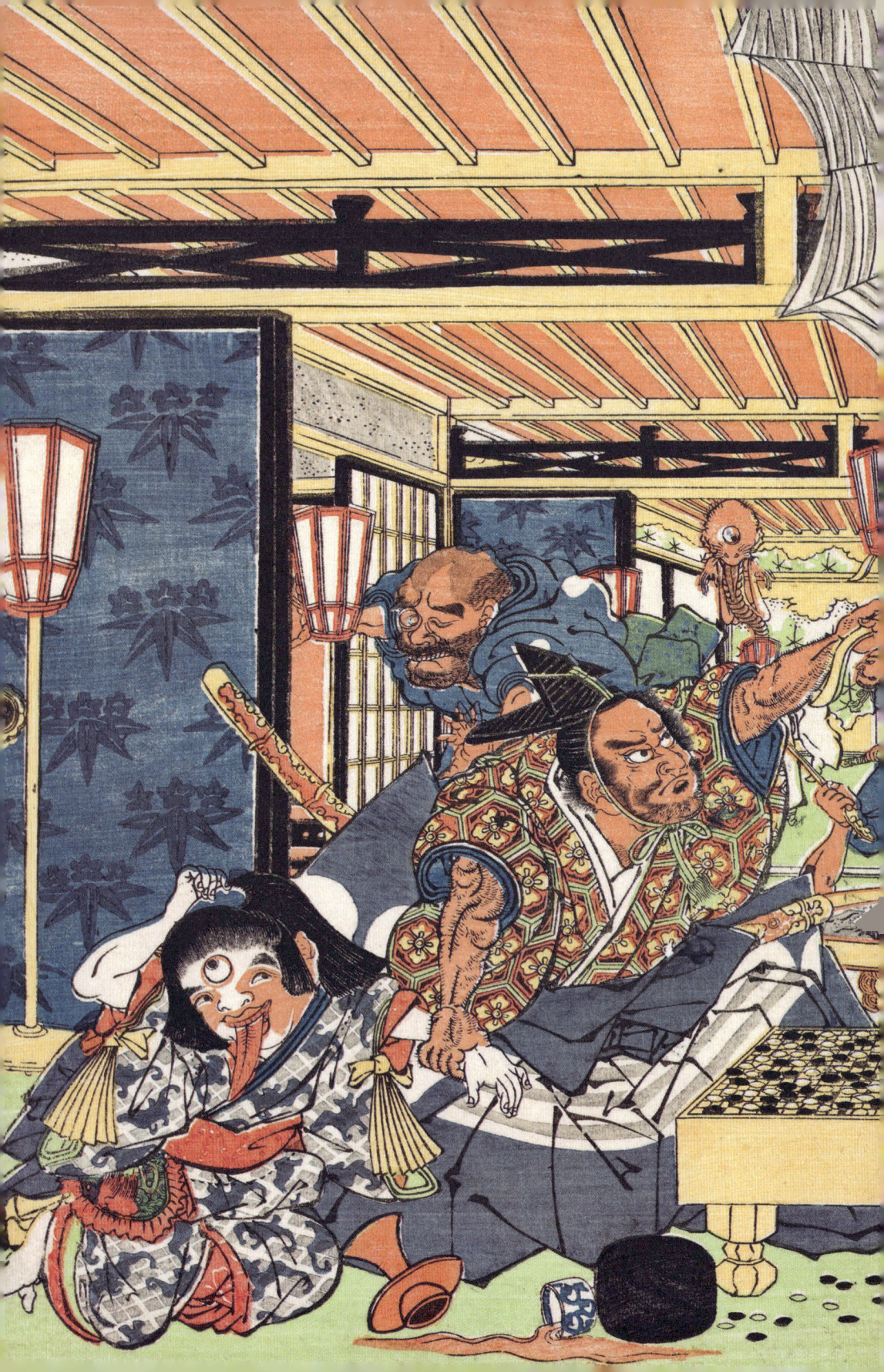

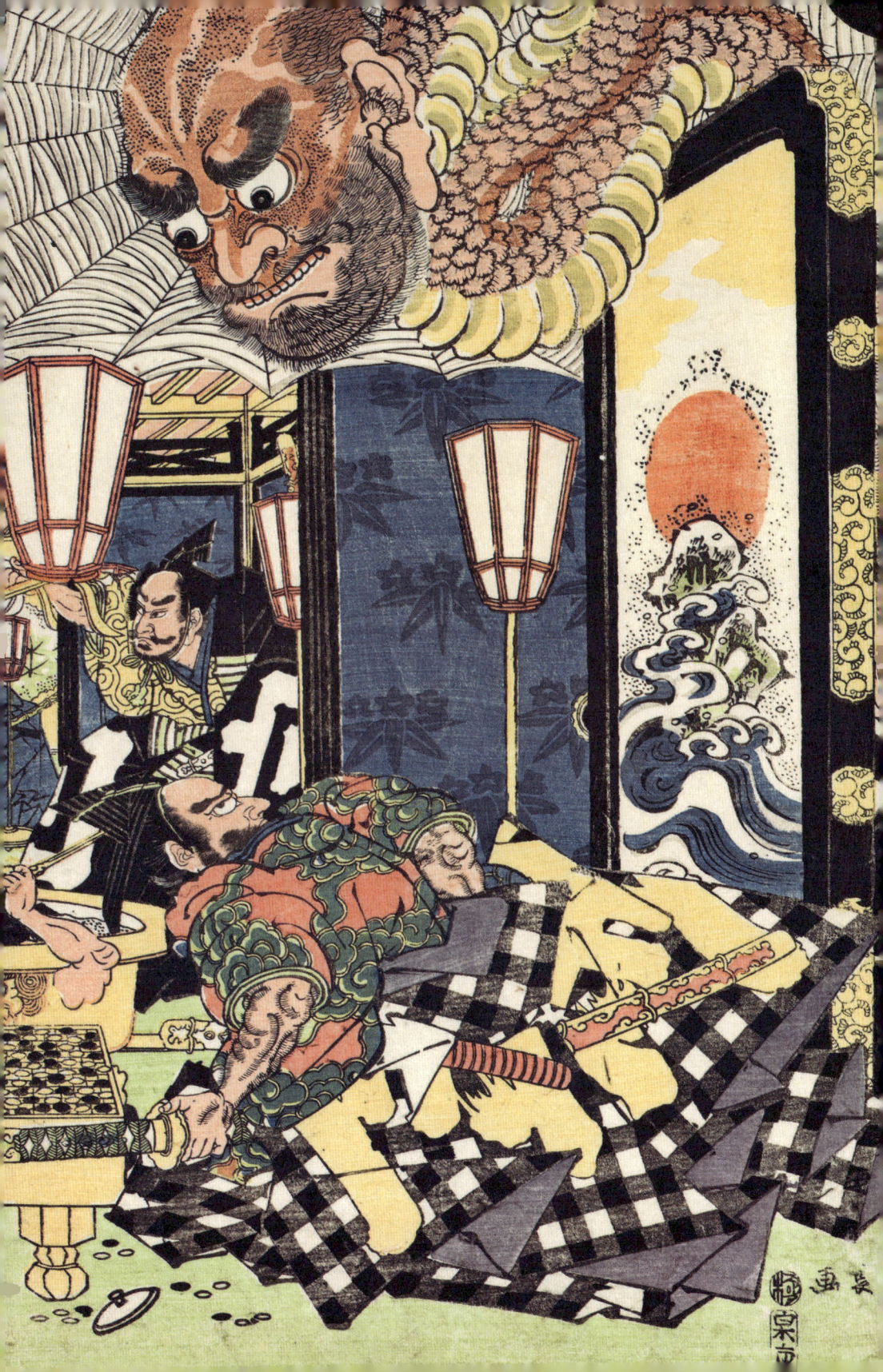

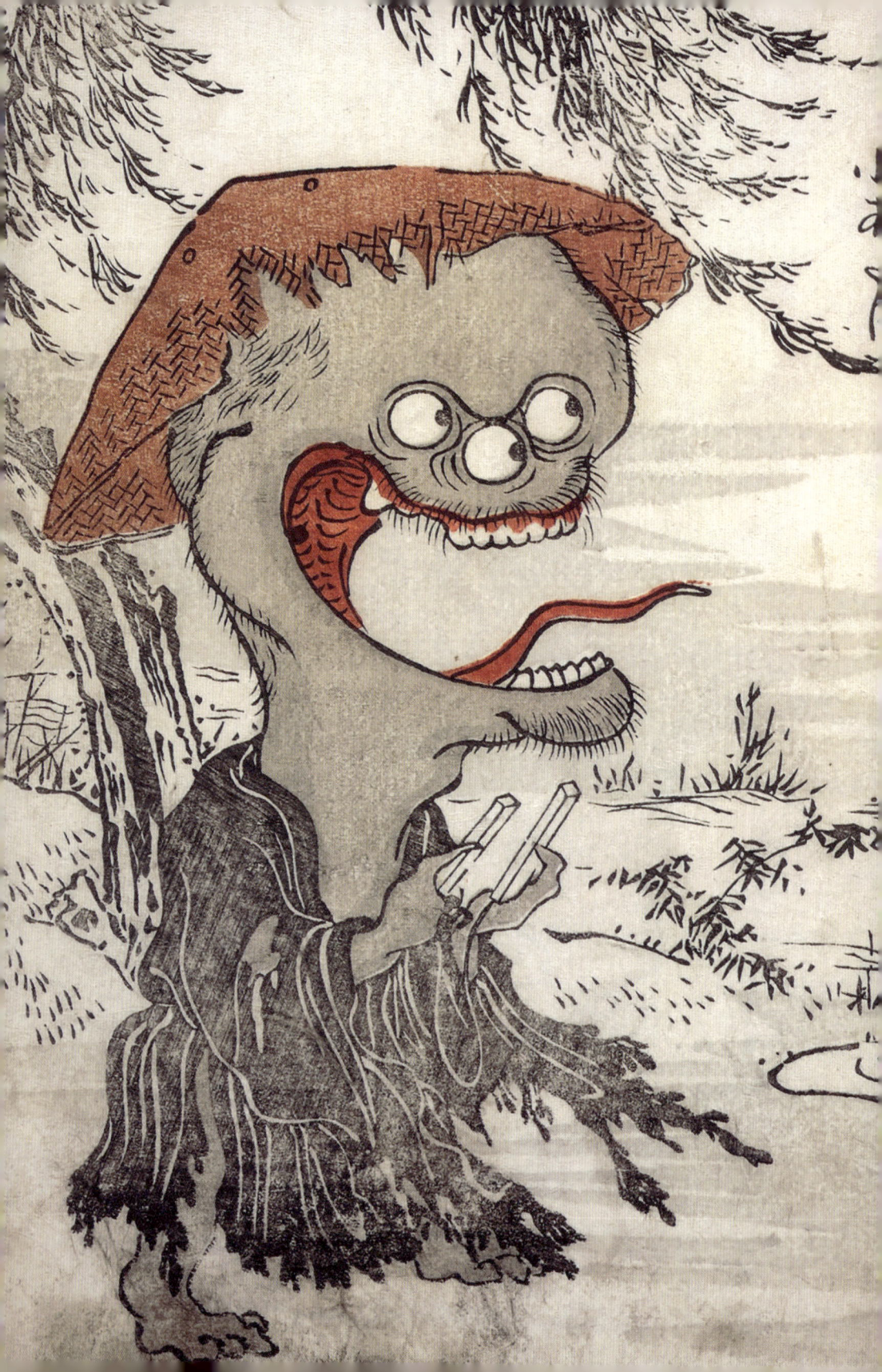

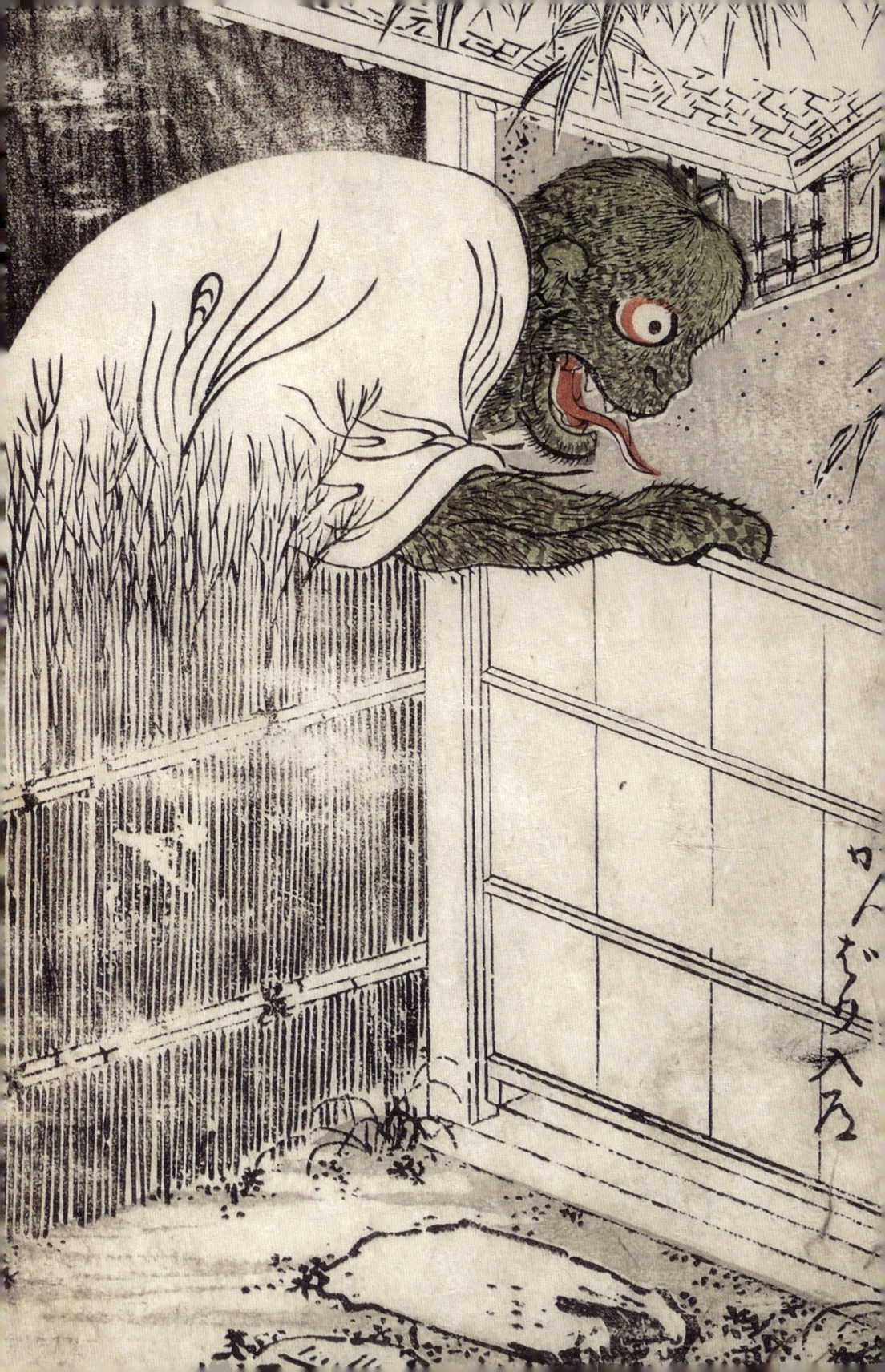

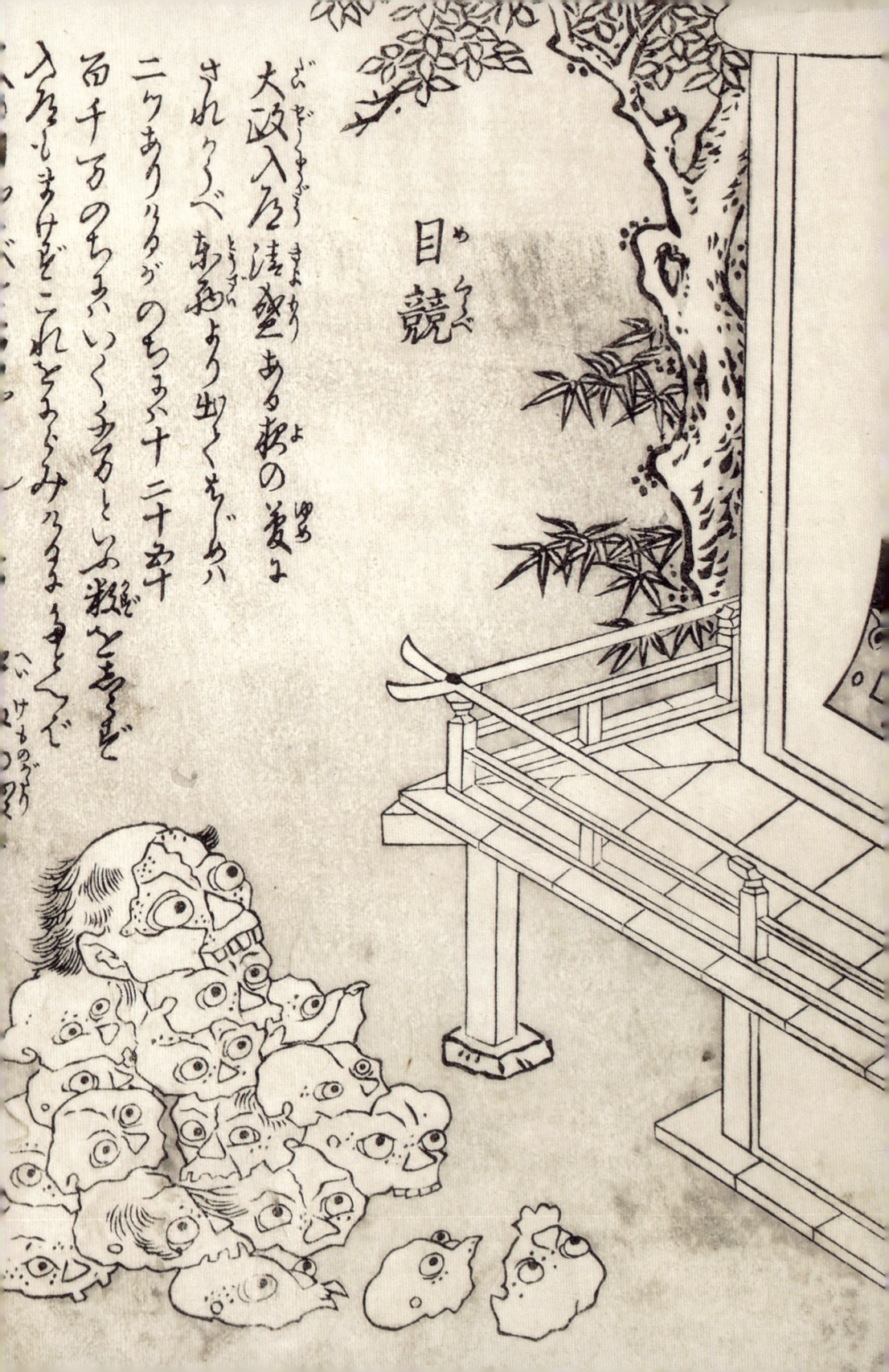

目競

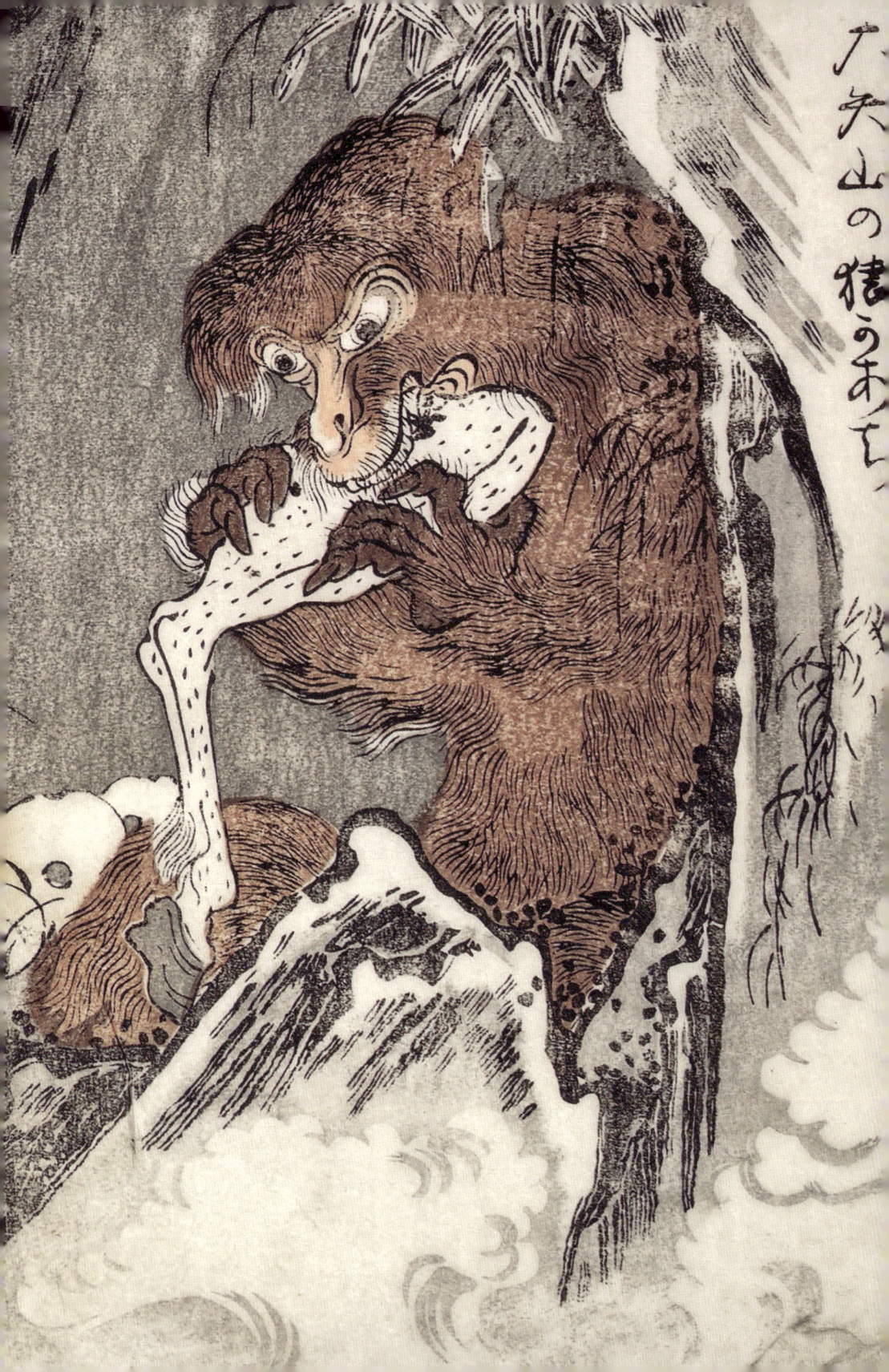

THE METAPHOR OF THE TONGUE-CUT SPARROW

•

In *Works and Days*, the Greek poet Hesiod recounts the story of Pandora who, driven by curiosity, opened a jar belonging to her father and released a scourge of misery upon humanity. The legend has a slightly different counterpart in Japanese tradition, with the *yōkai* as its malevolent protagonists.

    The tale starts with an old woodcutter working in a forest. He finds a wounded sparrow and takes the bird home to care for it, feeding it – against the wishes of his cantankerous wife – from the household's meagre stock of rice. A few days later, as the sparrow regains its strength, the woodcutter leaves for the mountains, leaving the bird in his wife's care. As soon as she goes outside, the sparrow eats every last grain of the rice, leaving nothing for the old couple. In anger, his wife cuts off the sparrow's tongue and hides the bird in the forest. When the woodcutter returns, he is dismayed and goes out in search of the wounded bird, eventually finding it. To thank him, without any resentment and touched by his concern, the sparrow invites him to its home to drink and dance. Later, as the woodcutter is about to leave, the sparrow decides to offer him a gift and gives him a choice of two closed baskets (*tsuzura*) – one large, one small. Out of humility, or perhaps not wanting to be too weighed down, the old woodcutter takes

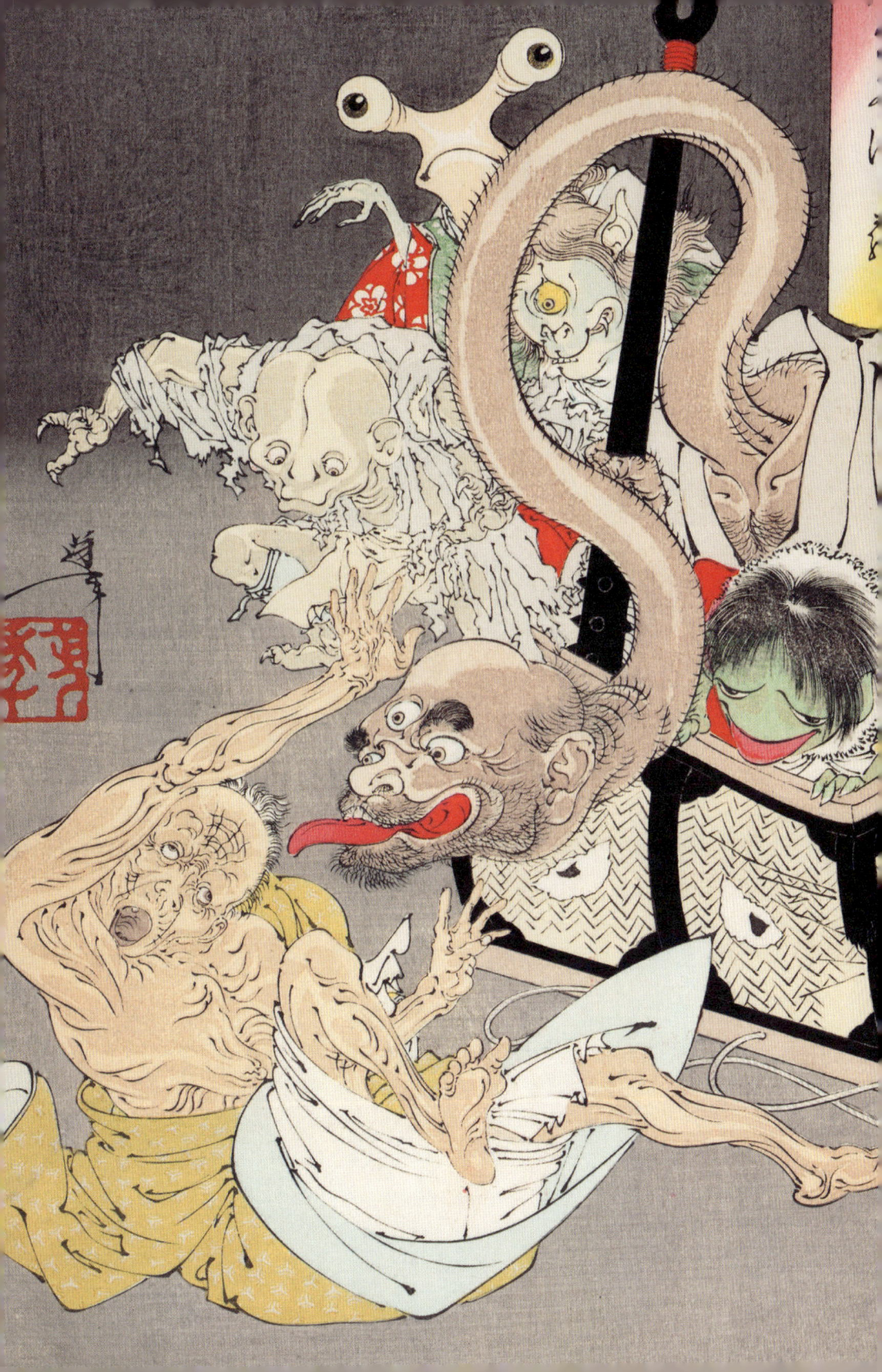

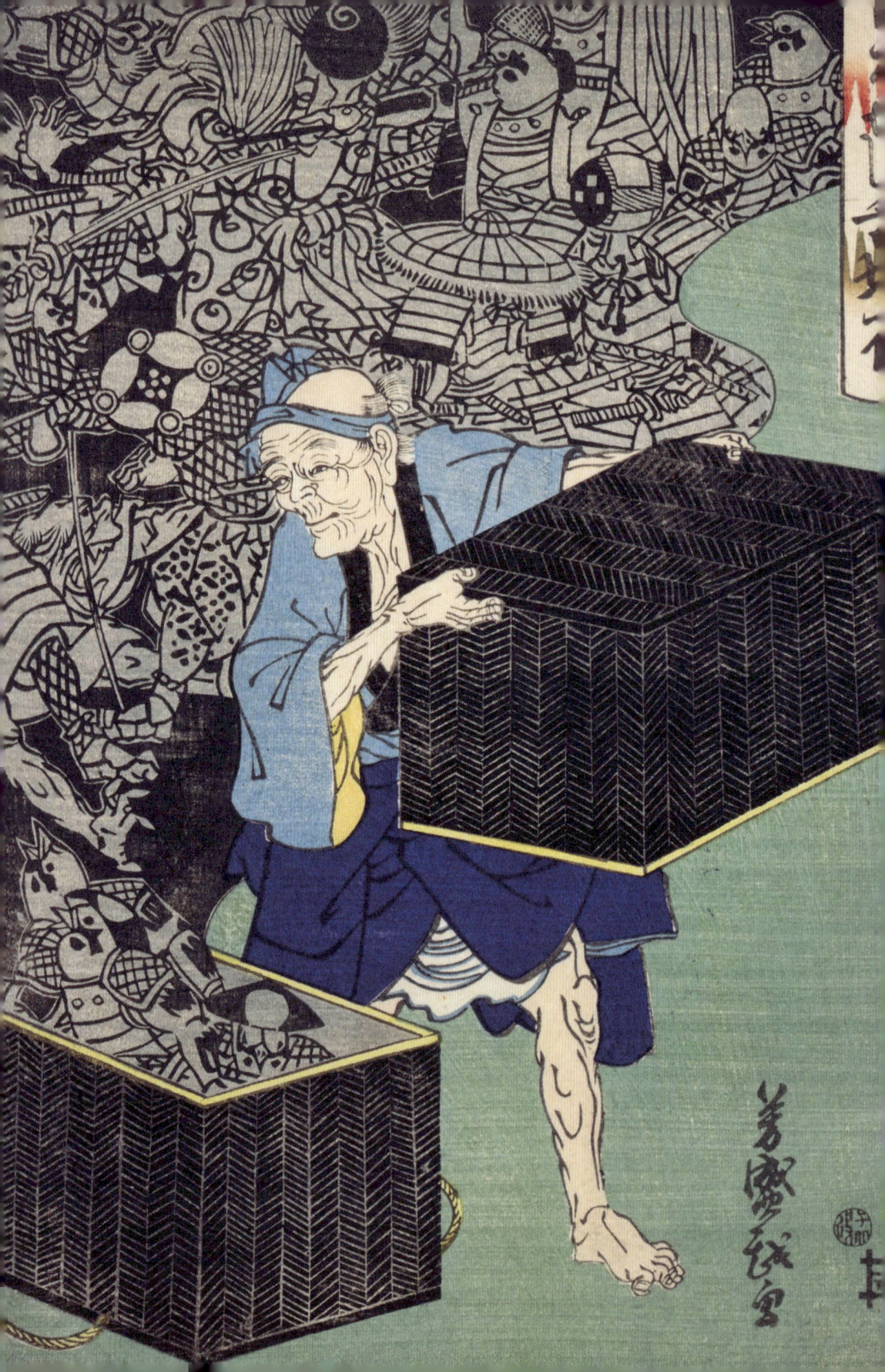

the smaller one and returns home. When he opens the basket in front of his wife, he discovers magnificent gold and silver treasures. Furious with her husband, the greedy old woman secretly goes and steals the other basket from the sparrow. But it is too heavy for her to carry, so she opens it on the way home. Out of it swarm horrific monsters that torment her to the end of her days, punishing her for her greed. Her suffering is so great that she repents before she dies.

Another, less dramatic version of the legend tells of a flock of sparrow warriors flying out of one basket to attack the *yōkai* emerging from the other basket.

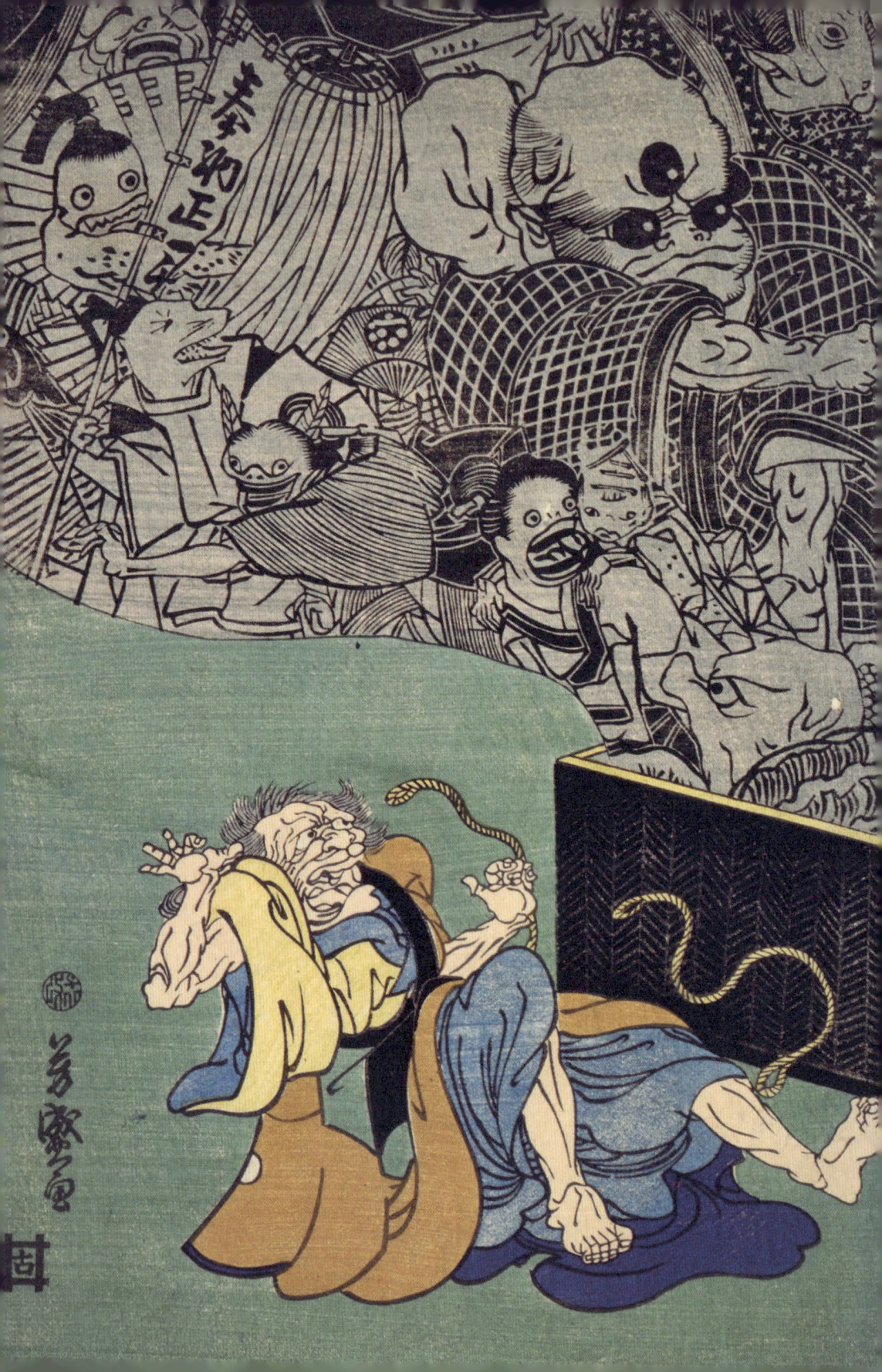

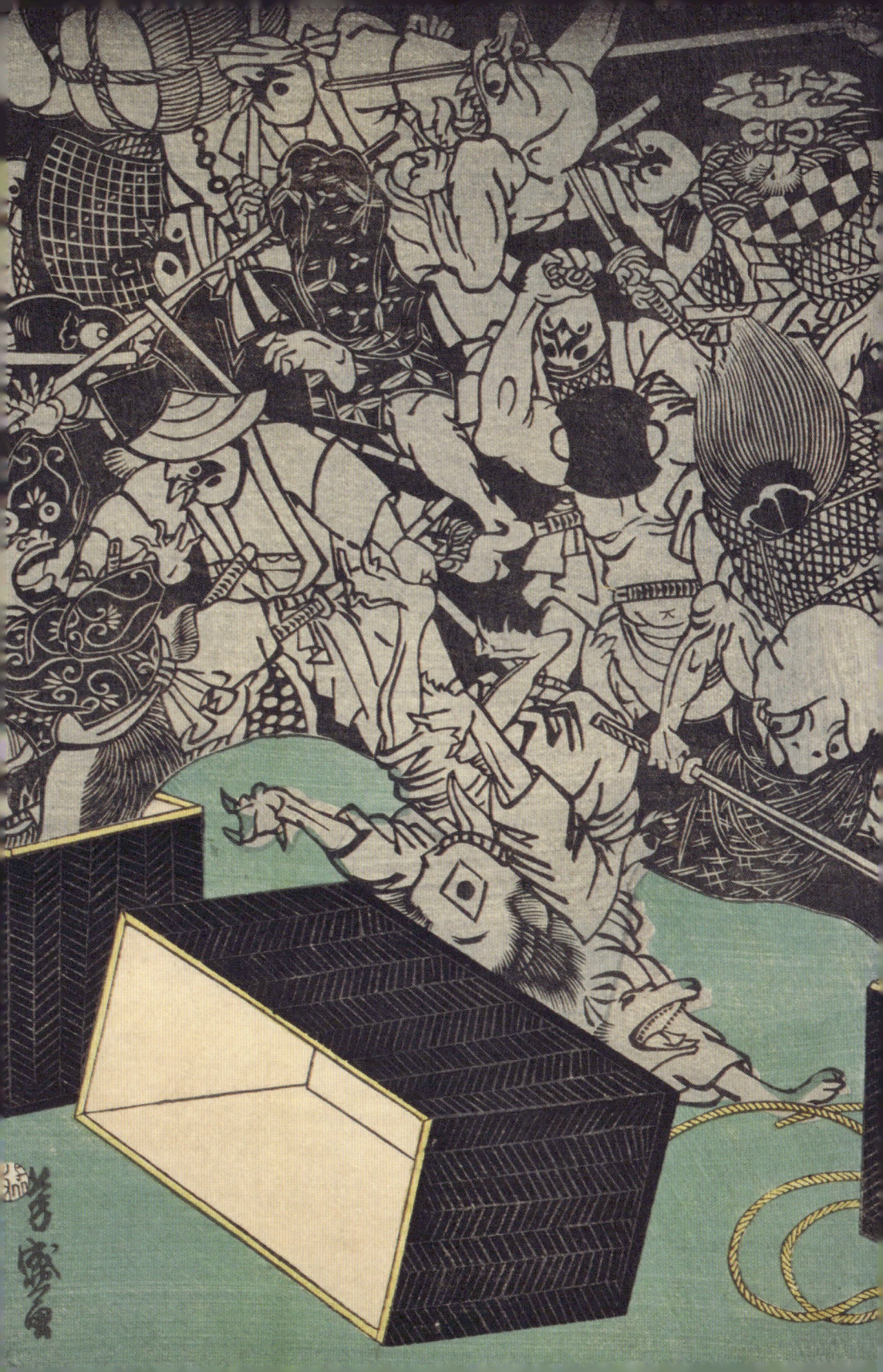

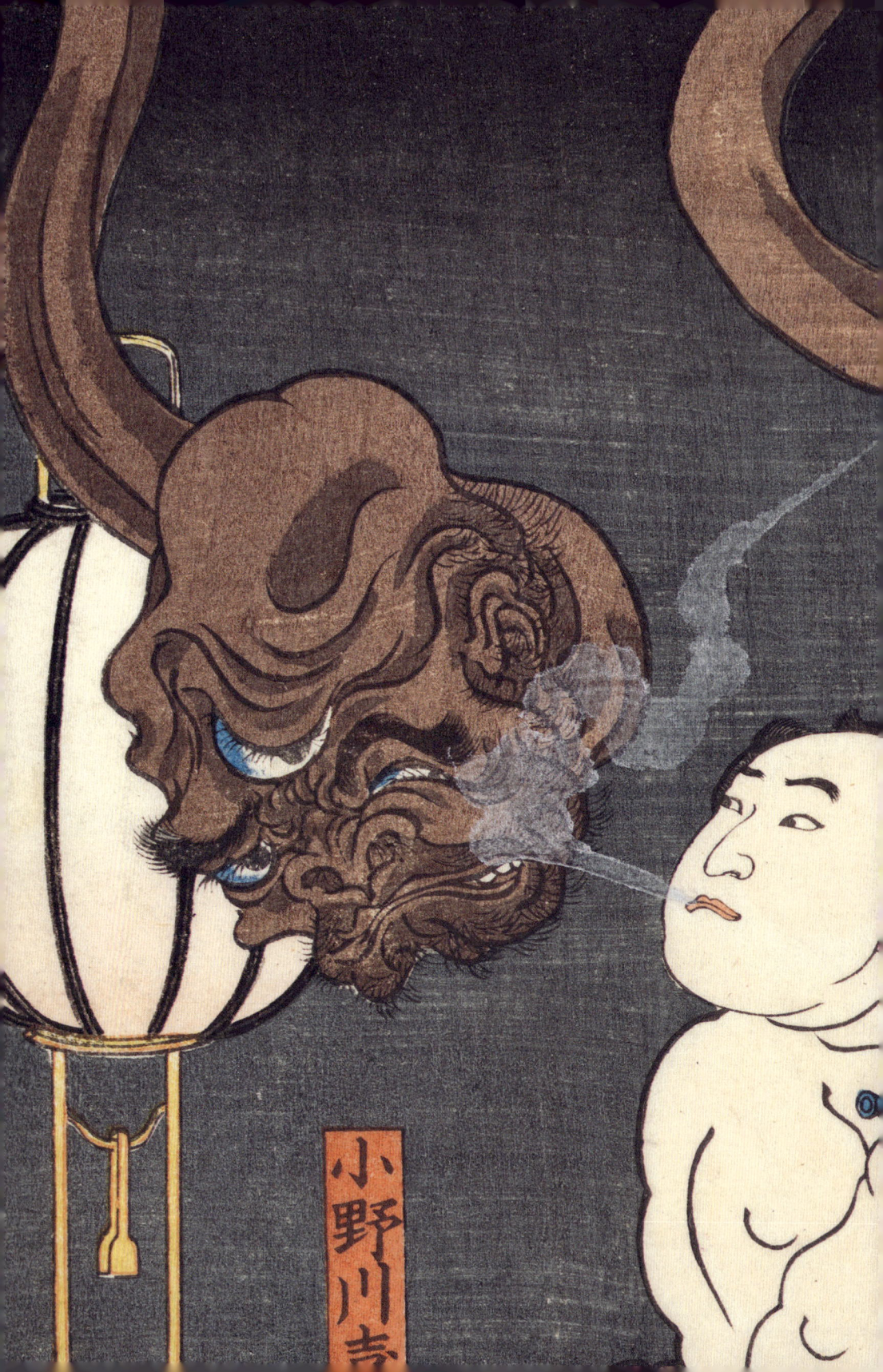

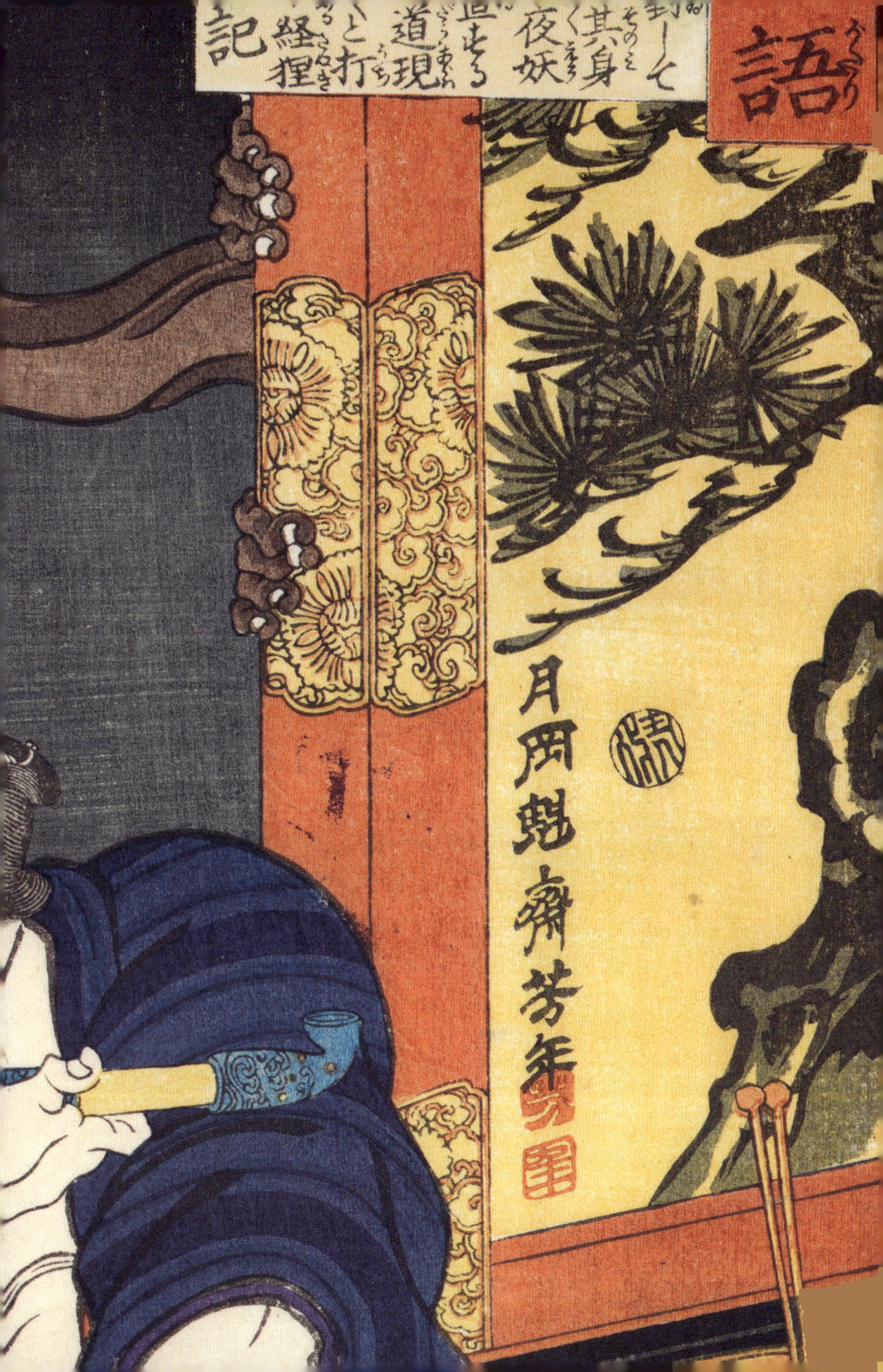

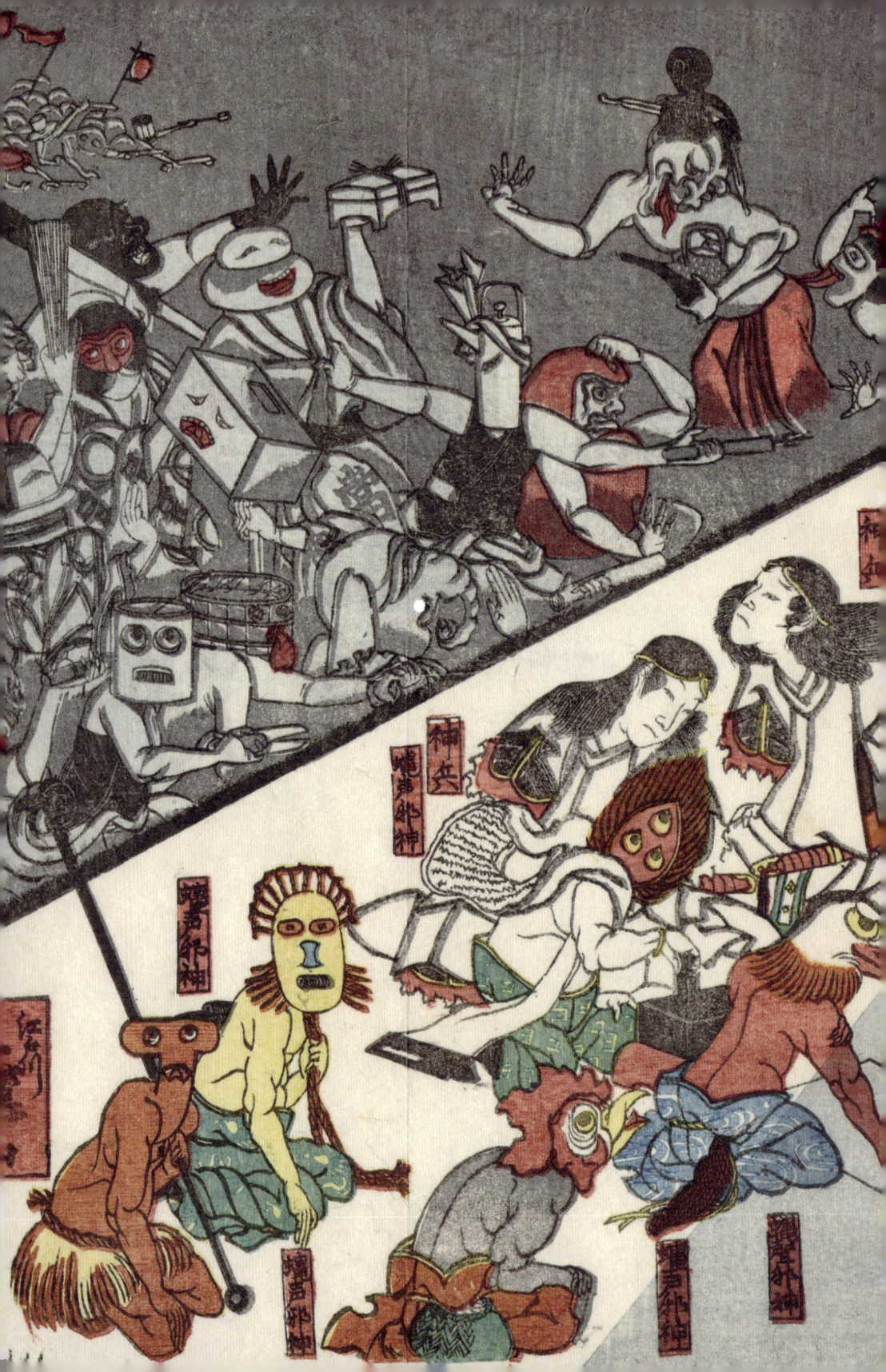

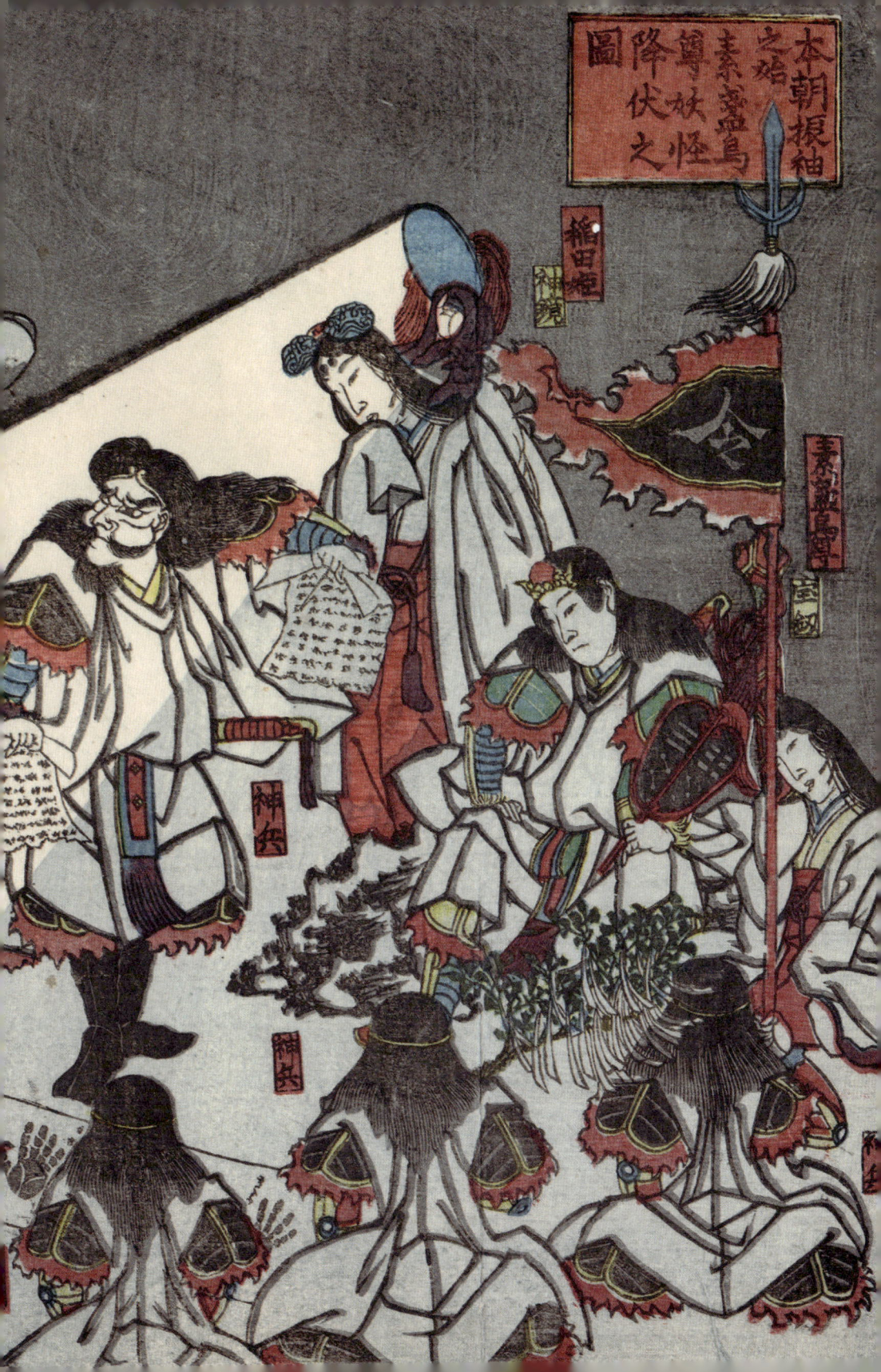

本朝振袖之始
素盞嗚尊妖怪
降伏之圖

稲田姫

素盞嗚尊

宝劔

神兵

神兵

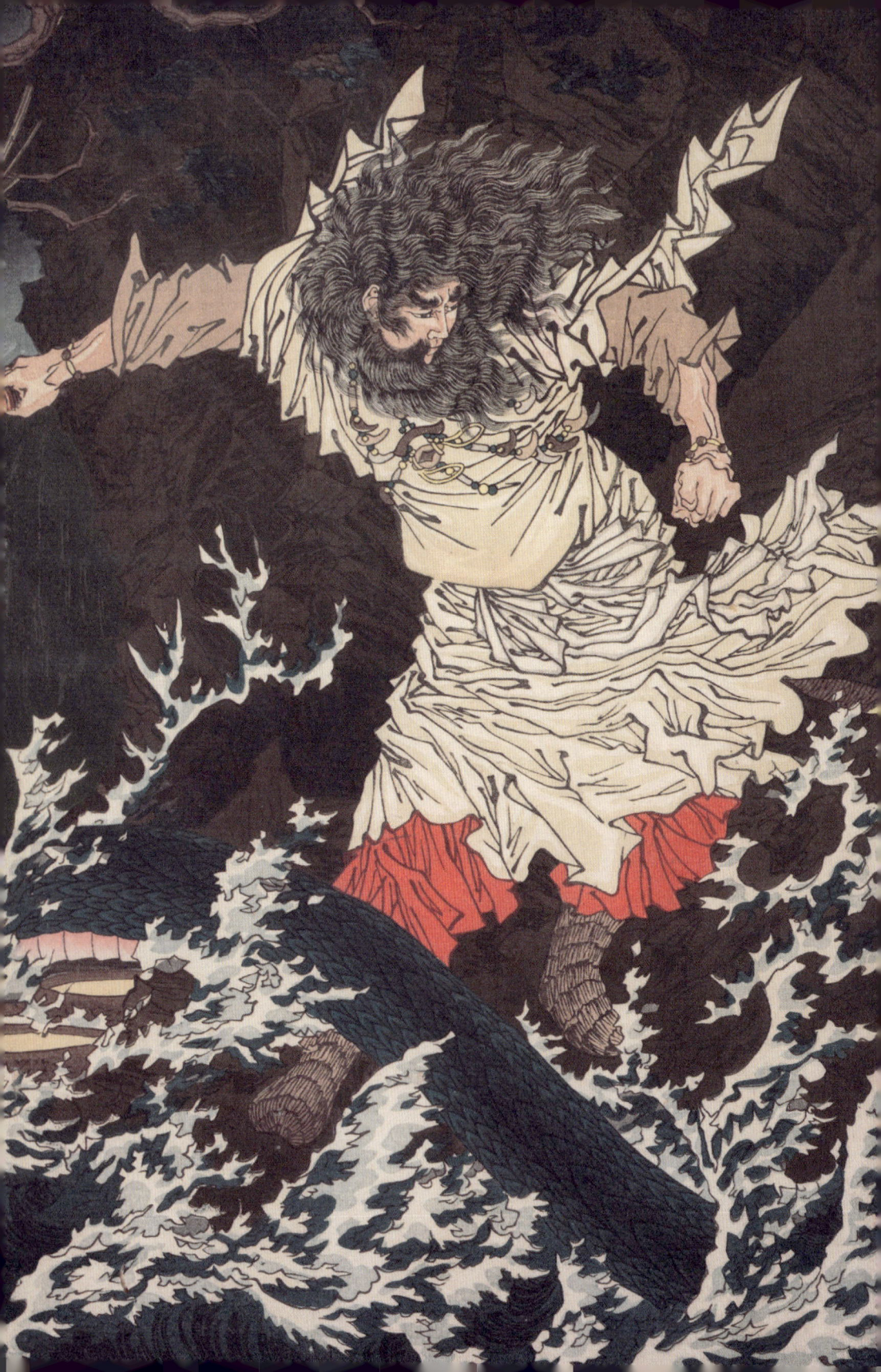

SON OF MUCUS

•

Susanoo-no-Mikoto is one of the most ancient Shinto deities (*kami*). When his father, Izanagi, creator of the world, returned from the land of the dead, he wished to cleanse himself of any contamination. As he washed his face, three children appeared: Susanoo-no-Mikoto, when he washed his nose; Tsukuyomi (god of the Moon), when he washed his right eye; and Amaterasu (goddess of the Sun), when he washed his left eye.

To say Susanoo-no-Mikoto is impetuous is an understatement. He is the very epitome of impetuosity. As god of the sea, storms and winds, he is constantly creating catastrophes. Banished from the underworld, where he went to see his father's first wife, he attempts to conquer the realm of his sister Amaterasu, then destroys paddy fields, spreads excrement over the Earth, skins a horse, and commits other vile acts. He is captured, forcibly shaven, and his fingernails are torn off. To redeem himself, he battles monsters (*yōkai*), most notably the dragon terrorising Koshi province.

One tale recounts the bravery and intelligent trickery of this deity, who is often compared to a *yōkai*. Transformed into a horseman, Susanoo-no-Mikoto stays with an elderly peasant couple. Seven of their daughters have been swallowed by the dragon Yamata no Orochi, leaving only their youngest daughter, Kushinada hime, due to be devoured the next day. Together with the local villagers, he decides to set a trap that will rid them of the monster once and for all. All around the farm, on the summit of Mount Sentsū, he constructs a palisade with eight gates. In front of each gate, he places a barrel of sake, which he splits open with an axe. The villagers hide and Susanoo-no-Mikoto has just enough time to transform

Kushinada hime into a comb and secure her in his hair before the monster arrives. Seeing nothing suspicious when it pokes one of its heads through the first gate, the dragon begins lapping up the sake with its other seven heads and soon it is completely drunk. With the monster now incapable of defending itself, Susanoo-no-Mikoto cuts its heads off, one by one, and soon the dragon lies slain. Searching the creature's carcass, the *kami* finds a magic sword in its tail (*Kusanagi no Tsurugi*), which he offers to Amaterasu as a token of reconciliation. This sacred sword, kept in the Atsuta Jingū Shrine in Nagoya, is now one of the three imperial regalia of Japan.

pp. 38–39: Tsukioka Yoshitoshi, *The Wrestler Onogawa Kisaburō Blowing Smoke at a One-Eyed Monster,* detail, 1865 Los Angeles County Museum of Art

pp. 40–41: Katsushika Hokki, *In the Play Honchō Furisode no Hajime, Susanoo no Mikoto Subdues the Monsters,* detail, 1851 Boston, Museum of Fine Arts

pp. 42 and 45: Tsukioka Yoshitoshi, *A Brief History of Japan: Susanoo no Mikoto Kills the Eight-Headed Serpent at Hirokawa in Izumo Province,* details, 1887 Philadelphia Museum of Art

pp. 46–47: Yōshū (Hashimoto) Chikanobu, *Susanoo no Mikoto Kills the Eight-Headed Serpent-Dragon from the Hino River in Izumi Province,* detail, ca 1880 Kyoto, Nishiharu

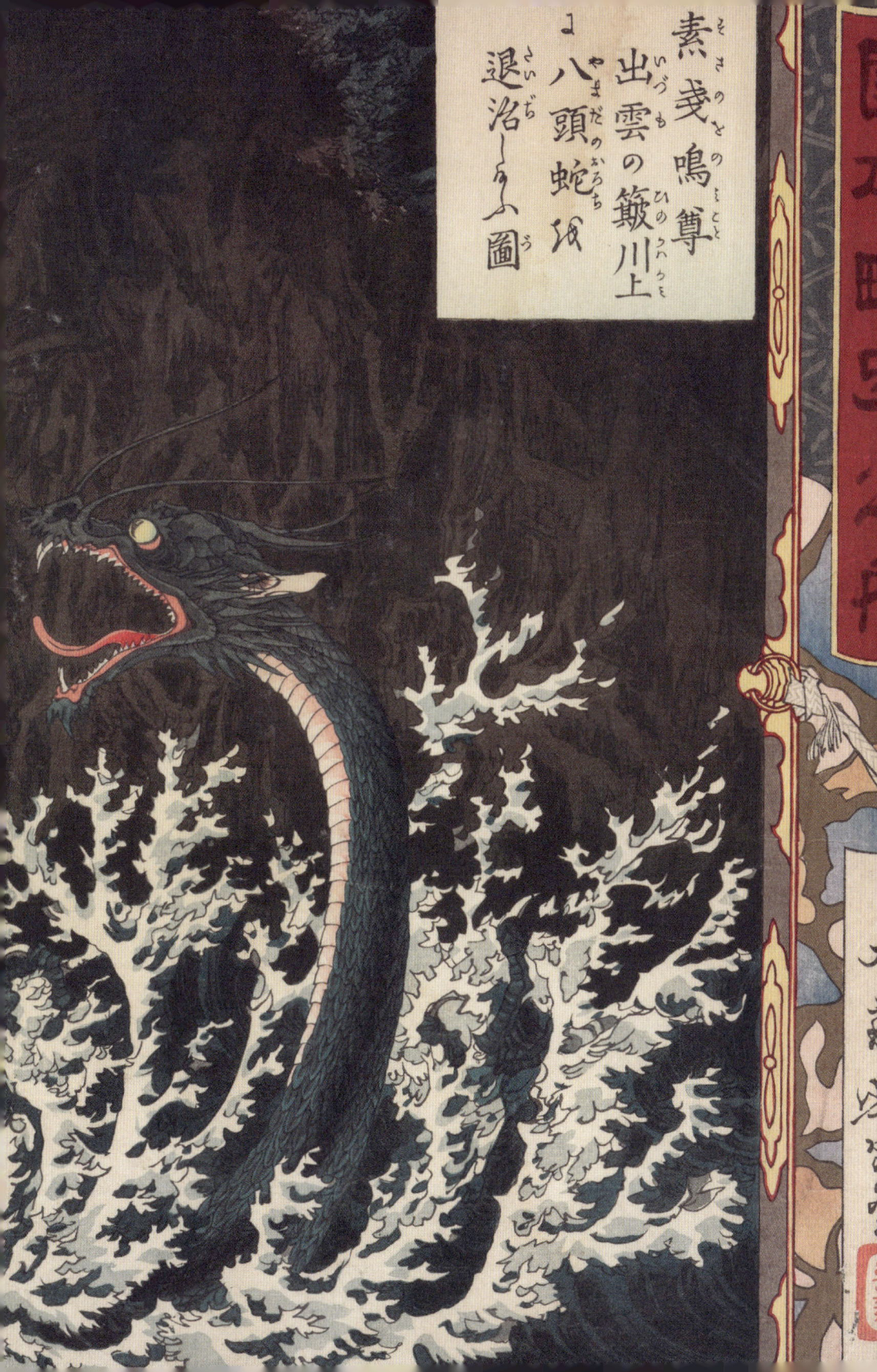

素戔鳴尊出雲の簸川上ニ八頭蛇を退治し給ふ圖

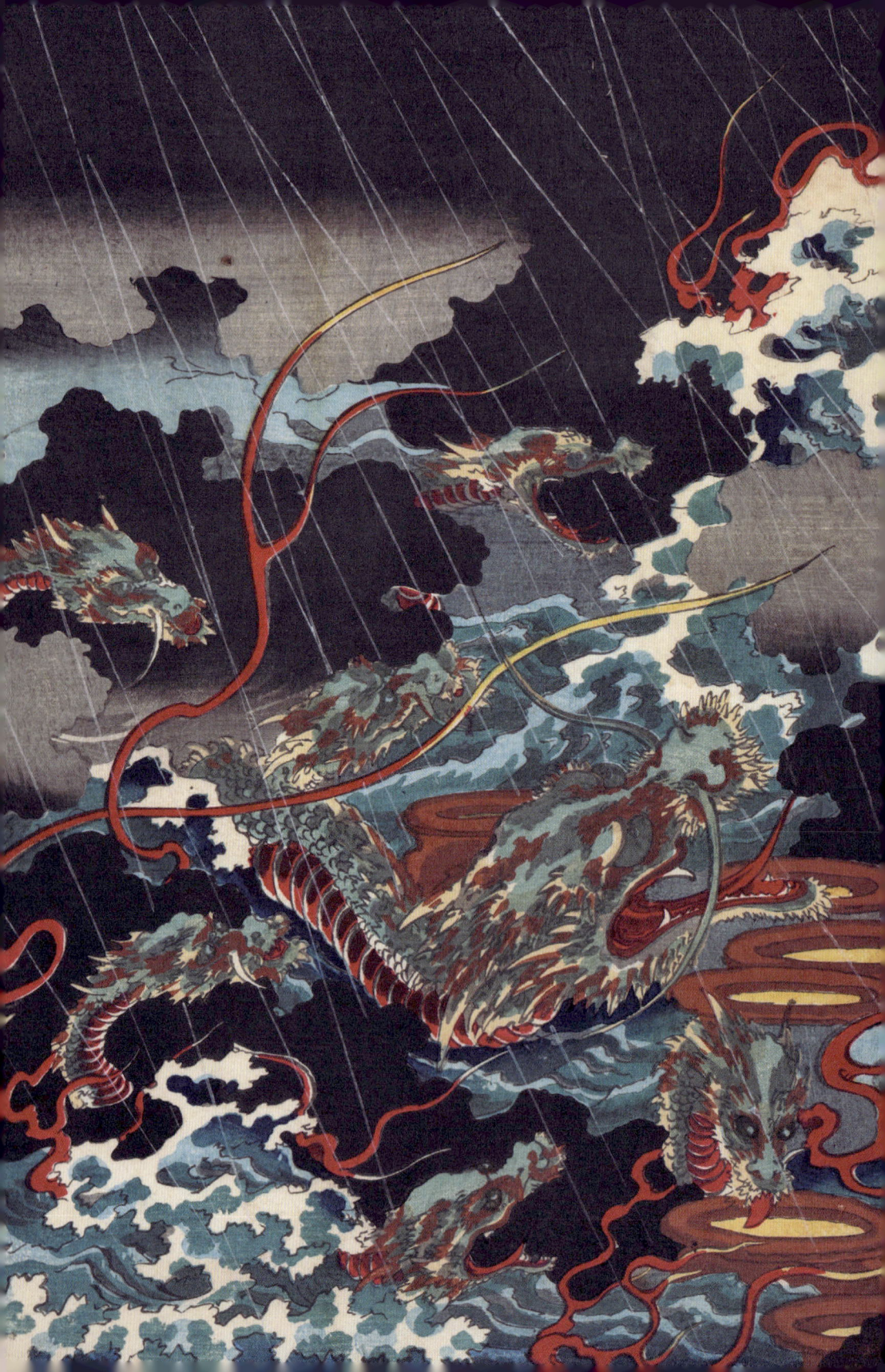

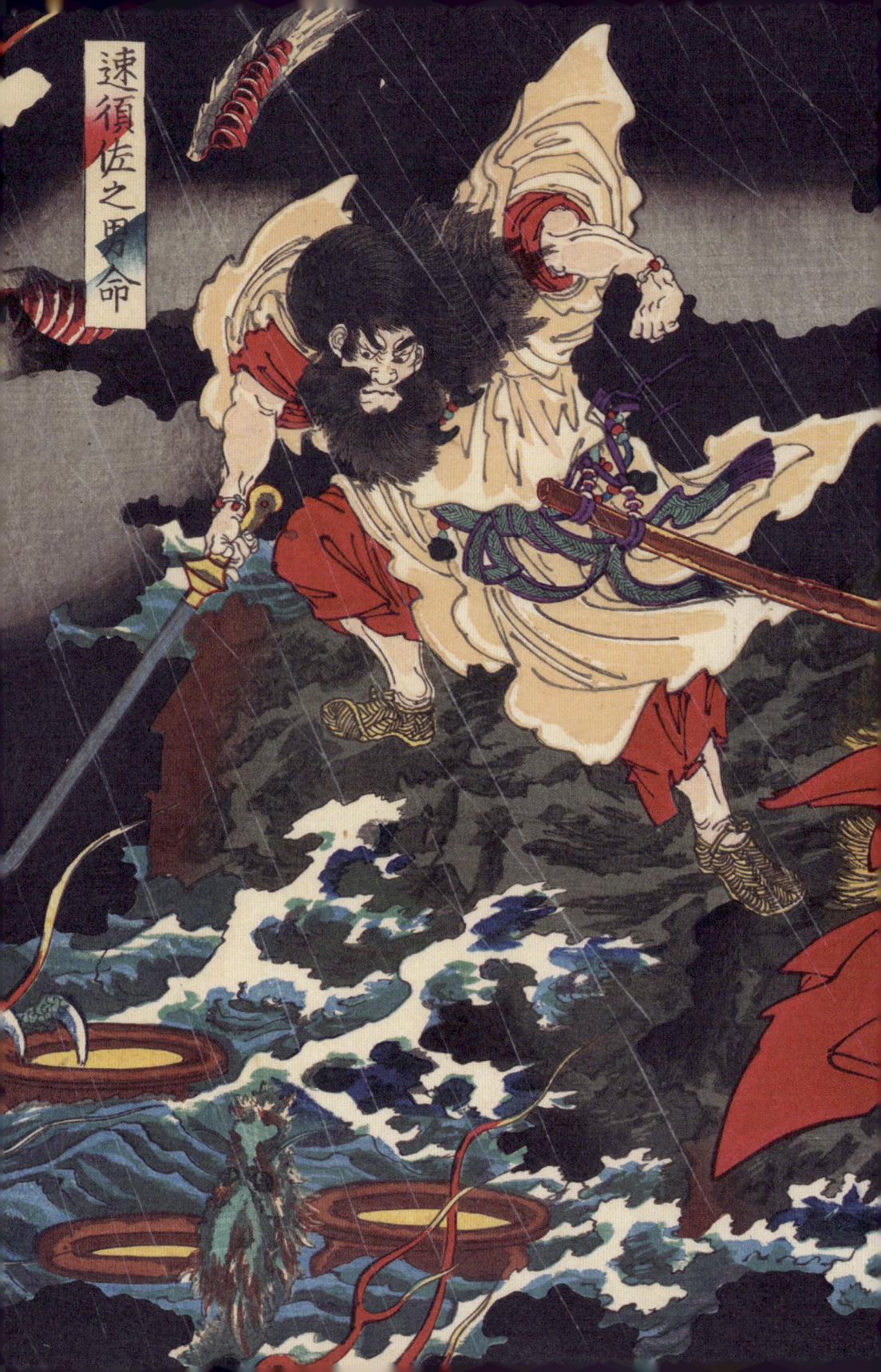
速須佐之男命

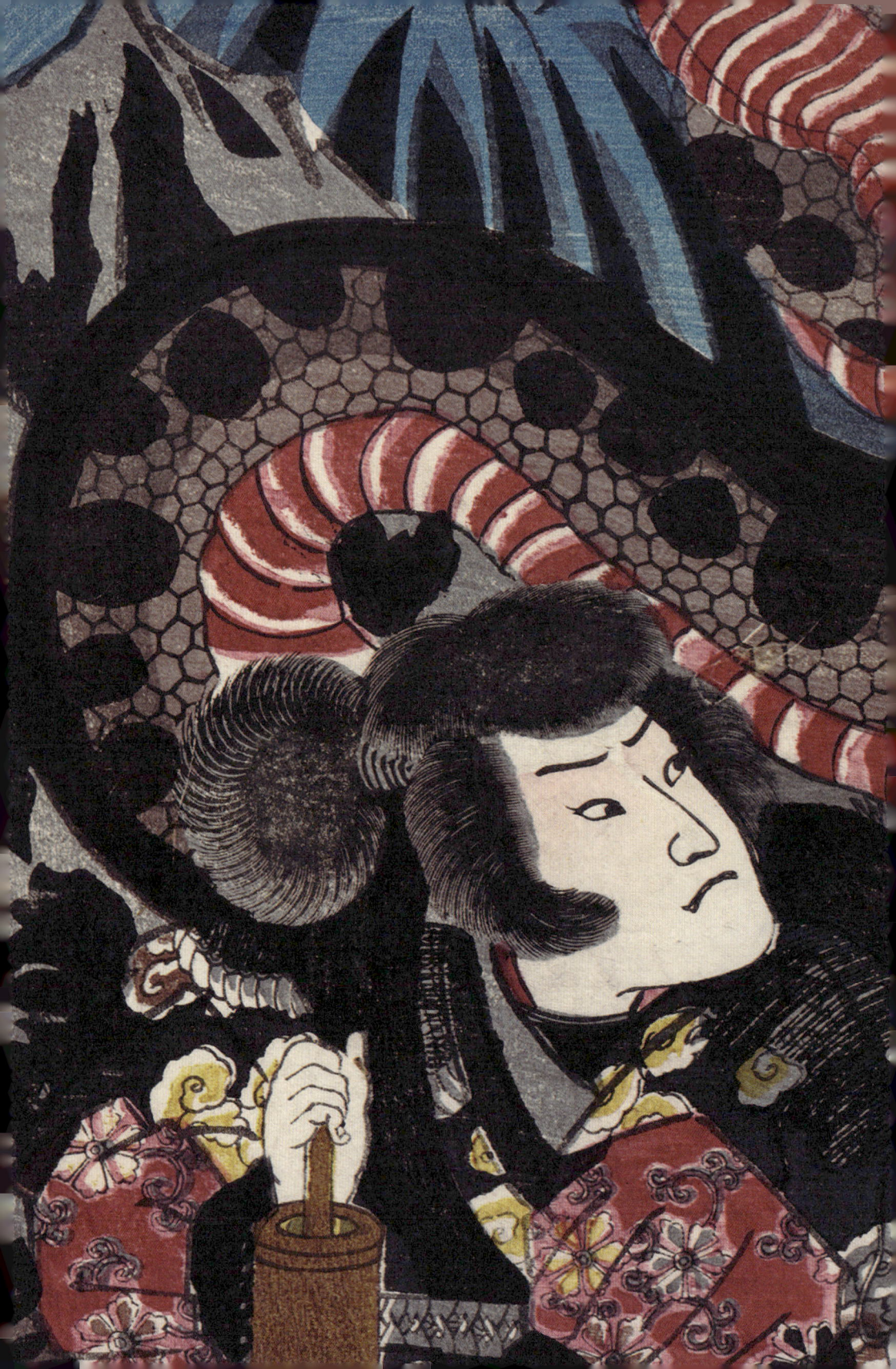

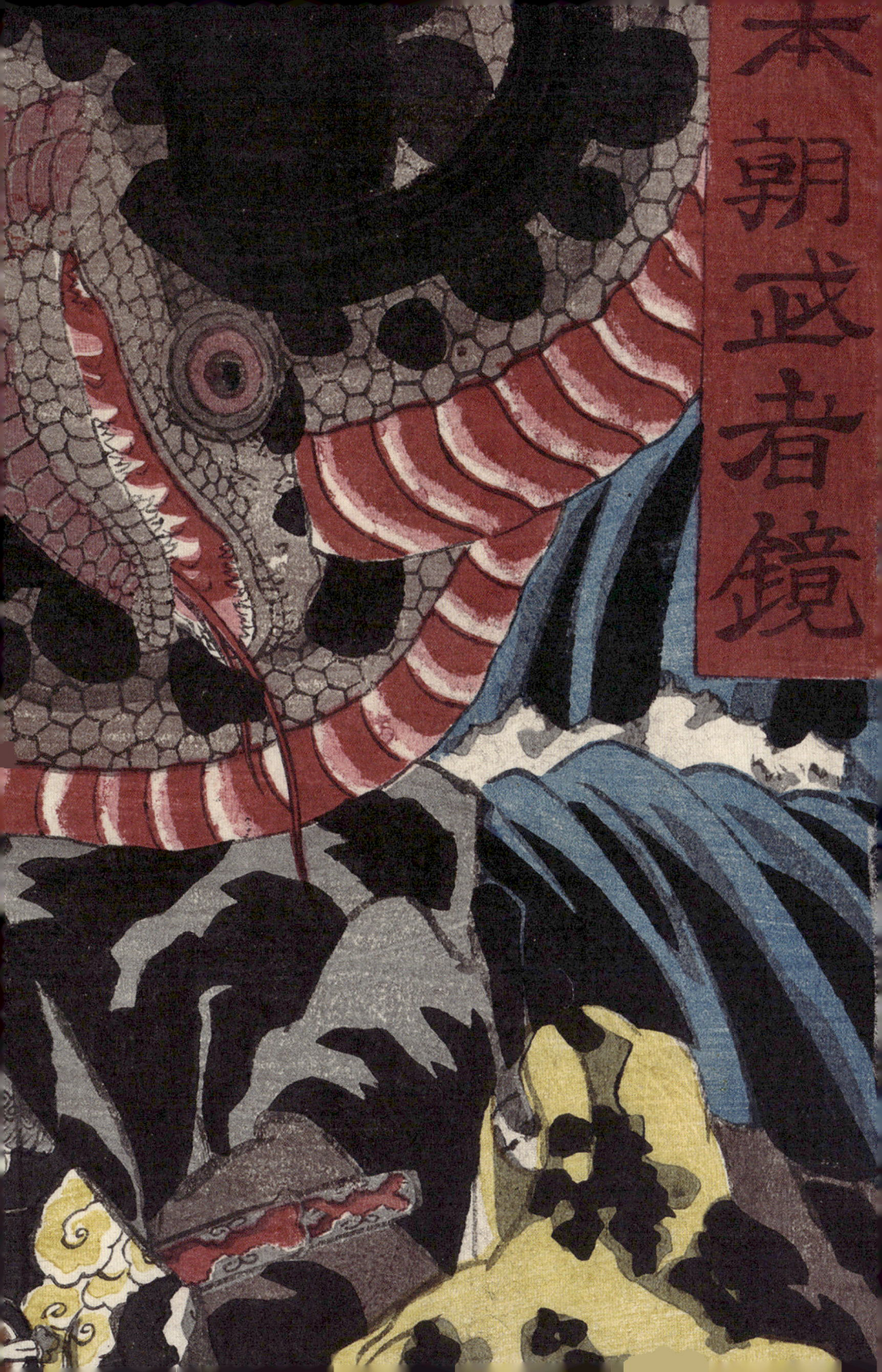

本朝武者鏡

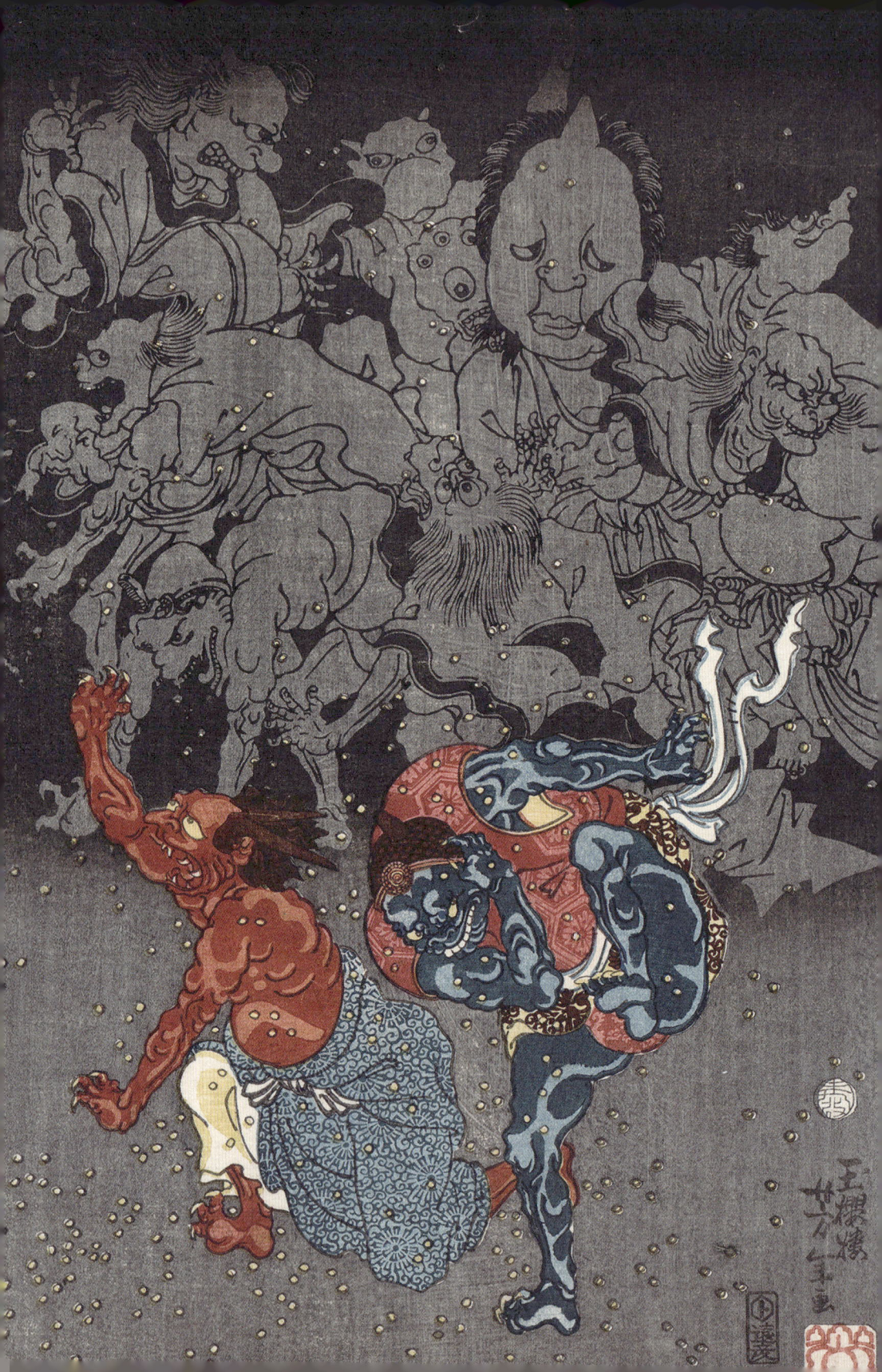

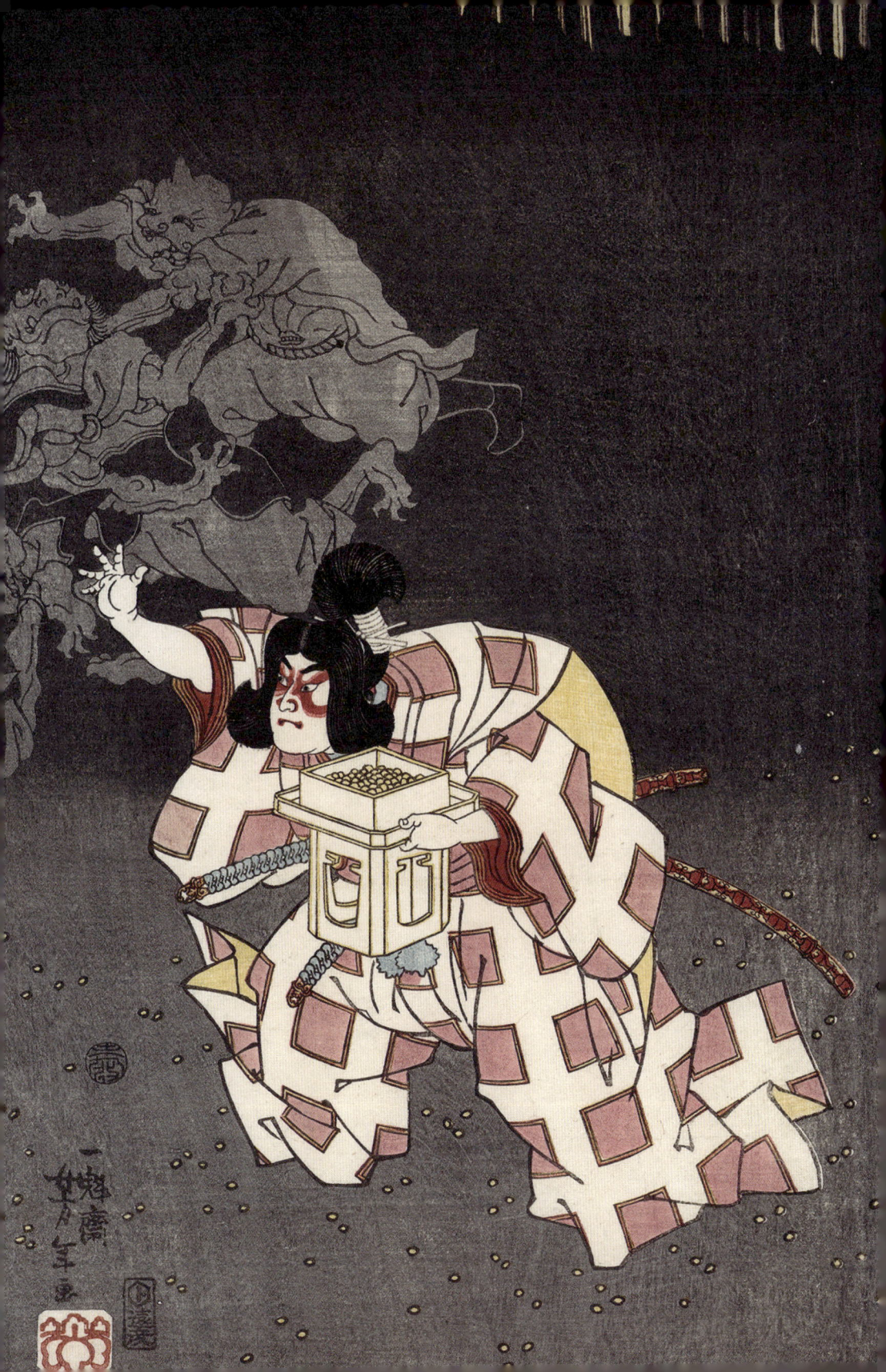

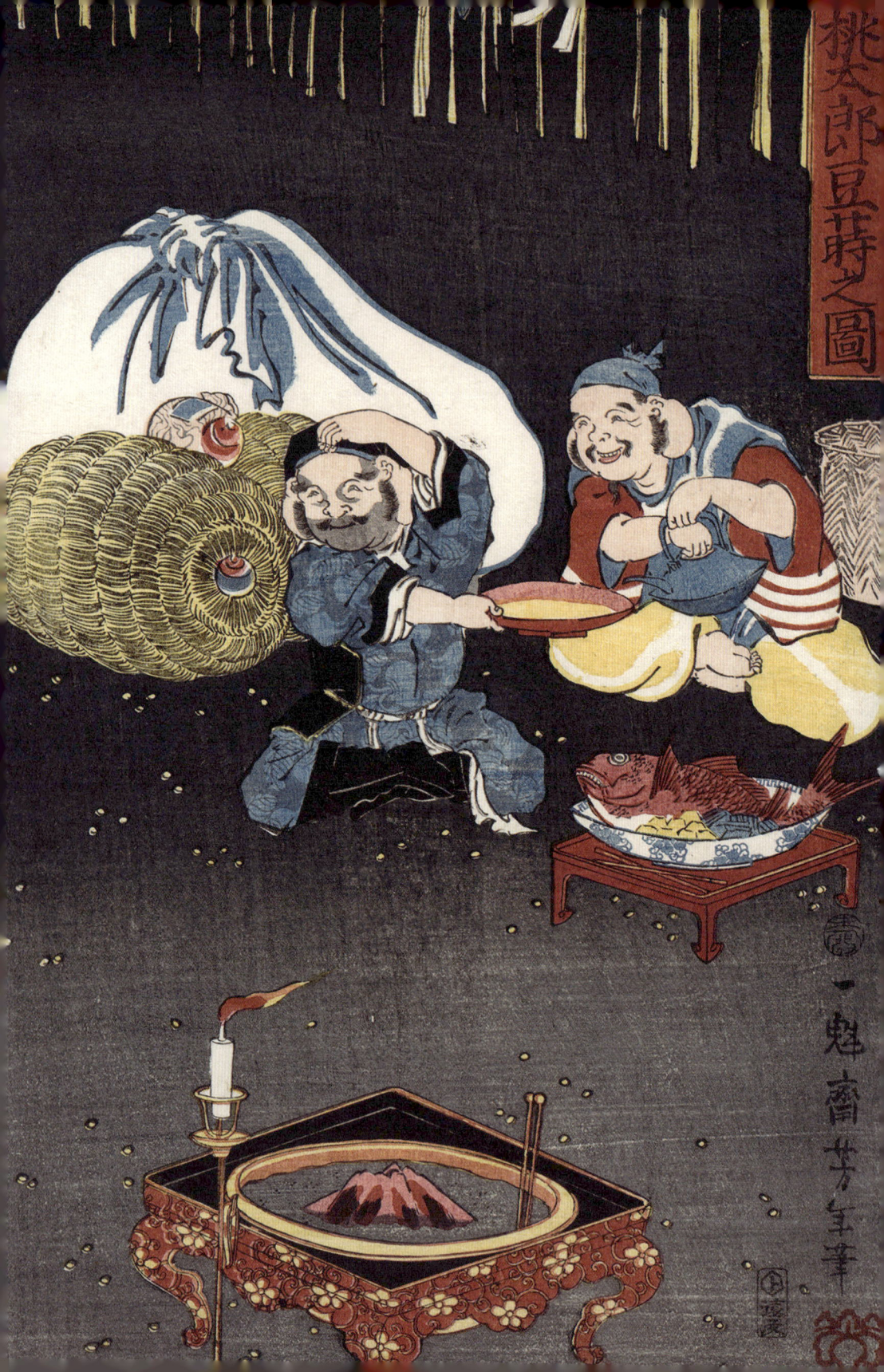

BEANS FOR
DEMONS

•

In *Fasti*, the Latin poet Ovid recounts that in ancient Rome rituals were performed each May during the Lemuria festival to expel malevolent spirits of the dead from the household. Around midnight, the *pater familias* – head of the family – would walk barefoot into the street, snapping his fingers to summon the spirits. Next, he would wash his hands three times in a public fountain, precisely at the moment when the streets were full of spectres and ghosts. He would then put nine black beans in his mouth and spit them out on the ground, one after the other, saying, 'These I cast; with these beans I redeem me and mine' (*Fasti*, Book V, ca 440, trans. J. G. Frazer, London 1931, p. 293). Because the close proximity of the dead was considered inauspicious, the father of the family would immerse his hands again in water and exhort the dead to leave, repeating nine times, 'Ghost of my fathers, go forth!'

Similarly, during the Japanese Setsubun festival in February, which marks the transition from winter to spring, people throw roasted beans to ward off demons (*oni*) and errant monsters (*yōkai*), shouting: 'Devils out, good fortune in!' (*Oni wa soto. Fuku wa uchi*). According to legend, it was through this clever ritual that a young boy, Momotarō – said to have been found inside a peach and to be as strong as he was lazy – succeeded with the aid of a dog, a cat and a pheasant in ridding the island of Onigashima of all the *yōkai* that had caused trouble there for years.

A more comical version of this legend has given artists even freer rein in their imagery. In this tale, a young man named Shinno, accompanied by a dog, a monkey and a bird, travels to an island plagued by clouds of troublesome *yōkai*. He

takes with him sacks full of sweet potatoes, persimmons and chestnuts. After obtaining an audience with the king of the *yōkai*, Shinno and the animals gorge themselves on these fruits and vegetables until their stomachs swell. Having plied the *yōkai* with great quantities of alcohol to put them to sleep, the heroes unleash a barrage of flatulence, almost suffocating the monsters in their sleep. Gasping for air, the creatures wake and quickly flee the island. The *yōkai* king declares that he has learned his lesson, vows to leave the humans in peace and retreats to the bottom of the ocean.

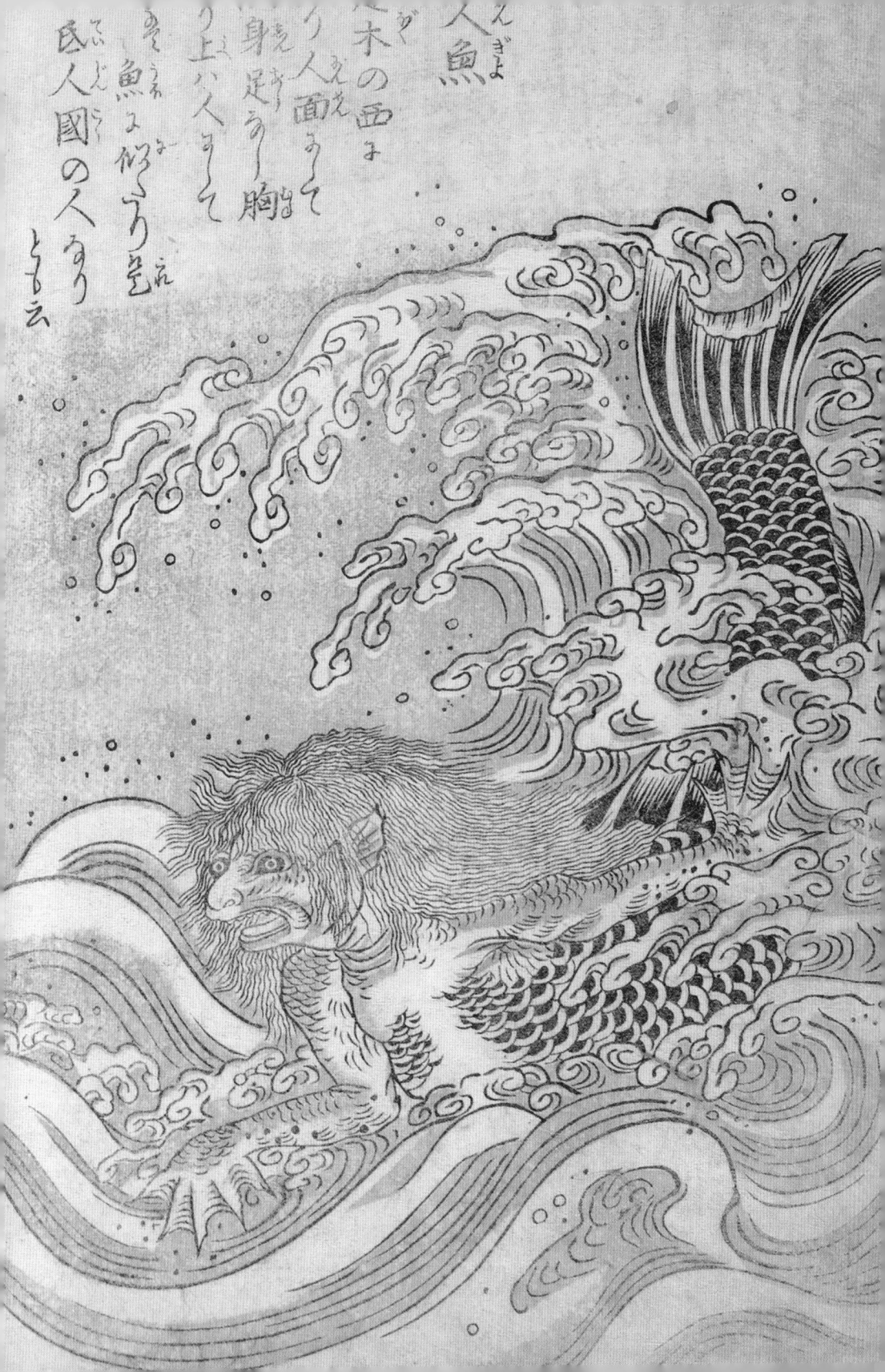

人魚

んぎよ

ぐ
リ木の西ま
り人面うて
ぎえる身足う胸
り上八人うして
えそれば
魚を怪うり至
ふ民人國の人すり
と云

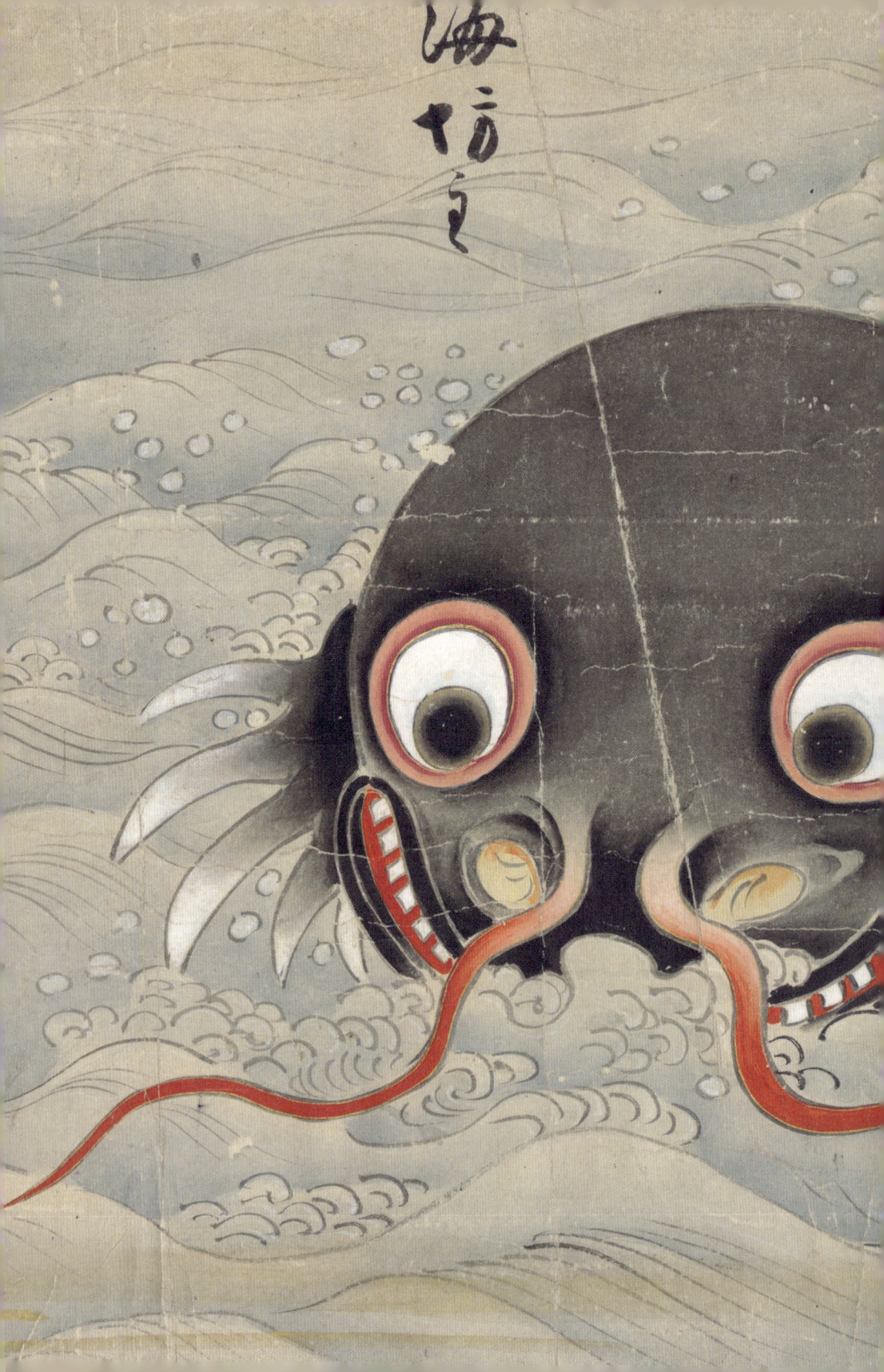

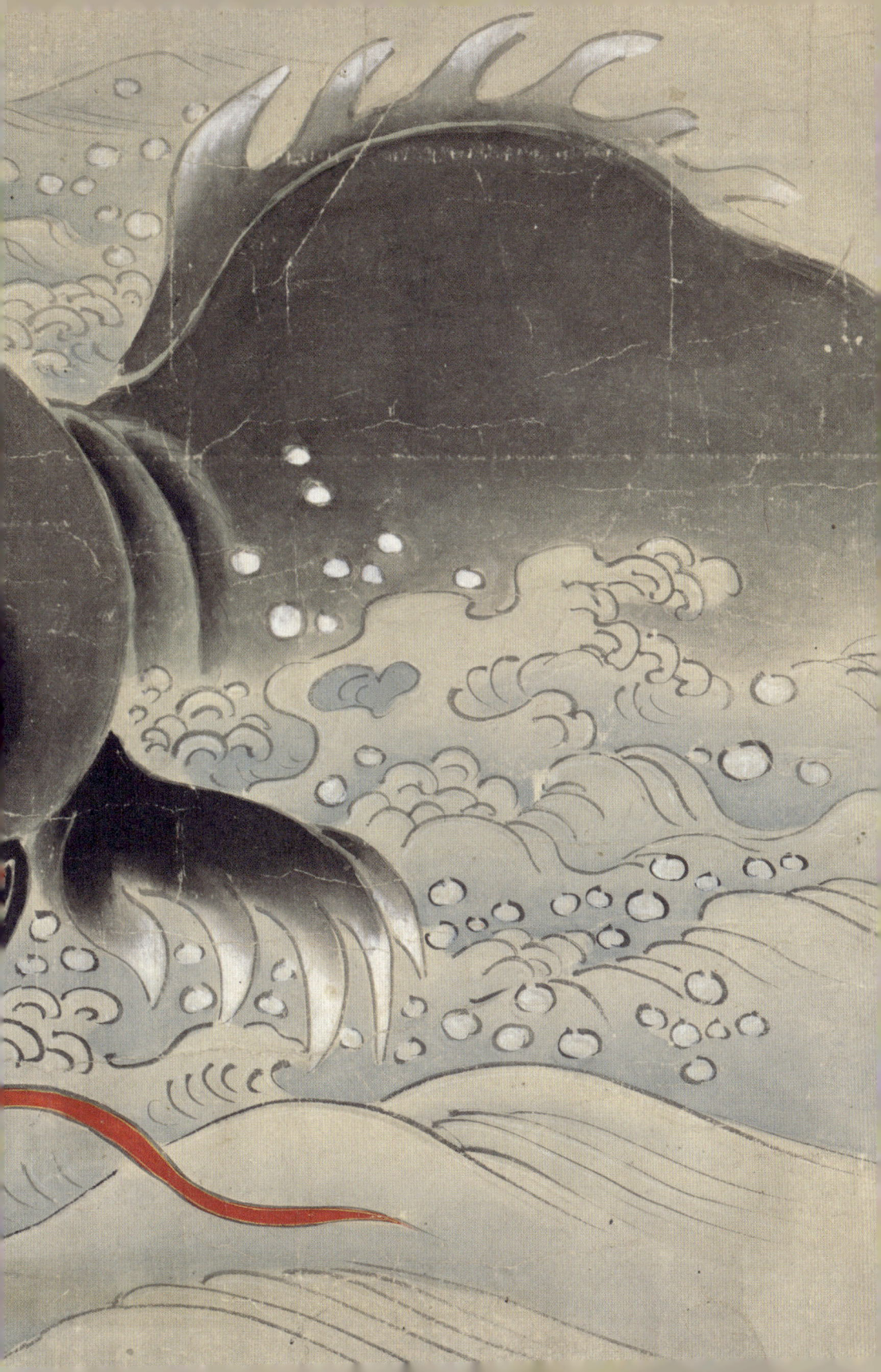

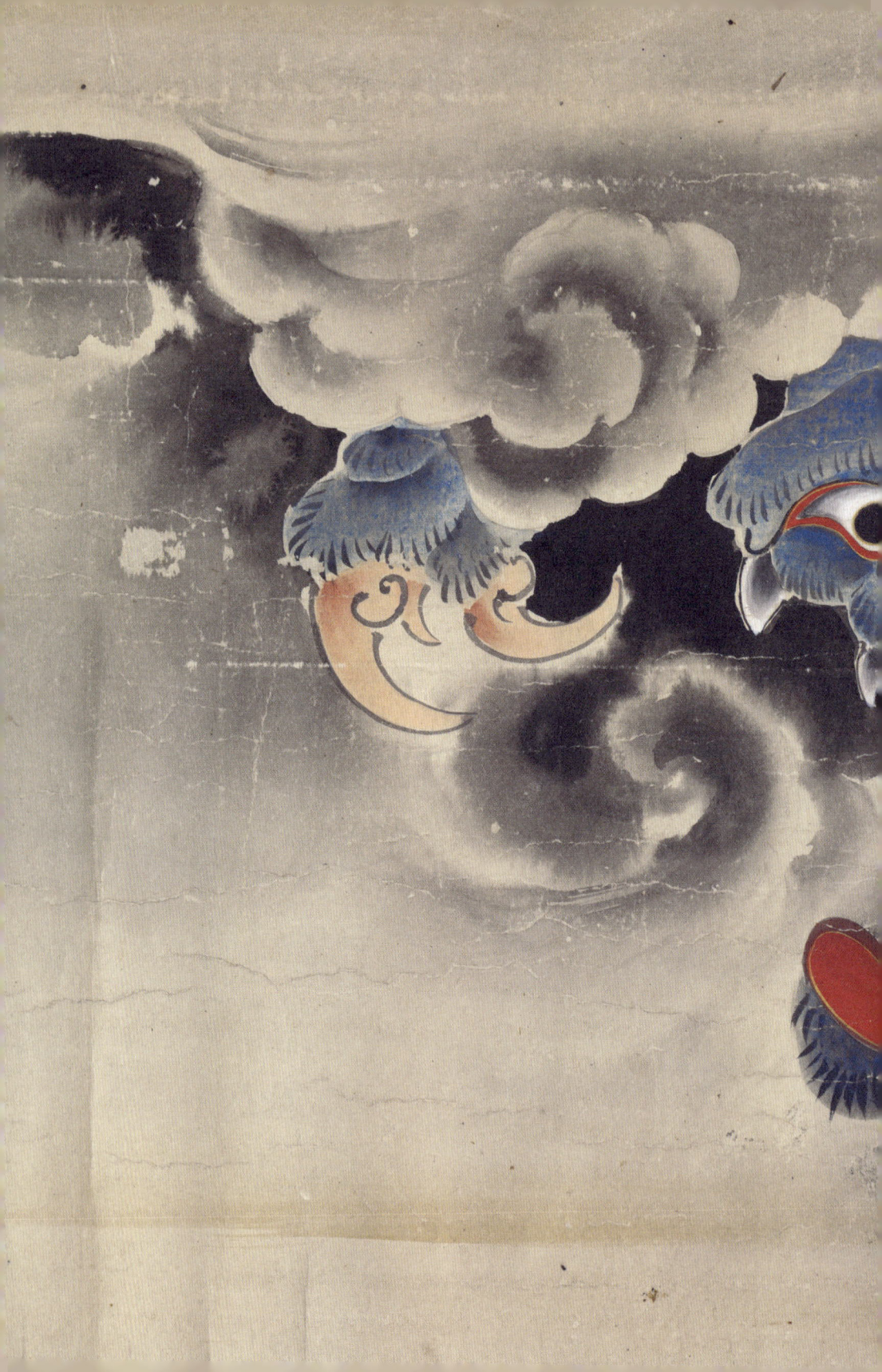

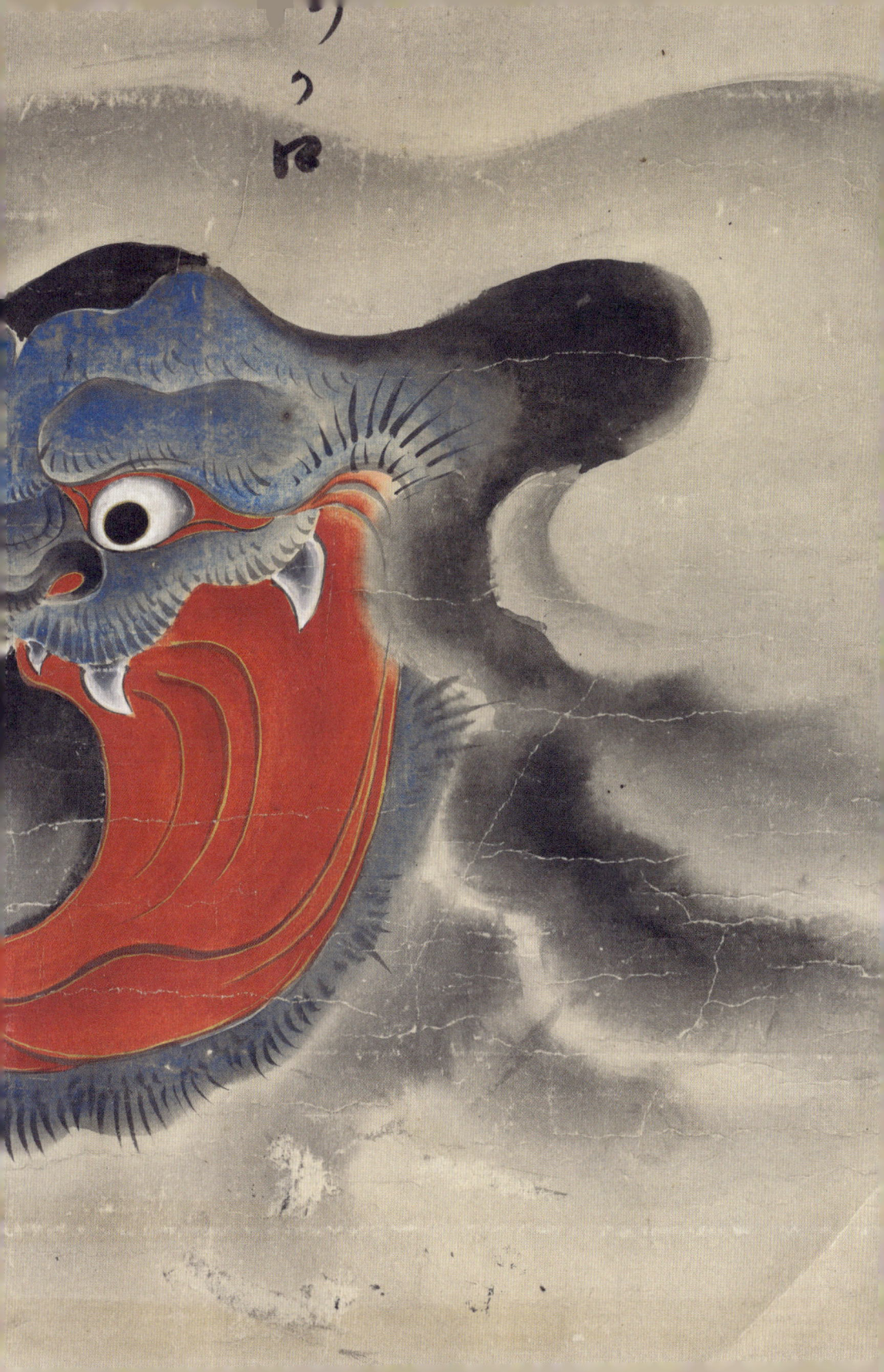

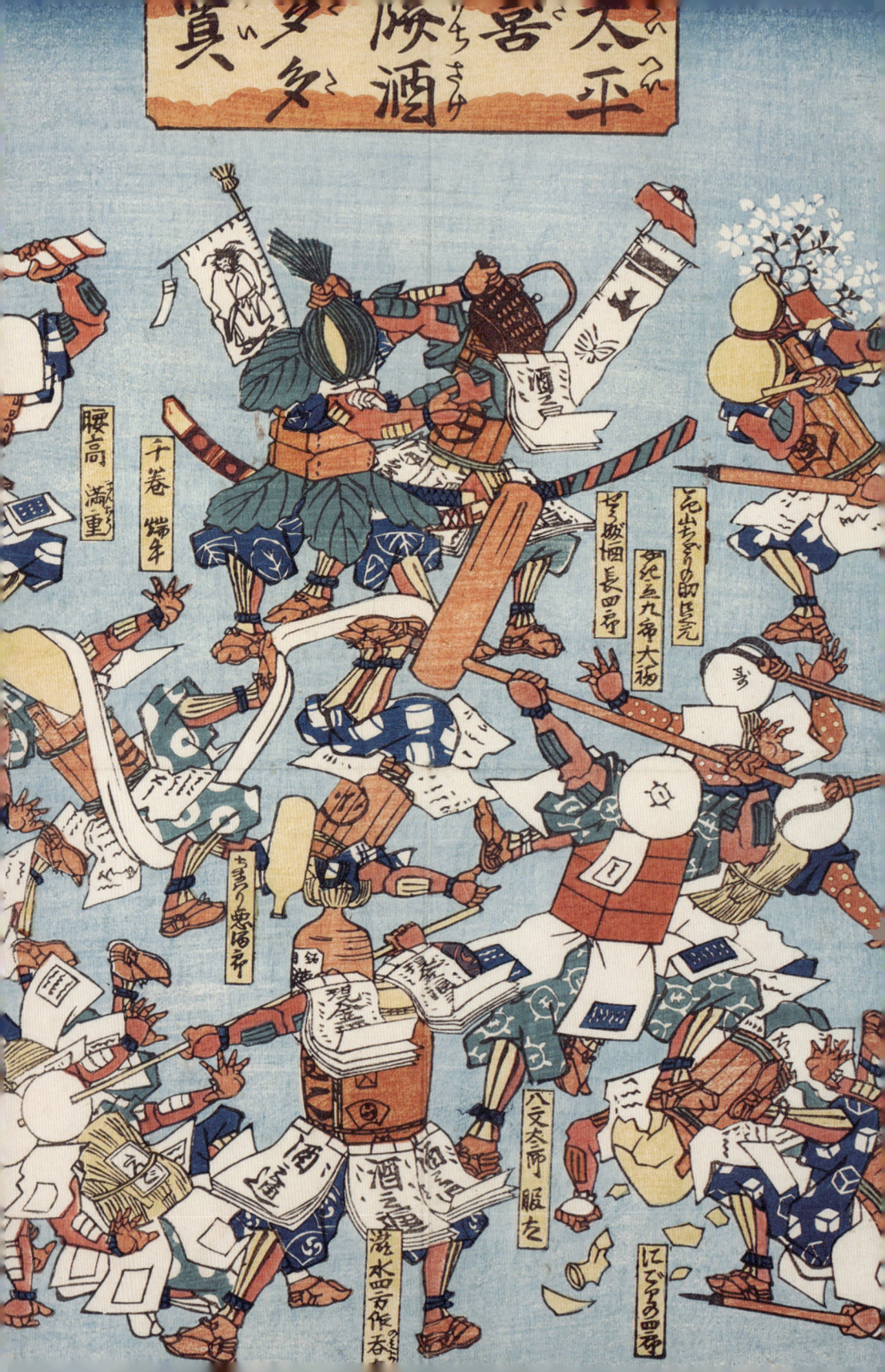

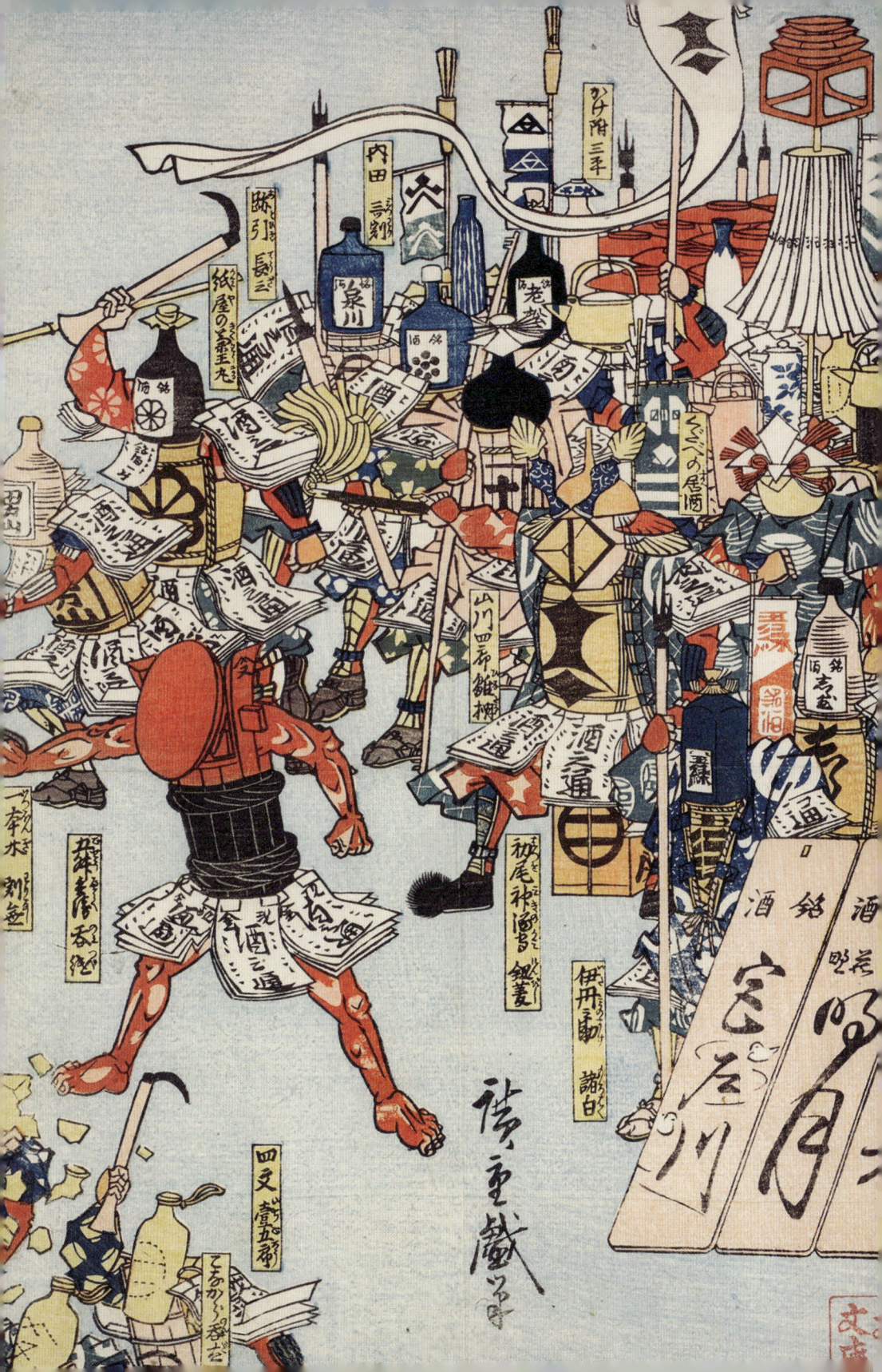

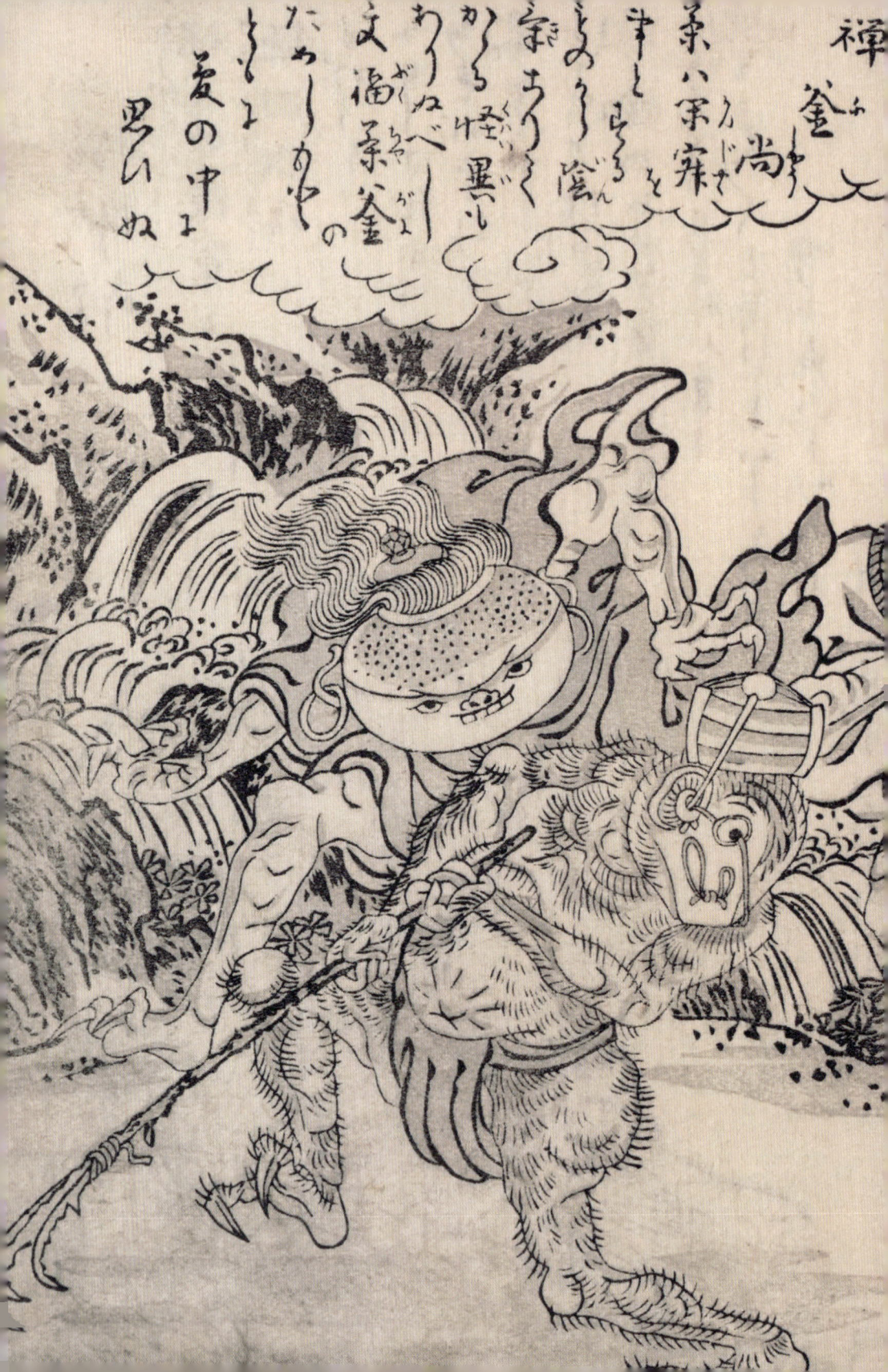

禅釜尚

弟ハ深く
まよう
ものう陰
まうりく
かろ怪異し
ありぬべし
ざうしゃうがう
文福茶釜
の
たゝうりや
ここと
ここと
爰の中よ
思いぬ

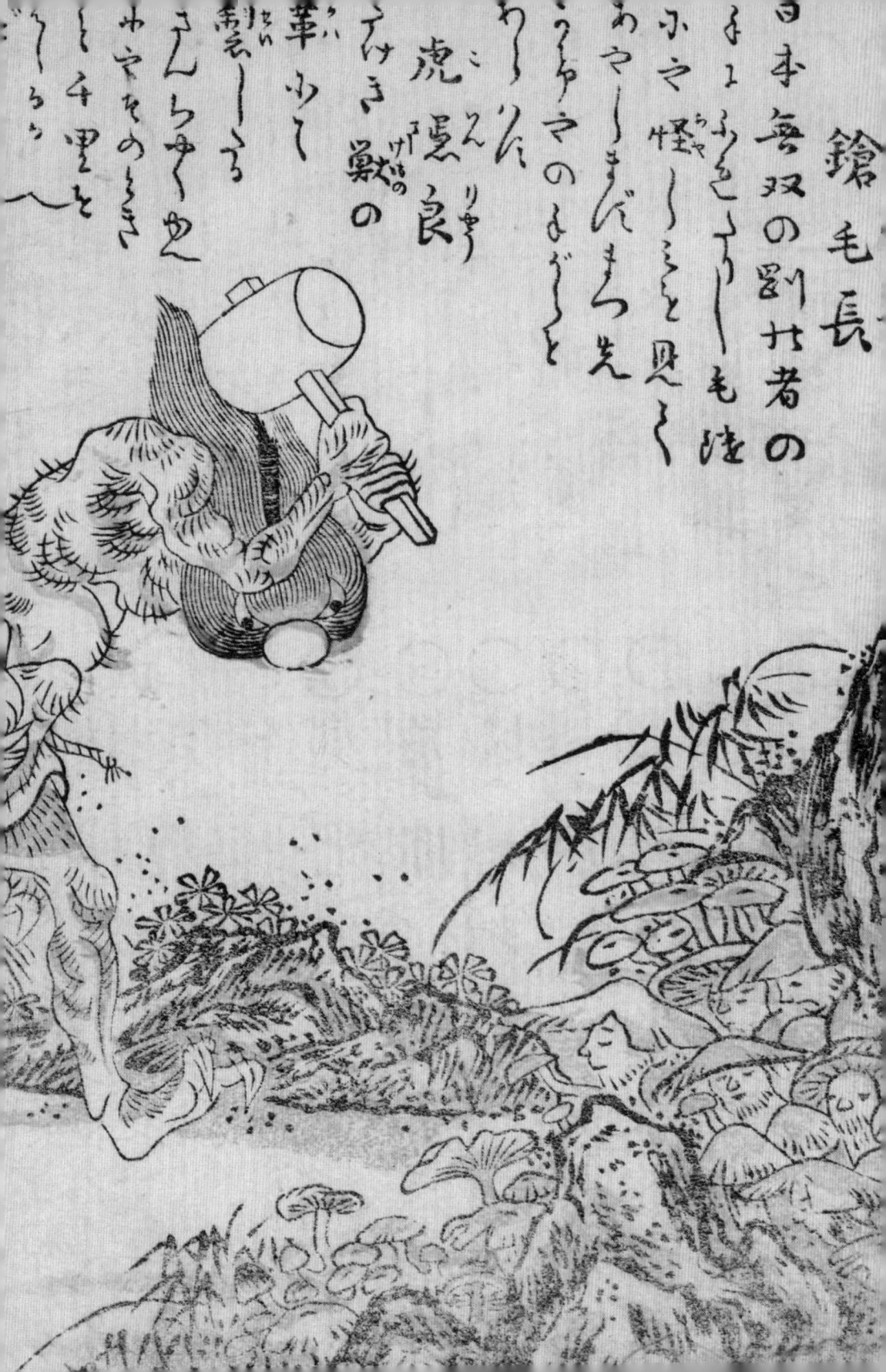

鎗毛長

日本無双の劔士者の
よくふるまうしも毛性
ふゝ怪しきを見く
あやしまぶるし光
うつゝのもぐゝと
りぬこと
虎隠良
えけき戦の
華少し
雲ふー
さんちうせ
ゆやそのゝき
ぐ千里と
こゝる

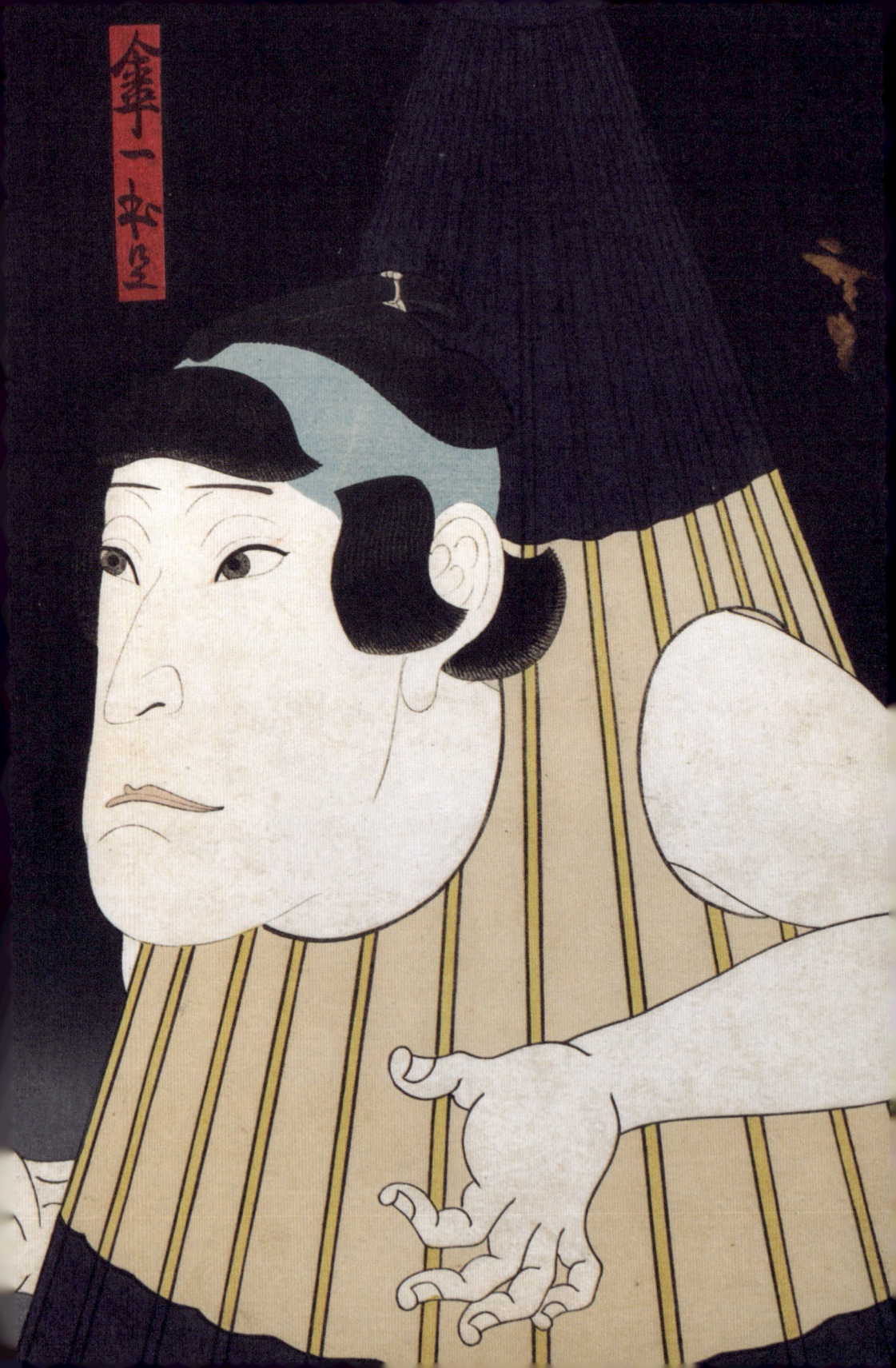

WHEN OBJECTS COME TO LIFE

•

It is said that as time passes, objects become imbued with human souls – like a patina not of age but of emotion, of the residue of human life and feeling. Little by little the objects begin to awaken, and by the time a hundred years has passed, they are fully animate. A chip, a crack, even a break does not prevent this transformation. On the contrary, everything conspires to make them little autonomous beings.

Some believe that every object possesses a soul from the start, one that demands complete respect from any human who handles it. If this basic rule is broken, the object seeks revenge by transforming into a *yōkai*. Now endowed with arms, legs and sense organs, it turns relentlessly against those who have wronged it.

Japanese prints often depict these animate objects – *tsukumogami* – which may include teapots, pieces of armour, brooms, lanterns, and more. They wait for the night to spring to life, emerging from drawers and cupboards, congregating for supernatural revels, and raising a joyous din before returning to their resting places by sunrise. Others, less well-behaved or even openly hostile, start hitting their 'master' (the man who owns the home) during his sleep, or setting traps for the woman of the house: an obstacle on the stairs, or a precariously balanced stack of dishes. Is it vengeance for some thoughtless act, when a human took out their frustration on a harmless object? Perhaps.

And yet nothing is ever entirely lost. Despite their mischief or malice, these animate objects are still capable of attaining Nirvana through the power of their devotion.

Many people, fearful that their belongings may become *tsukumogami*, choose to do discard them before they reach the fateful age of one hundred years, but this only increases the frustration and anger of the abandoned objects towards their former owners.

During my last visit to Japan, it felt as though I may have encountered a few of these *tsukumogami*. I was staying at Nagiso, in an old house on the banks of a rushing mountain stream. For several nights running, I heard vibrations coming from a drawer in an old wooden cabinet, home to a Singer sewing machine dating back to 1880. Inside was a timeworn toothbrush, its bristles blackened by the solution of vinegar and iron filings once used by married women to darken their teeth, a tradition known as *ohaguro*.

On the road towards Magome Pass (the old route between Tokyo and Kyoto), there was a long-abandoned teahouse. Through the broken windowpanes, I could make out piles of plates, saucepans and cutlery. Everything was coated with a thick layer of dust except for these surprising objects, as if their nocturnal processions shook off the grey veil. But a look at the worm-eaten floorboards convinced me not to go inside.

On Mount Koyasan, in a building adjoining the Shojoshin-in monastery, a small bronze incense burner, no larger than a child's fist, wandered near my futon each night, leaving a trace of faint metallic green on the pristine whiteness of the tatami. And then in Paris there was the tiny tea bowl that I bought for next to nothing at the Hôtel Drouot auction house. I put it on my bedside table between two piles of books and found it on the floor one morning broken into four pieces (the number of death). Was it the vibrations of the Métro trains passing beneath the building, or some magic at work?

In historical prints, artists gave free rein to their fantasies, often adding comical features

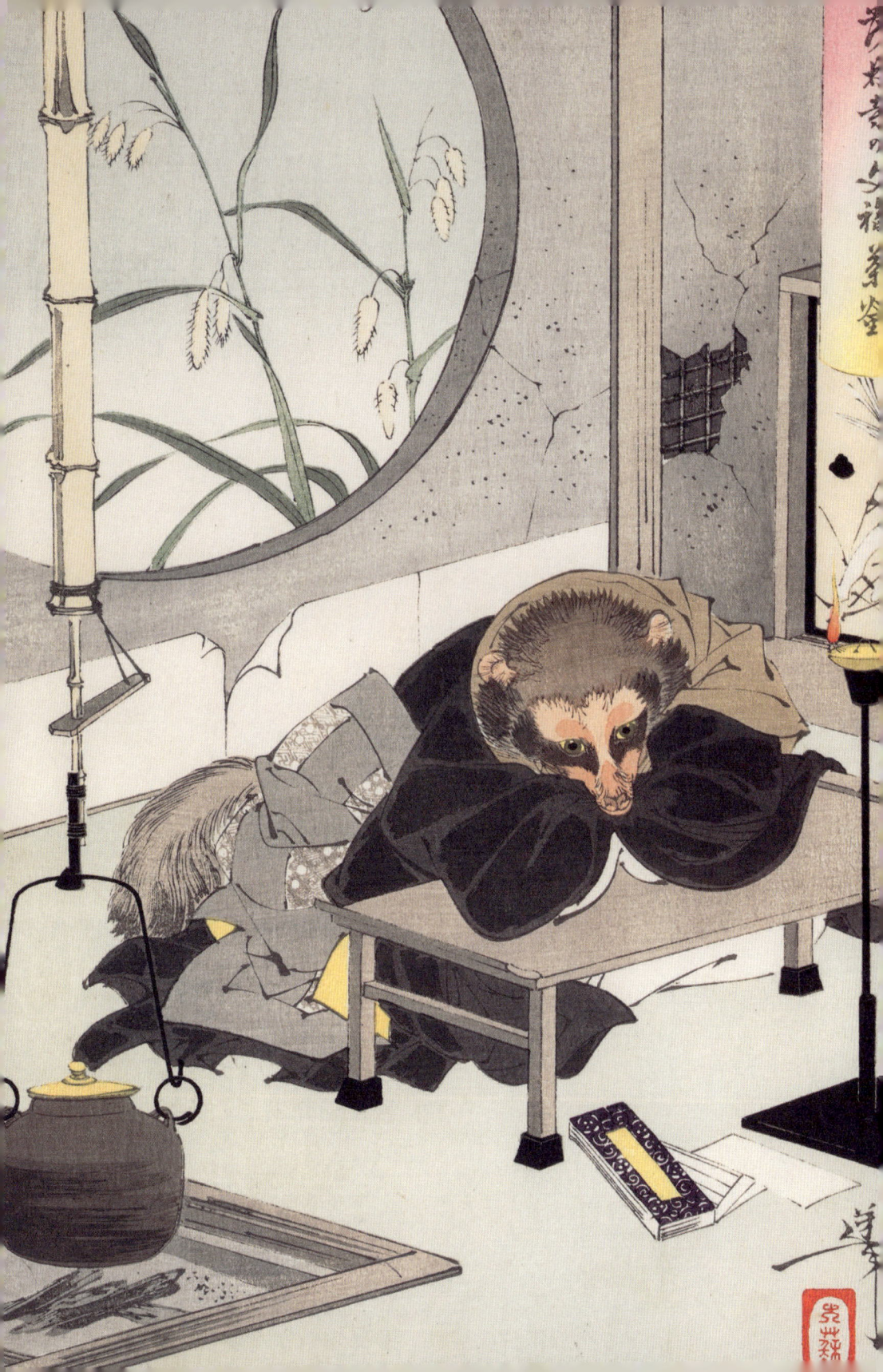

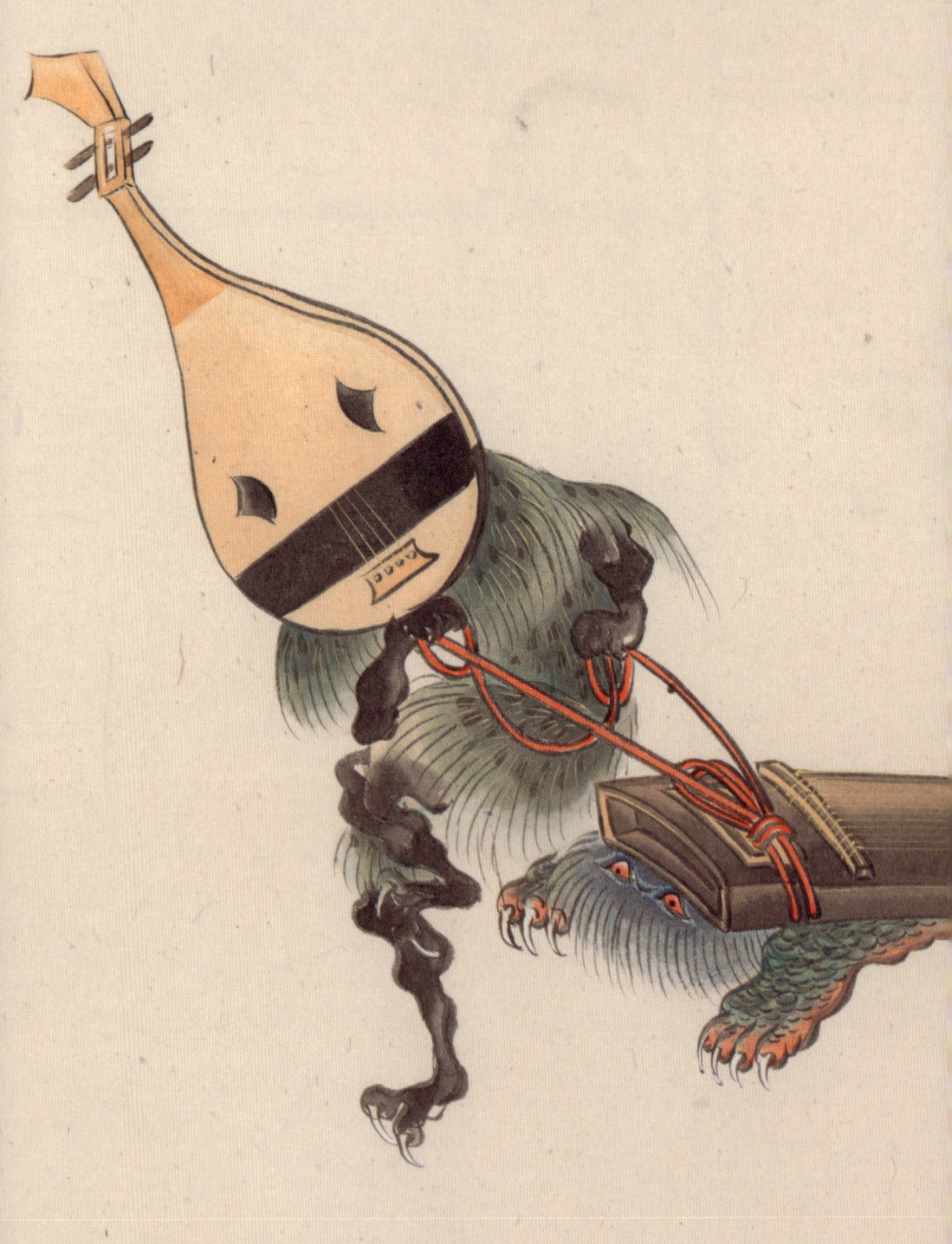

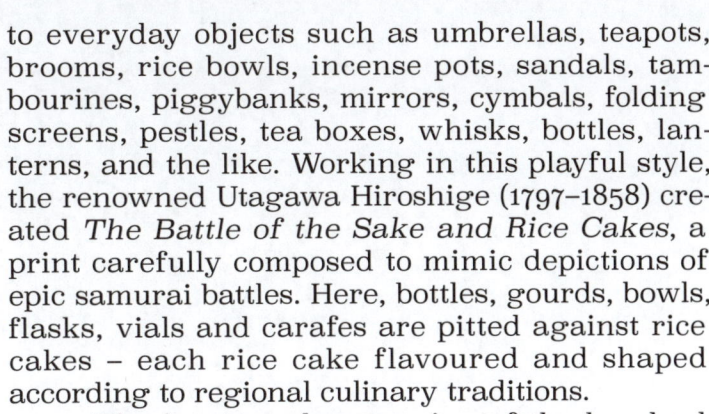

to everyday objects such as umbrellas, teapots, brooms, rice bowls, incense pots, sandals, tambourines, piggybanks, mirrors, cymbals, folding screens, pestles, tea boxes, whisks, bottles, lanterns, and the like. Working in this playful style, the renowned Utagawa Hiroshige (1797–1858) created *The Battle of the Sake and Rice Cakes*, a print carefully composed to mimic depictions of epic samurai battles. Here, bottles, gourds, bowls, flasks, vials and carafes are pitted against rice cakes – each rice cake flavoured and shaped according to regional culinary traditions.

The 'nocturnal procession of the hundred demons' (*Hyakki Yagyō*) is a central motif in Japanese art and storytelling, involving a parade of *tsukumogami* in the streets of Edo, Kyoto, Osaka, Nagasaki and more remote regions on certain cursed nights. This monstrous march is composed of a succession of a hundred animate objects making a hellish noise and hurling imprecations at any human unfortunate enough to cross their path. It is above all in the height of summer, during the Obon festival honouring the dead, when heat, humidity and storms descend upon Japan, that the *yōkai* come out after dark to parade through towns and cities, giving vent to their mischievousness.

The earliest representation of the *Hyakki Yagyō* theme, painted by Tosa Mitsunobu (1430–1522), is now in the Shinju-an Daitoku-ji Buddhist temple in Kyoto. This seminal work became the model for a long tradition of illustrated scrolls, each showcasing the imagination and technical skill of the artist. Every detail carries meaning, such as the tip of a bushy tail protruding from a fold in a kimono, indicating that the harmless courtesan is in fact a dangerous fox (*kitsune*).

One question is often asked: Where do these hellish processions begin? It is likely that geomantic considerations come into play, pointing to a spiritually harmful spot where a building's negative energies are concentrated – a place well-suited for *yōkai* to meet and for the march to depart. This location is the north-east corner of the building; it is traditionally trimmed or cut back, and salt is scattered or placed there for protection and

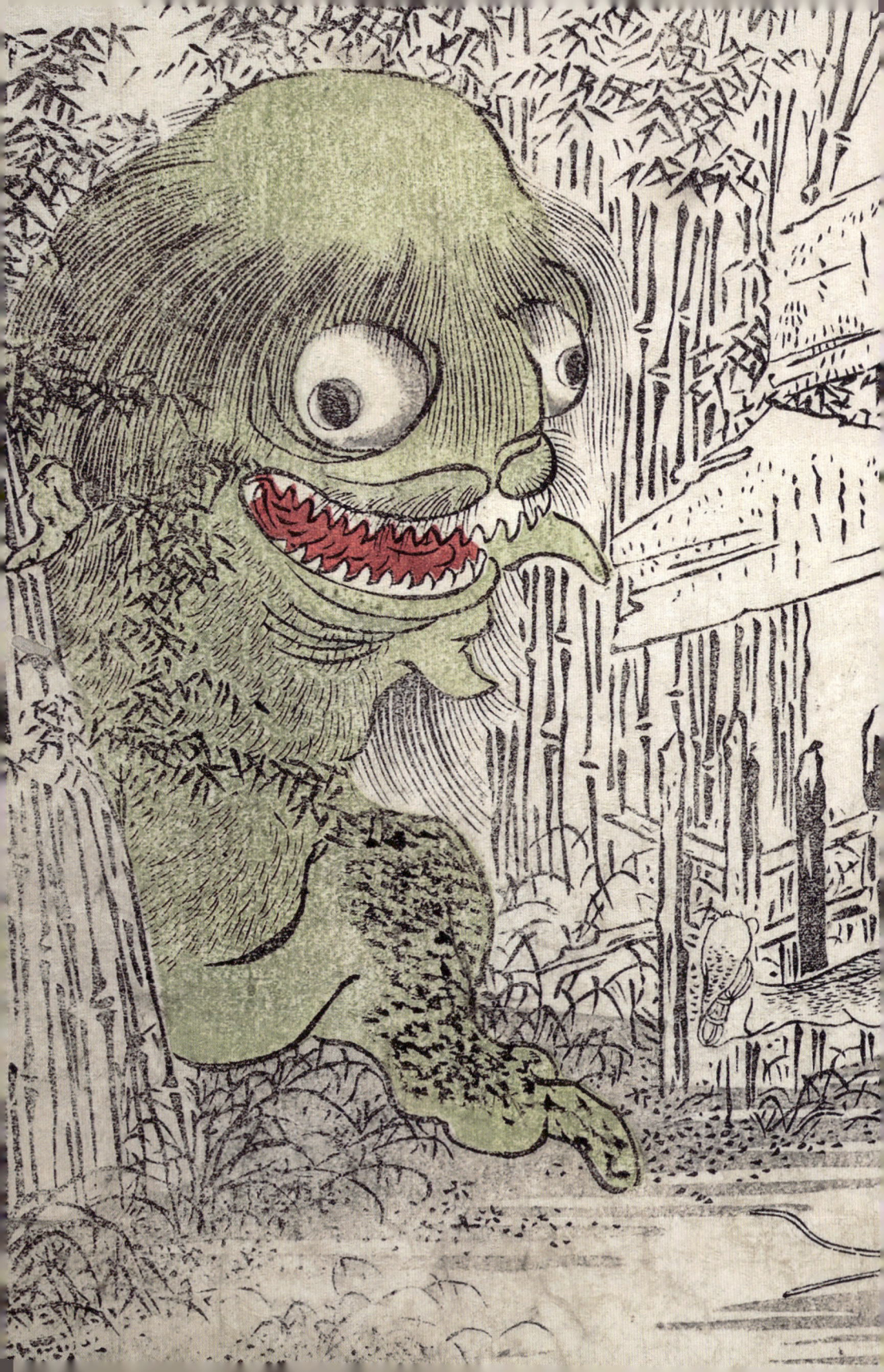

purification. Similarly, the enclosures of imperial palaces are often truncated at this same corner and furnished with a wooden statue of a monkey (*saru*). Because the sound of the Japanese word for 'monkey' is very similar to the word 'leave', the statue is believed to help drive away evil spirits (Koyama-Richard, 2017, p. 36).

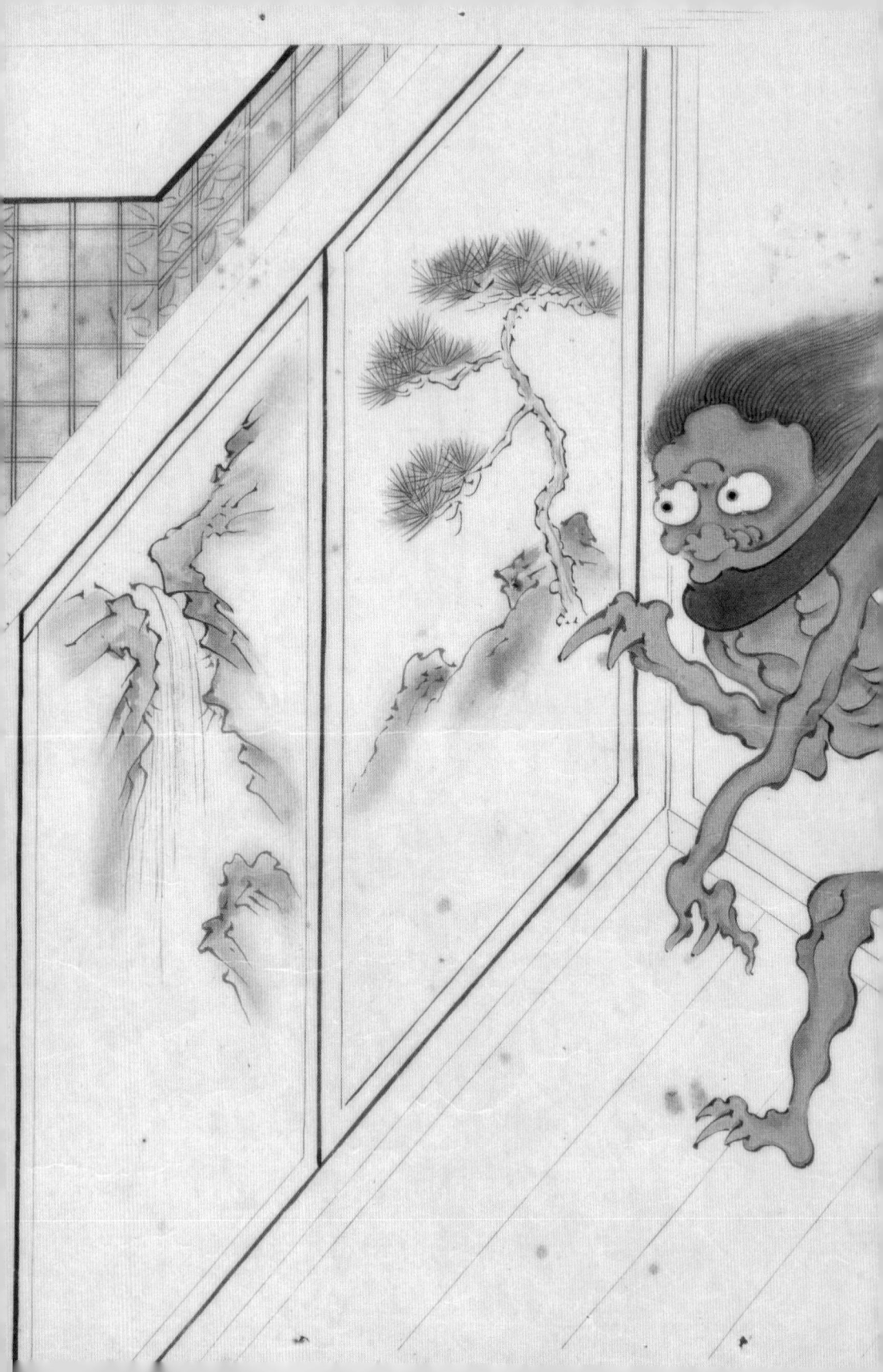

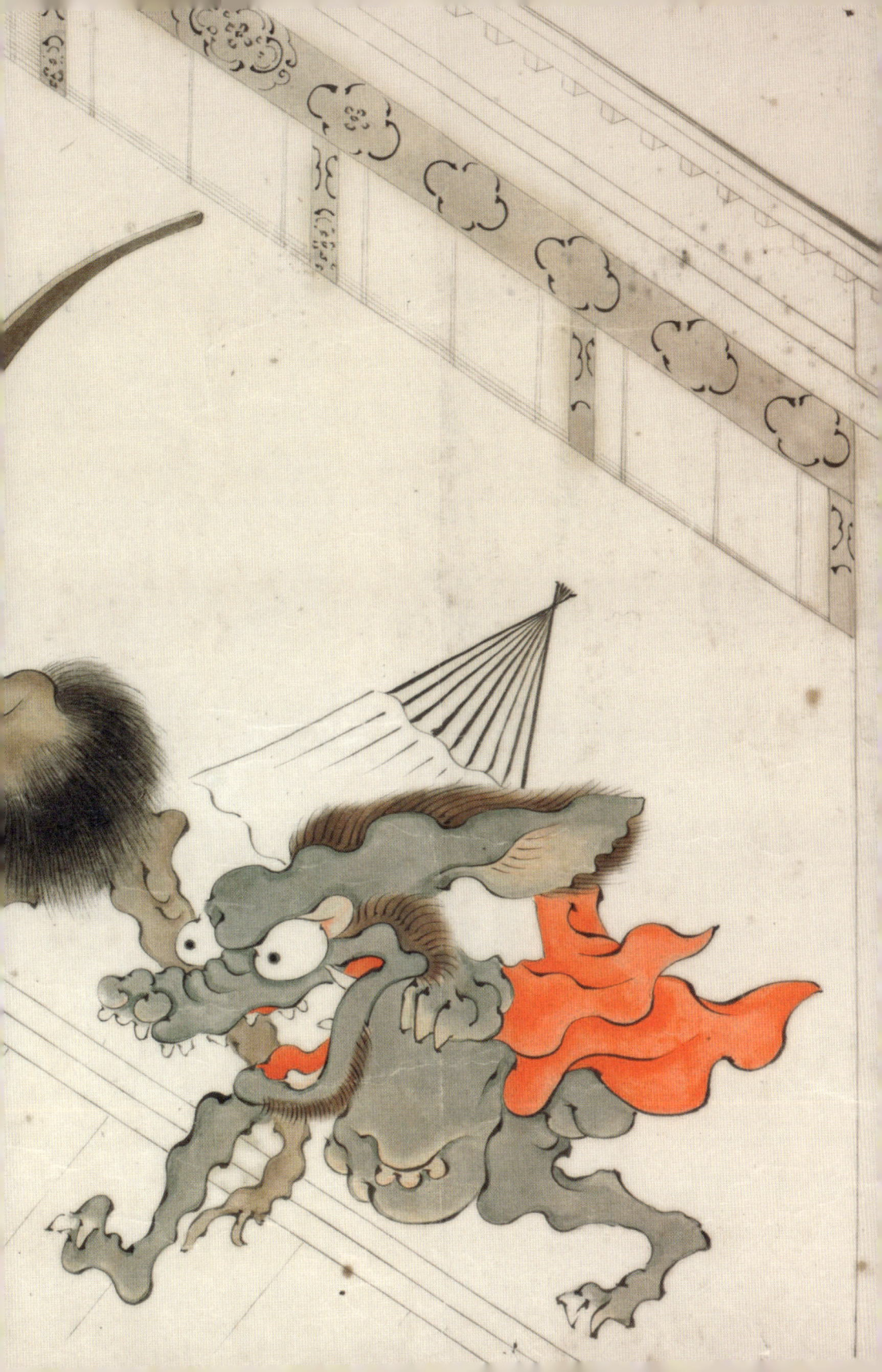

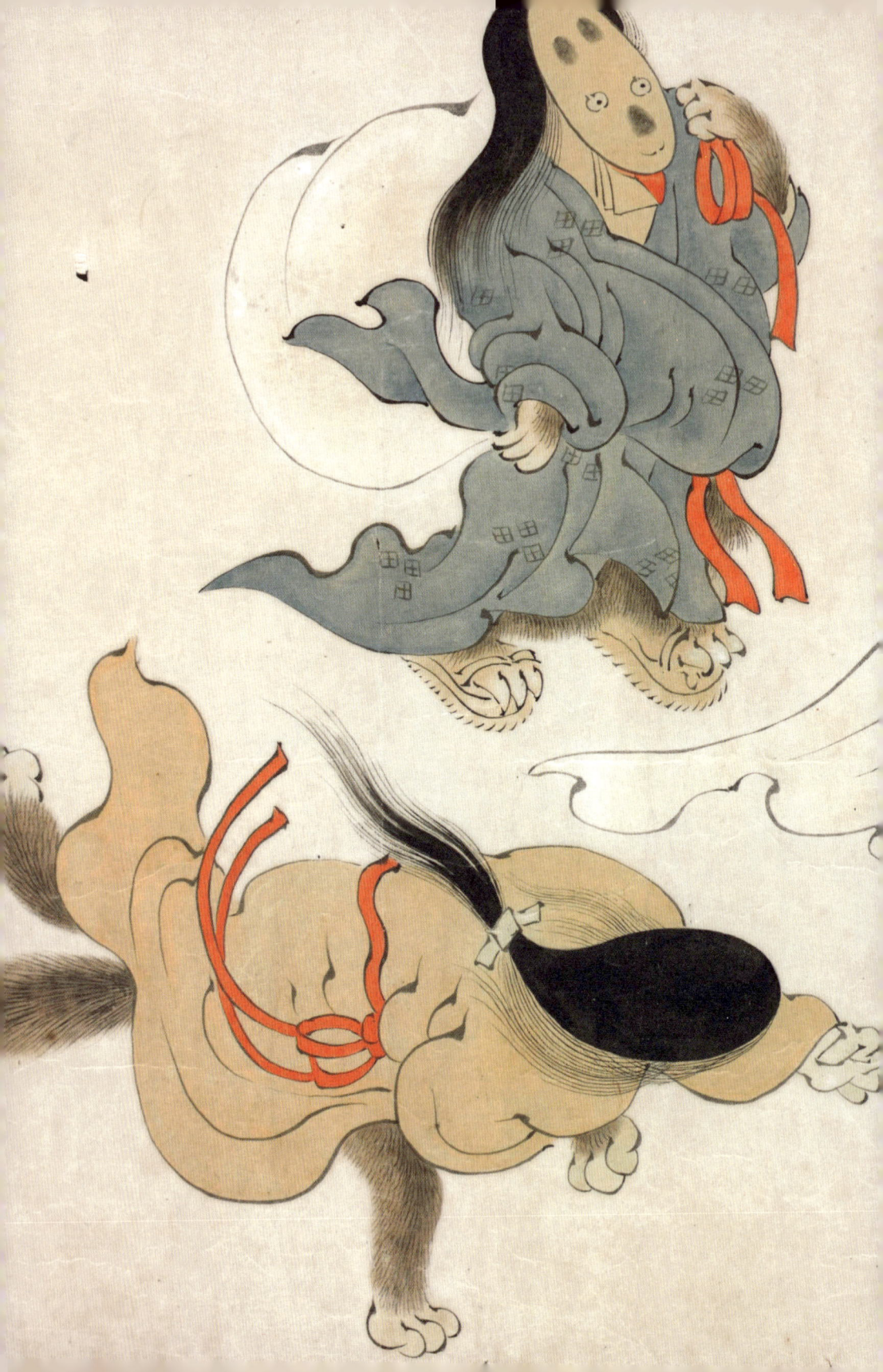

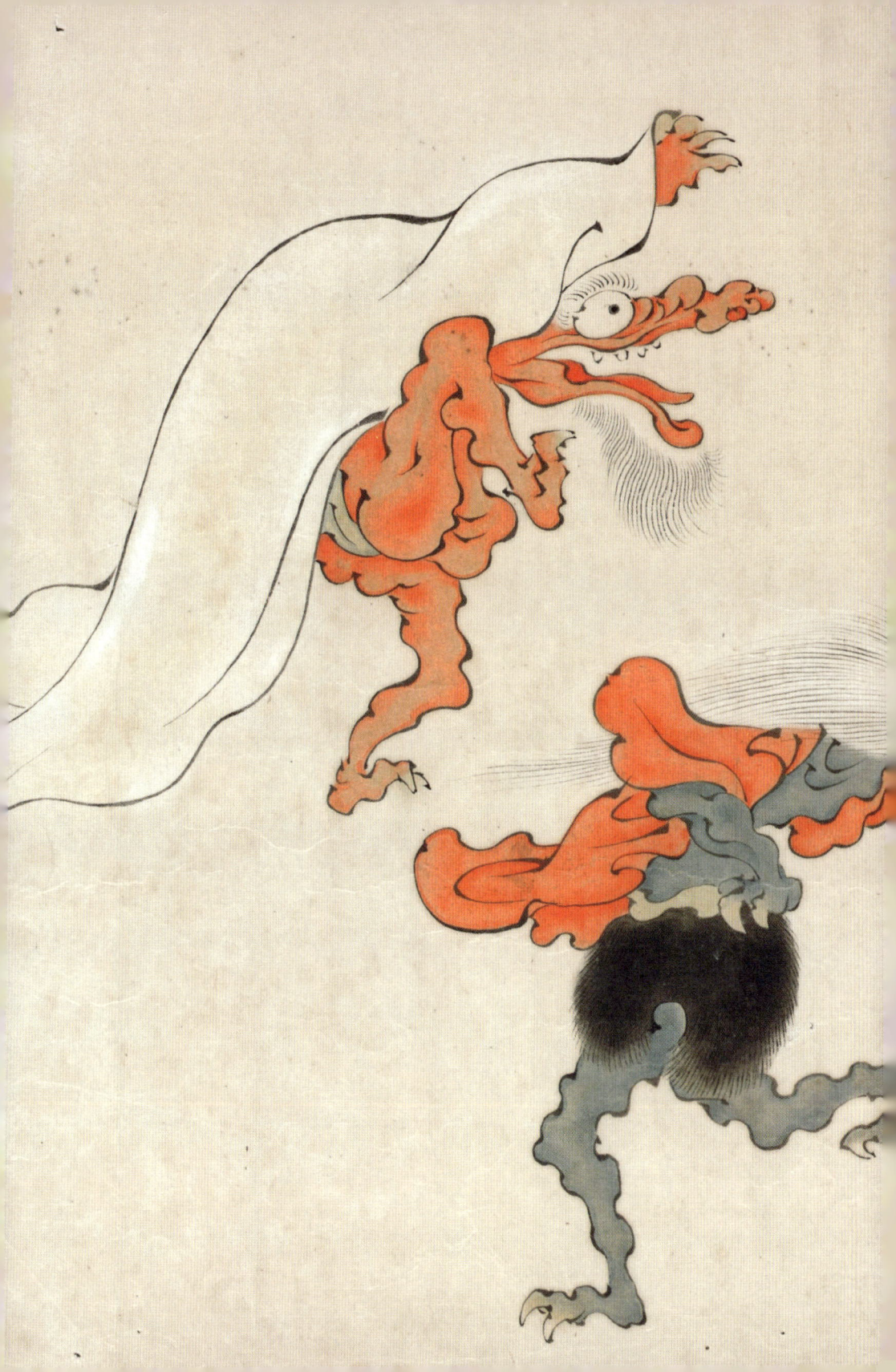

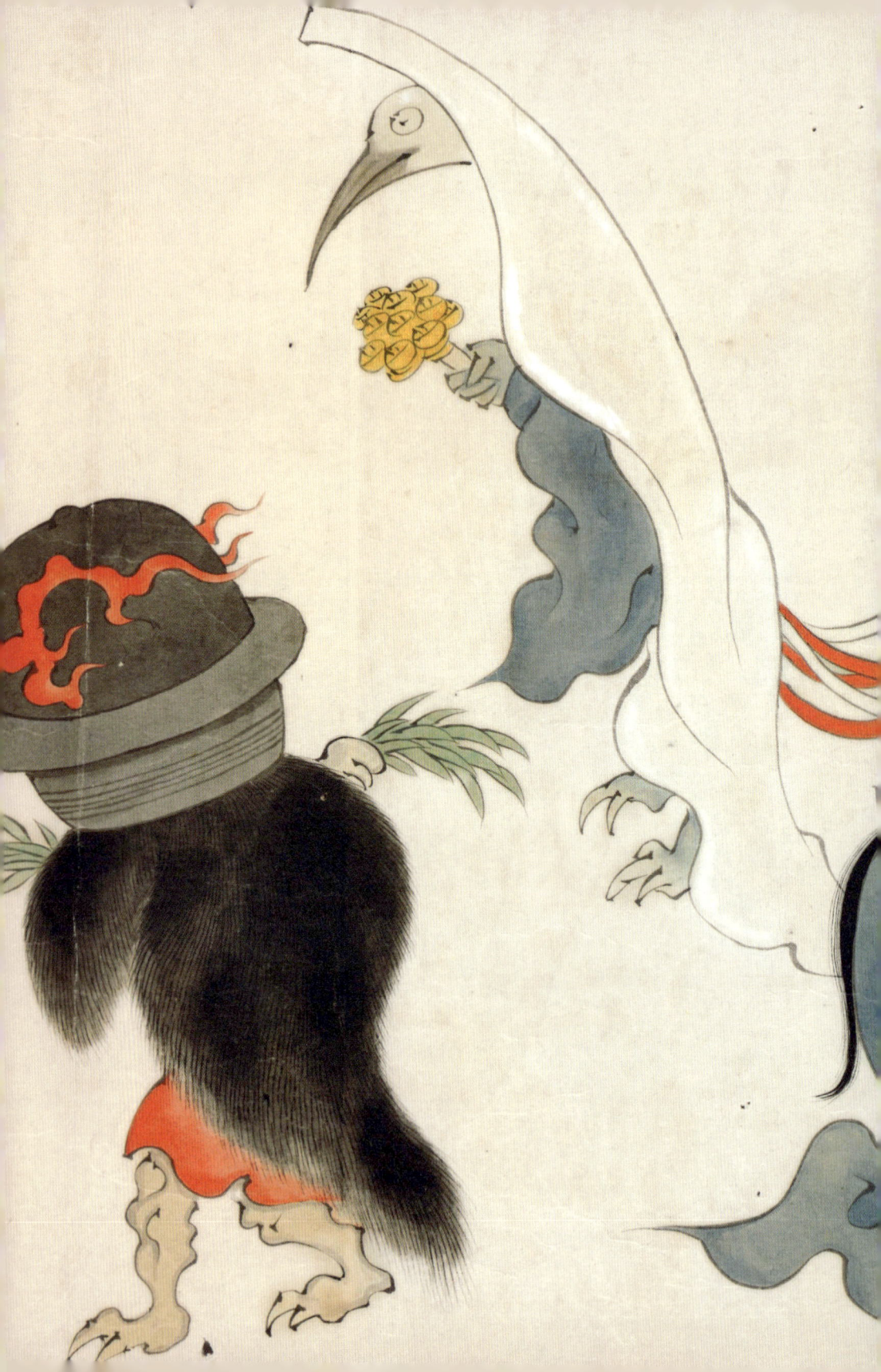

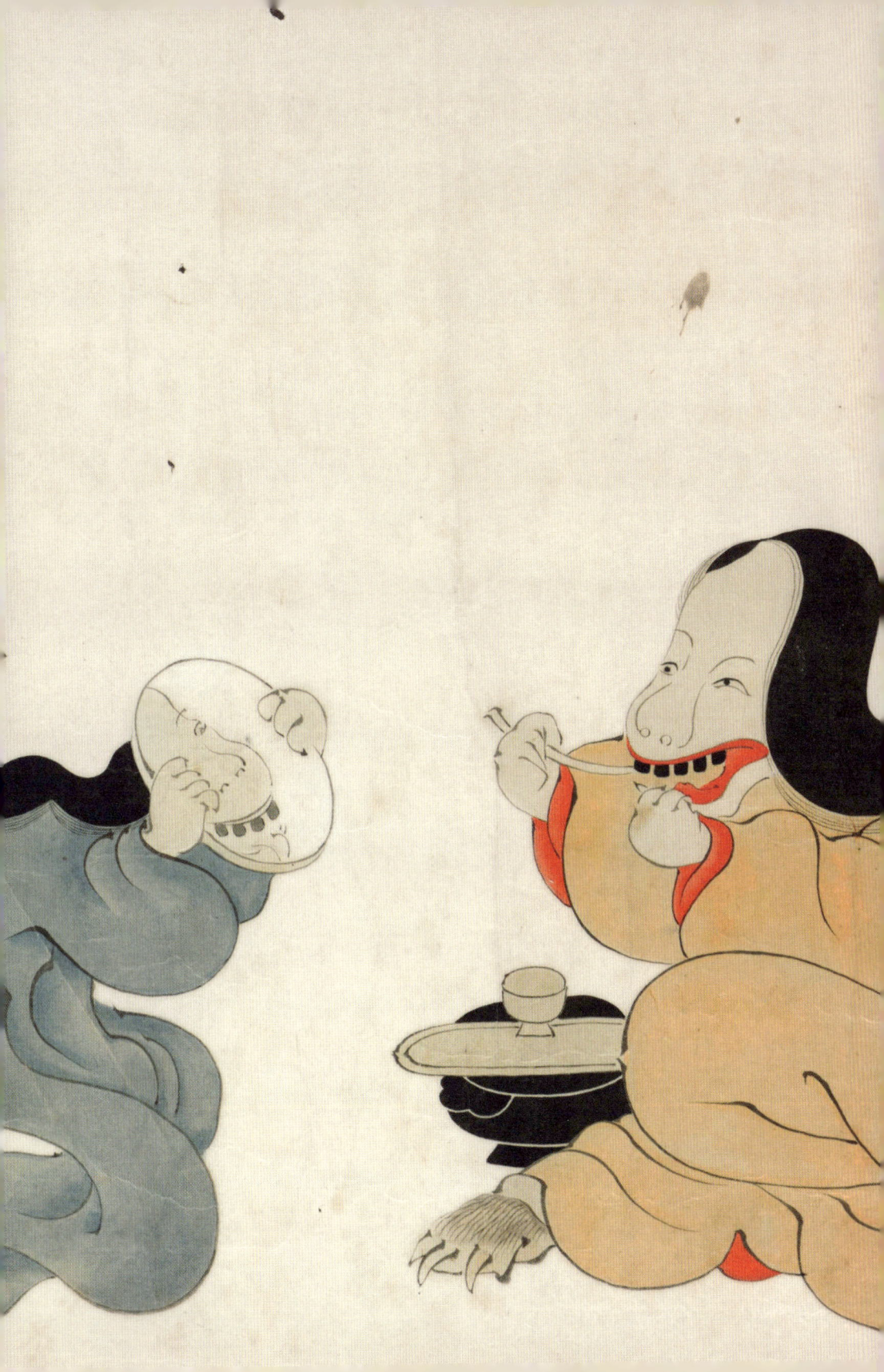

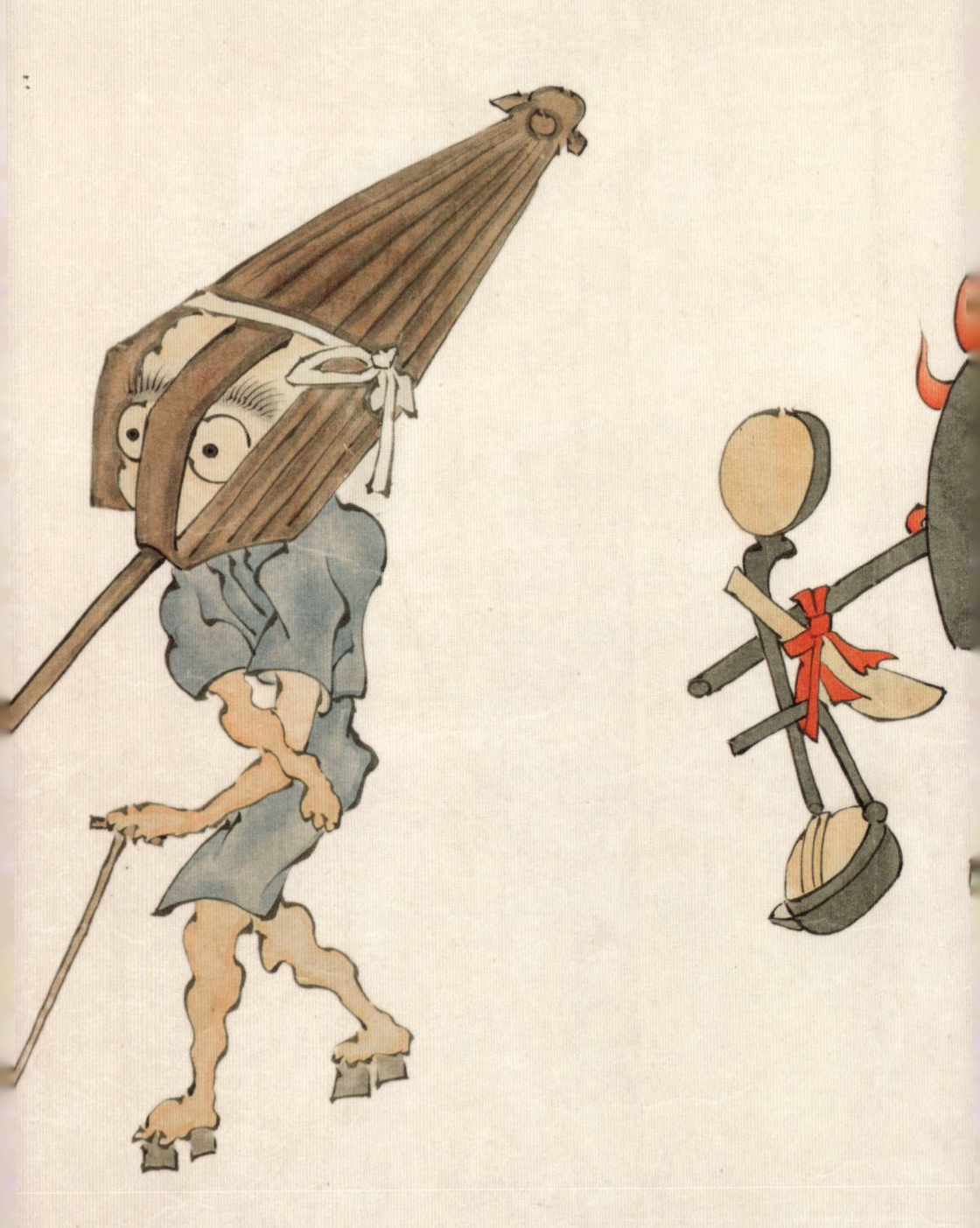

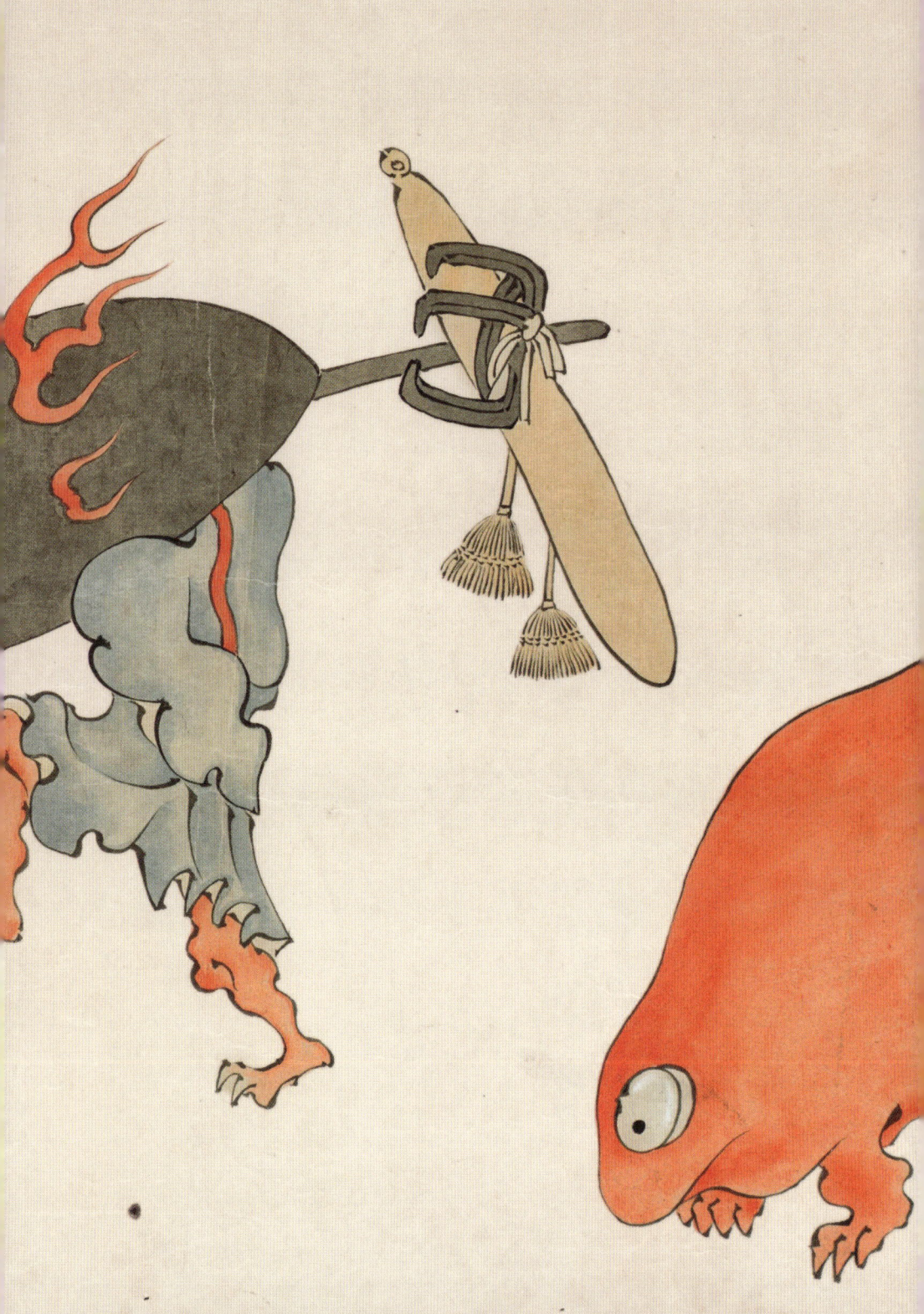

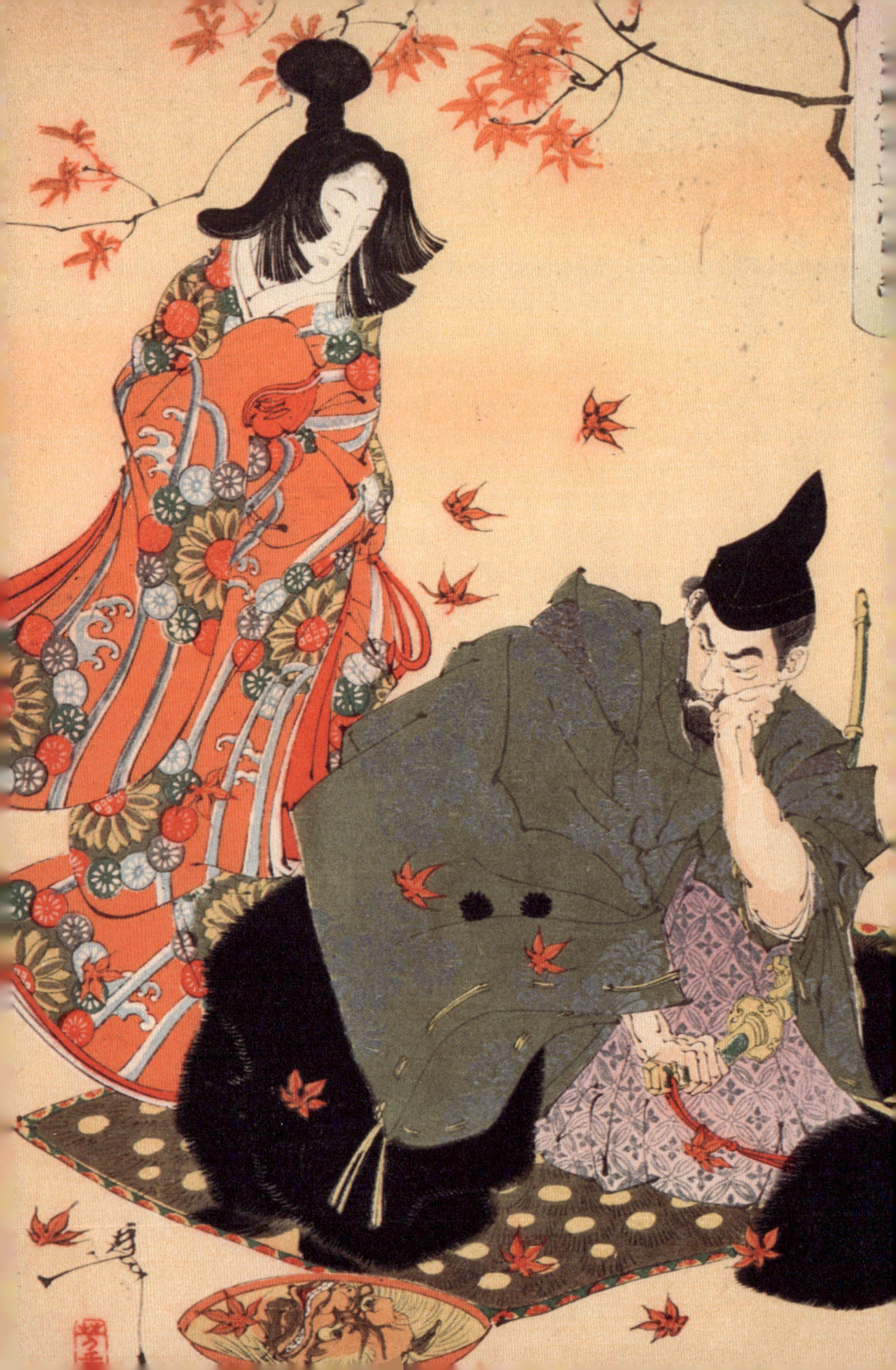

DEFYING
THE
UNKNOWN

•

When the philosopher Athenodoros moved into a supposedly haunted house in Athens in the first century, attracted by the low rent and probably also to test the rumours, he soon perceived what appeared to be the pleas of a ghost. He had the garden dug up and unearthed the skeleton of a slave who had been unceremoniously buried there. After giving the deceased a proper ritual burial, the apparitions ceased, as if by magic (Pliny the Younger, Letters, Book VII, letter 27).

A story in every way comparable took place a few centuries later in Japan, though this time involving not *yūrei* (ghosts) but *yōkai*. It is part of the famous *Anthology of Tales Old and New* (*Konjaku Monogatarishū*), an eleventh-century compilation of Japanese stories. Its hero is none other than the state official Miyoshi no Kiyotsura, also known as Zen Saisho. 'Despite protests from his entourage, this eminent man of letters acquired a very dilapidated and reputedly haunted house in Horikawa Street, near Fifth Avenue in the ancient capital of Kyoto. He sent all his people away and remained there alone. A great connoisseur of the teachings of Yin and Yang [*onmyōji*], he had chosen an auspicious day to move in and considered that he had nothing to fear. Yet when night came, as he was falling asleep, faces appeared in the squares formed by the ceiling's crisscrossing beams. Unperturbed, he watched them quietly and they vanished. Shortly after, tiny creatures arrived on horseback, crossing the floorboards of the porch from east to west. He remained impassive. The next to appear was a very tall and very

beautiful woman, a fan concealing her lower face. Still, Saisho remained serene, unmoved by the scent of her bewitching perfume. As she withdrew, leaving the way she had come – sliding on her knees – she lowered her fan to reveal horrible fangs, then disappeared. Soon after, dawn came and an old man came to greet Saisho. He prostrated himself, handed him a letter and declared that he had lived in the house for a very long time. Furious, Saisho replied that true demons knew how to behave more properly, adding that he was the current owner of the property and that nothing could force him to leave. His courage and wisdom got the better of the monsters, who abandoned the place forever.' (Koyama-Richard, 2017, pp. 64–65, translated by David Wharry).

These two examples show that both philosophy (through observation and accurate interpretation of the facts) and traditional esoteric cosmology (through respect of the prohibitions and powers of the natural sciences and occultism) can succeed in annihilating the forces of evil, beginning with the *yōkai*. Nothing is ever truly lost; there is always a way to purify a place and banish those who create chaos instead of order.

pp. 72–79: Unknown artist, *Nocturnal Procession of the Hundred Demons* (Hyakki yagyō), details
Tokyo, National Diet Library Digital Collections

p. 80: Tsukioka Yoshitoshi, *Taira no Koremochi Subjugates the Evil Devil at Mount Togakushi*, detail, 1902
Los Angeles County Museum of Art

p. 83: Katsushika Hokusai, *One Hundred Ghost Stories in a Haunted House* (*Shinpan uki-e bakemono yashiki hyaku monogatari no zu*), detail, 1780
Boston, Museum of Fine Arts

pp. 84–85: Utagawa Kuniyoshi, *Three of Minamoto no Raiko's Retainers, Sakata no Kintoki, Usui Sadamitsu, and Watanabe no Tsuna, Playing Go, with Attempted Interruptions by the Earth Spider's Demons*, detail, mid-19th century
London, The British Museum

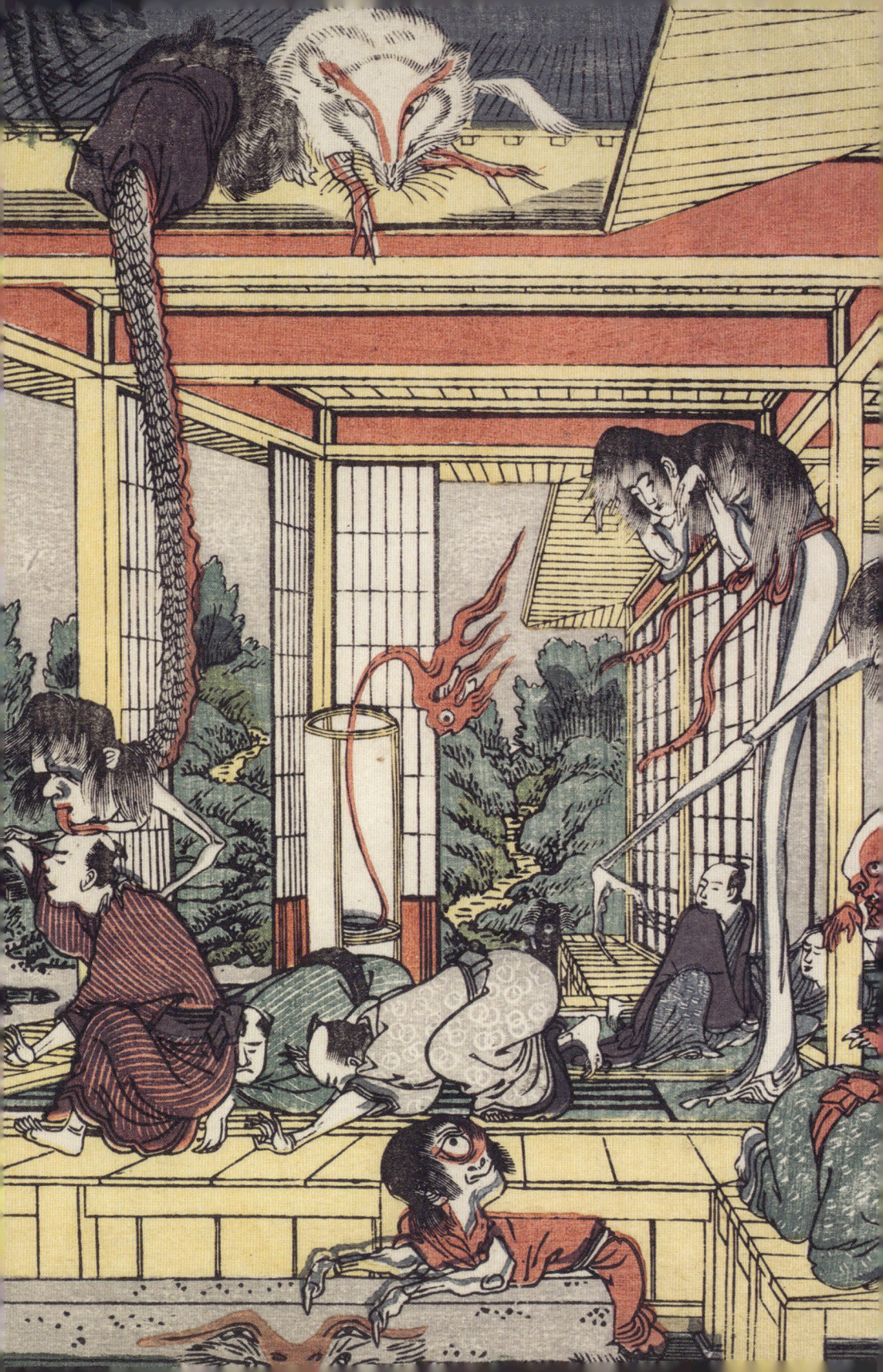

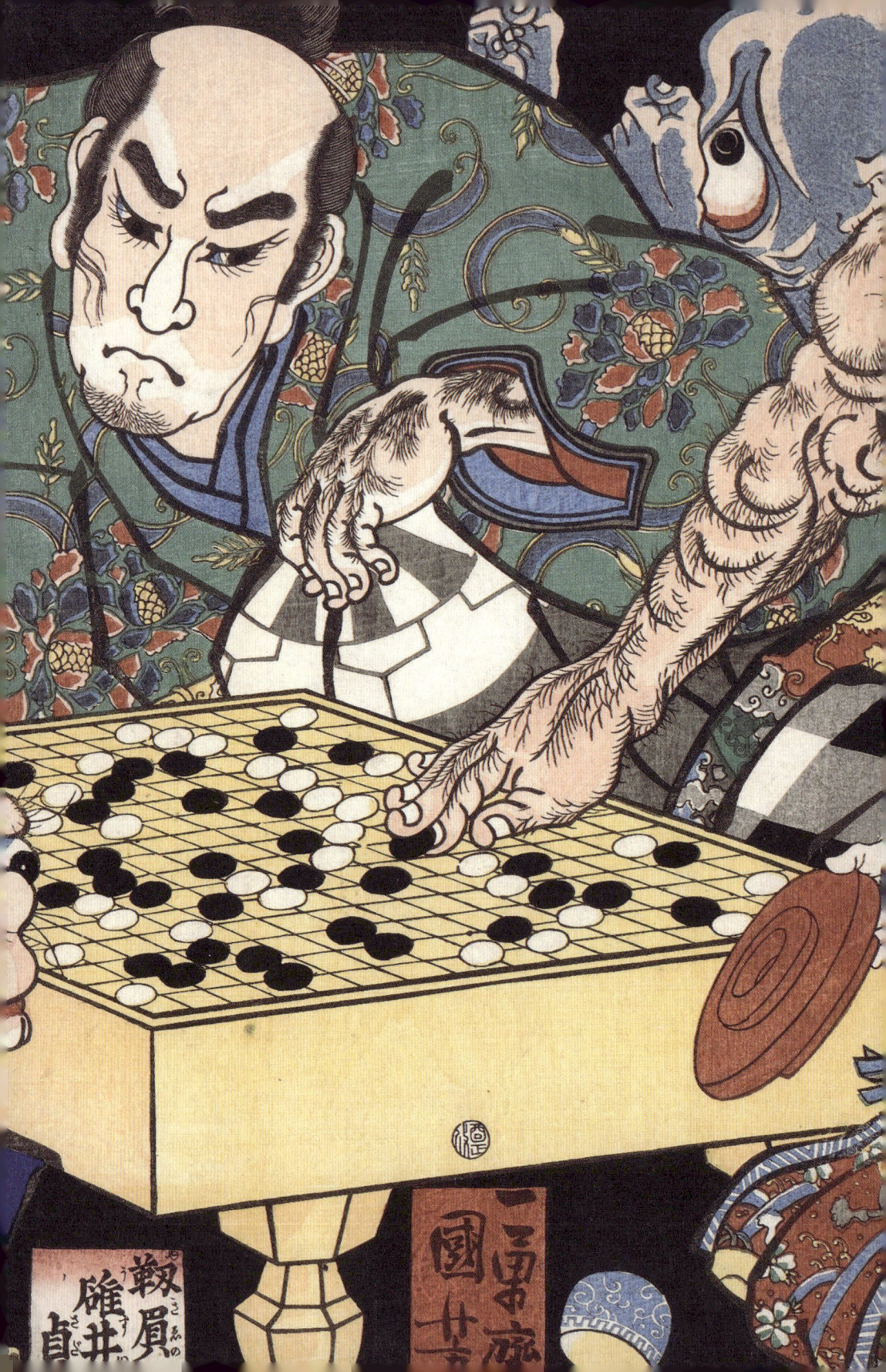

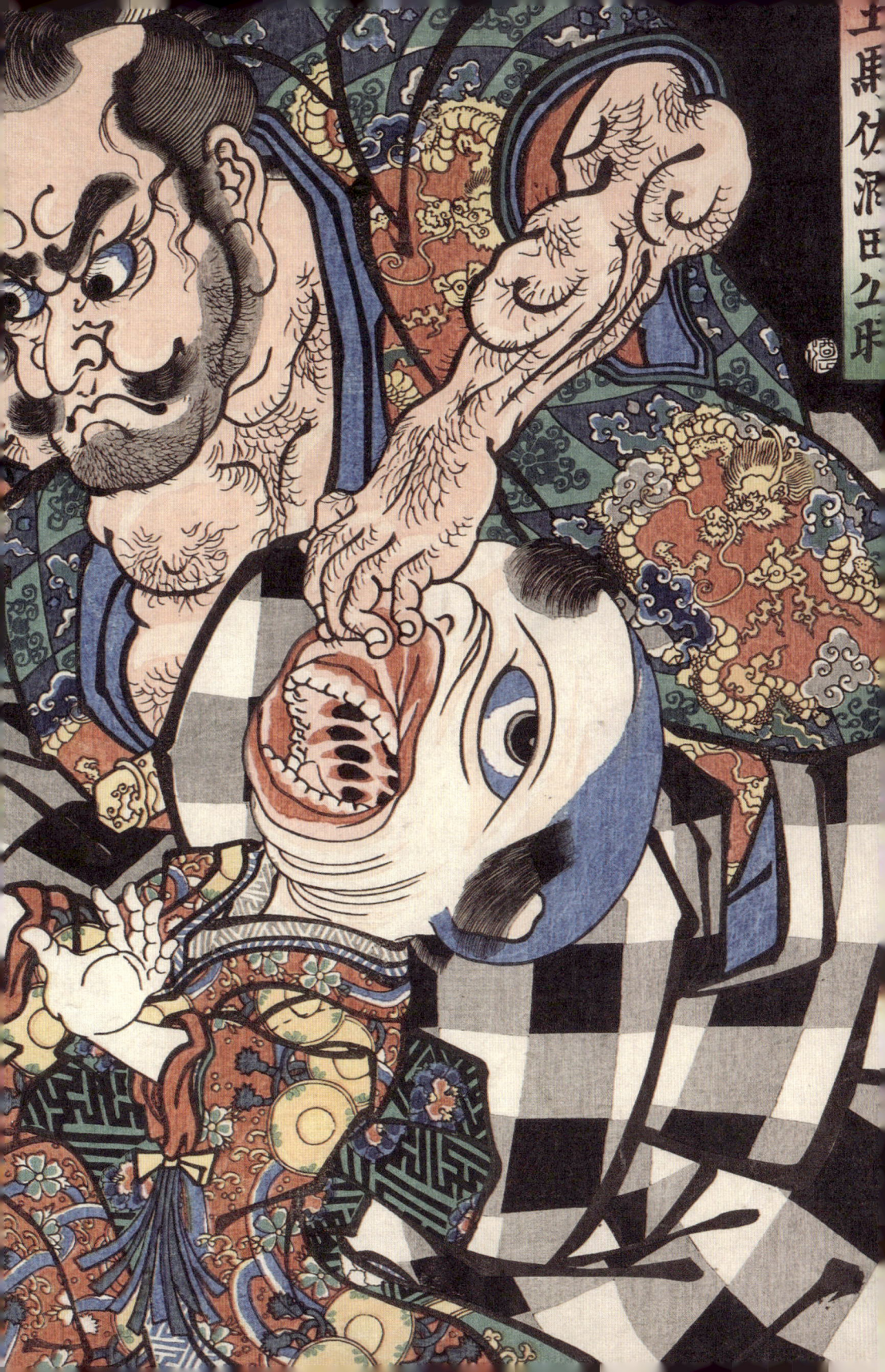

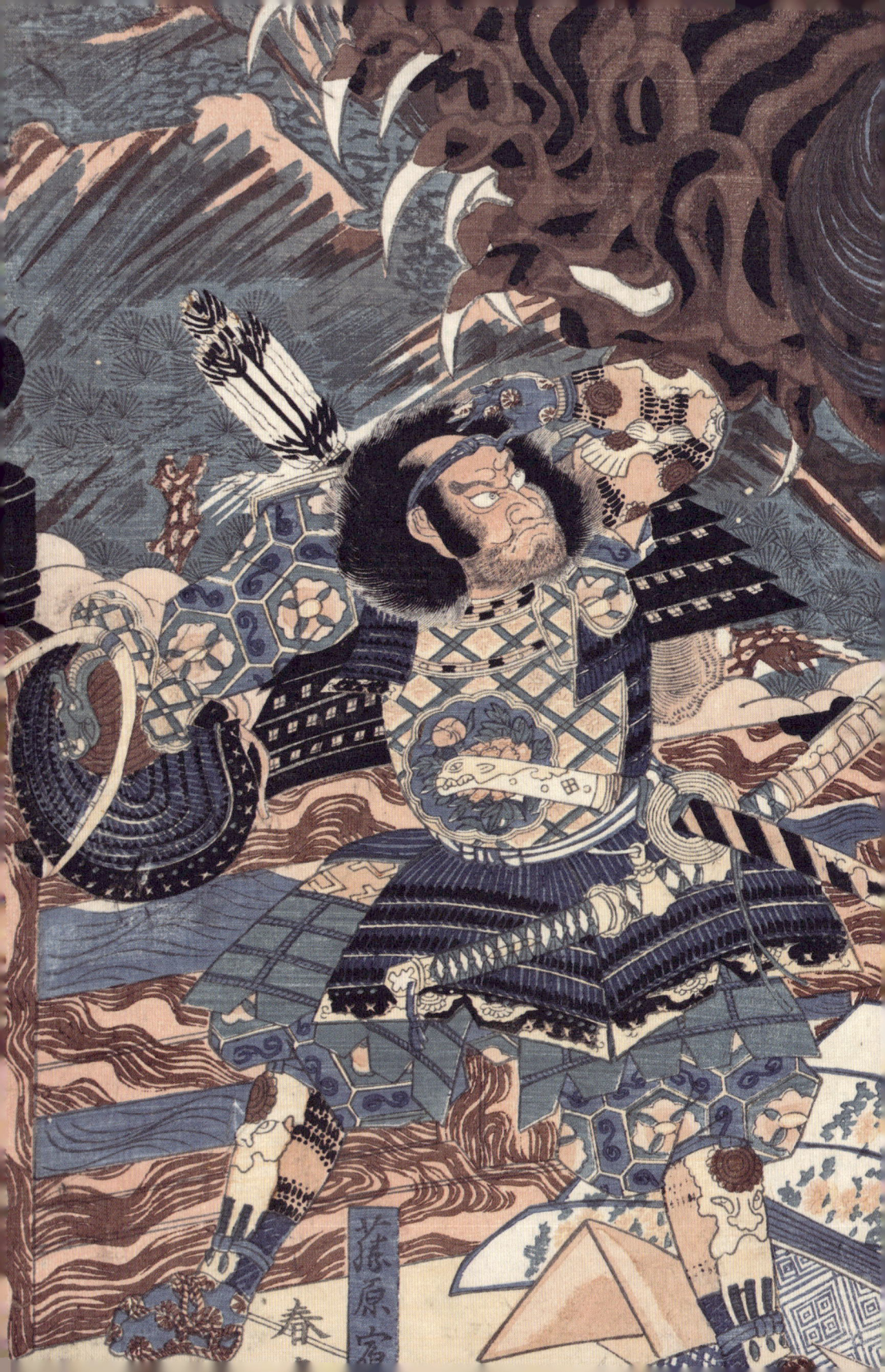

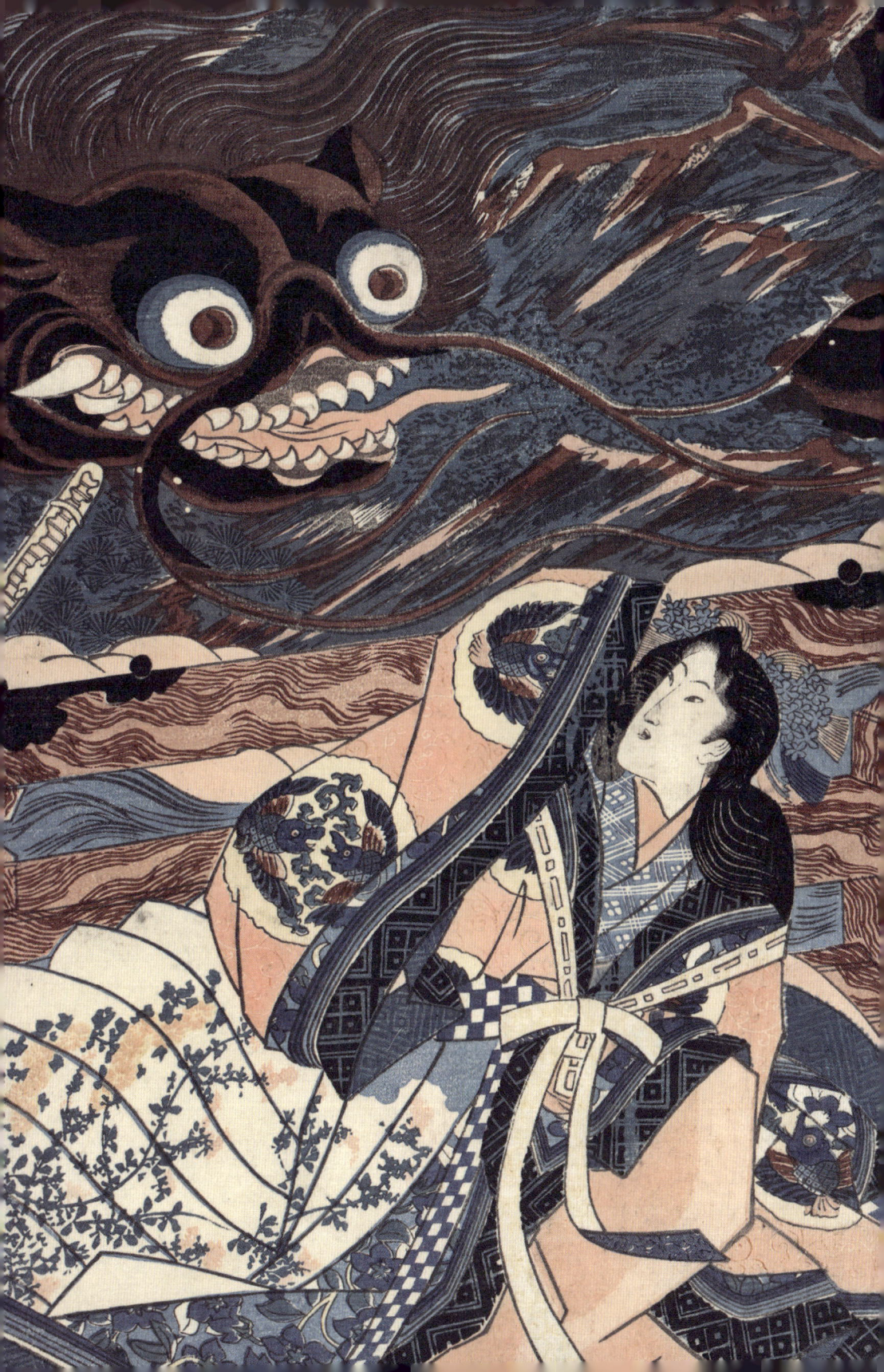

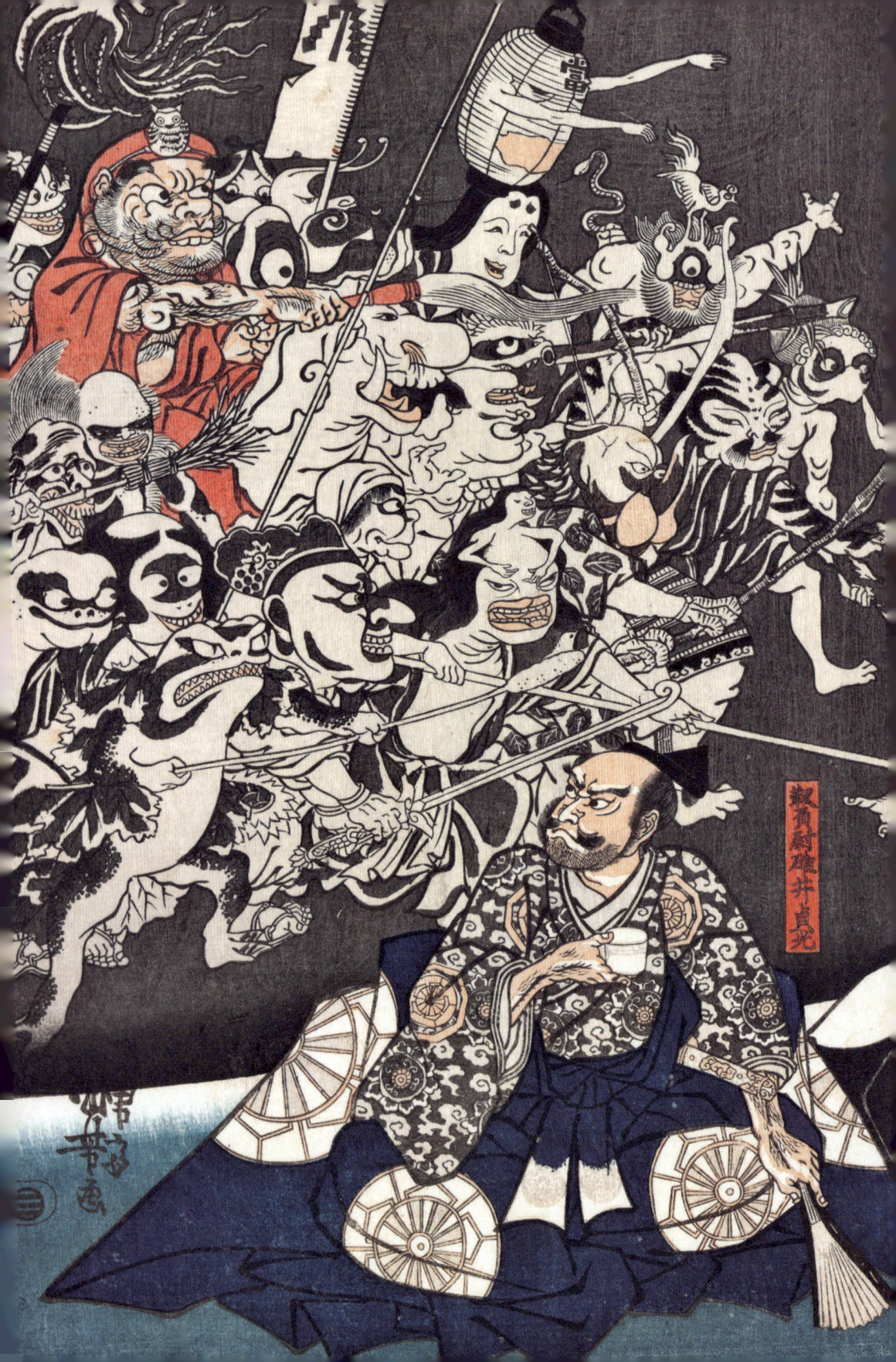

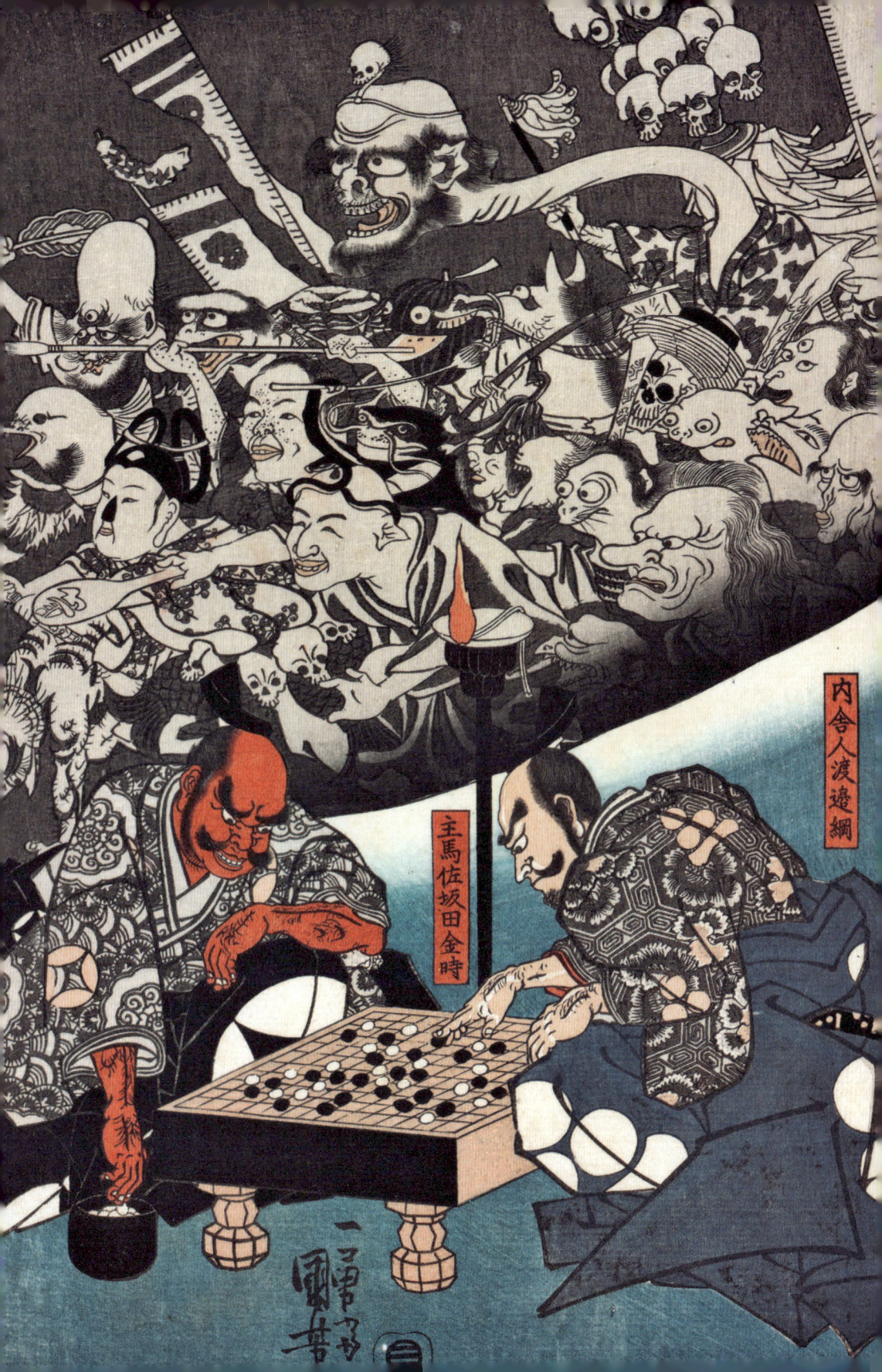

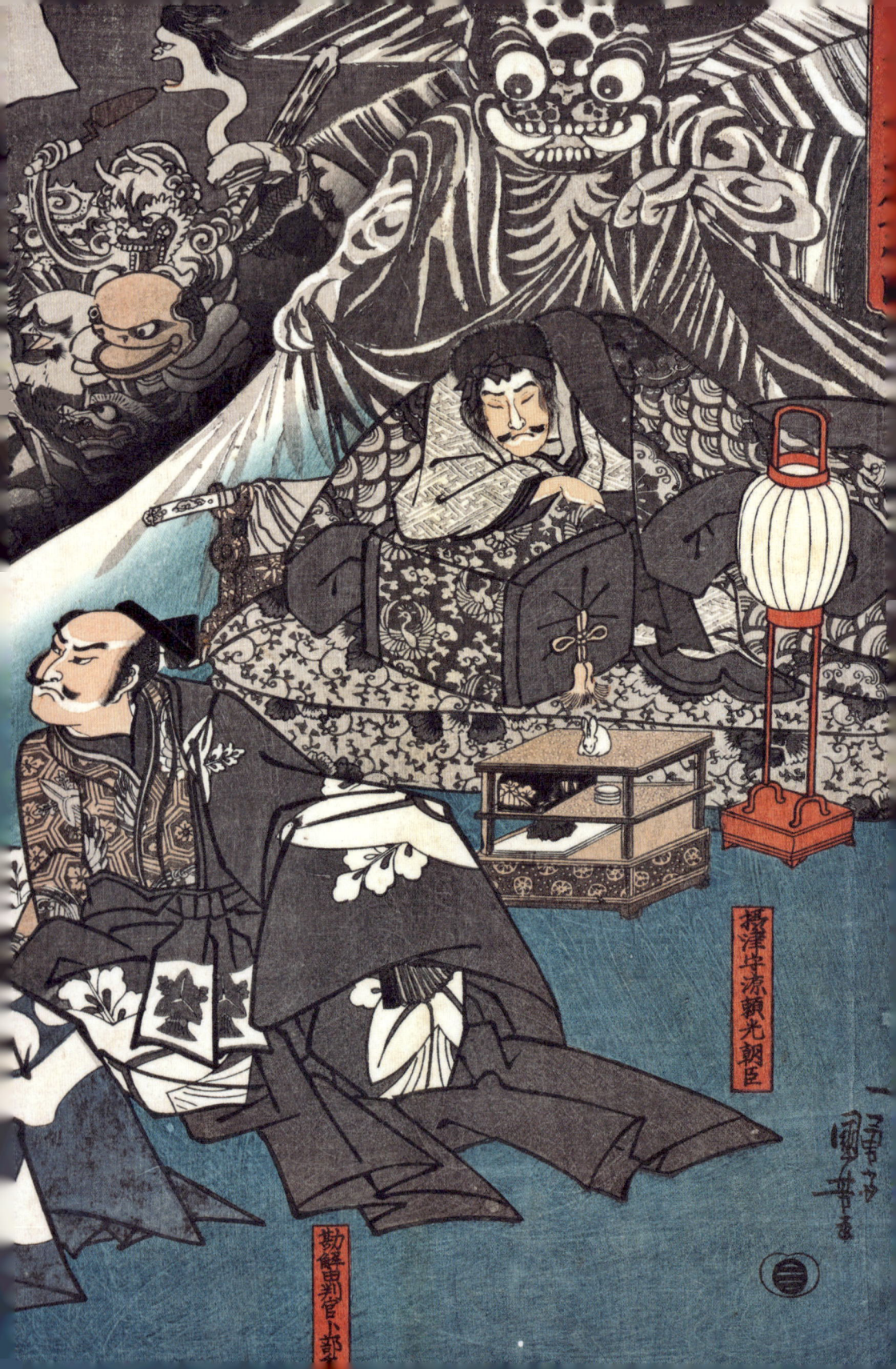

THE EARTH
SPIDER

•

This legend is rooted in historic fact and centres around a powerful military chief, Minamoto no Yorimitsu (948–1021), also known as Raikō. Over the centuries, fact and fiction became confused, or rather the truth was embellished with extraordinary details, elevating certain elements of his life to the realm of legend and wonder. This was the case with his battle against the bandit Hakamadare, who derived his strength and menace from a giant snake. The following story of the giant spider comes from the same collection of fantastic tales.

The first version recounts how Yorimitsu, bedridden with a fever, receives a visit from a monk who has come to heal him. But when they are left alone for the healing ritual, the monk begins tying Yorimitsu to his bed with thick ropes. Seizing his sword, Yorimitsu immediately strikes his attacker, who flees. Without delay, his companions follow the monk's trail (he is losing blood with each step) and find him in the mountains. To their astonishment, he is no longer a man but a giant spider (*Tsuchigumo*), and his metamorphosis is complete. They put him to death and impale him; in an instant, Yorimitsu's fever subsides and he is healed.

In another version, Yorimitsu and his men one day see a human skull floating on the surface of a pond in front of an abandoned house at Kitayama, near Nara. When they enter the house, they come face to face with an enchanted woman surrounded by a cloud of monsters and demons. This woman is strikingly beautiful and Yorimitsu, dumbstruck, stands gazing at her for a long moment. Captivated by his stare, she begins casting small clouds at him that cling to his skin, armour and weapons. Sensing danger, he wakes from his stupor and begins to defend

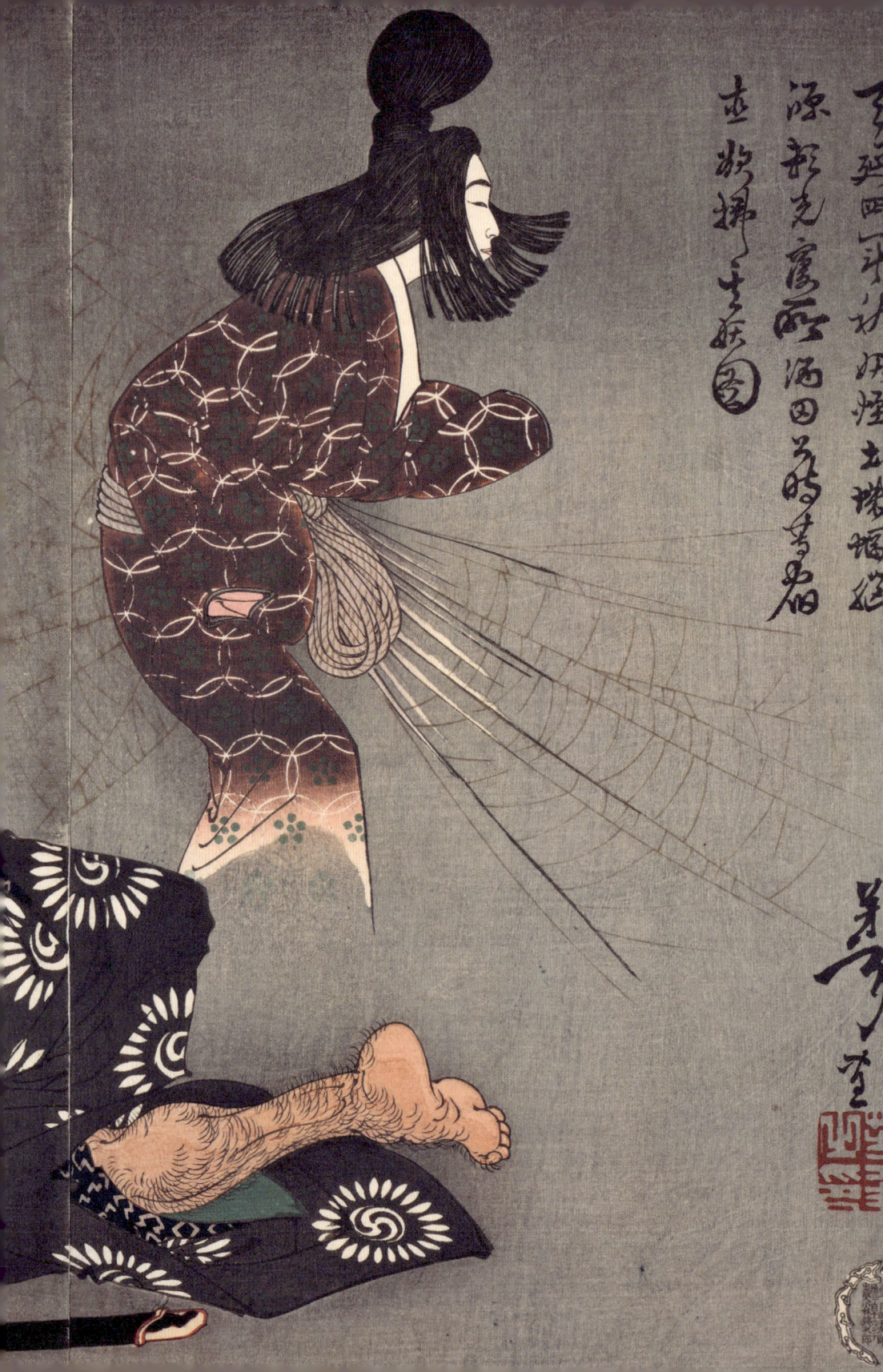

himself, striking the woman with his sword. As she flees, she leaves a long trail of blood behind her. Following the trail, Yorimitsu and his companions come to a cave carved out of the mountain, where they find a giant spider. They immediately put it to death, only to see spilling from its wounds the skulls of its human victims, along with tiny girl-spiders, which they kill one by one.

A giant spider also features in the legend surrounding the famous fourteenth-century warrior Ōmori Hikoshichi. This lieutenant of the great warlord Ashikaga Takauji joined the rebellion against Emperor Go-Daigo and killed his fiercest general, Kusunoki Masashige. But Kusunoki's ghost soon returns to haunt Ōmori Hikoshichi, appearing first in the form of a woman of incredible beauty, then transforming into a horrifying witch or giant menacing spider. This legend was performed on stage in kabuki plays in the Edo and Meiji periods, most notably by the celebrated actor Ichikawa Danjuro IX in the late nineteenth century.

pp. 86–87: Katsukawa Shuntei, *The Warrior Fujiwara Hidesato Battling the Giant Centipede*, detail, between 1815 and 1820
Washington, Library of Congress

pp. 89–90: Utagawa Kuniyoshi, *The Earth Spider Conjures Up Demons at the Mansion of Minamoto Yorimitsu*, details, 1843
Washington, National Museum of Asian Art, Smithsonian Institution

p. 92: Tsukioka Yoshitoshi, *Sakata no Kintoki (Kintaro) and the Earth Spider*, detail, 1886
Amsterdam, Rijksmuseum

pp. 94–95: Utagawa Kunisada I (known as Toyokuni III), *Actor Arashi Rikaku II as Hananomura no Chigusa, actually Toriyama Shūsaku* (left); *Bandō Shūka I as Shiranui Daijin, Wakana hime* (right), detail, 1853
Boston, Museum of Fine Arts

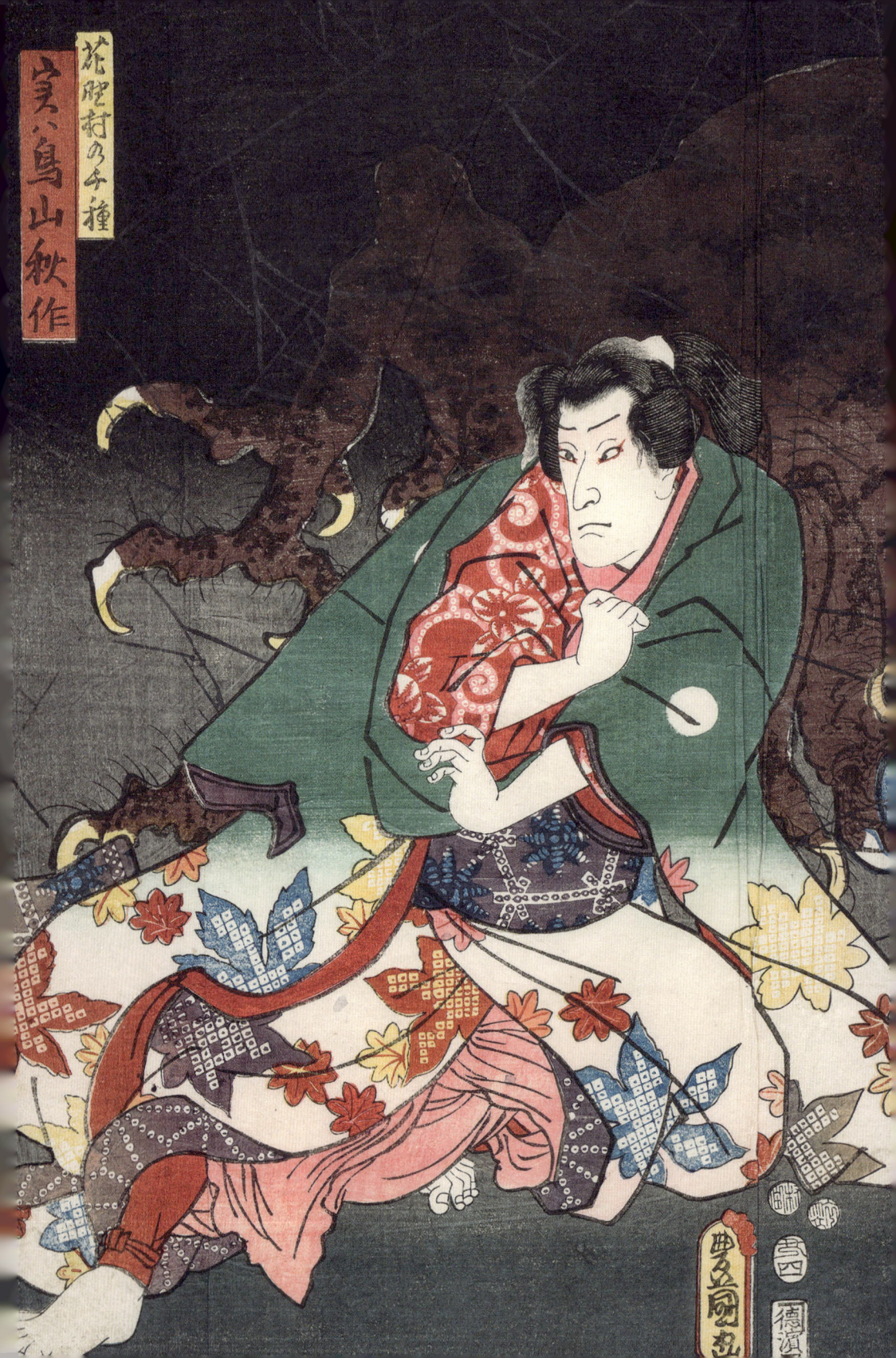

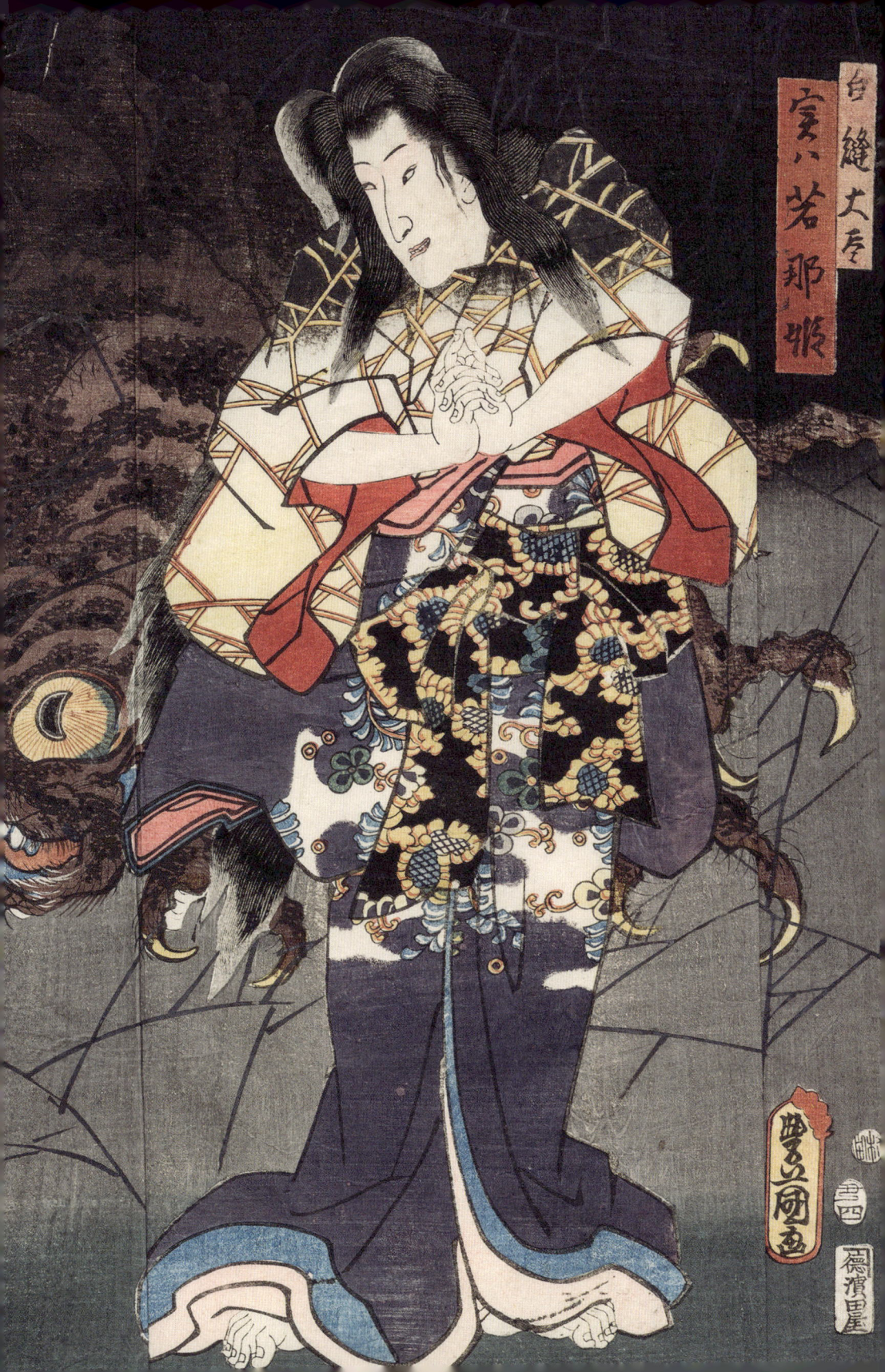

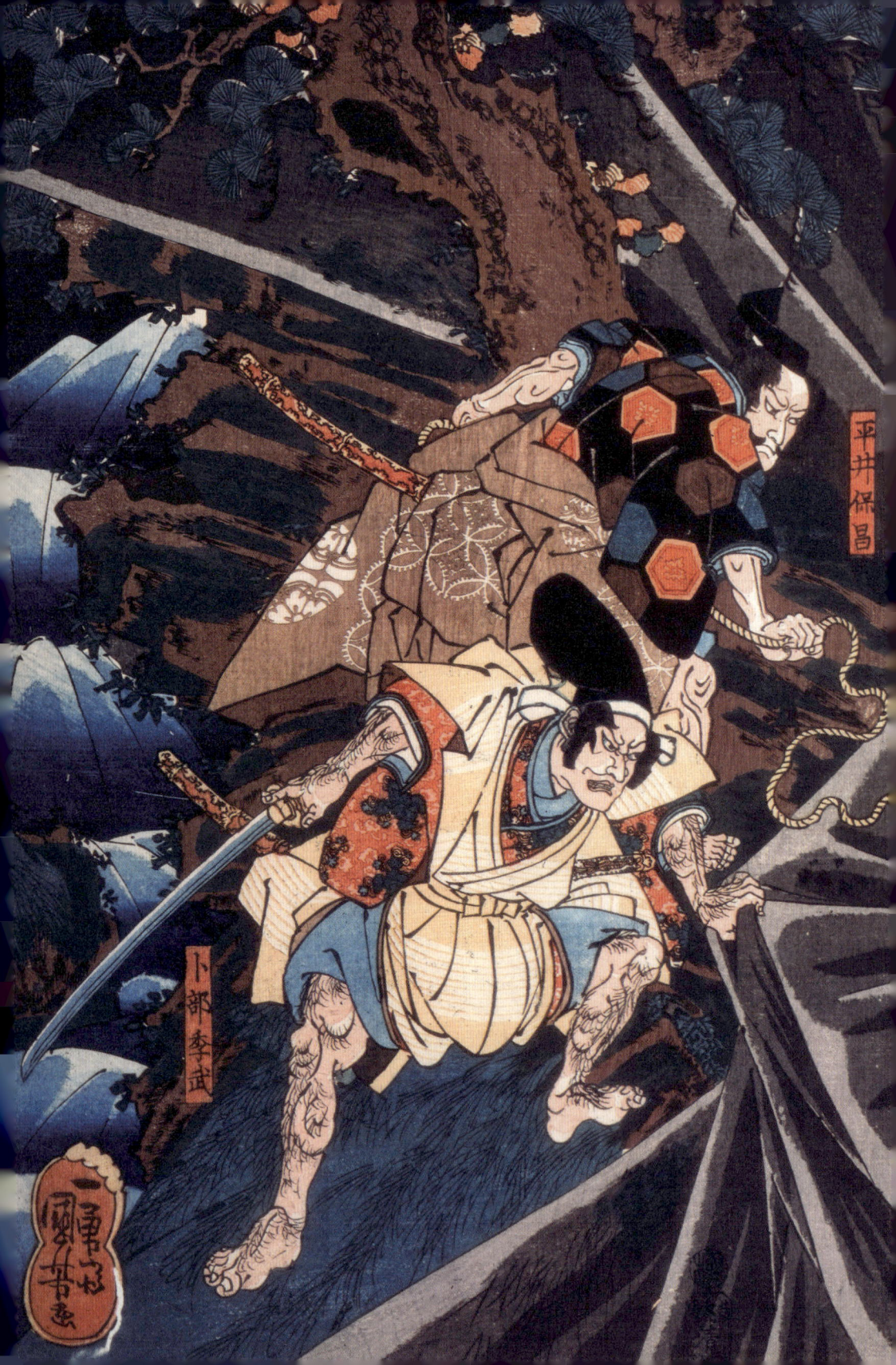

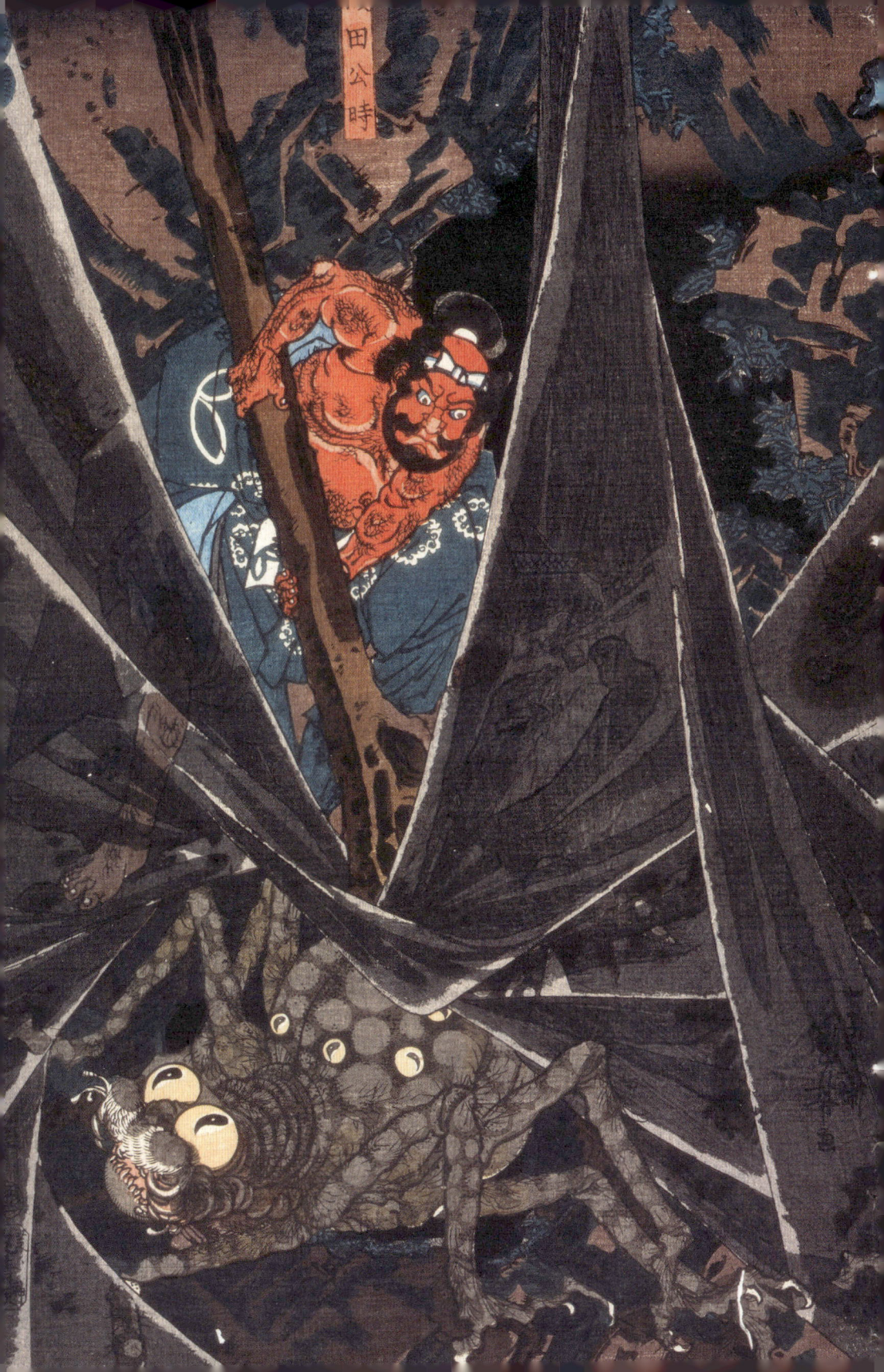

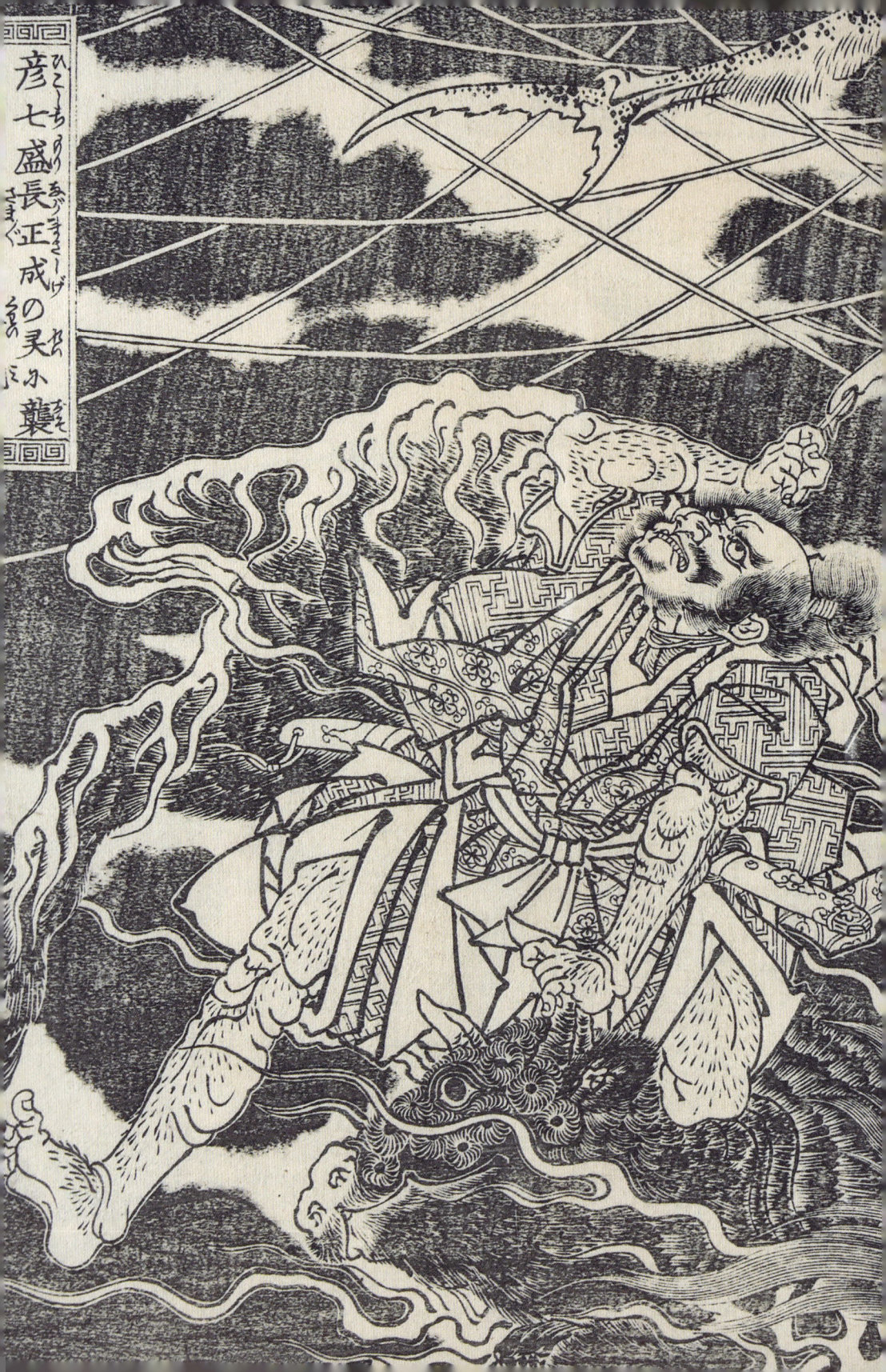

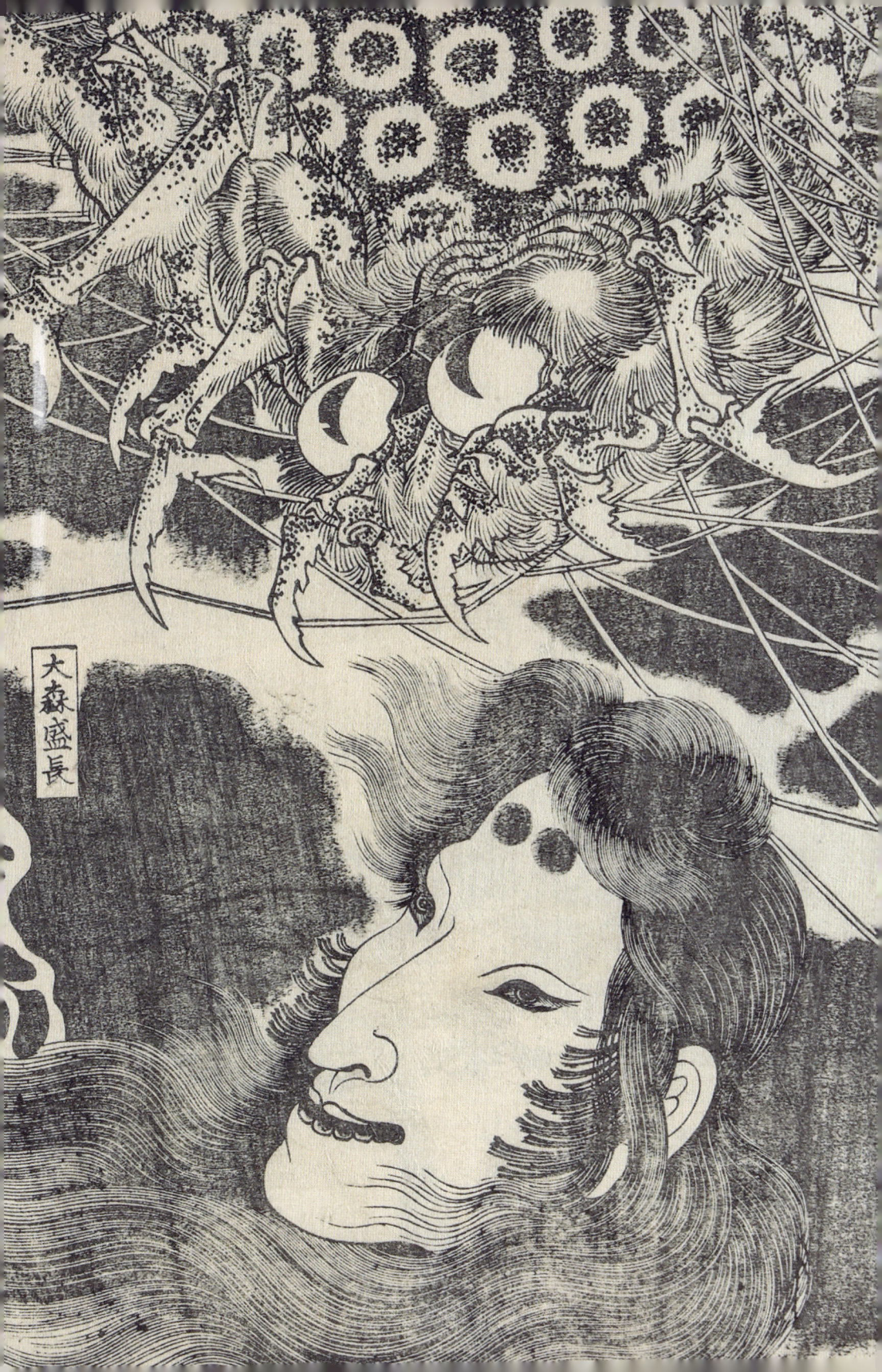
大森盛長

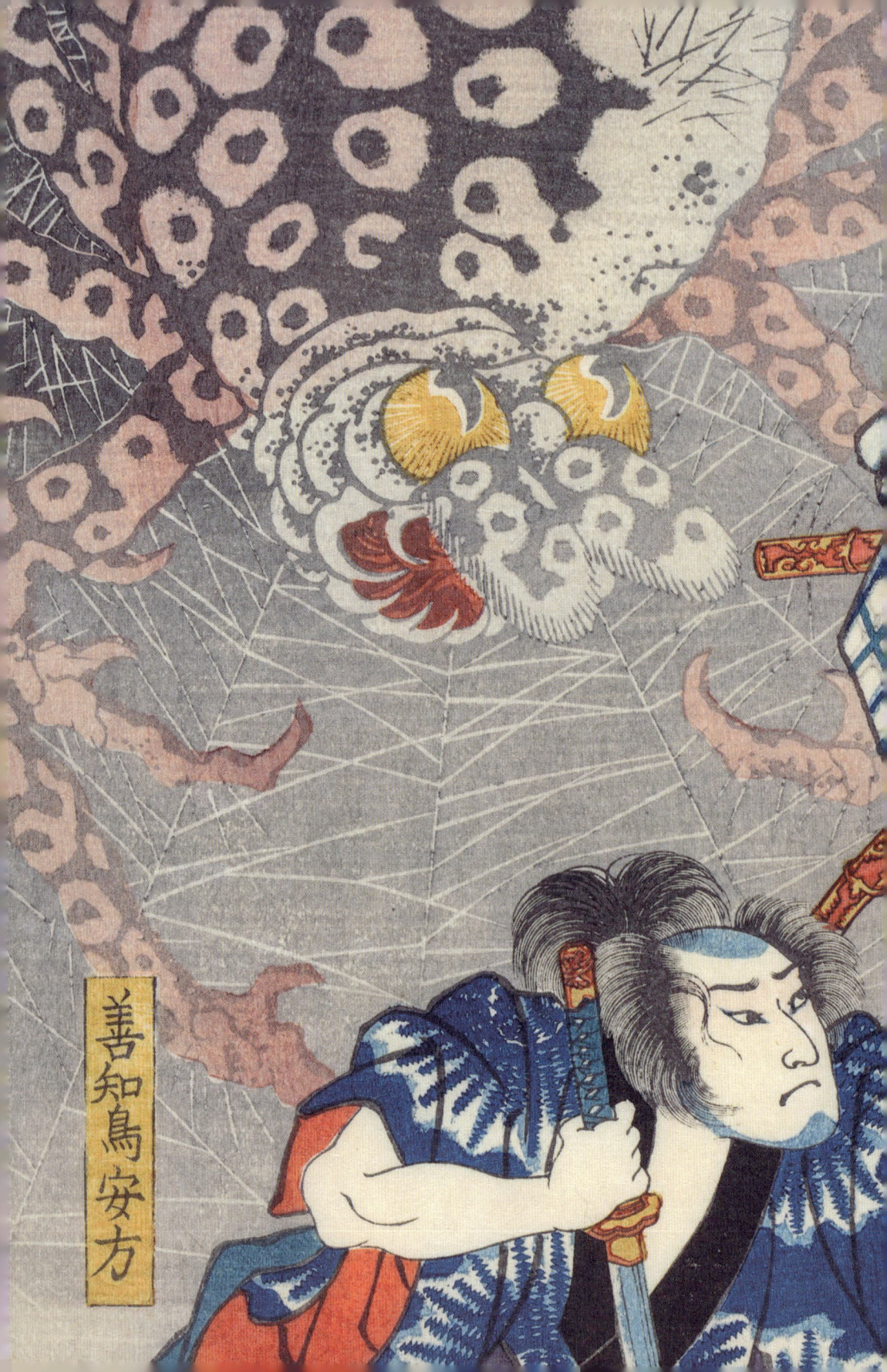

善知鳥安方

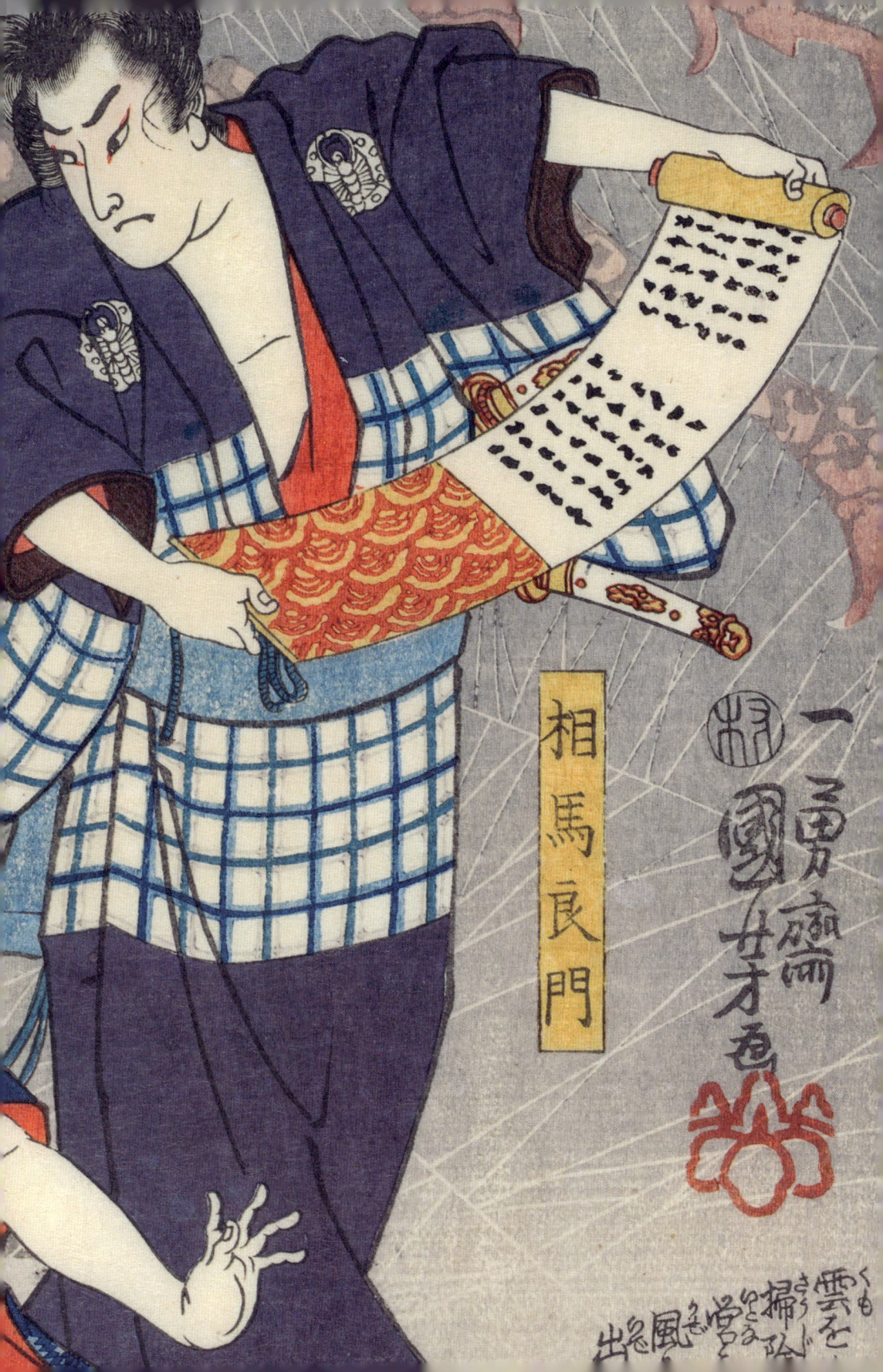

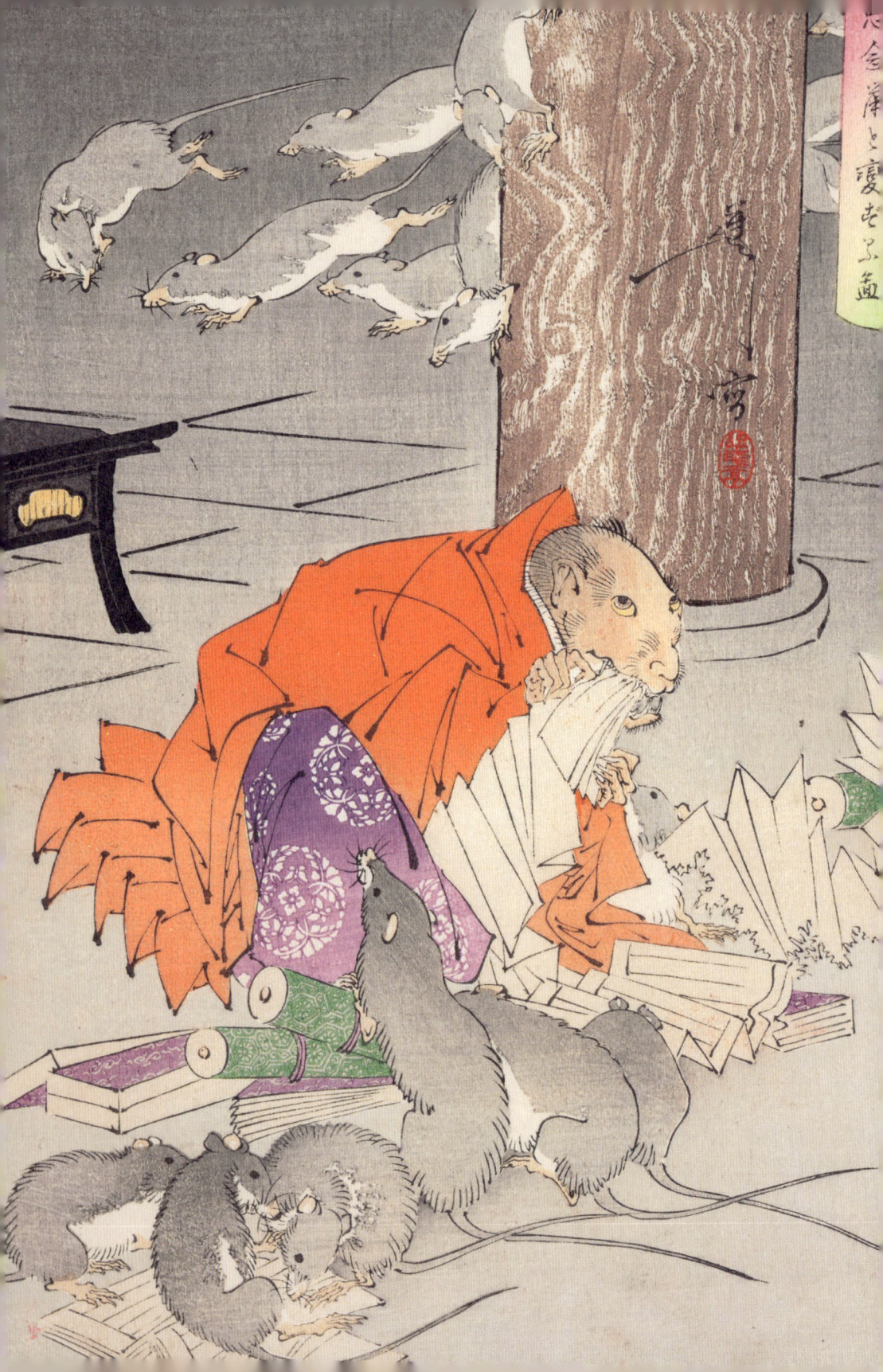

SPITEFUL MONK, YOU KILLED ME

•

Not all monks are saints, some are even demons. When they are driven by dark desires, their spirit warped by malevolent deities or weakened by the appetites of the flesh, they transform into dangerous *yōkai*, which appear before the living, intent on drawing them into shadow.

Yōkai often take on the appearance of *nyūdō*, that is, apprentice Buddhist priests who have started on their religious path and undergone tonsure but not yet been ordained. They manifest in fearsome variations of this form: towering giants called *ō nyūdō* or eerie figures with elongated skulls known as *mikoshi-nyūdō*, strange and unsettling to behold.

There are also examples of creatures adopting the *nyūdō* form to deceive or manipulate others, like the badger who, according to one tale, took this shape to trick his enemy, a famous warlord. Then there is the priest Raigō, who, consumed by resentment and rage, was transformed into a rat.

This last story deserves to be told in greater detail. Raigō, a monk in the Miidera temple at Otsu, at the foot of Mount Hiei near Kyoto, was a member of the Fujiwara family and in charge of discipline at the monastery. When he was appointed advisor to Emperor Shirakawa (1053–1129), Raigō's prayers helped the emperor's wife conceive an heir to the throne. As a token of his gratitude, the emperor promised to have a new building put up in the temple, but later broke his word, claiming that the neighbouring monastery, Enryaku-ji, was already sufficiently endowed. Mad with rage, Raigō fasted

103

until he died. Shortly afterwards, his soul full of resentment, he transformed himself into a repulsive *yōkai* – a metallic rat known as *tesso* – that led an army of real rats to Enryaku-ji, where they devoured its sacred texts as an act of posthumous revenge.

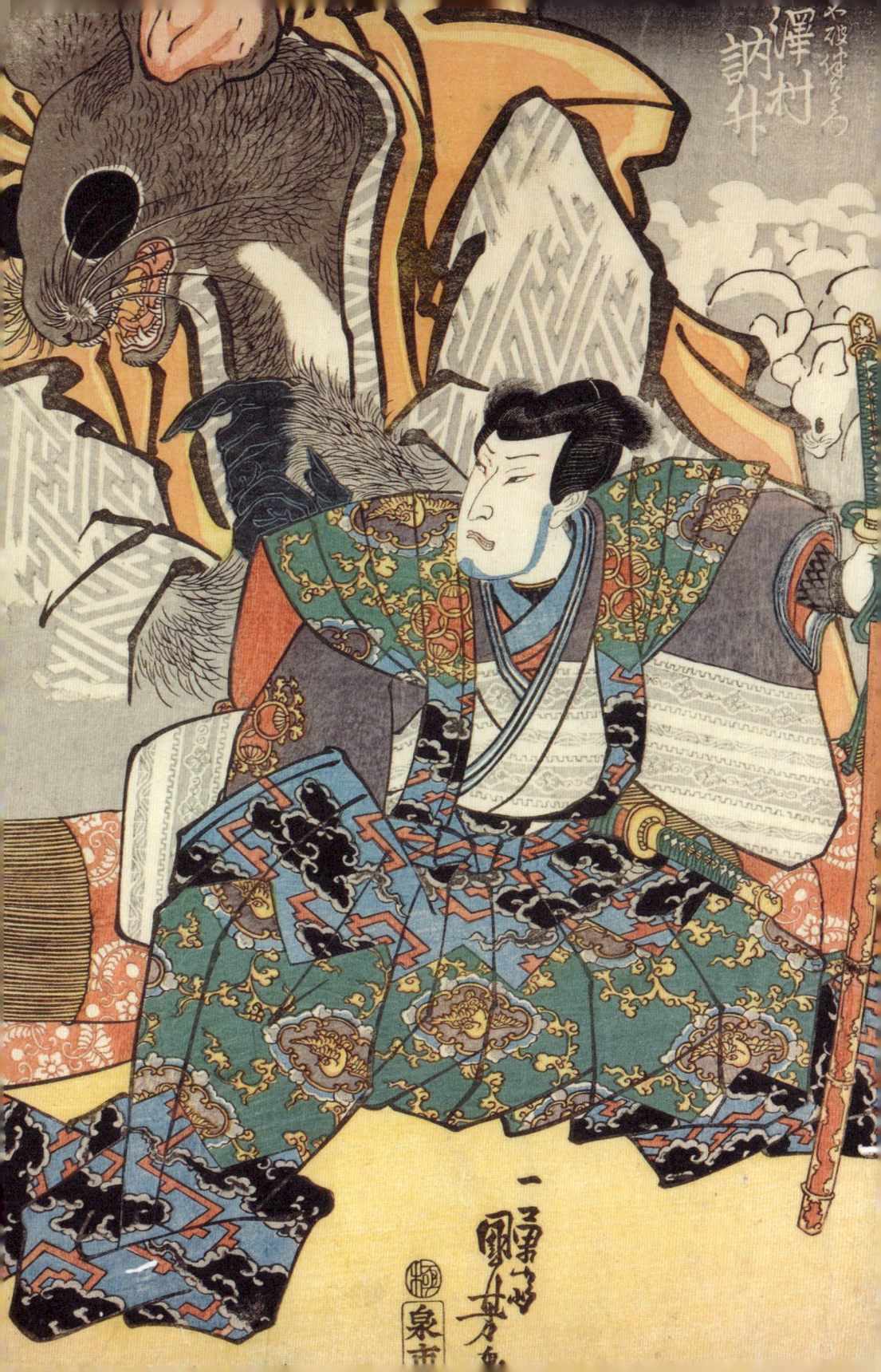

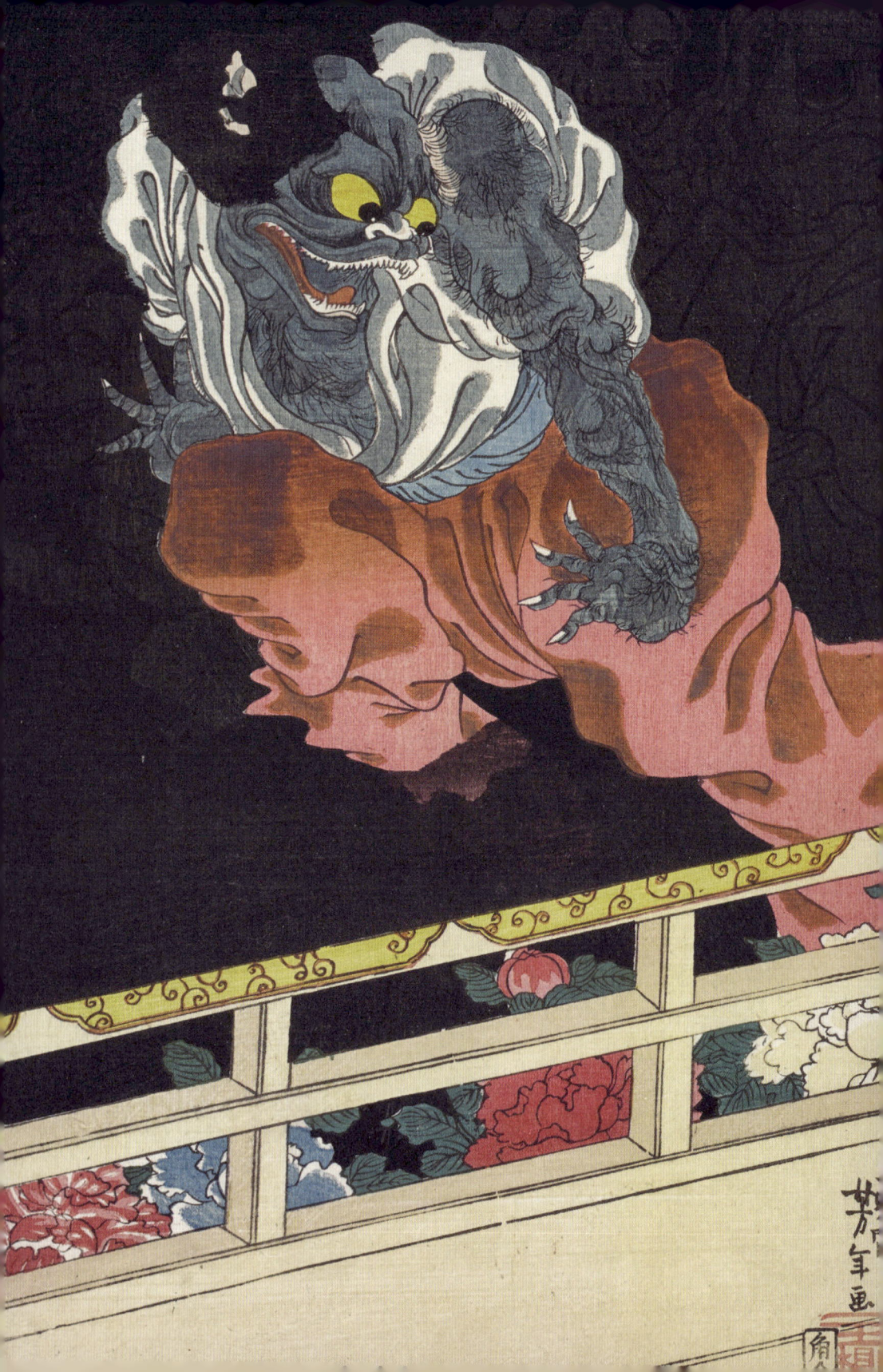

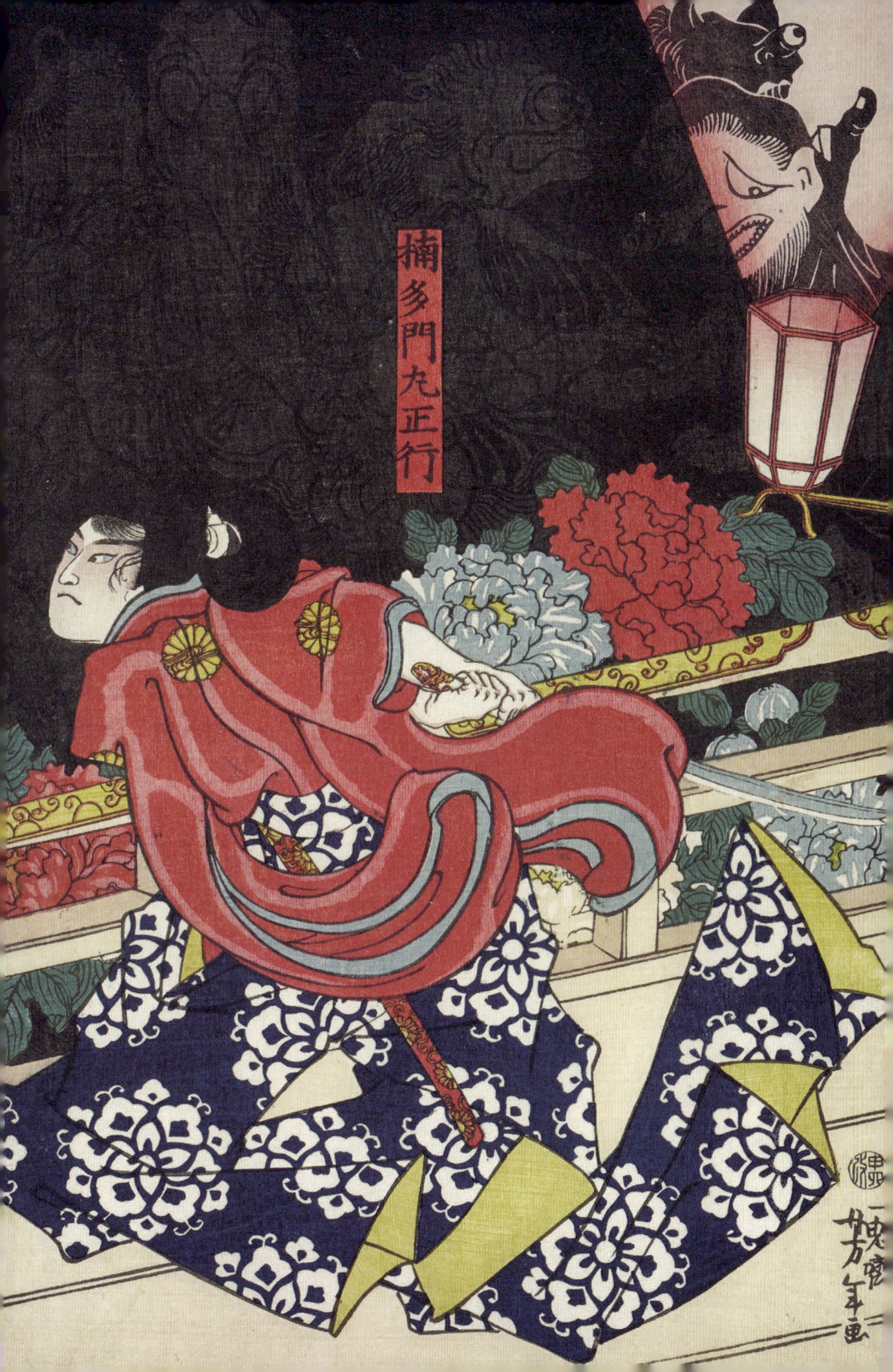

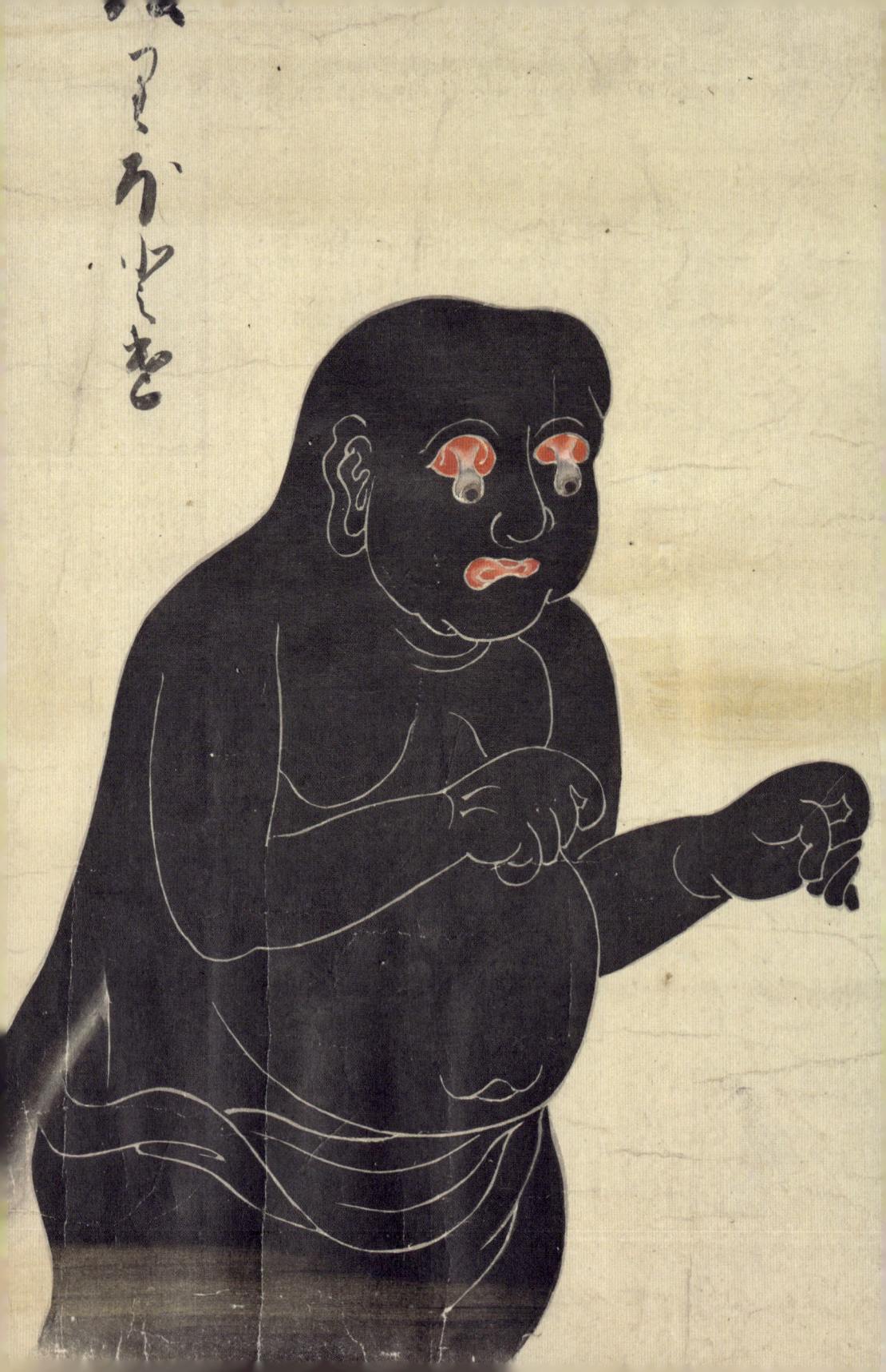

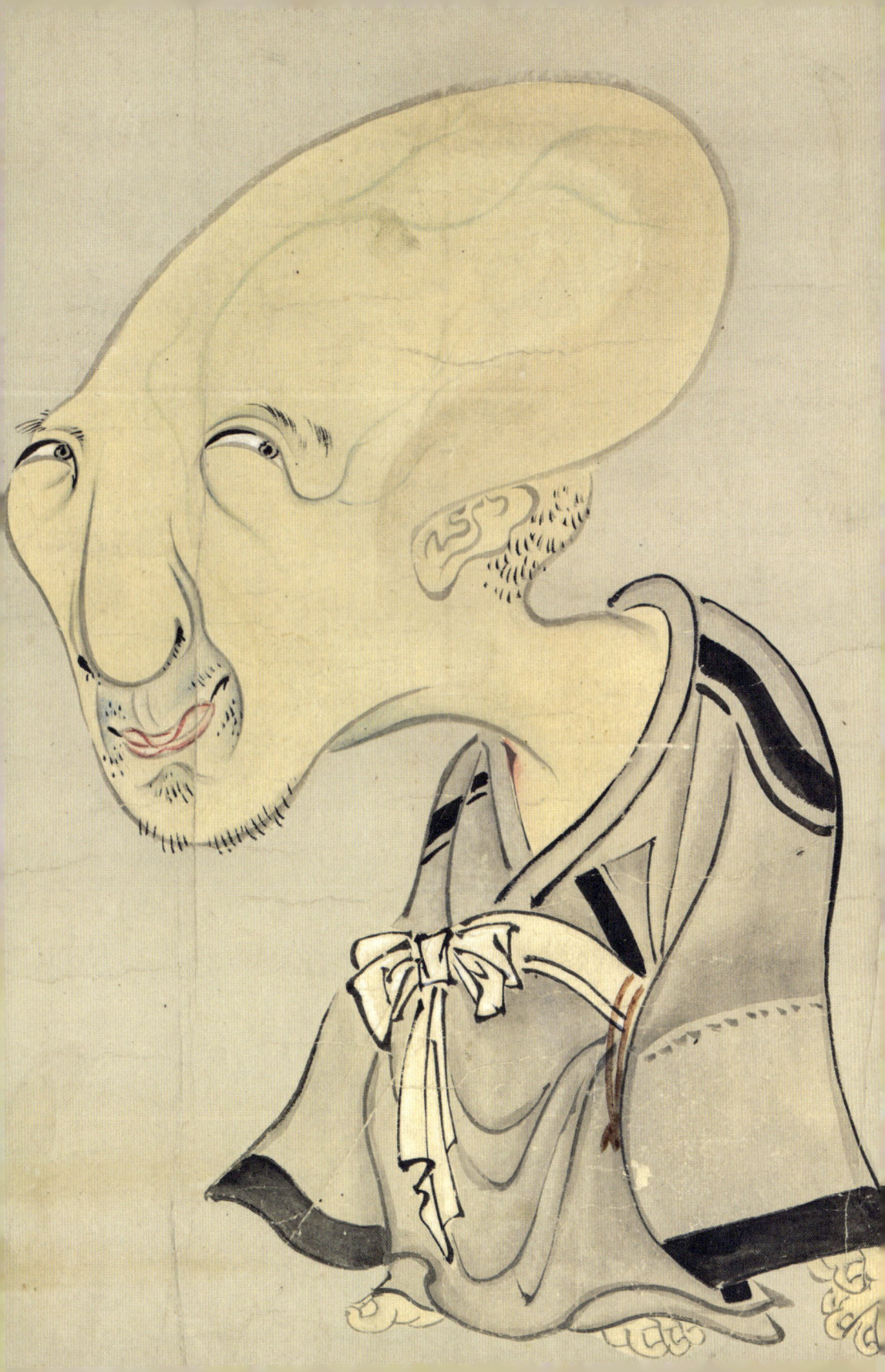

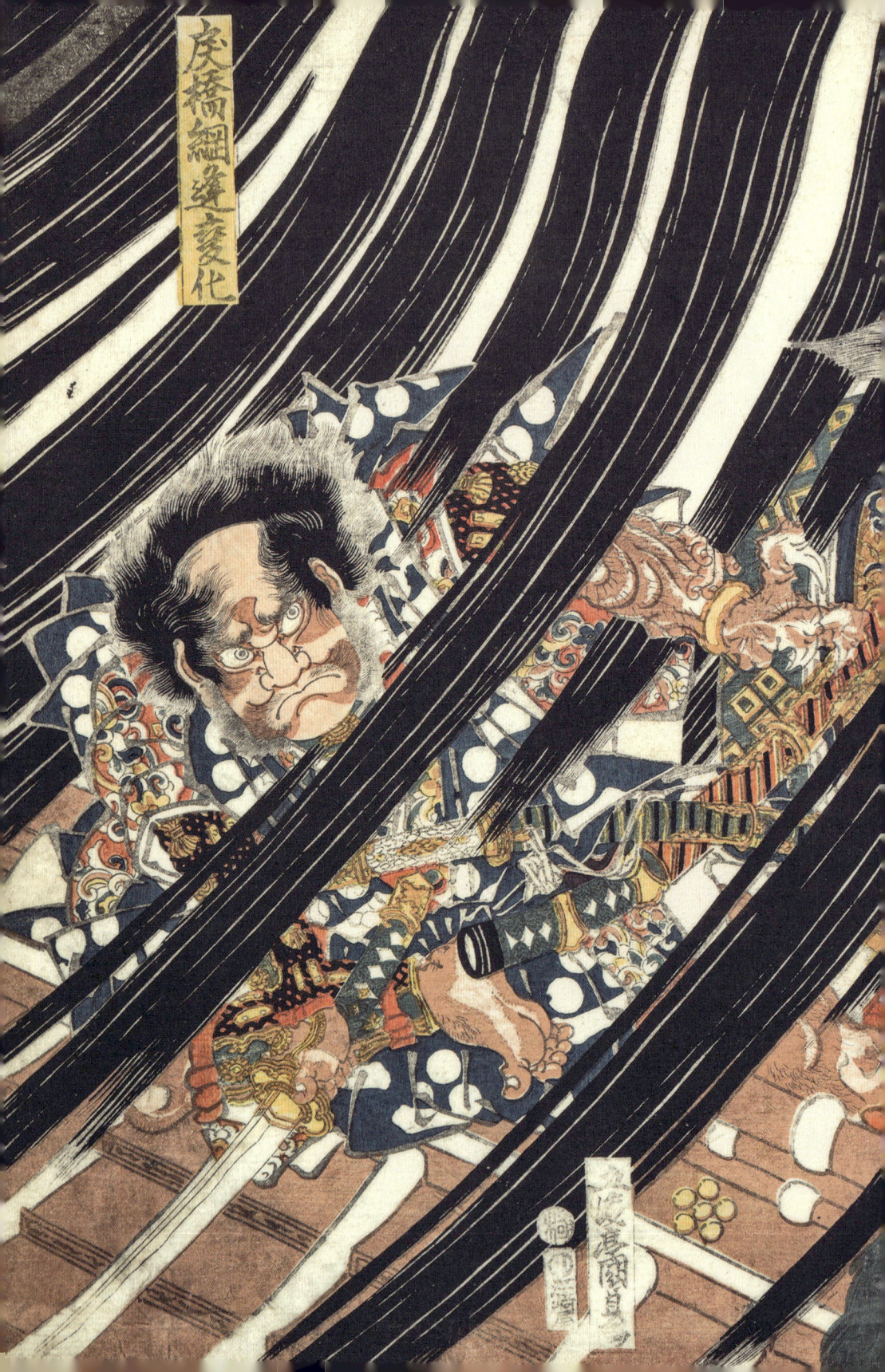

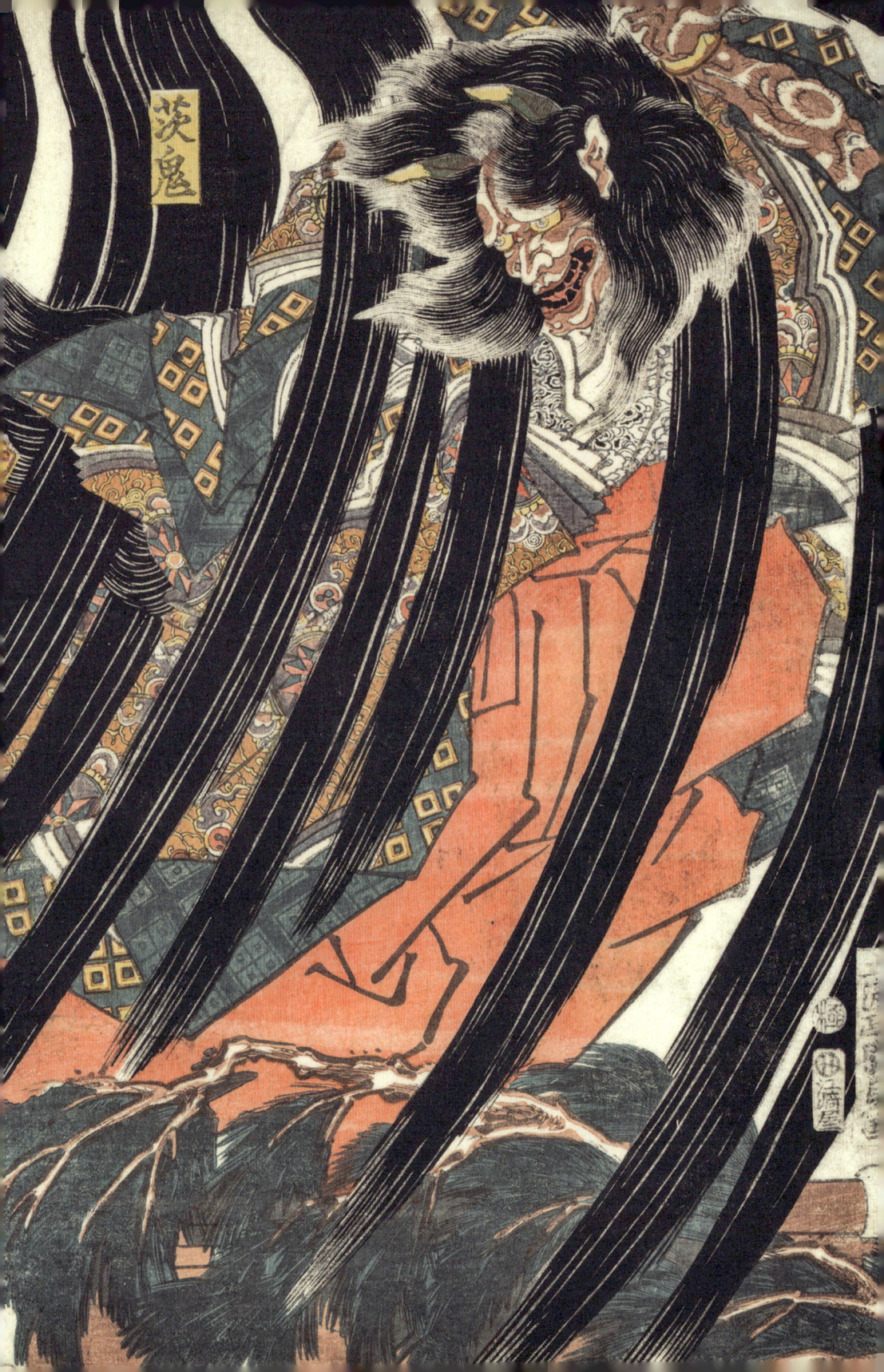

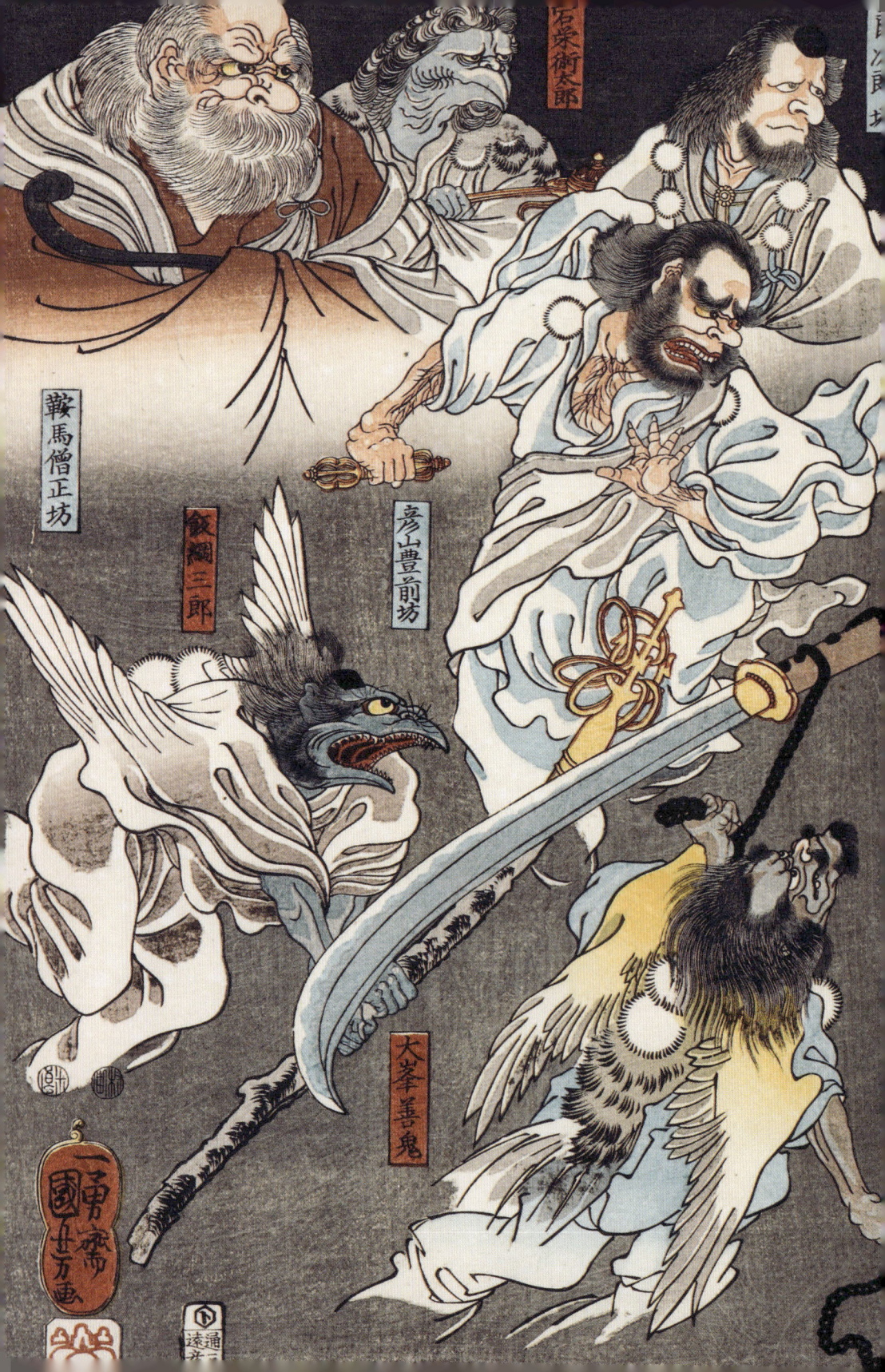

○
てんぐ
天狗

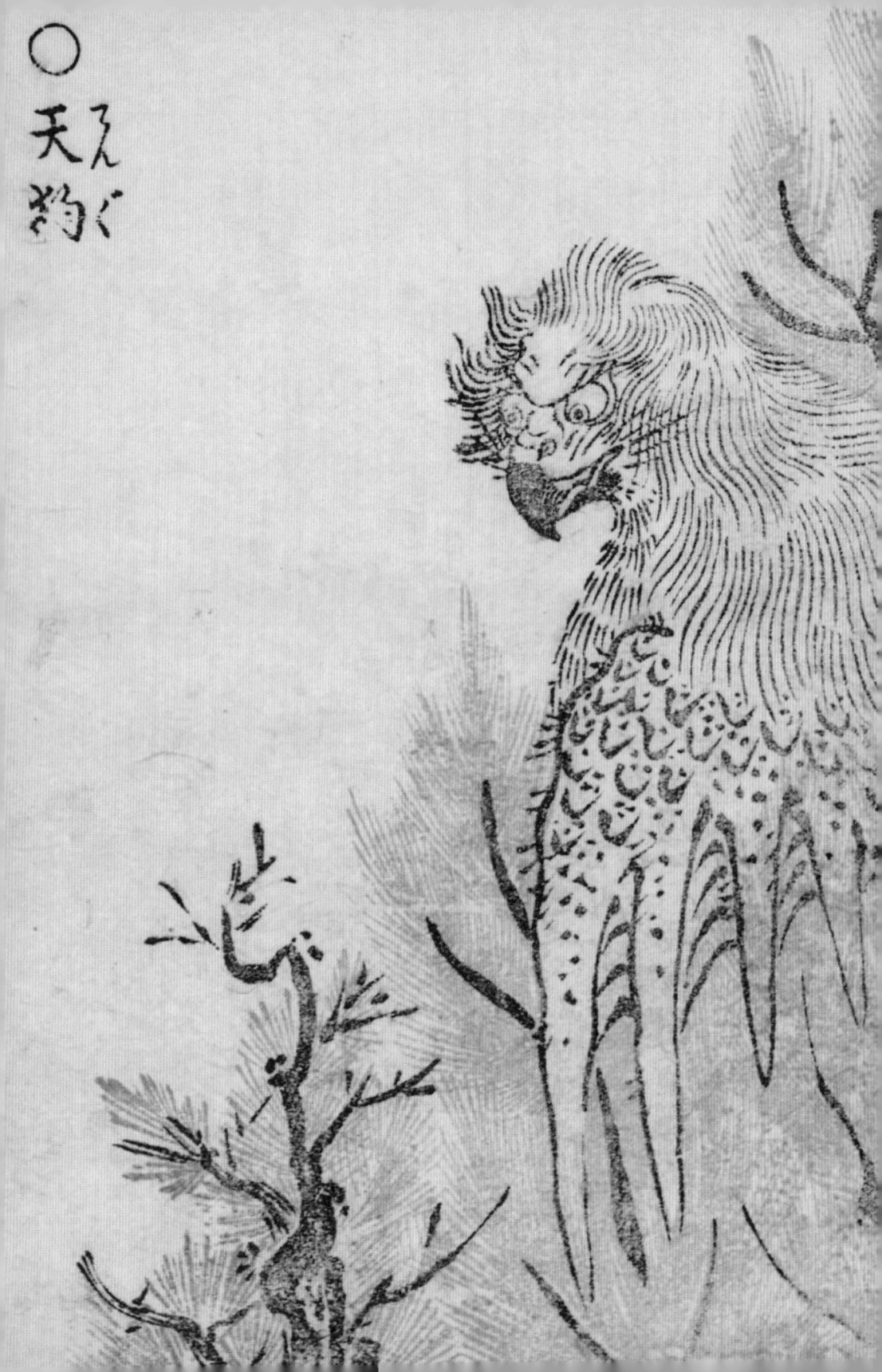

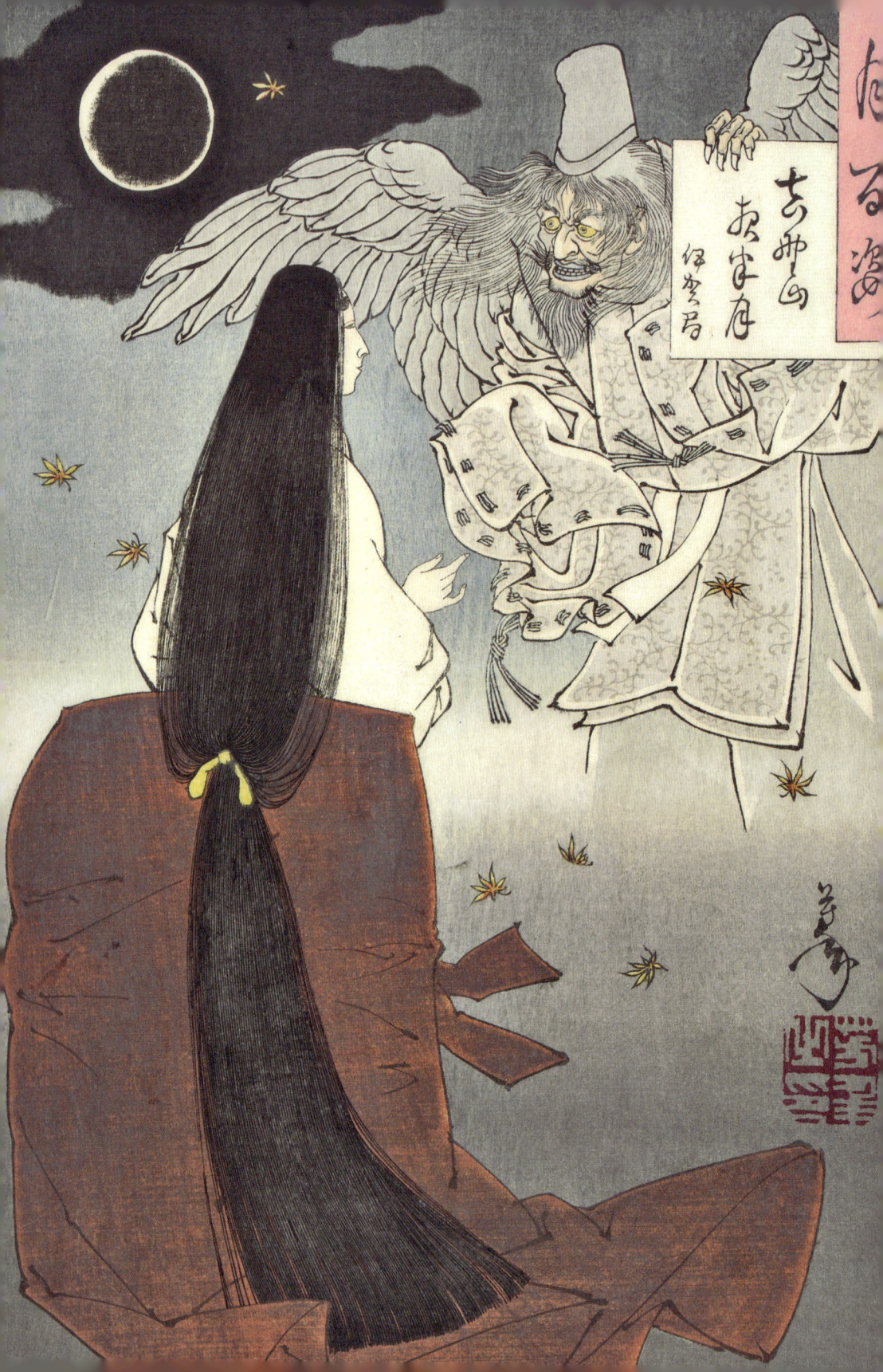

TENGU

•

Literally 'heavenly dogs', the *tengu* are supernatural entities that defy easy classification, existing somewhere between Shinto deities (*kami*) and monsters (*yōkai*). Consequently, it's never quite clear if we should fear them or revere them. Thought to originate from shooting stars heralding a cortège of political and military disasters, the *tengu* later took the form of giant human-like birds, possibly influenced by Garuda, the mythical bird-mount of the god Vishnu. Over the course of time, the beaks of these fantastic creatures transformed into the long noses seen in Japanese prints and the masks worn during dance rituals in Japanese shrines.

For a long time, *tengu* – often described as 'winged demons of the mountains' – were associated with Buddhist priests and mountain ascetics (*yamabushi*), whose distinctive clothing and accessories they adopted. Chief among these was the fan, possessing the magical power to unleash violent storms, or to enlarge or shrink a person's nose. The *tengu*'s link with religion is also reflected in literature and oral traditions, in anecdotes of them setting traps for monks and lay worshippers. In one story, a *tengu* possesses the mind of a courtesan to seduce a devout priest; in another, it steals sacred objects from a temple or disguises itself as a priest or nun to lead the faithful astray.

Japanese prints teem with such *yōkai*, notably in depictions of the warrior Ushiwakamaru. Taught the art of swordsmanship by a band of *tengu* working under the supervision of their king Sōjōbō, Ushiwakamaru, also known as Minamoto no Yoshitsune, received unparalleled training. Empowered with these skills, he succeeded in defeating the giant Musashibo Benkei on Gojō Bridge in Kyoto.

Another popular print illustrates the tragic love story of a fourteenth-century man who dies of

a broken heart, then returns as a ghost resembling a *tengu* to haunt the imperial palace in Yoshino. One night, the *tengu* confesses to one of the empress's ladies-in-waiting, Iga no Tsubone, that his true love was the empress. She promises that she will go with the empress to bow at his grave, and the *yōkai,* appeased, disappears forever.

Spiritual guardians of the mountains, the *tengu* are hybrid creatures who haunt remote valleys, appearing as leafy *konoha-tengu,* crow-like *karasu-tengu,* or long-nosed *hanadaka-tengu,* but they can also be the manifestation of a tormented soul. The shogun governor of Sagami Province, Hōjō Takatoki (1303–1333), is a striking example. At the end of his life, this morally corrupt man is persecuted by clouds of *tengu* and clumsily attempts to ward them off with his fan.

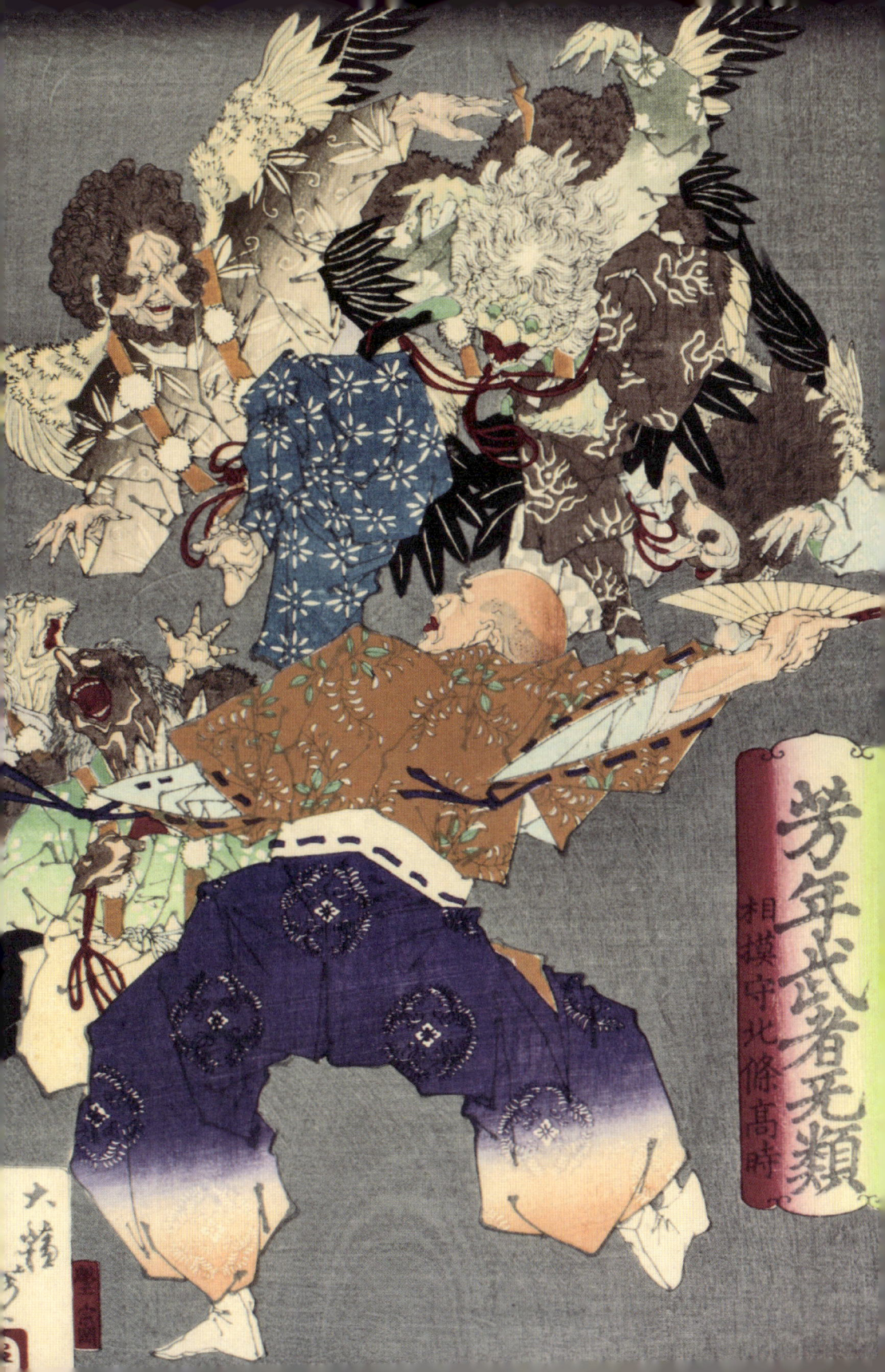

芳年武者无類

相模守北條髙時

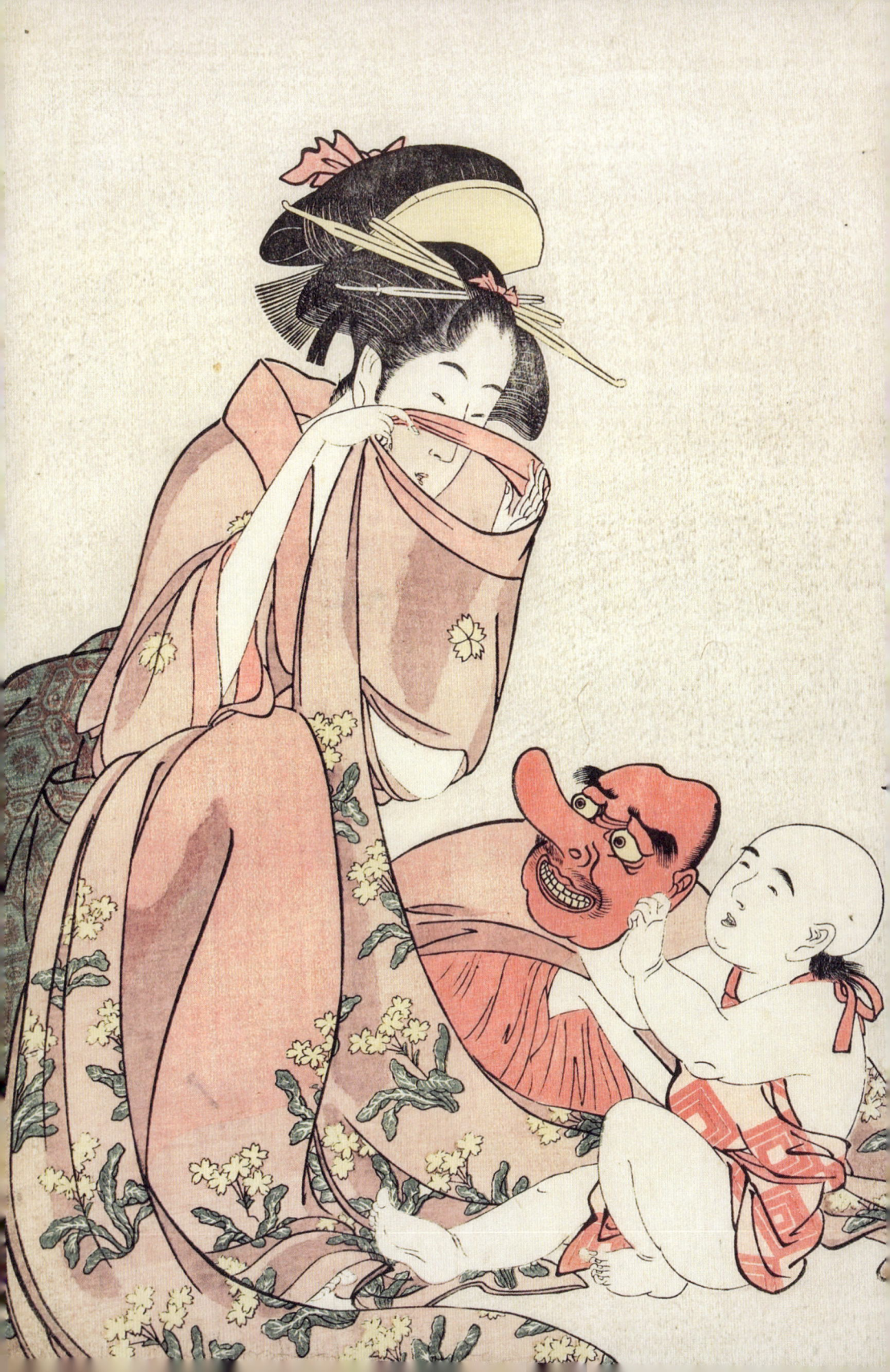

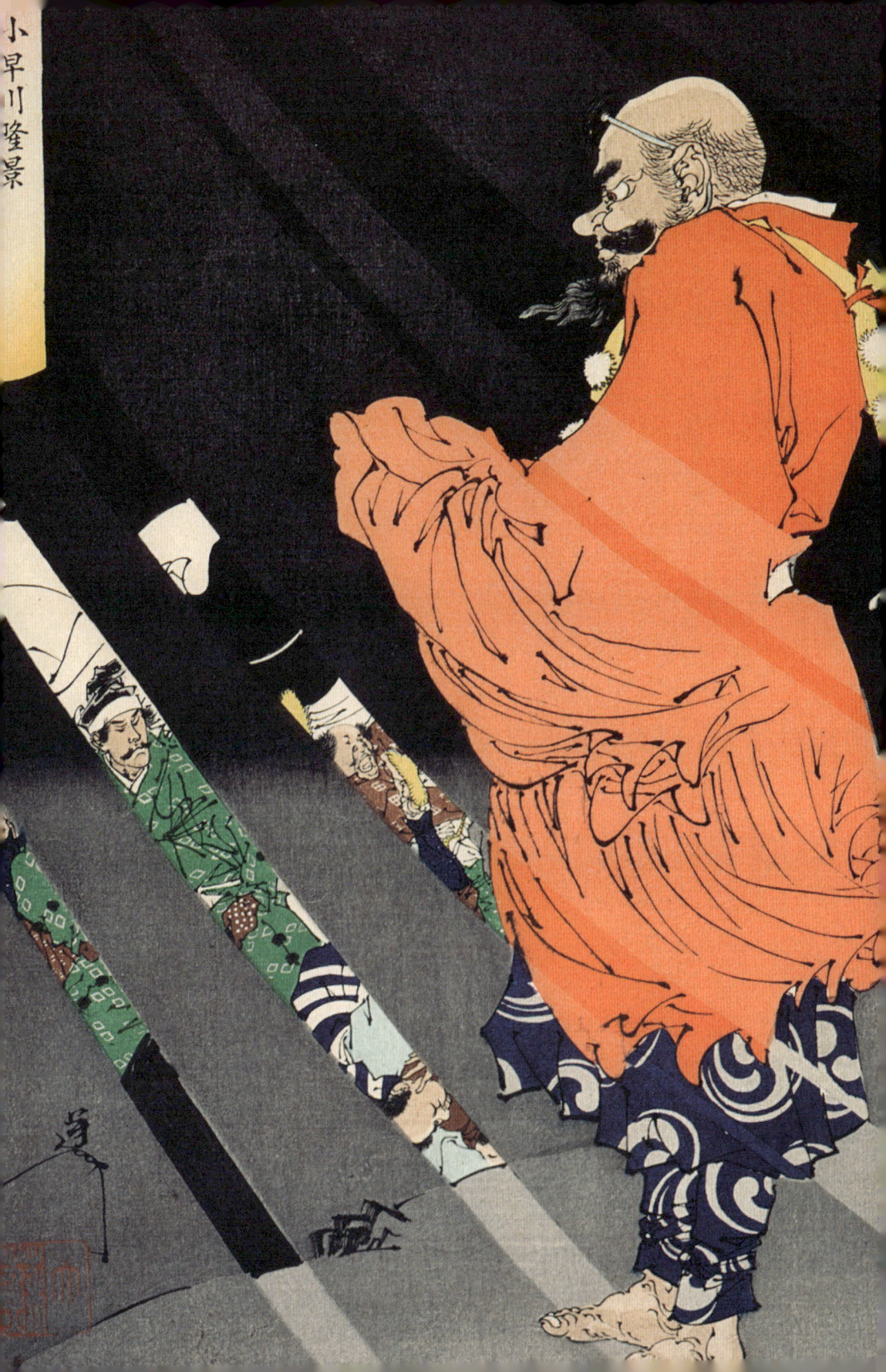

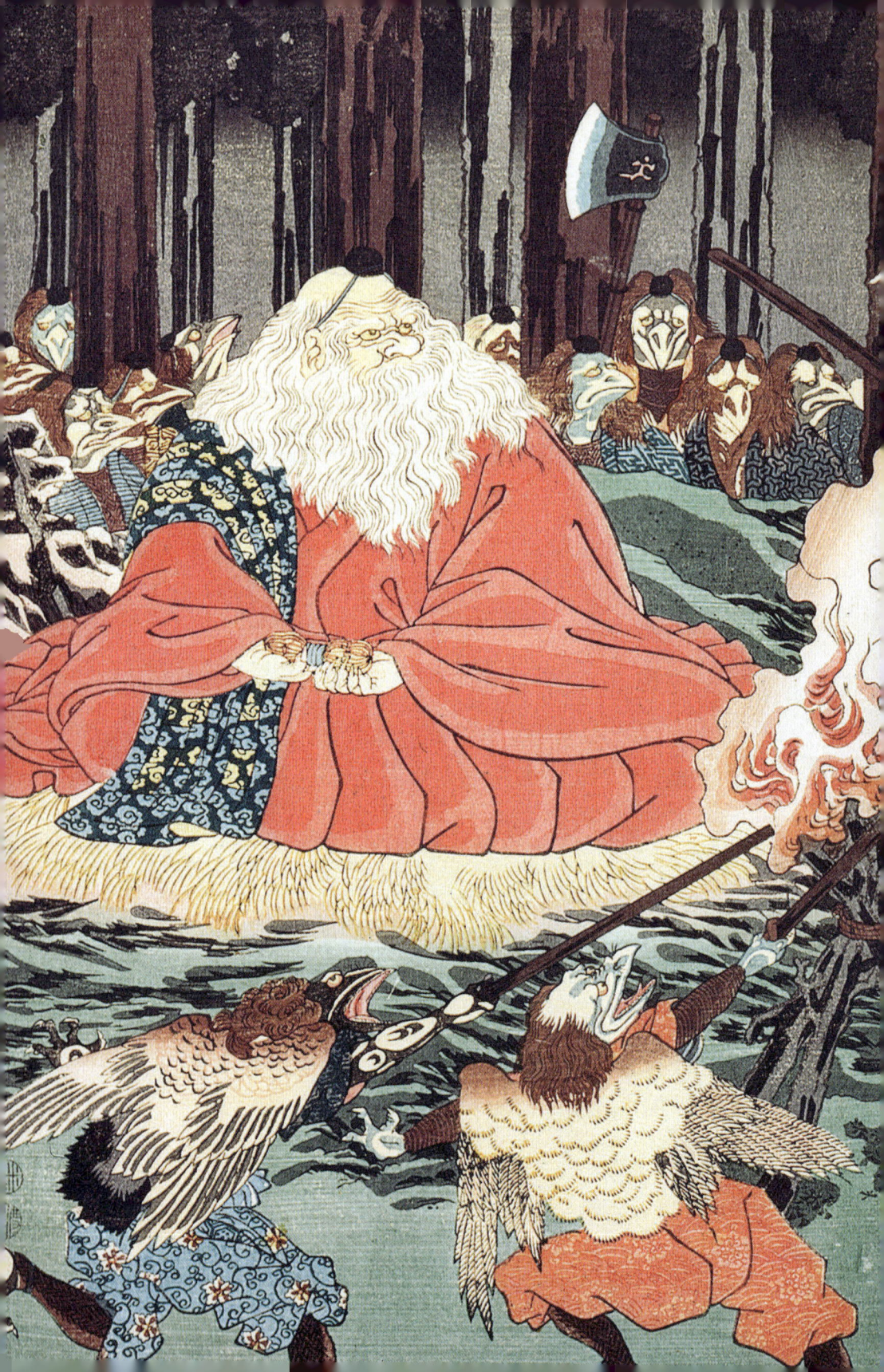

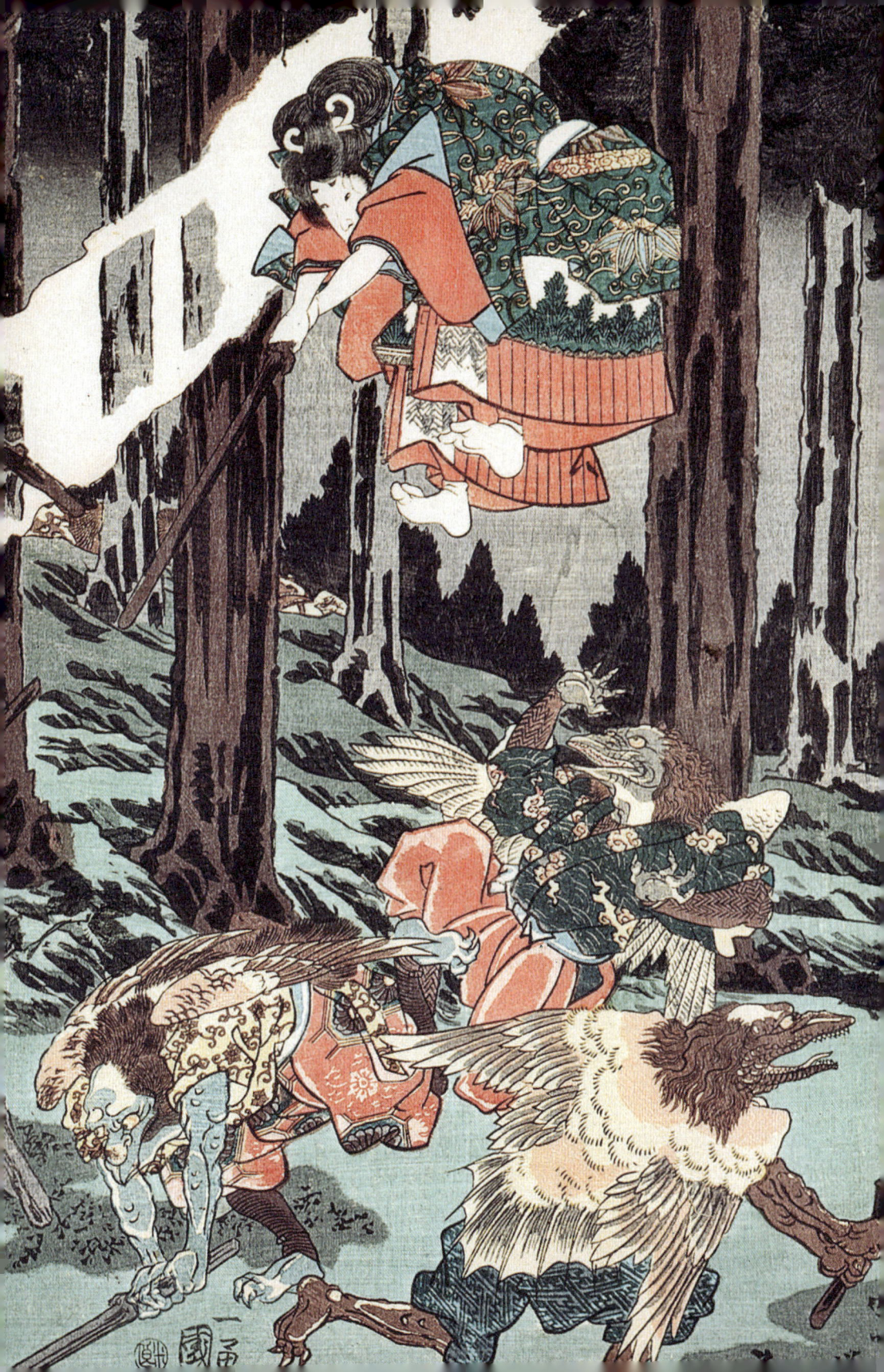

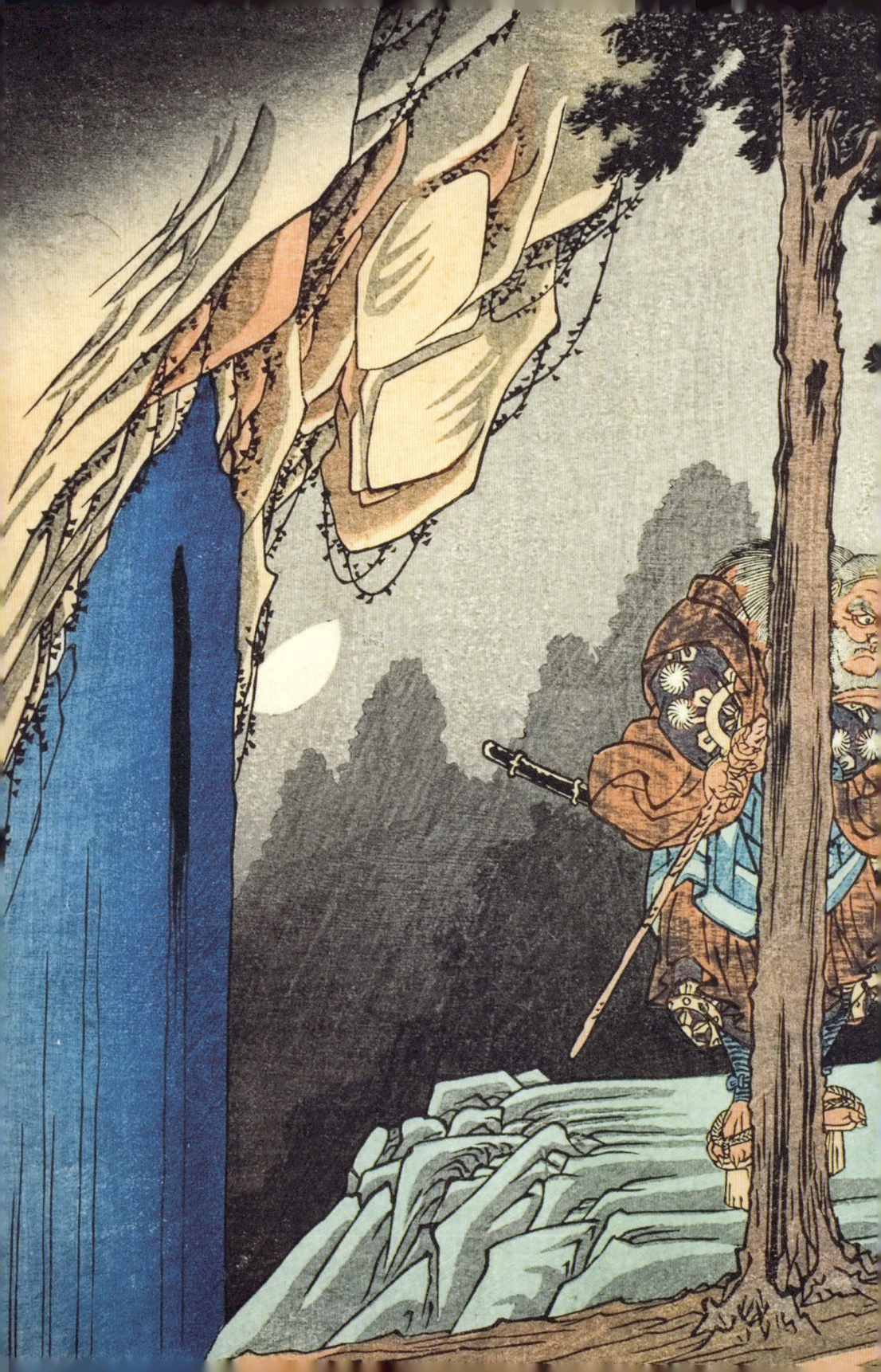

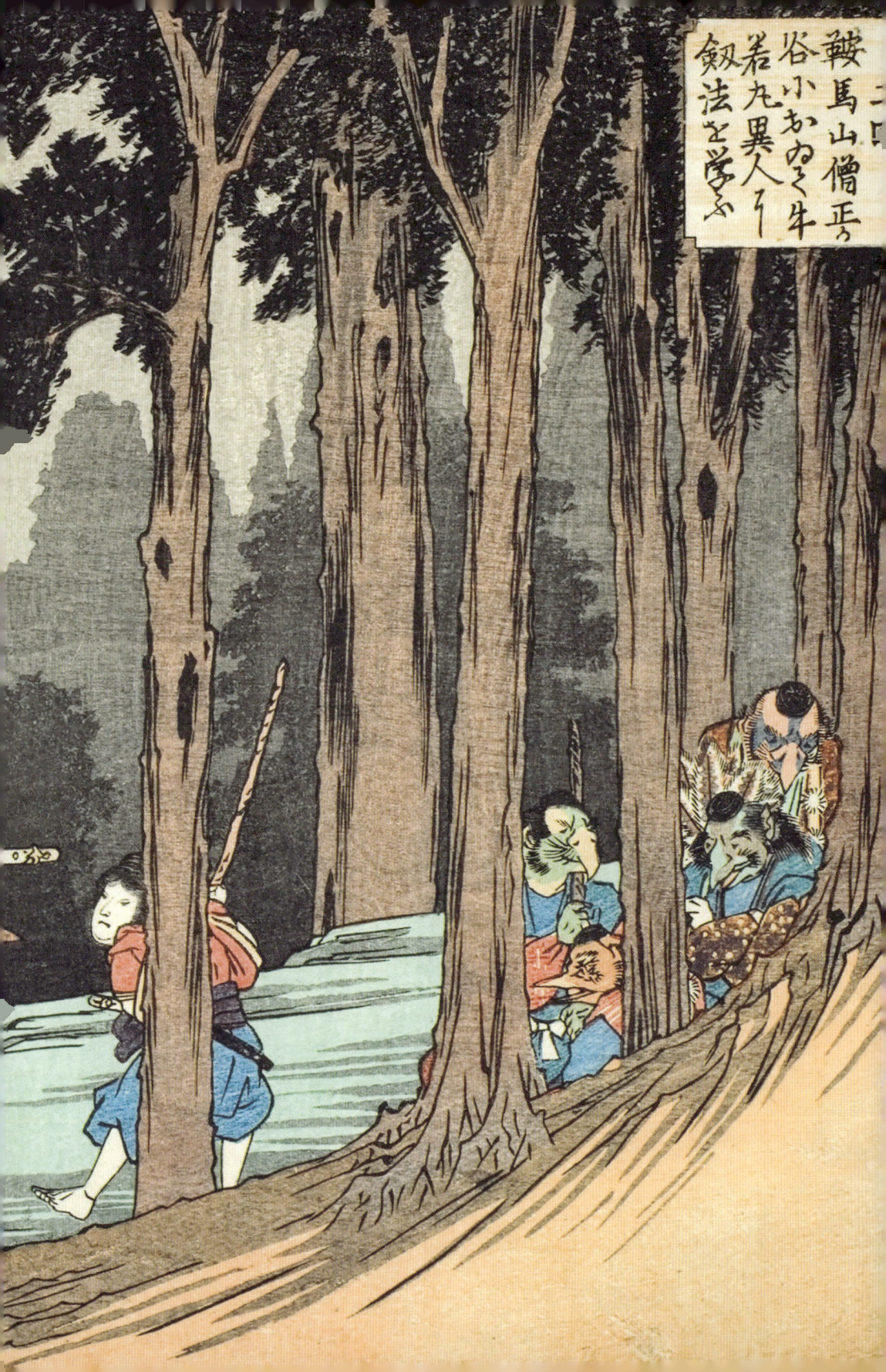

鞍馬山僧正ヶ
谷小おぬく牛
若丸異人ら
剣法を学ぶ

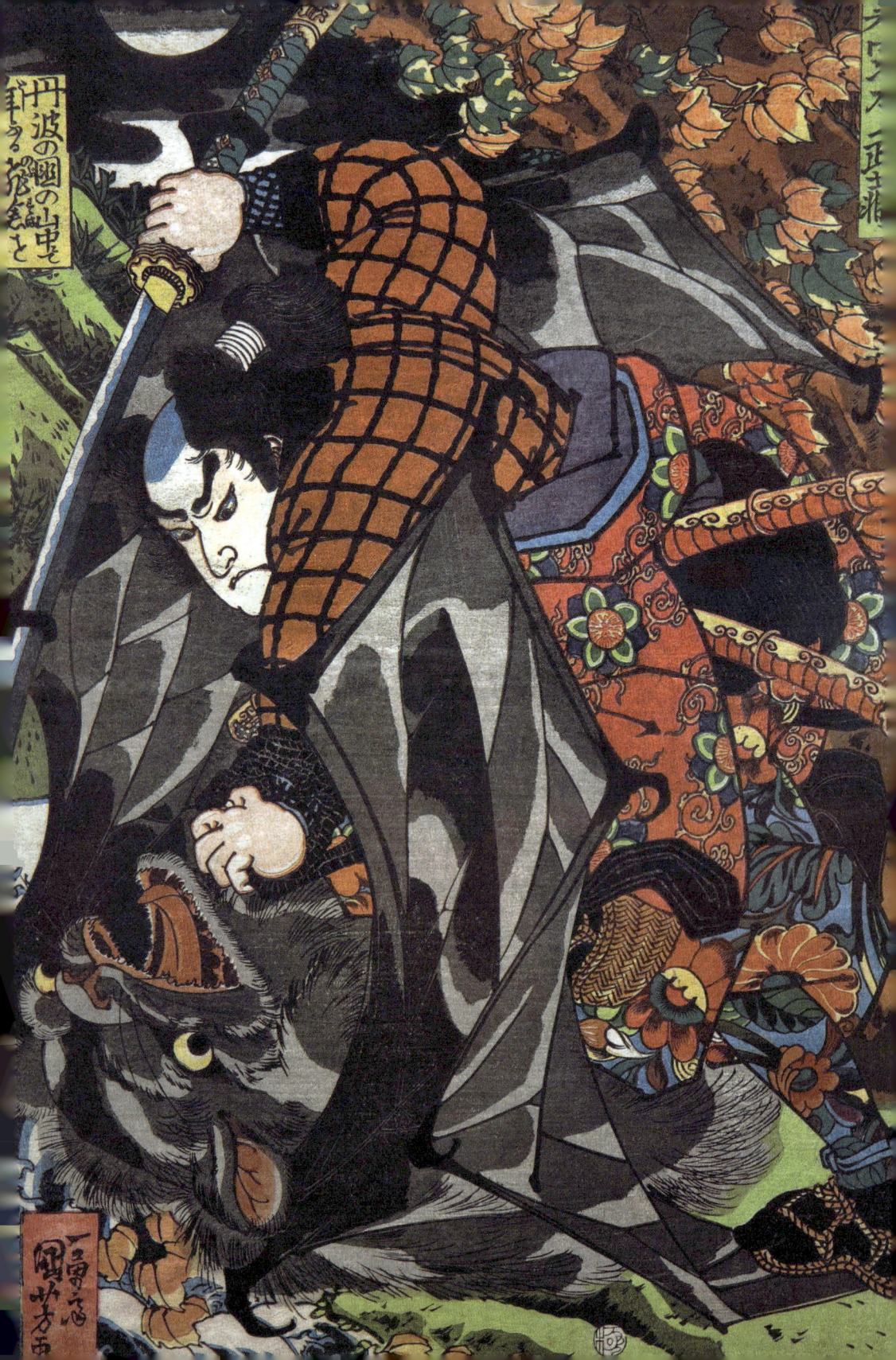

NOBUSUMA

•

According to legend, bats that live for several thousand years or more transform into terrifying *yōkai* known as *nobusuma* – demonic flying squirrels that harass travellers by blowing out their torches and plunging them into darkness. These creatures feed on nuts and fire, and they also greedily suck the blood of cats.

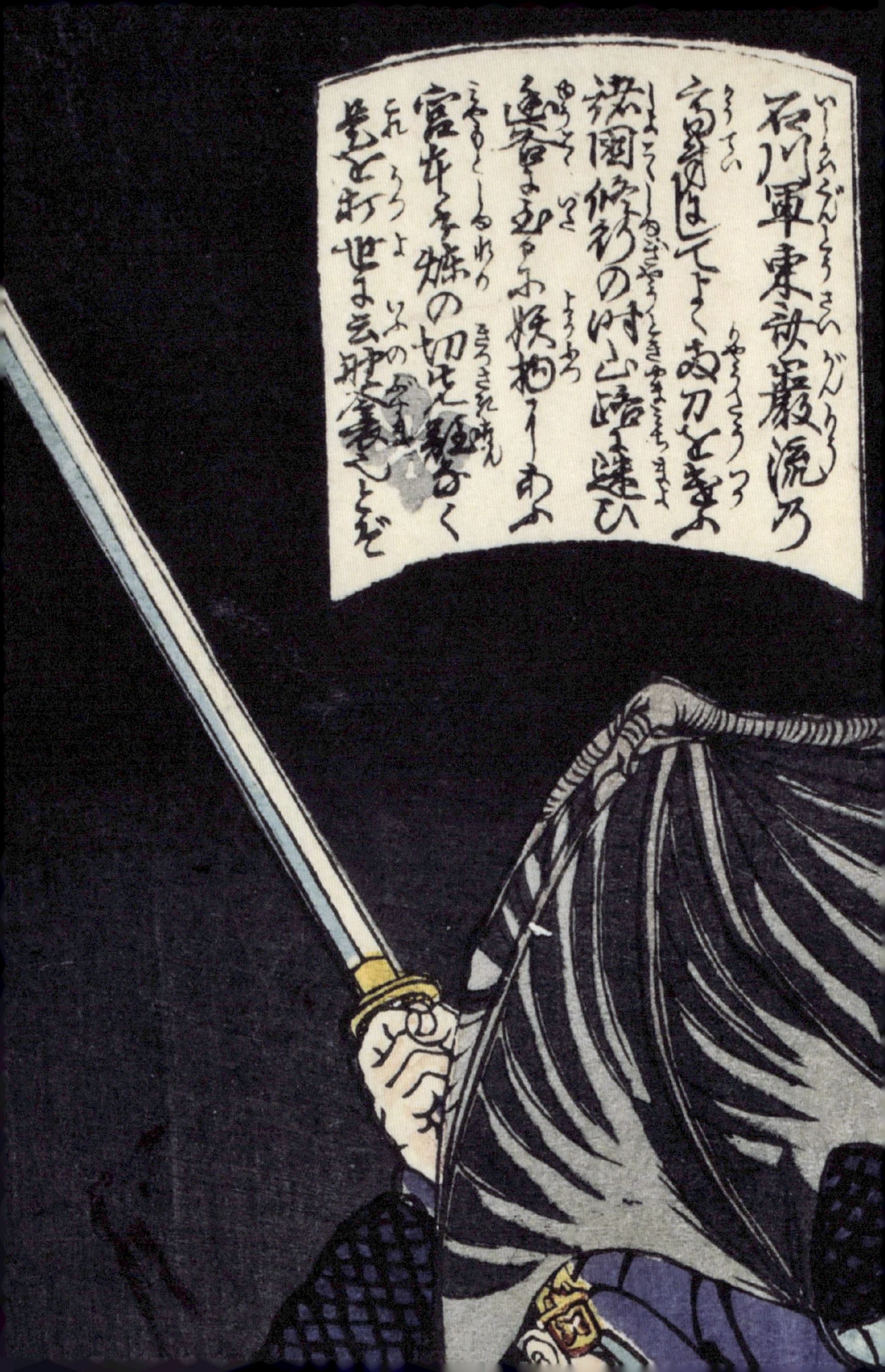

石川軍東訳巌流乃

いしかわぐんとうやくがんりう

高軍のは一てよくあ刀とまふ

かうくん　　　　　　　りやくさう　つ

諸国修行の州山路で選ひ

しよこくしゆぎやう　とき　すしやま　しらみえ

運番の亭戸不候柄て一あ

うんばん　　　えど　　ふ　　ようろう

宮本を嫌の切れに延べく

みやもと　　きら　　きれ　　　のべ

益を新せま云州義とぞ

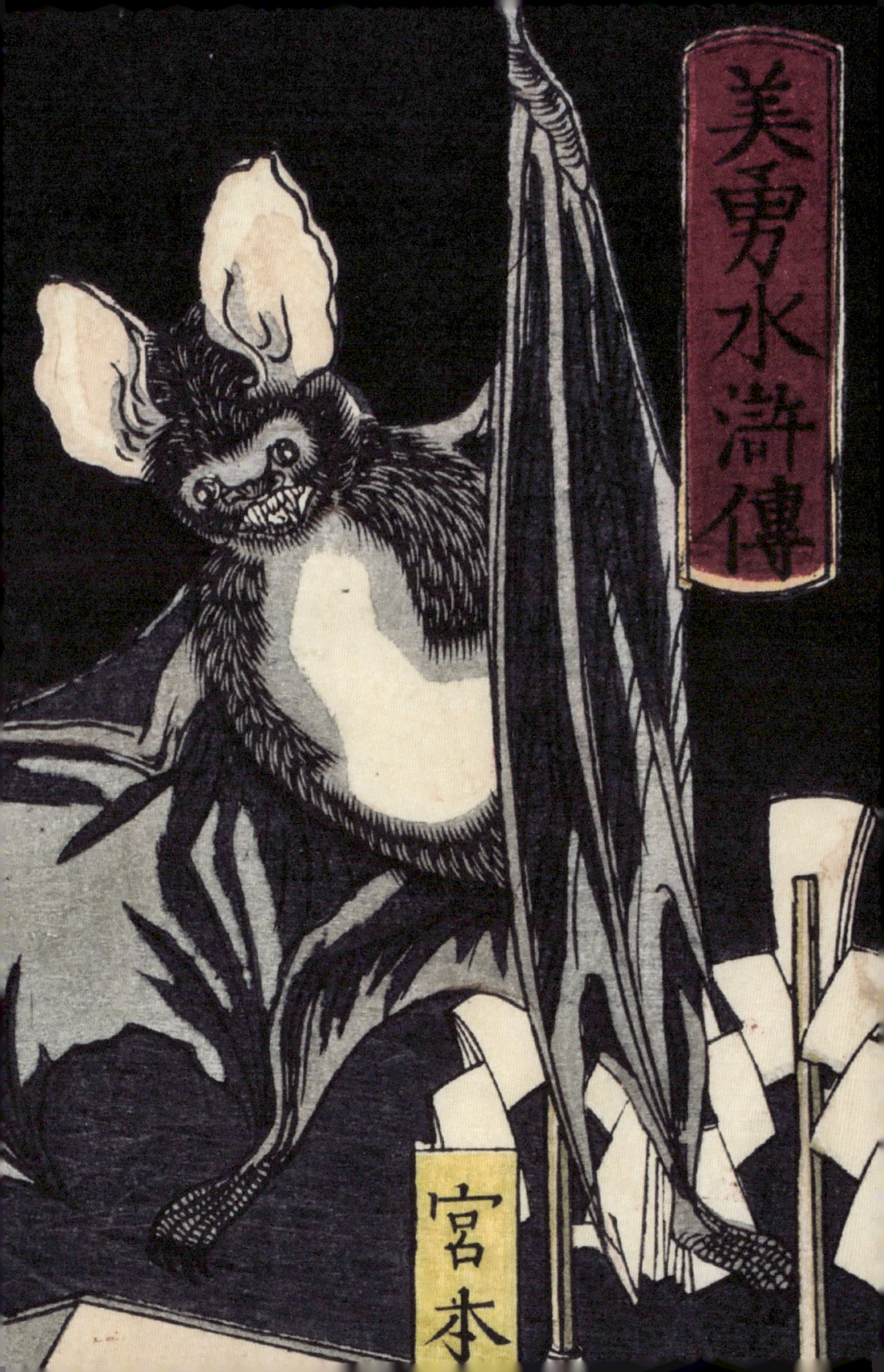

美勇水滸傳

宮本

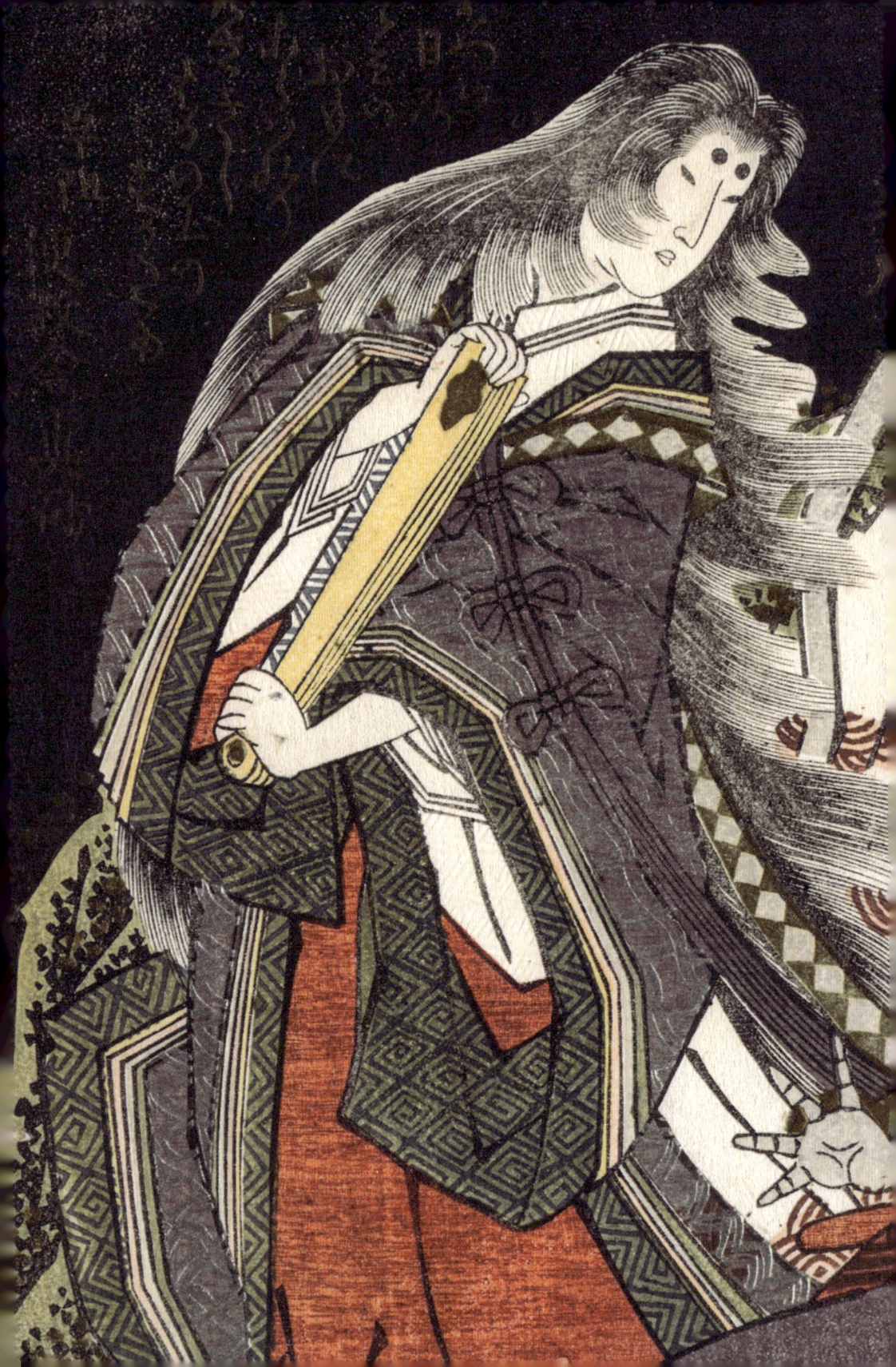

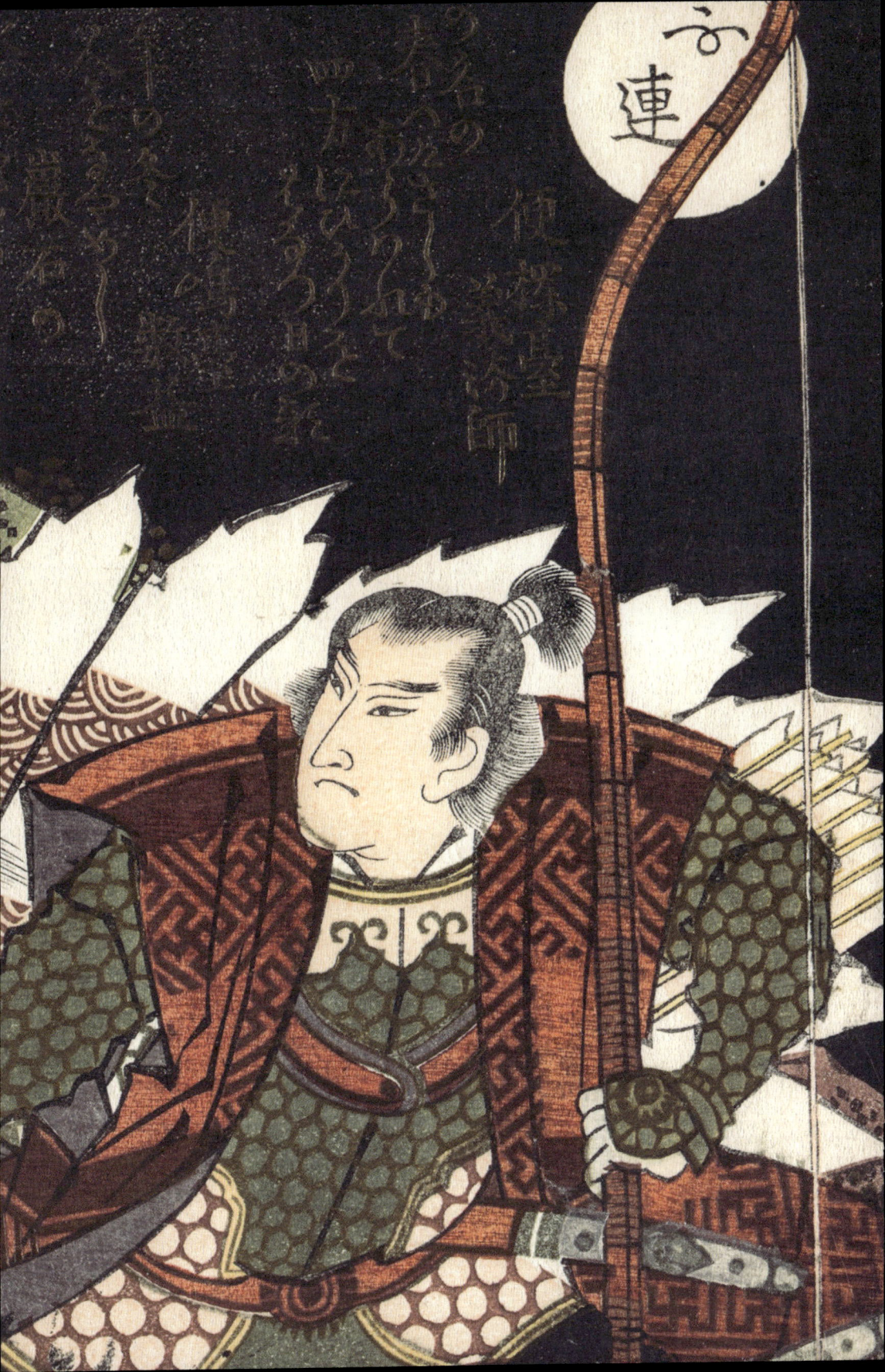

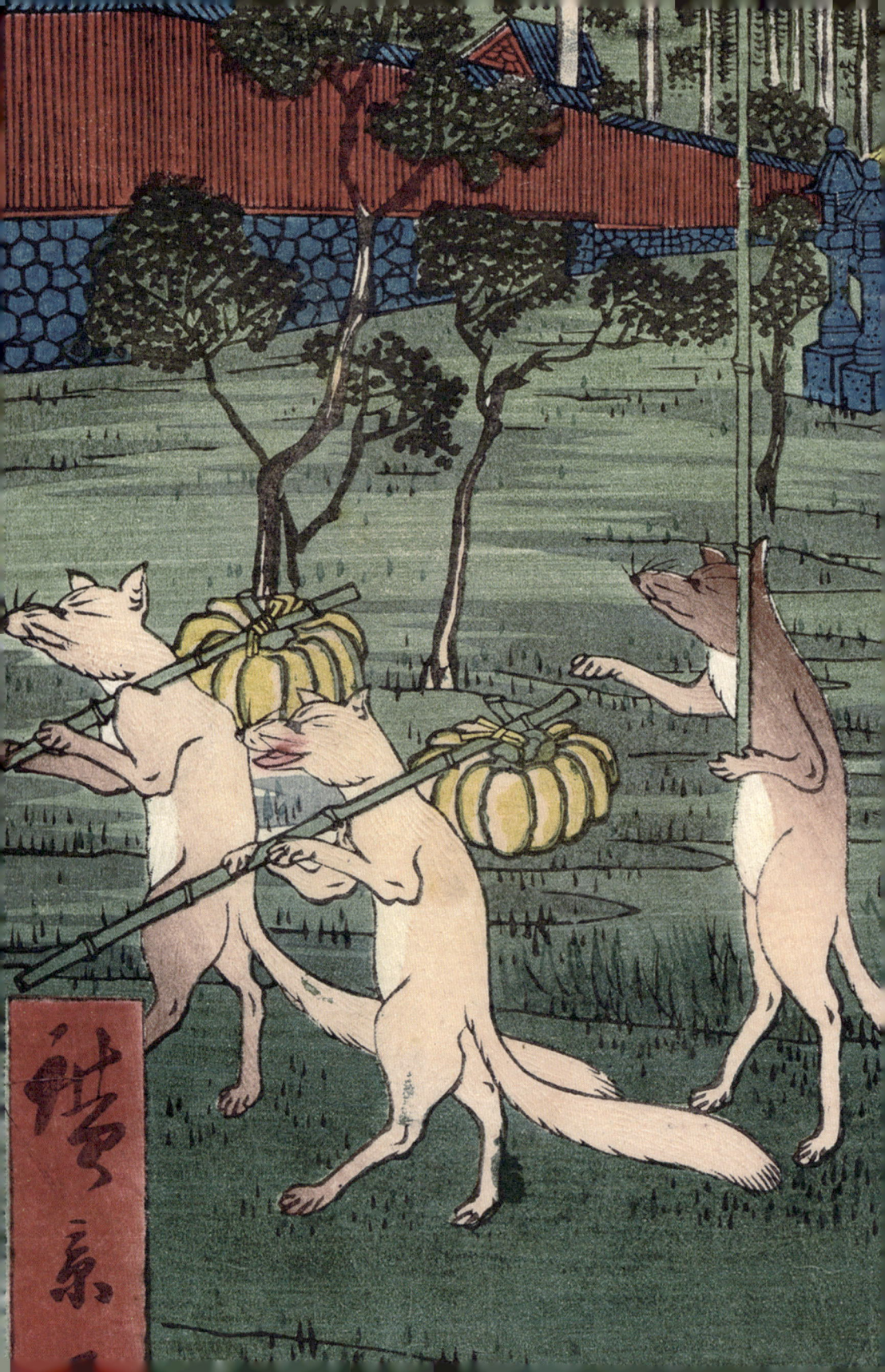

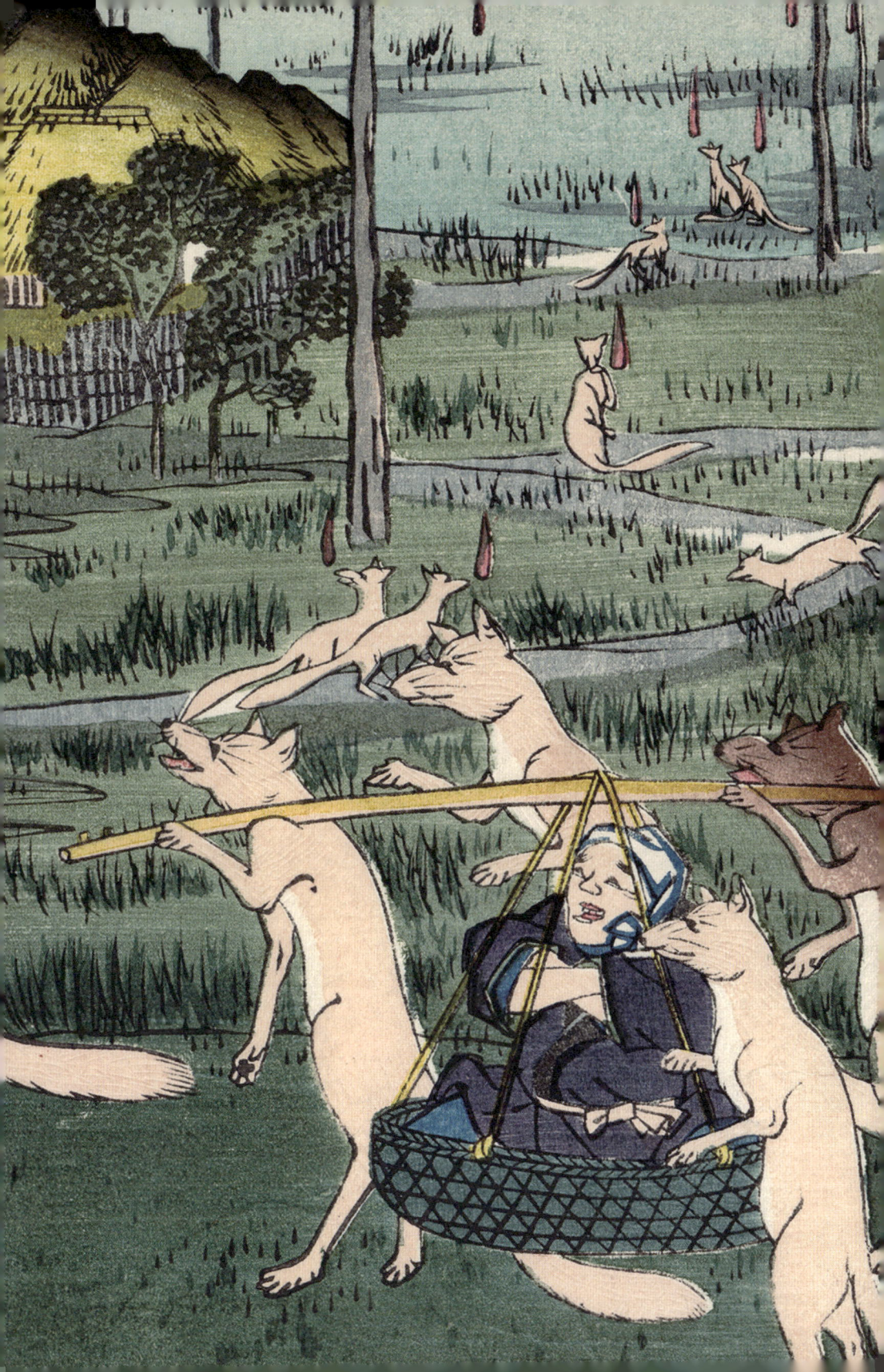

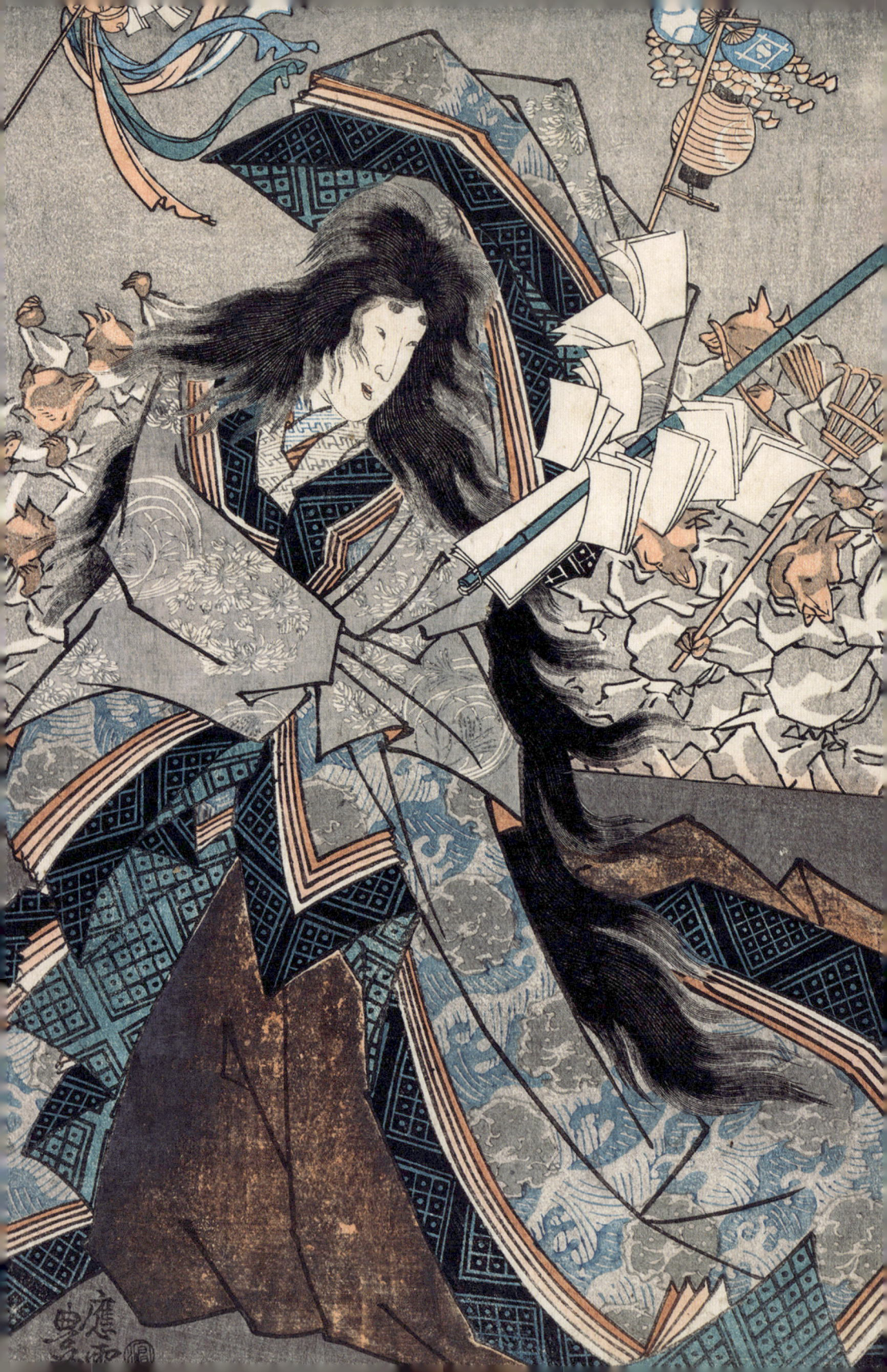

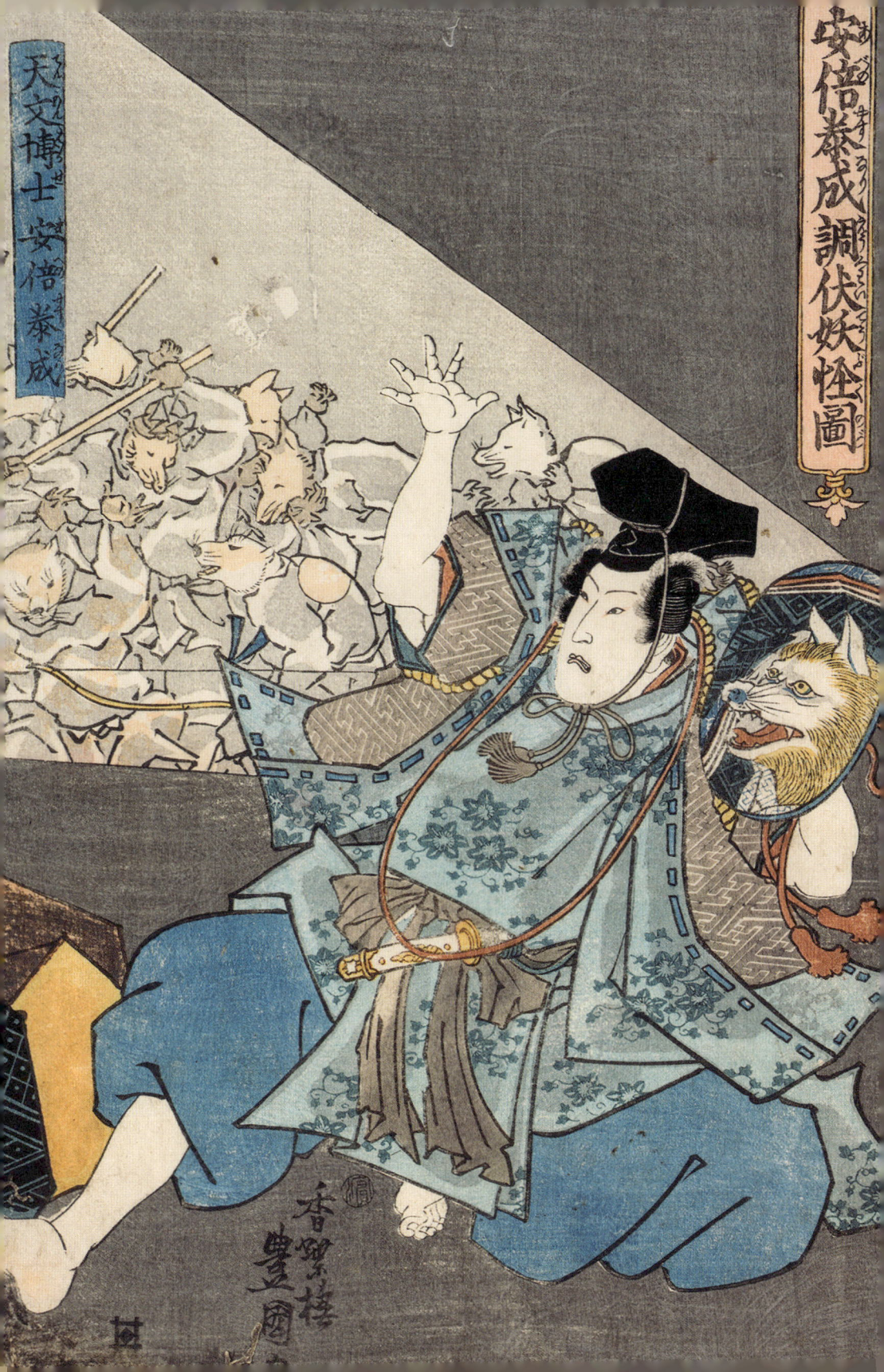

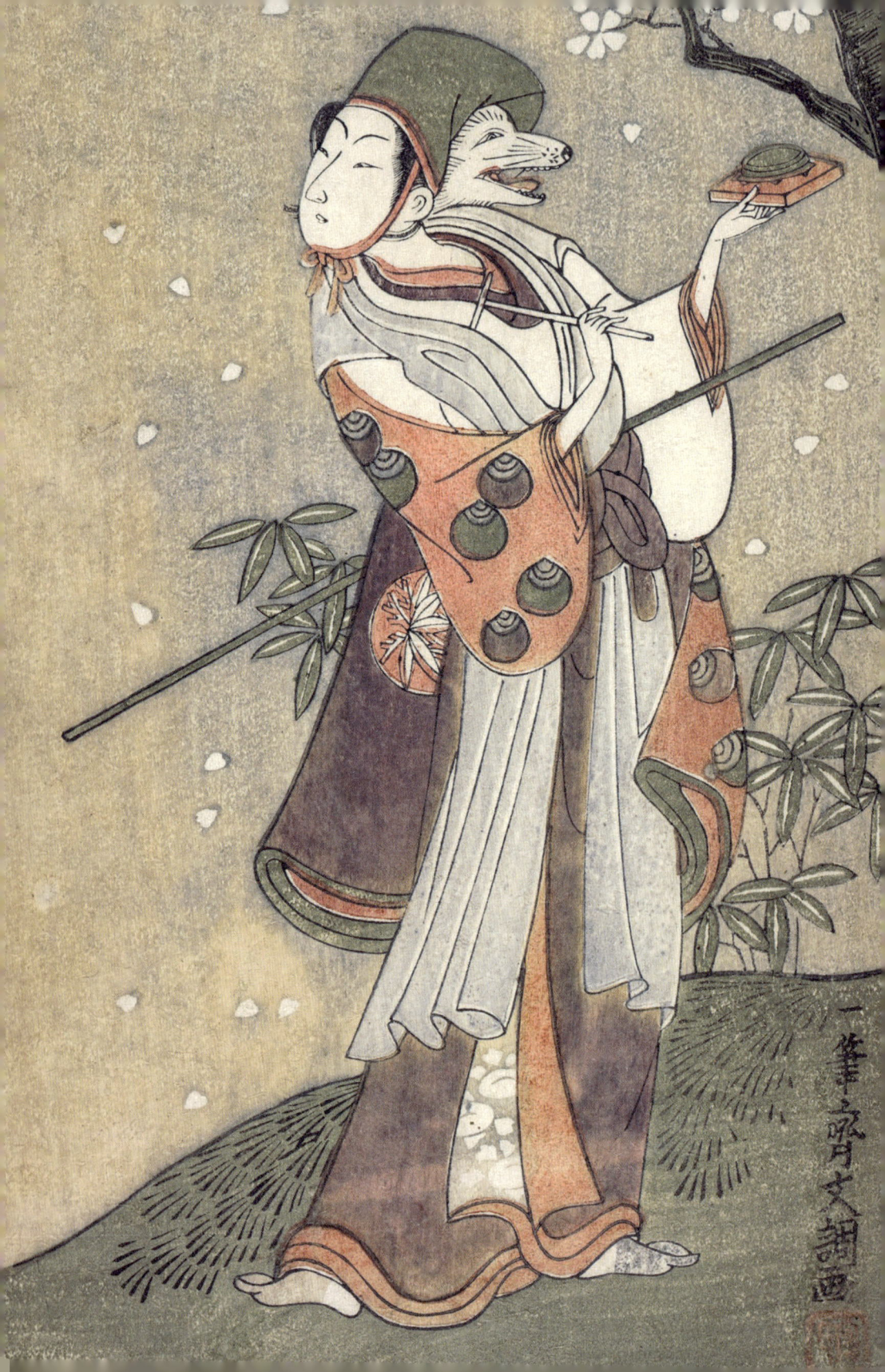

KITSUNE

•

'Beware of pretty girls' is the eternal advice repeated to all men from generation to generation, in all civilisations. The Noh play *Admire the Autumn Foliage* (*Momijigari*) tells the story of the warrior Taira no Koremochi who, while travelling through a forest, meets a group of beautiful young women and stops for a while with them. Having eaten well, drunk freely and laughed much, he falls asleep. During his slumber, a deity warns him that his companions are in fact not women but ill-intentioned demons. When he wakes, he kills them, one by one and without hesitation. The print *Taira no Koremochi Conquering the Devil Woman on Mount Togakushi* by Tsukioka Yoshitoshi depicts the moment he kills one of the *yōkai*, including a very striking detail: in the stream beside them, the reflection of one of the beautiful women reveals her true monstrous form.

Foxes have taken the art of metamorphosis to extraordinary heights. They appear throughout the *yōkai* stories from century to century, at times beguiling, at times repelling those who cross their path. Ever-present in the background is Inari Daimyojin, the Shinto deity of rice and fertility, often with fox-like features. Thus, the *kitsune* is deeply sensitive to justice, commitment and loyalty. These qualities are illustrated in the story of Abe Yasuna. A nobleman at the court of Emperor Murakami (926–967), Yasuna one day saves a fox – an animal hunted for its liver, which is used in traditional medicine. Wounded as a result of his efforts, Yasuna is aided by a strikingly beautiful woman, Kuzunoha, who takes him to her home to care for him. They become inseparable, eventually marry and have a son, Dojimaru. When he reaches the age of five, he understands that his mother is the fox his father saved and that she possesses supernatural powers. Yasuna also becomes

135

aware of the true identity of his wife. One day, when they are together in the forest where the fox was saved, Kuzunoha entrusts her husband with a golden casket and a crystal ball, then disappears, abandoning them forever. Equipped with these two treasures, Yasuna becomes an *onmyōji* – that is, a master of *onmyōdō*, an occult, esoteric art that he employs in the service of his emperor. His son eventually surpasses him in this knowledge and power, also becoming a 'master of Yin and Yang' under the name Abe no Seimei.

A print by Tsukioka Yoshitoshi, *The Fox-Woman Kuzunoha Leaving her Child* (*Kuzunoha kitsune dōji ni wakaruru no zu*, 1890), subtly shows the transformation – or rather the hybrid nature – of this *kitsune*, whose human form fades behind a paper screen, revealing a faintly lit fox-like profile. At her feet, a child on all fours sadly tries to hold his mother back, clinging to the hem of her purple kimono. At the top of the image hangs a branch of *Pueraria lobata*, or kudzu (*kuzu* in Japanese), which the fox had once said would be enough—if touched—to summon her in a dream, should her husband ever find himself longing for her.

The fox with nine tails (*kyūbi no kitsune*) is a unique form of *yōkai*, the result of a very long and gradual maturation of the fox's intellectual and physical capabilities, passed down from generation to generation, from life to life. With each new stage of growth, spanning centuries or even millennia, a new tail appears, culminating in the emergence of the ninth. The *kitsune* has now reached the peak of its development and is endowed with immense material and spiritual powers. It is capable, for instance, of transforming itself into a woman to deceive men, like Tamamo no Mae, who fools the warrior Miura no Suke. It can also conjure ghostly flames – will-o'-the-wisps – to frighten lonely travellers or to protect those it favours. In the kabuki play *Honchō Nijūshikō*, for example, the fox aids Princess Yaegaki as she walks across a frozen lake to rescue her lover, the son of Takeda Shingen, a deadly rival of her father. Some believe there are several foxes with nine tails, others that there is only one. Like the

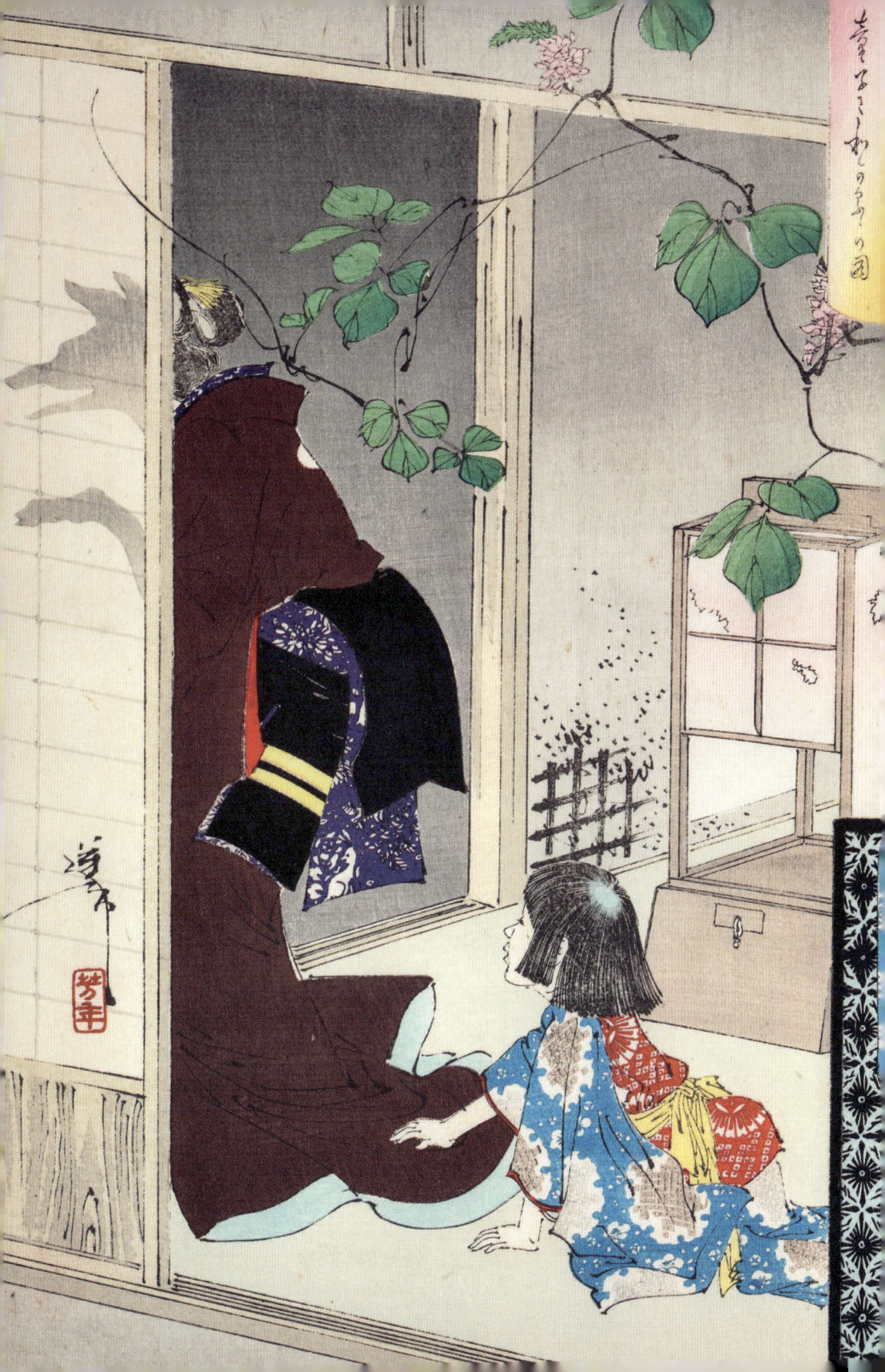

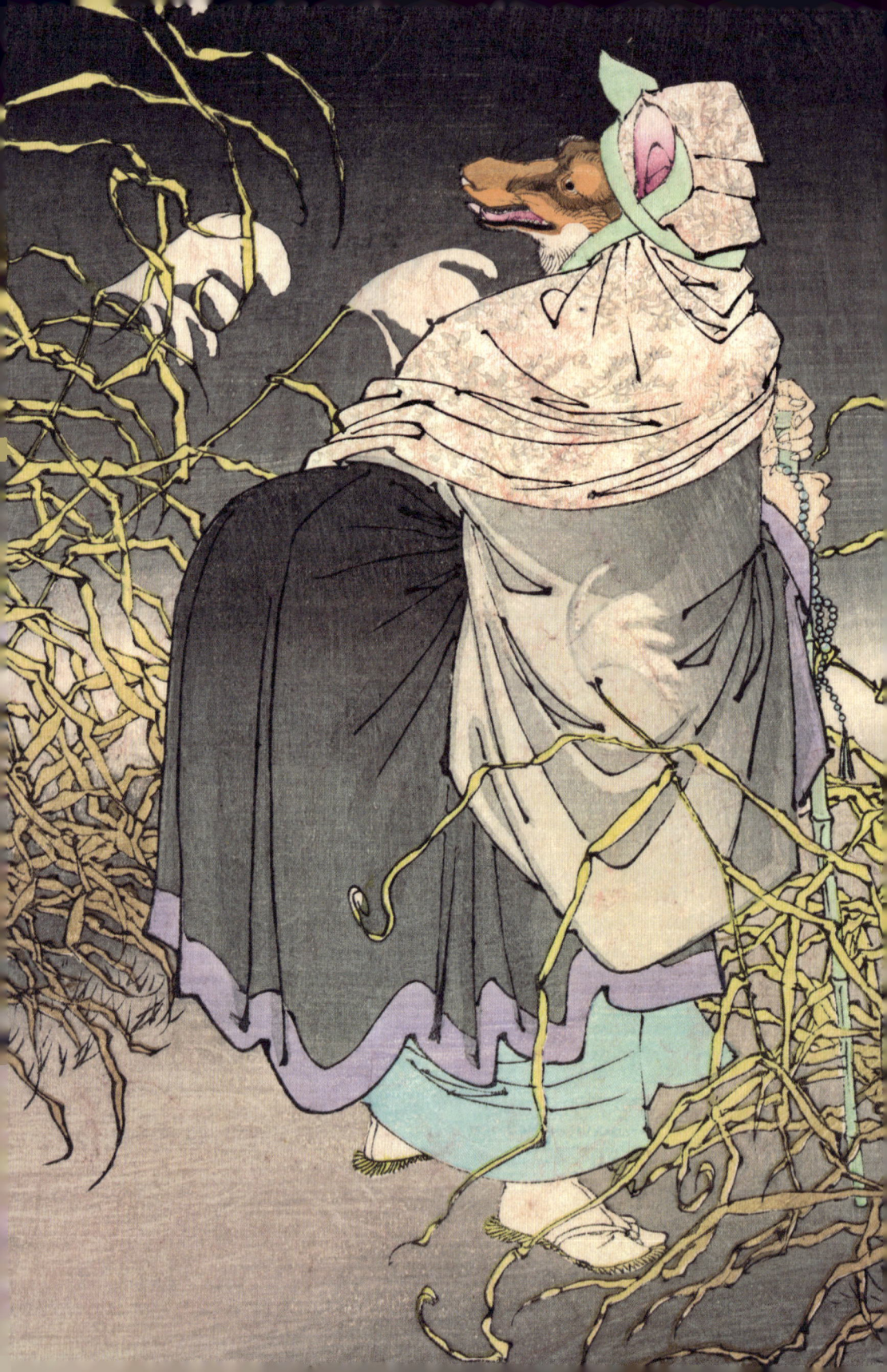

Wandering Jew (Ahasverus) of Western mythology, *kyūbi no kitsune* must roam the world for centuries. Unable to die, or eternally reborn like a phoenix, it appears again and again across the ages.

This fox – or rather vixen, for it is female – is said to have been seen for the first time in China in the eleventh century, then in India, again in China and finally in Japan. There, she seduced numerous monarchs, bringing about their ruin and the fall of several dynasties. As she was slowly poisoning the emperor Toba (1103–1156), a sorcerer succeeded in neutralising her. He forced her to transform into stone – a toxic, even lethal stone that killed anyone who came too close to her. Only incantations, performed some two centuries later, put an end to her. But for how long?

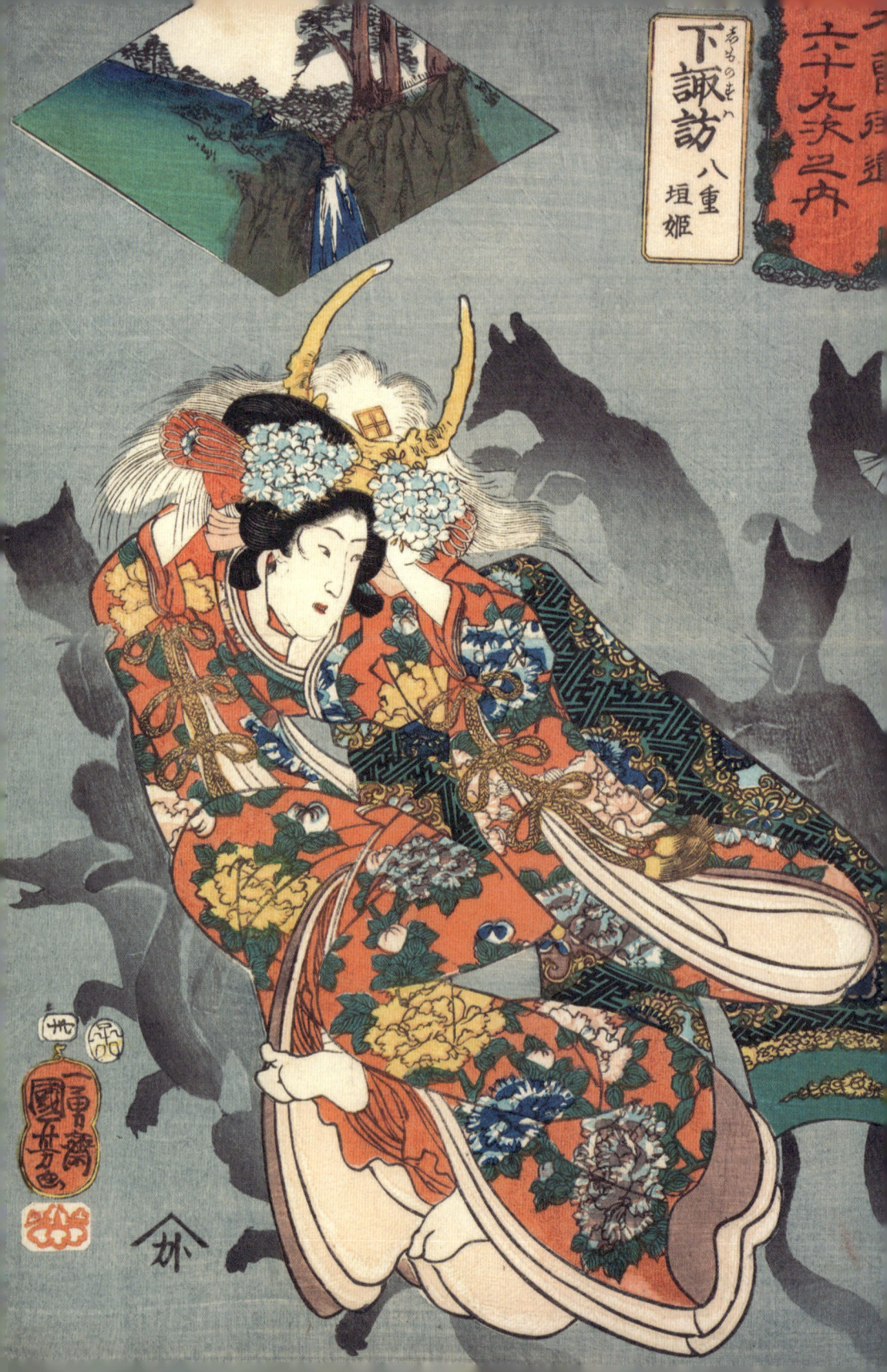

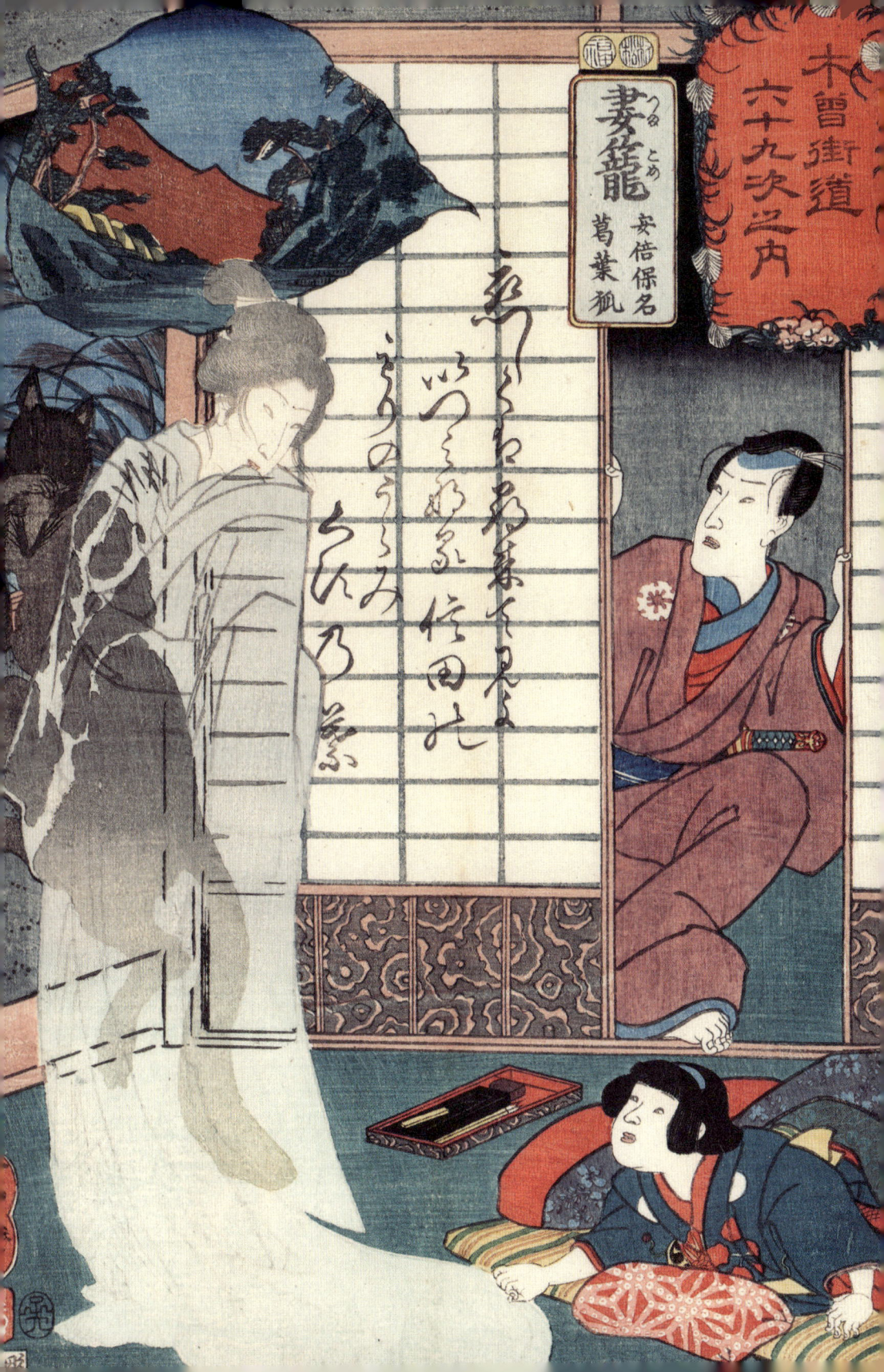

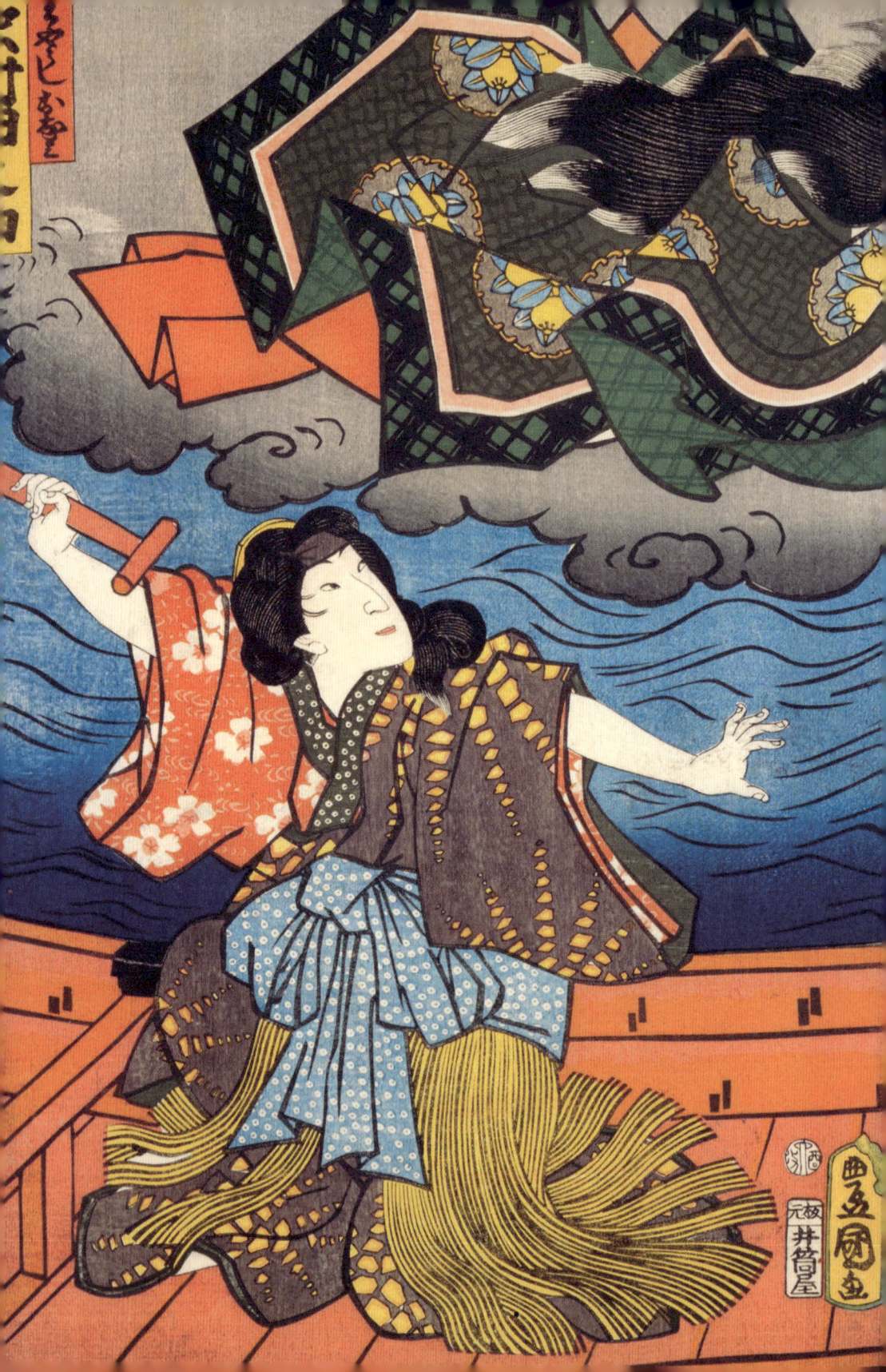

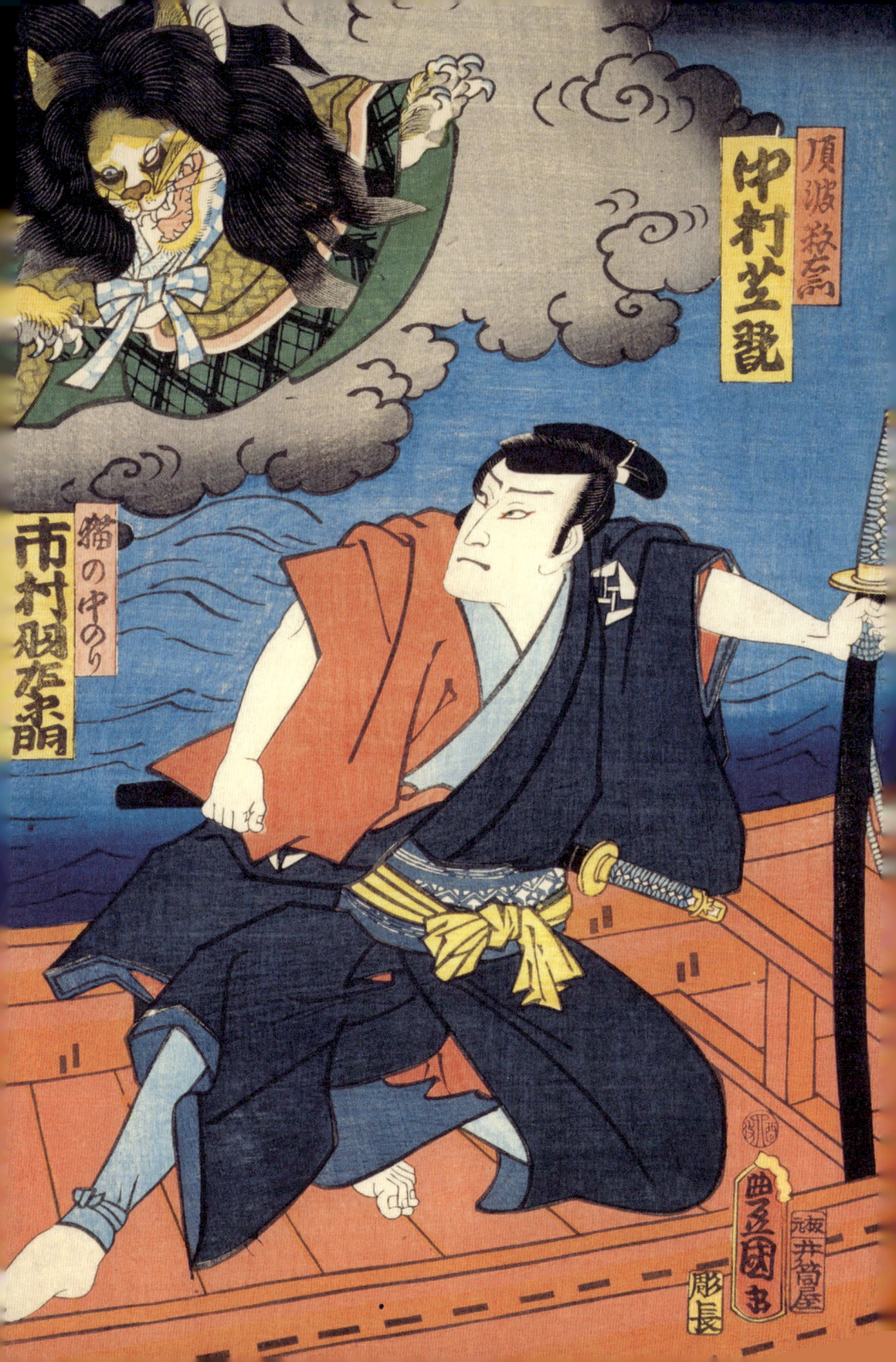

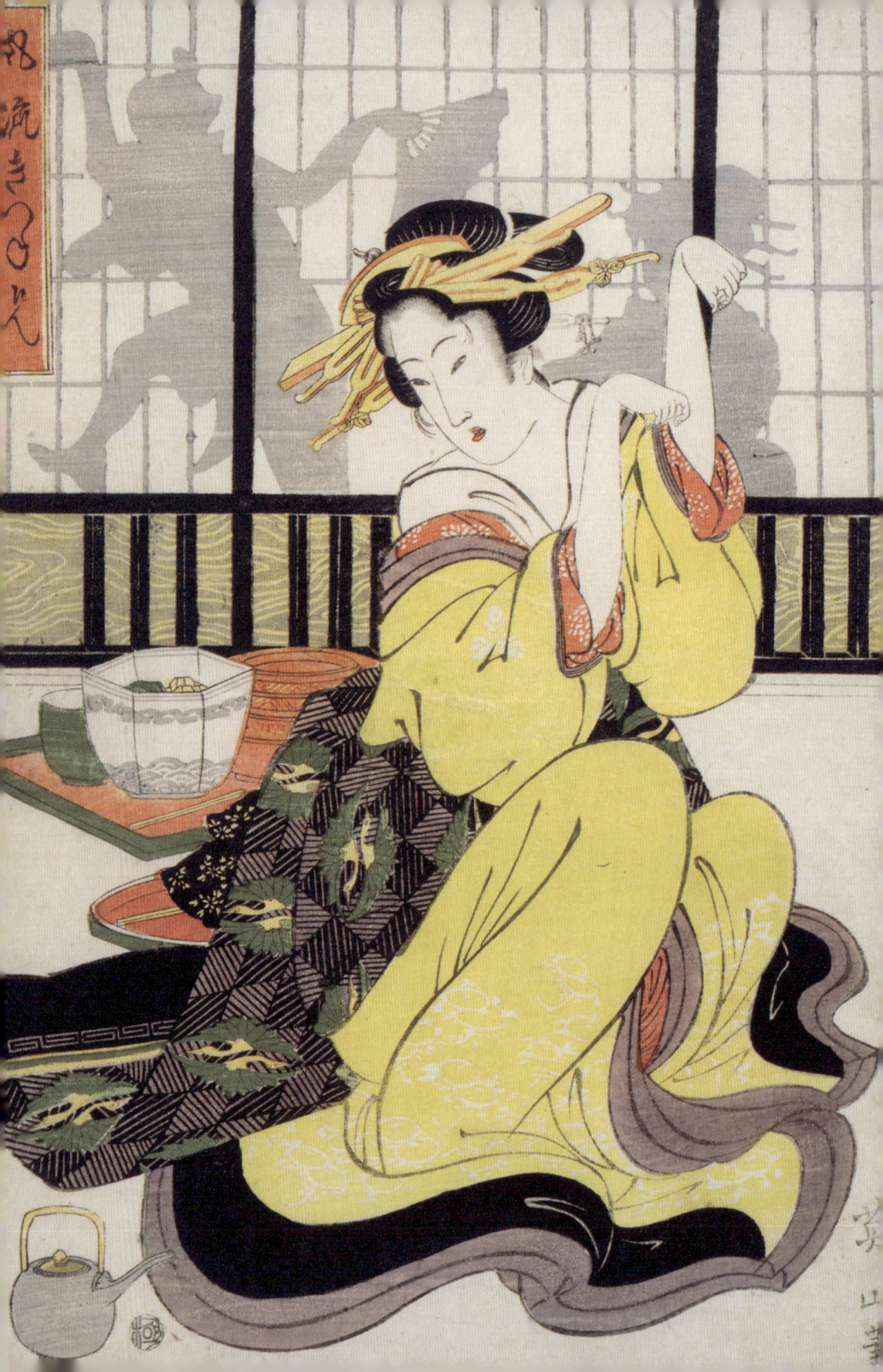

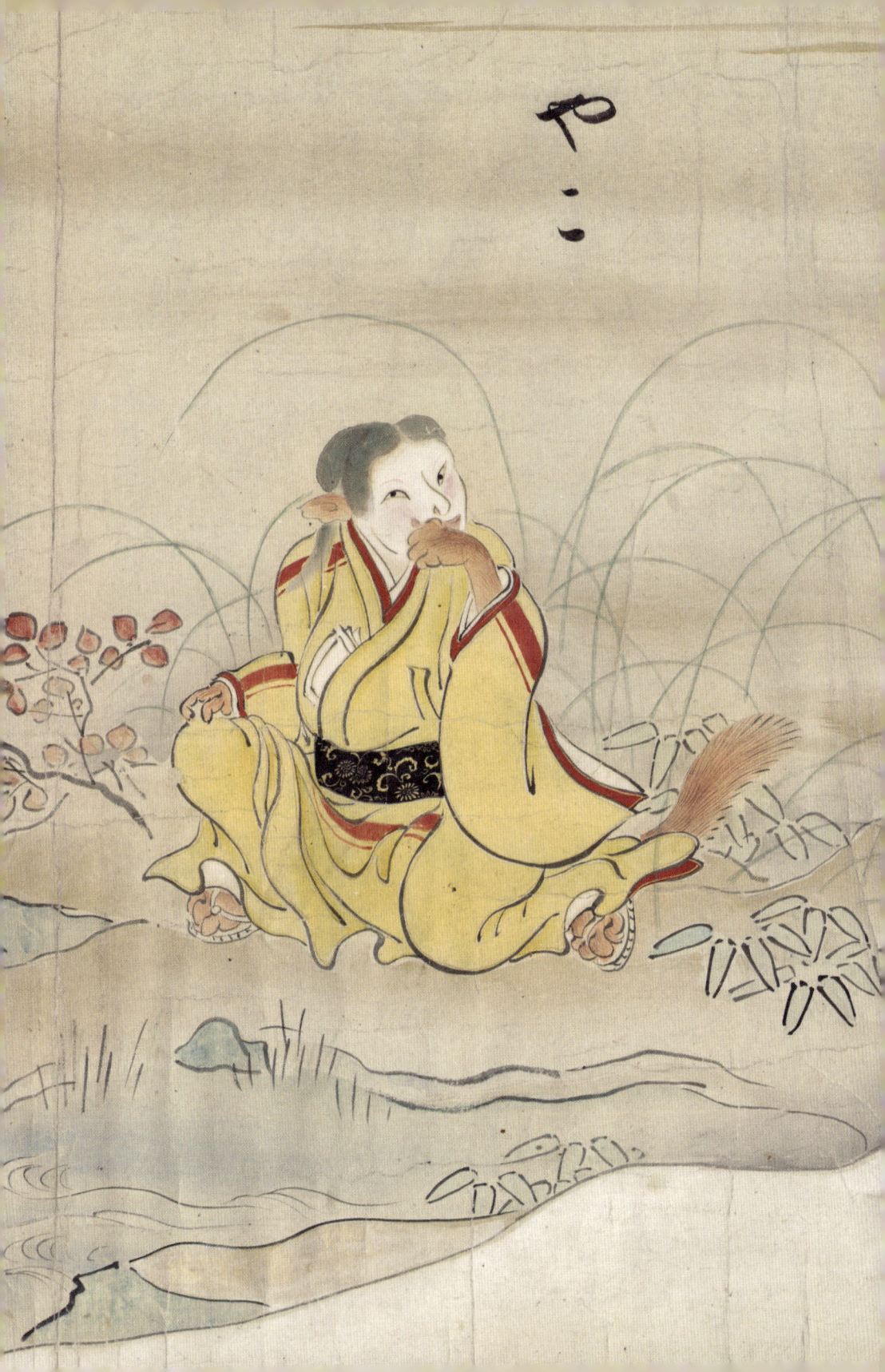

DEMON
MAIDENS

•

Obedience can mean survival – but sometimes curiosity wins out, and with knowledge comes despair. This is the lesson of the 'heron maiden' print, which recalls the story of a young man who saves a heron from certain death and shortly afterwards meets a beautiful young woman whom he eventually marries – on the strict condition that he never looks at her when she is weaving brocade. Everything goes wonderfully until the day when, burning with curiosity, he dares to glance at his wife working, only to realise that she is a heron, weaving the silk fabric with her feathers. The heron takes flight and he never sees her again.

And the other female demons? They reign over remote territories, scaring travellers and pilgrims who stray from the path. One such spirit on Mount Togakushi transforms into a beautiful princess to seduce the noble warrior Taira no Koremochi. Another is the *rokurokubi*, a type of demon known for her very long neck, which can wind its way anywhere. One print by Hokusai (from his sketchbook or *manga*) shows two images of her: in one, she is lying on the floor, her head hovering far above her body, smoking a pipe; in the other, she is seated, knitting, with her head stretched far away from her body, mischievously distracting a blind musician.

Others are born of a transformation caused by resentment or some other dark emotion. This is true of Kiyohime, a young widow who falls in love with the monk Anchin during his pilgrimage to the Kumano shrine at the summit of Mount Nachi. When the young man, accompanied by another monk, stays overnight in her house, she joins him in his bed. He rejects her and, in order to free himself of her, promises to return at the end of his

146

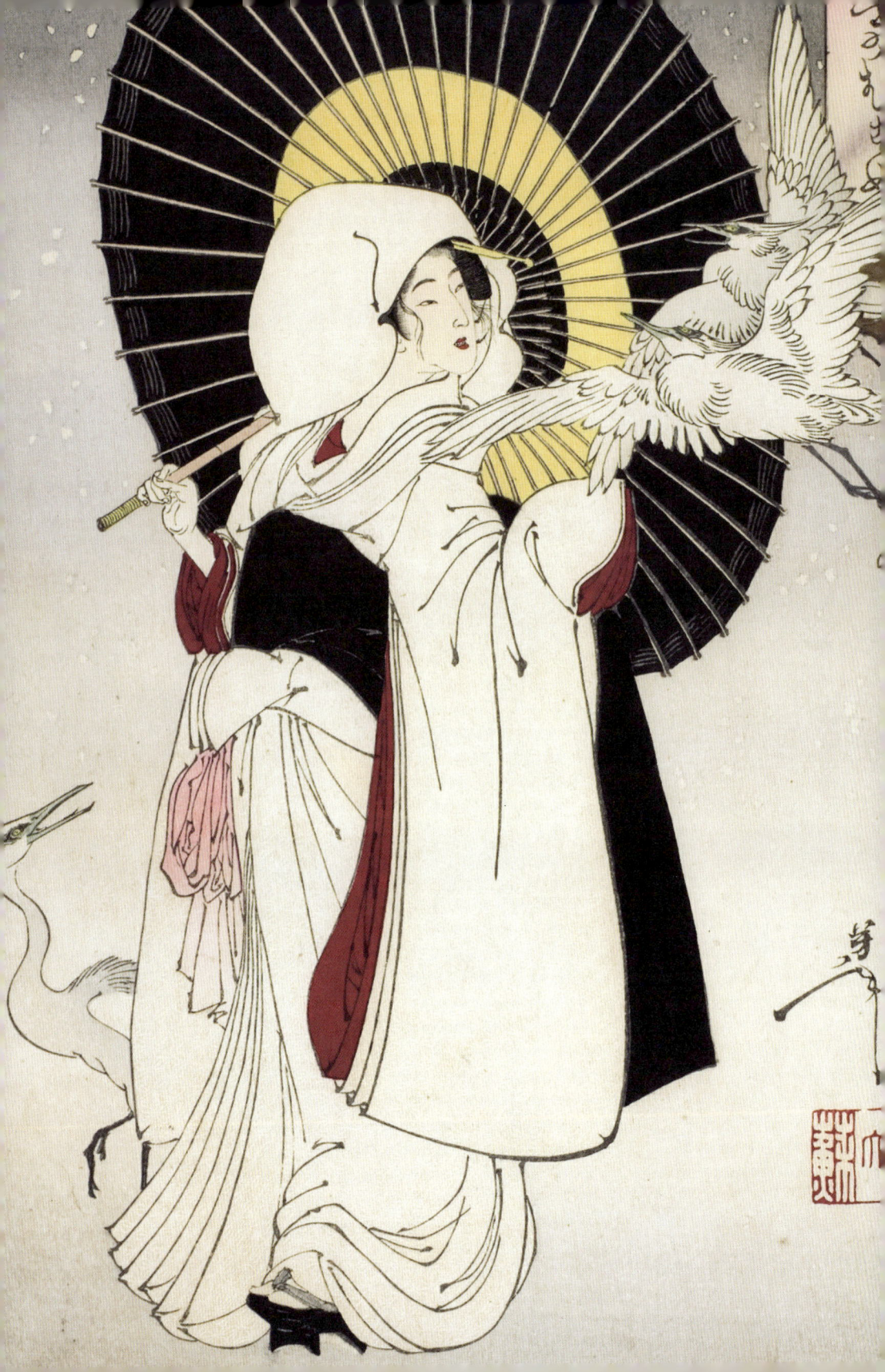

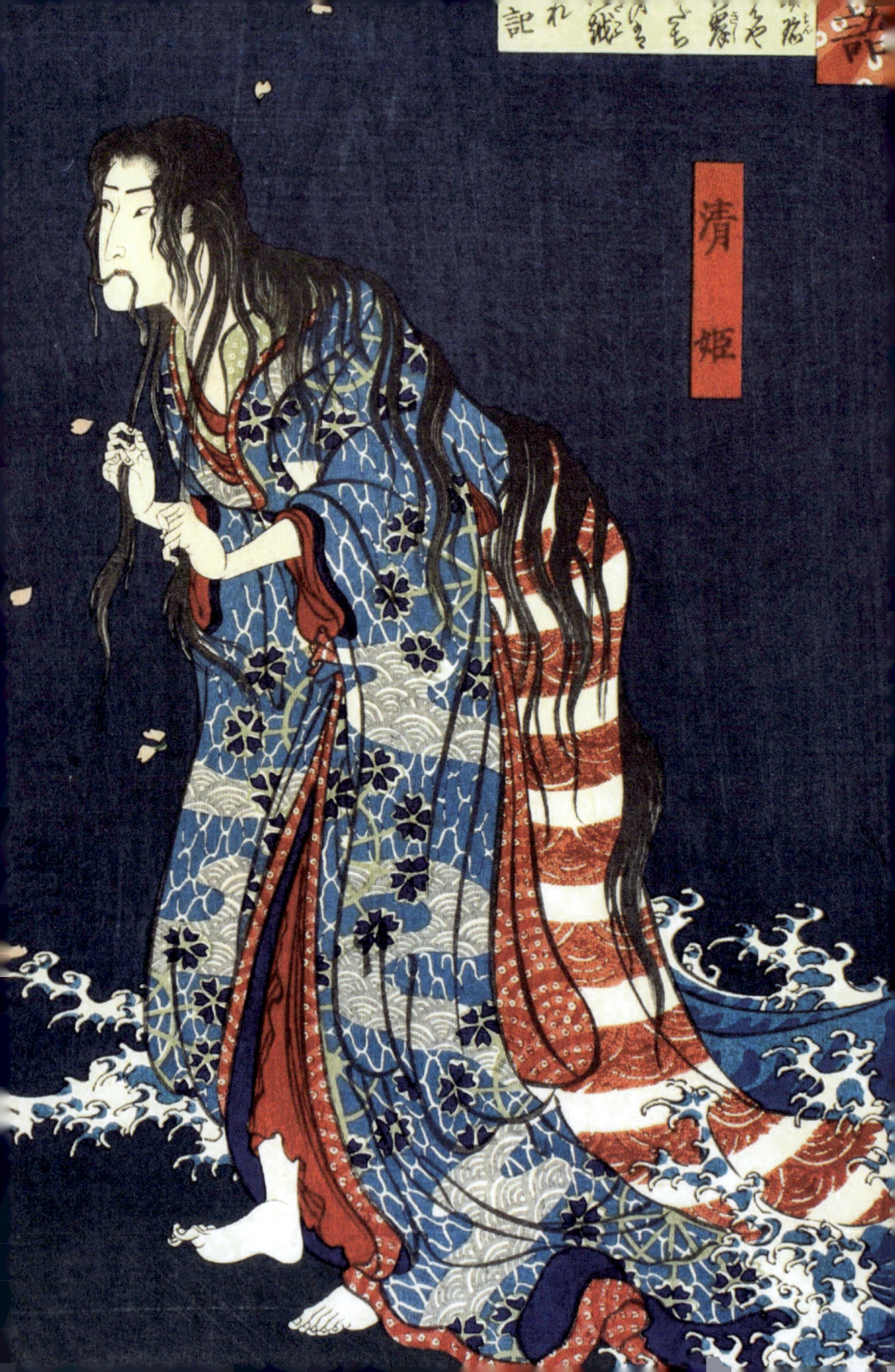

pilgrimage. But, faithful to his monastic vows, he never does. Enraged by his rejection, the beautiful widow pursues her forbidden love, but with each step she takes transforms into a horrific giant white serpent (or dragon, depending on the version of the story). Crossing rivers and streams, she finally corners him in his temple (Dojo-ji, at Hidakagawa, to the southwest of Honshū). Sensing his presence beneath a bronze bell, she coils herself around the green-tarnished metal and, spitting fire as tears stream from her eyes, heats it until she burns the monk alive. When monks pour ice-cold water over the bell to cool it, they discover Anchin's charred corpse beneath. Over the ensuing weeks, the abbot of the monastery has several dreams. In the first, Anchin appears to him, damned, under the malign influence of the woman-serpent Kiyohime, imploring the abbot to pray for his soul – a plea the abbot immediately answers upon waking. In the second dream, he sees Anchin and the woman-serpent in an enchanted place and understands that they have found peace together in the next world. In Noh and kabuki plays inspired by this legend, the actor's robe often features patterns that evoke the serpent's scales, an allusion to Kiyohime's transformation.

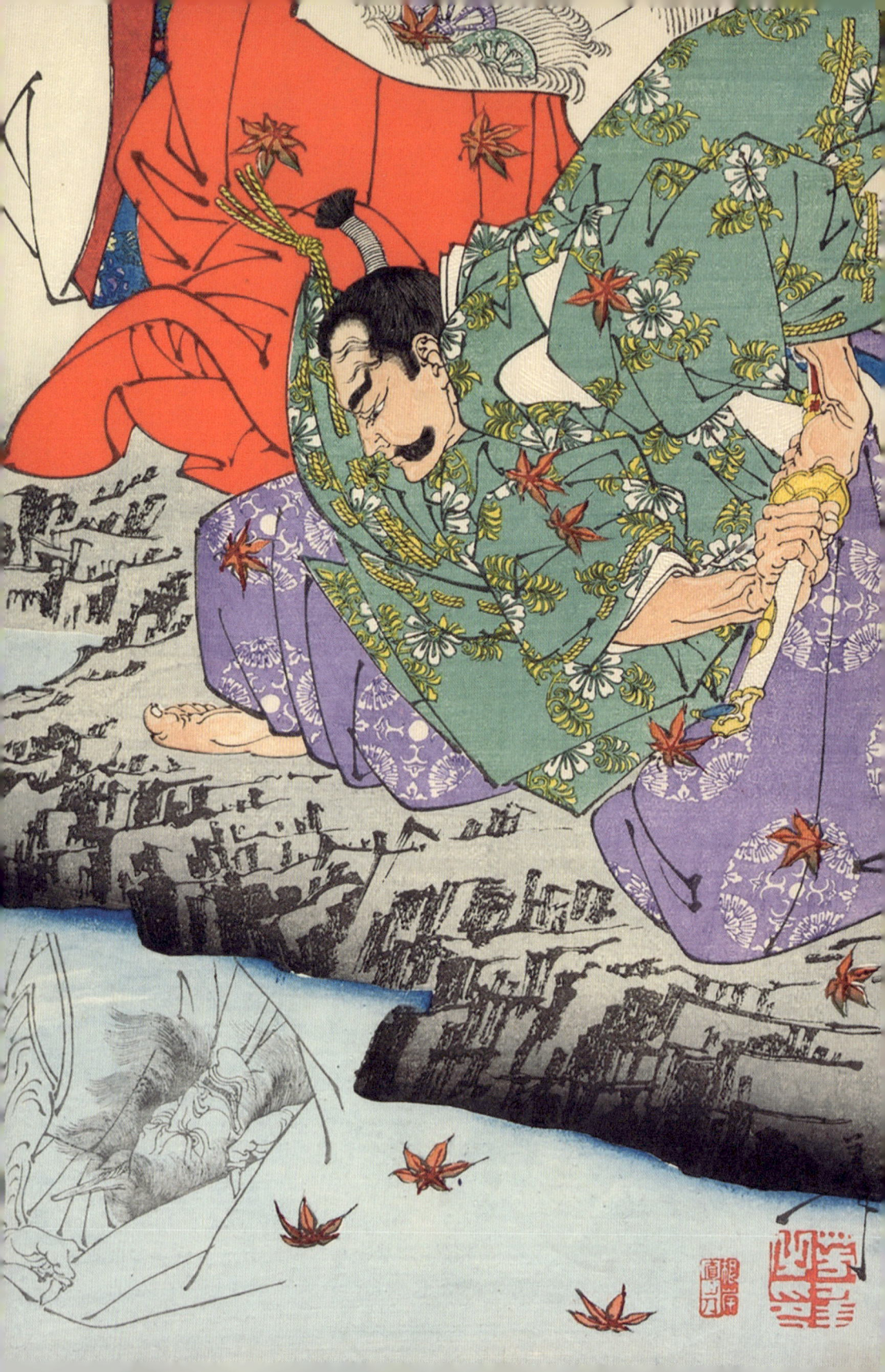

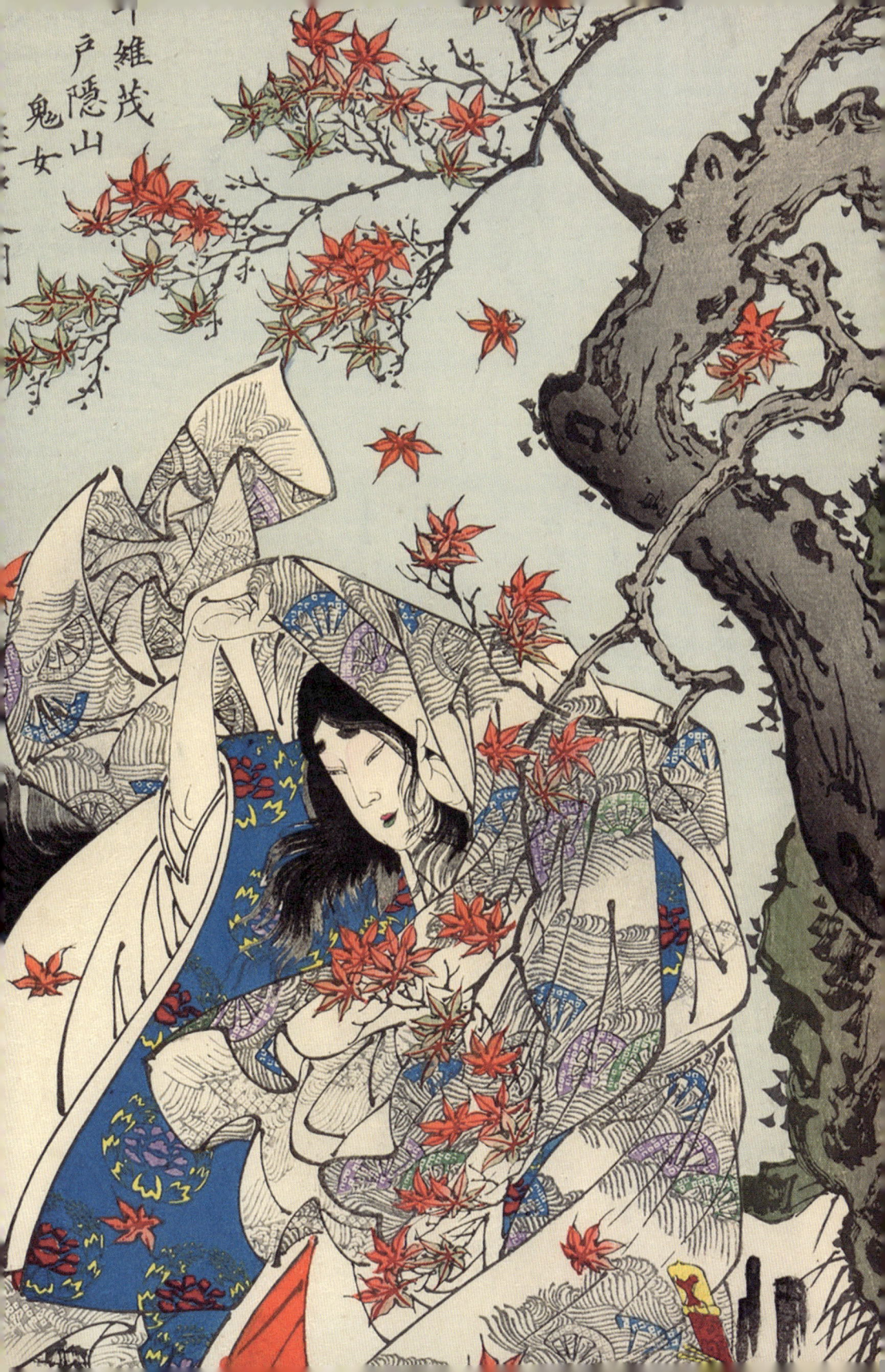

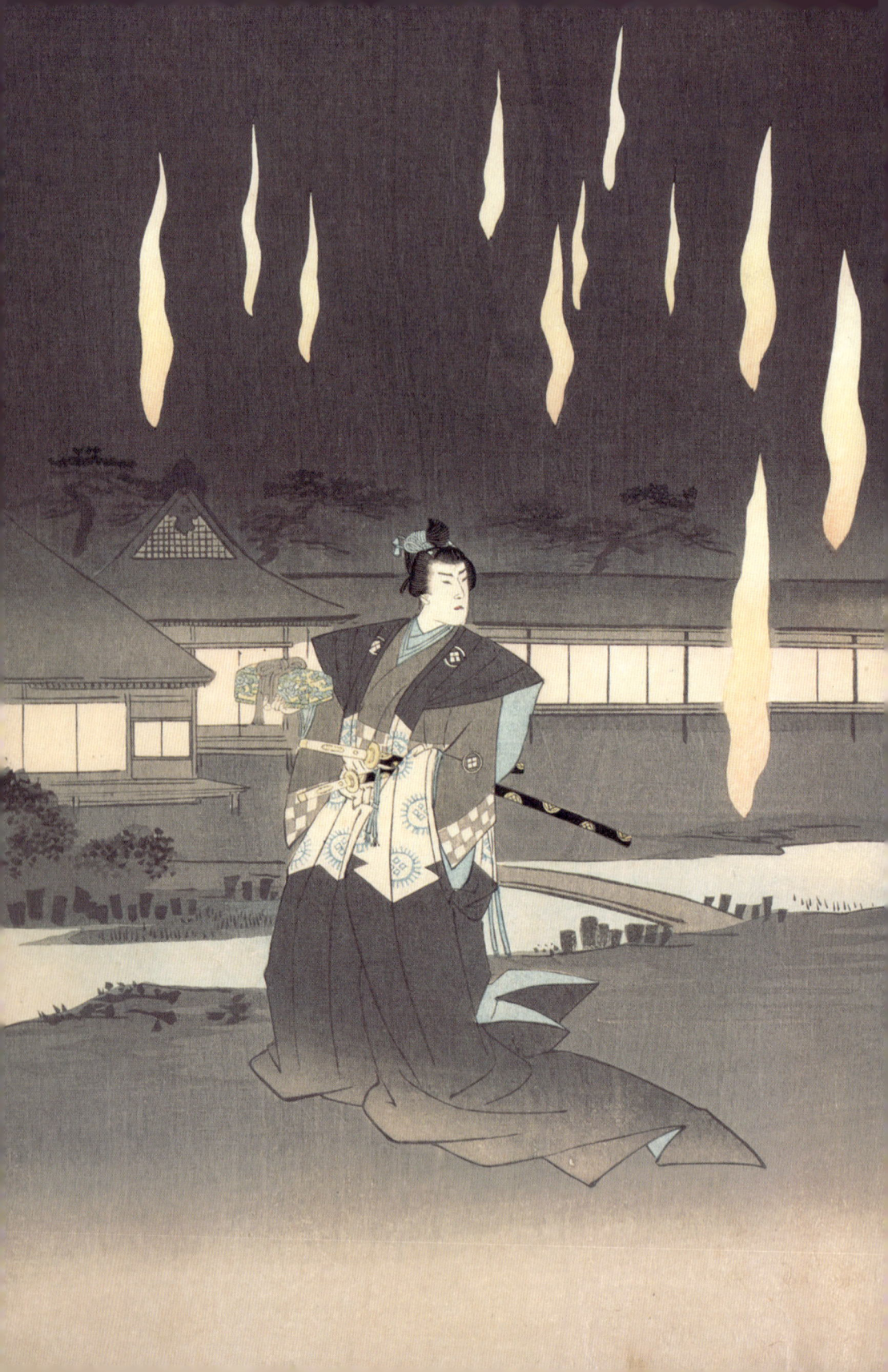

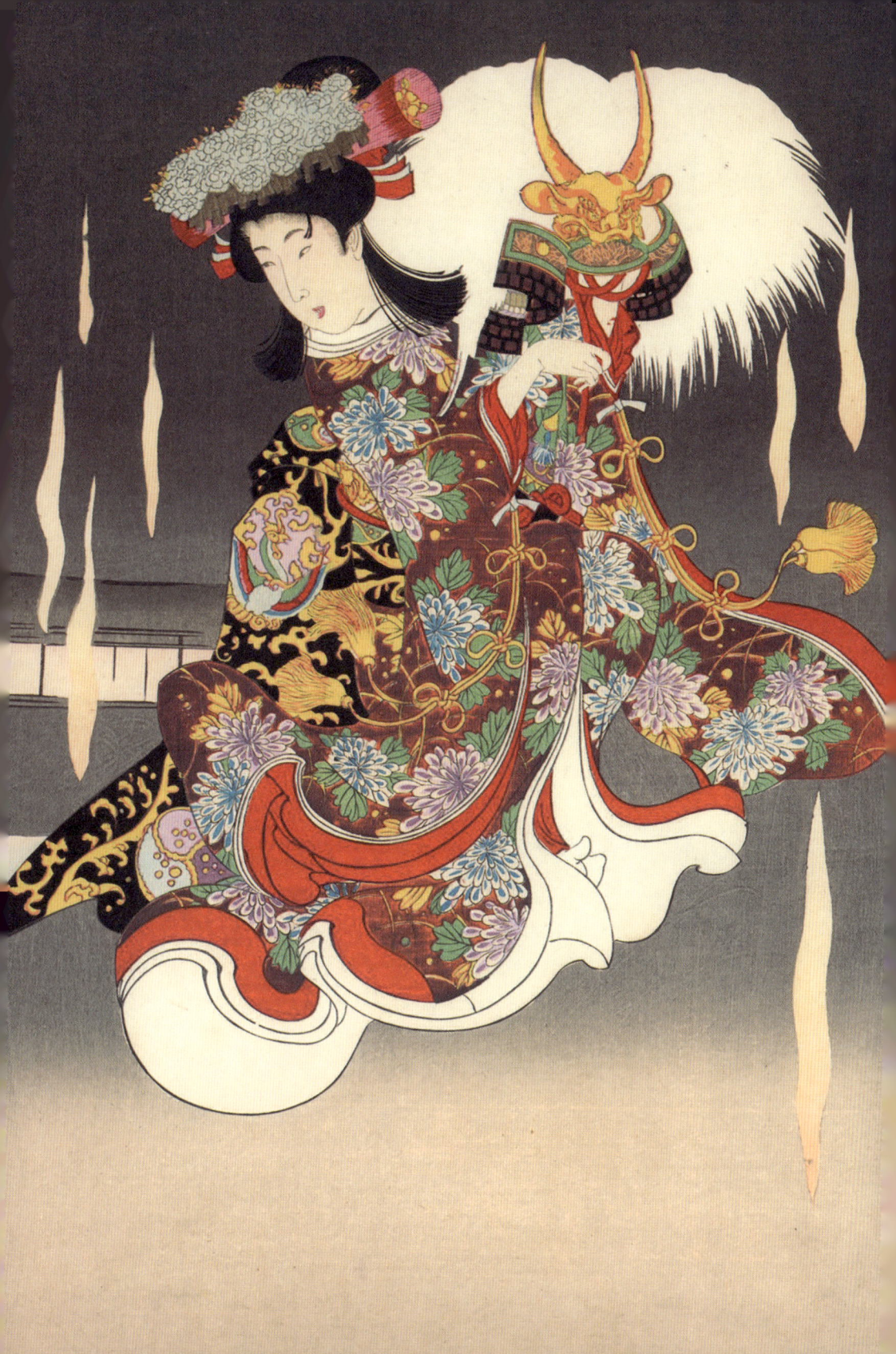

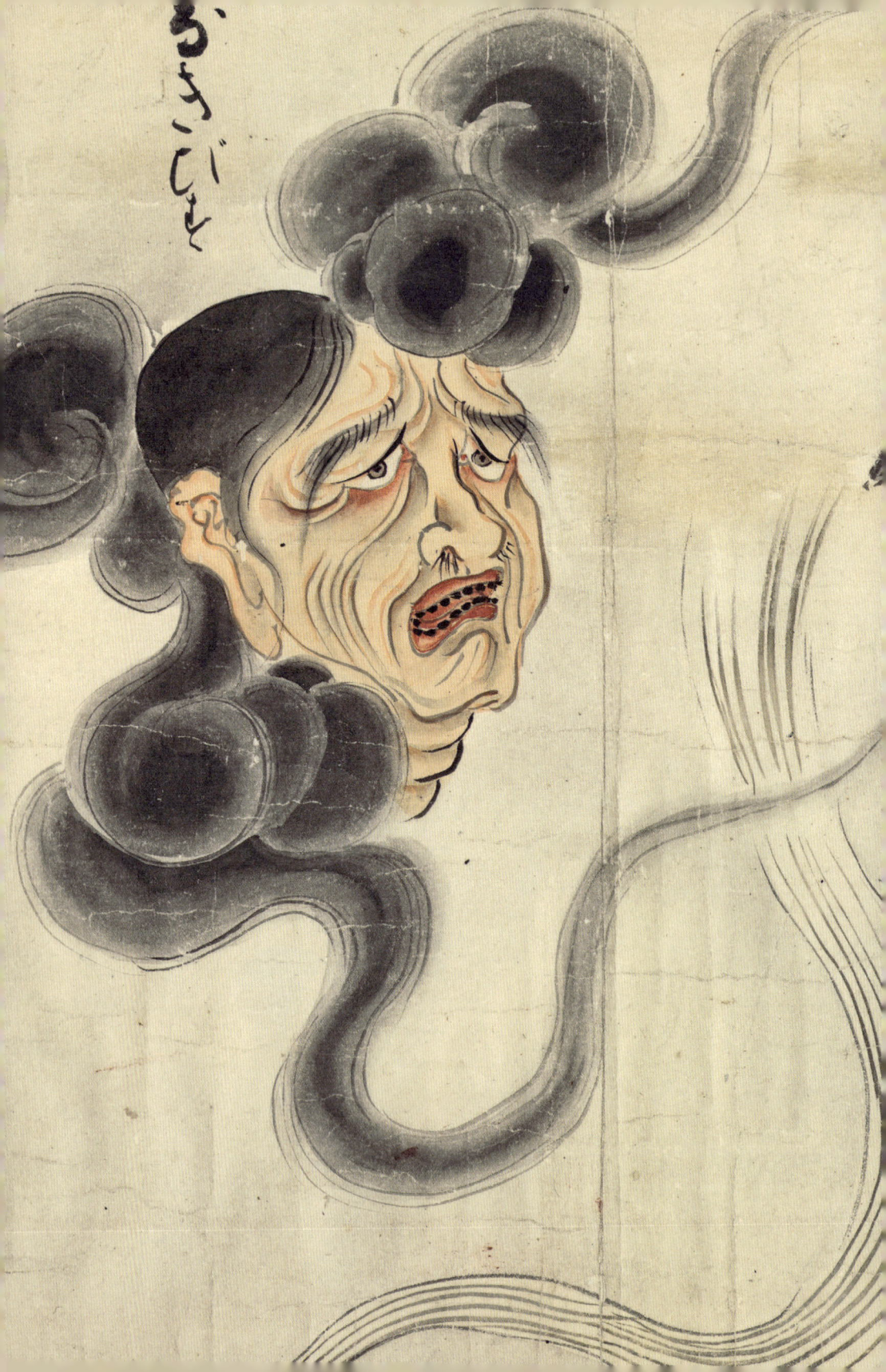

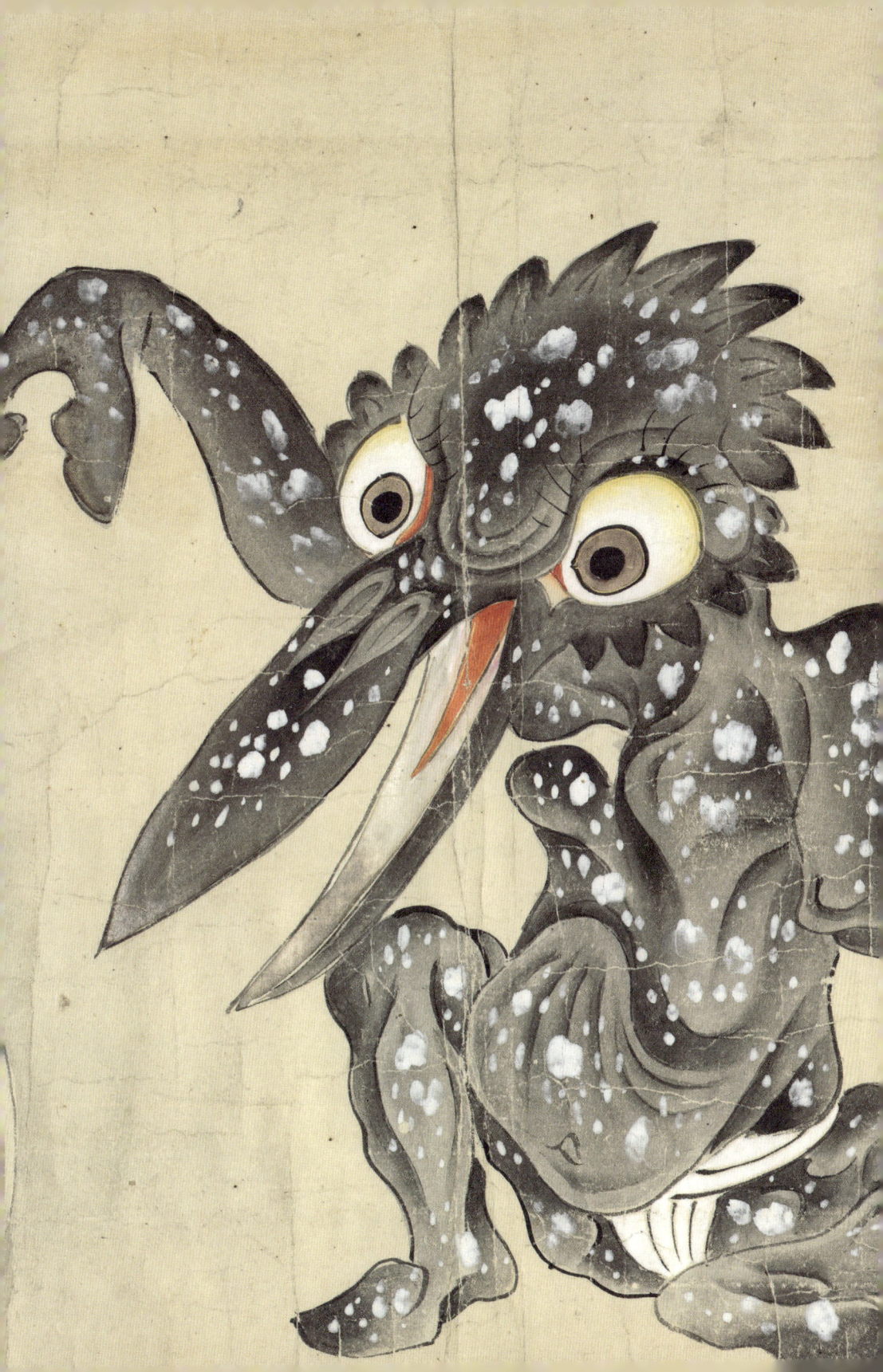

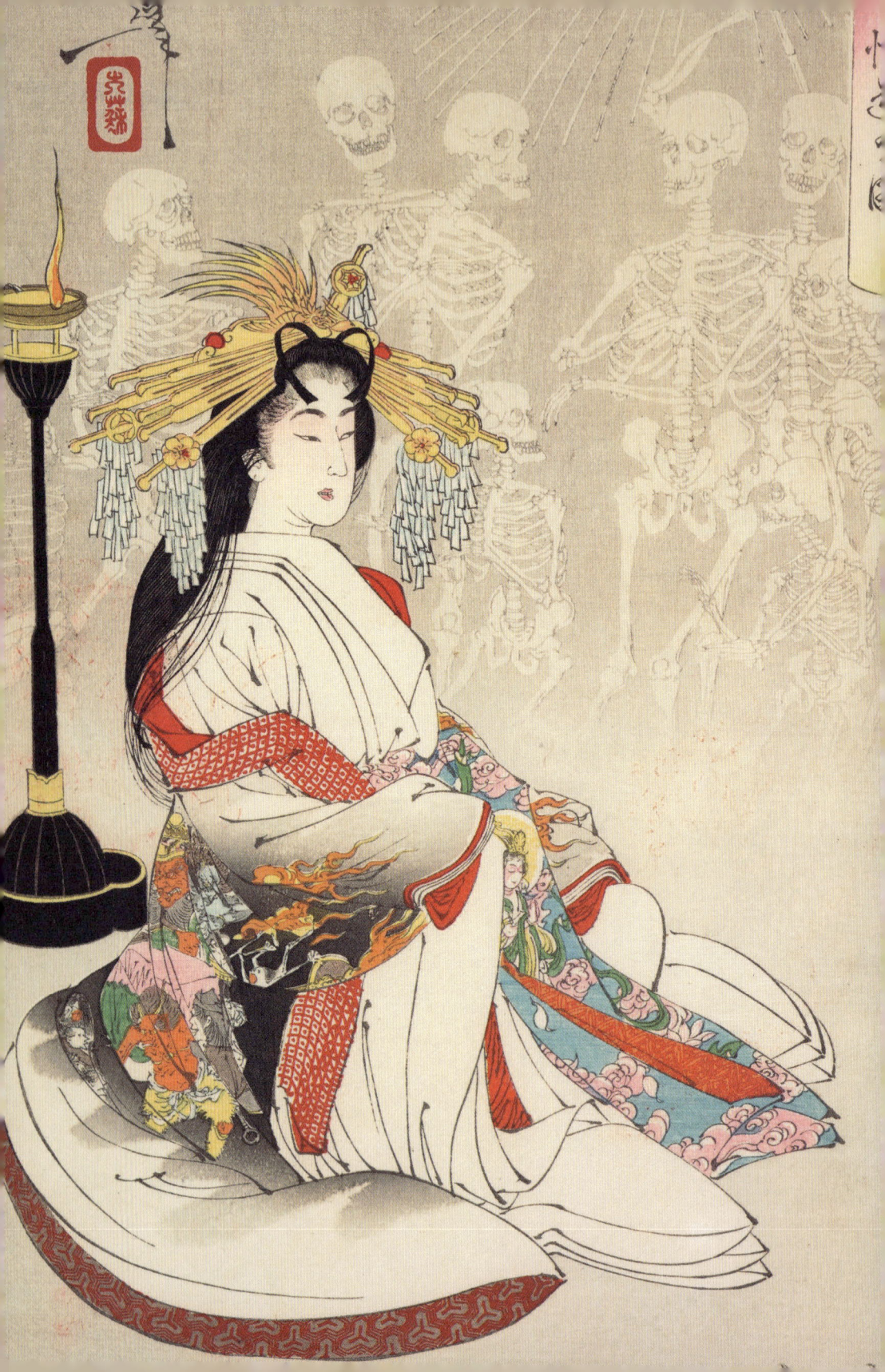

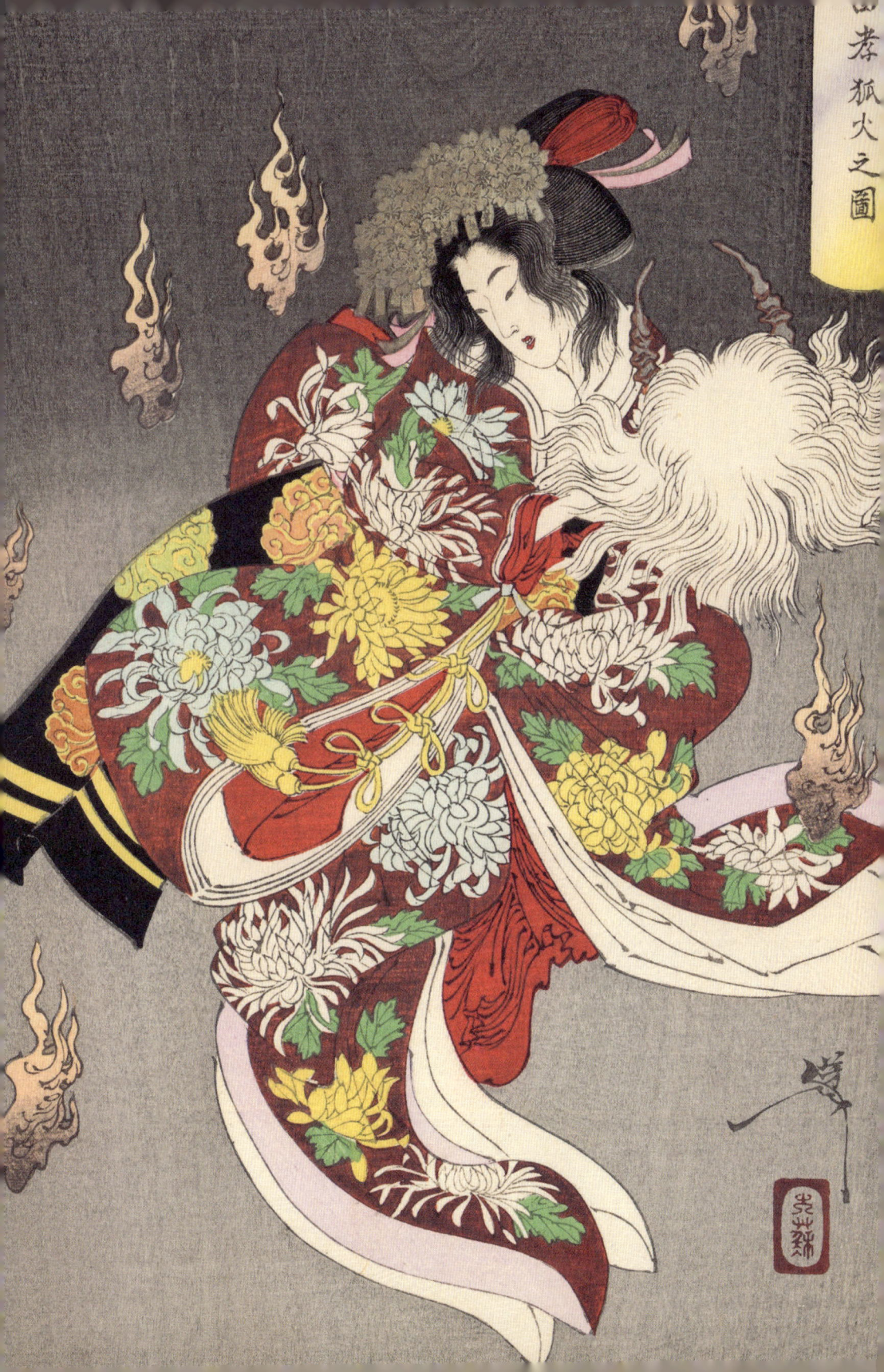

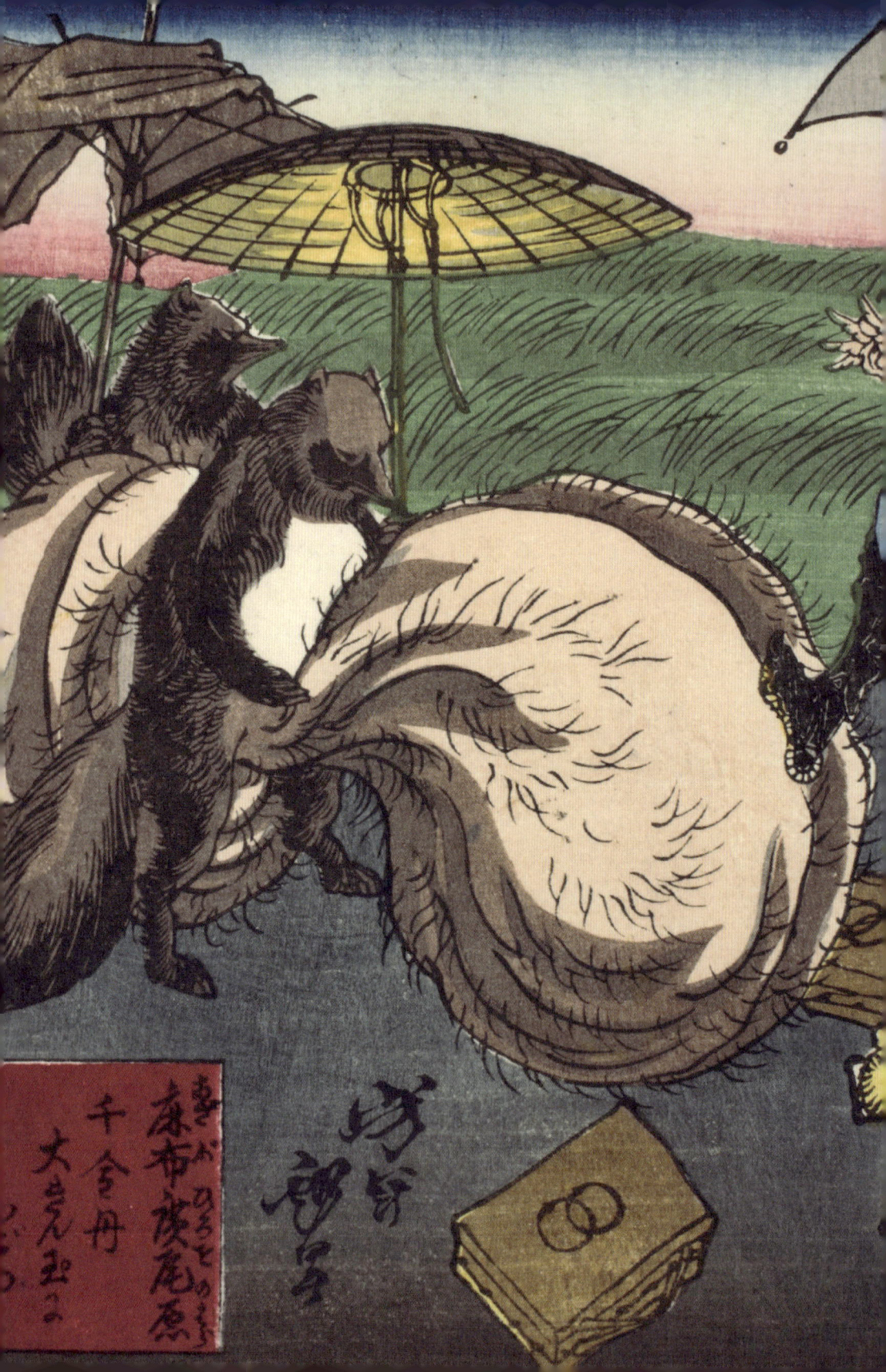

GARBED IN HIS OWN TESTICLES

•

The *tanuki* are magical raccoons (or raccoon dogs) who are fond of scaring pilgrims with their giant testicles, sometimes even making garments out of them. They enjoy drinking rice wine (*sake*), playing tricks on strangers and mischievously indulging in the art of metamorphosis. But they can also be moved by gratitude and inspired to acts of kindness, as illustrated by the story of one transforming itself into a teapot to thank a compassionate woodcutter.

What follows, however – an episode from *The Kachikachi Mountain* (*Kachi Kachi Yama*) – is a tale not of kindness but of cruelty. One day, an old woodcutter comes across a *tanuki* by chance and captures it, planning to have it later for dinner. Once home, he lets his children play with it and then gives it to his wife to cook. Taking advantage of the woodcutter's absence, the *yōkai* offers to amuse his wife with a comical dance. When she frees it to dance for her, it immediately kills her, assumes her likeness and throws her corpse into the cooking pot. When the husband returns, he hurriedly sits down to enjoy his dinner. Though puzzled by the size and shape of the bones, he eats several servings, after which the *tanuki* reverts to its original form and reveals to the woodcutter that he has just eaten his wife. In despair, and horrified by this act, unintentional though it was, he confides in his three household pets – a dog, a rabbit and a cat – who urge him to exact revenge. The rabbit takes the lead and sets a trap for the *tanuki*, paying it to renovate the woodcutter's house and asking it to transport straw to thatch the roof.

When the *yōkai* is in a boat with the straw on his back, the rabbit secretly sets fire to it. Desperate, the *tanuki* cries out for help but to no avail. The rabbit reaches the riverbank unharmed, and the wicked *yōkai* is either burnt alive or drowns.

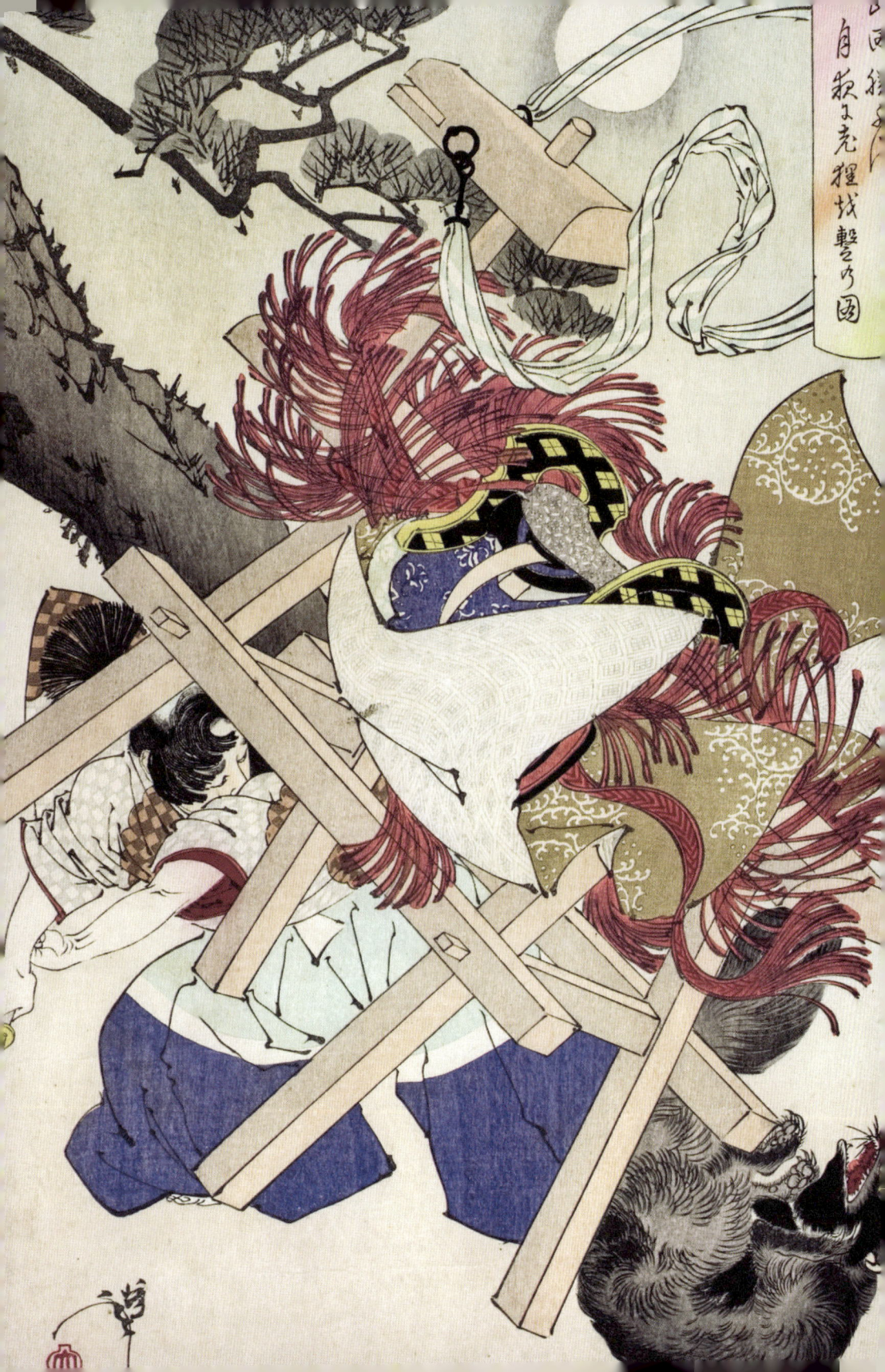

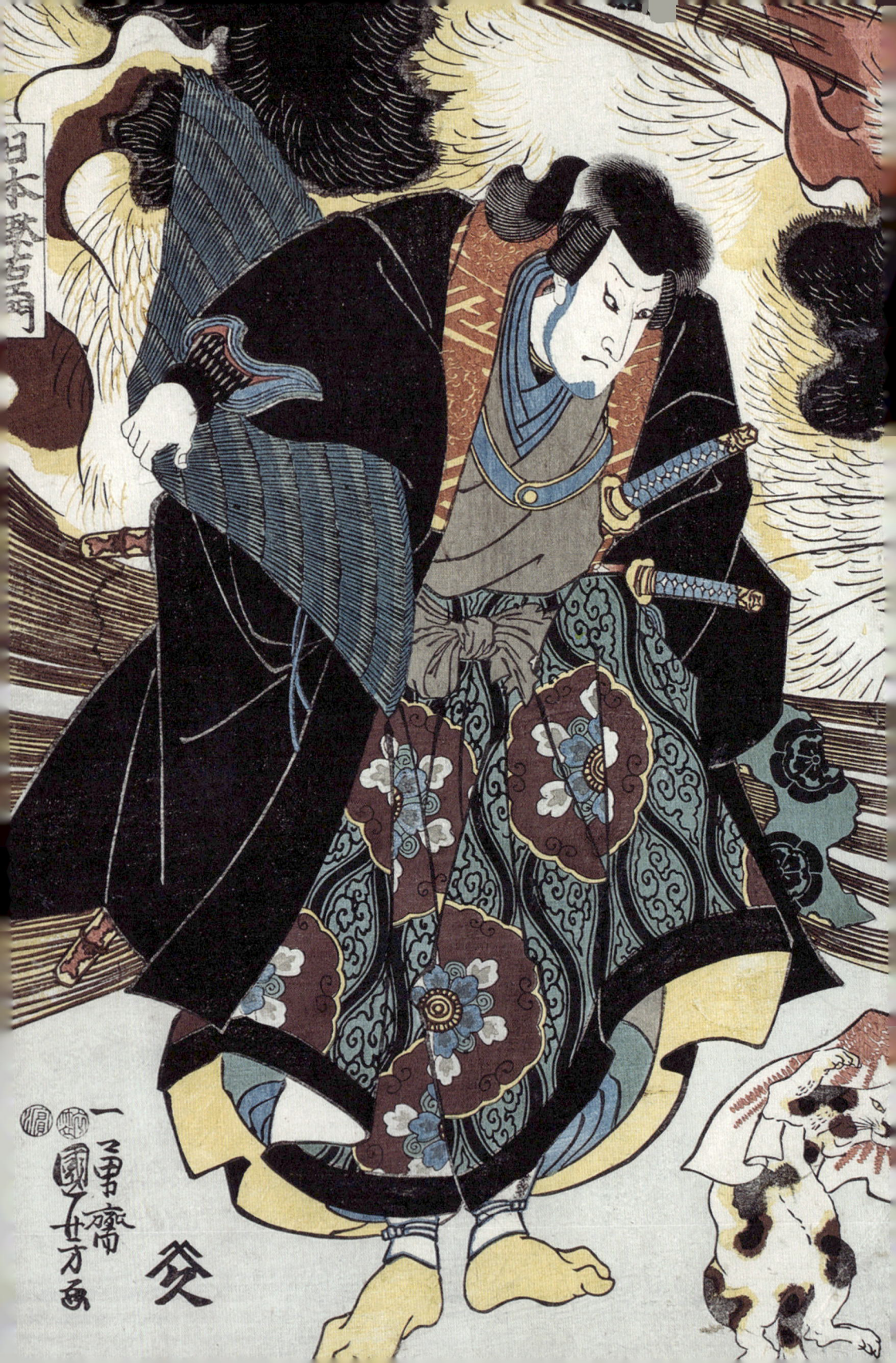

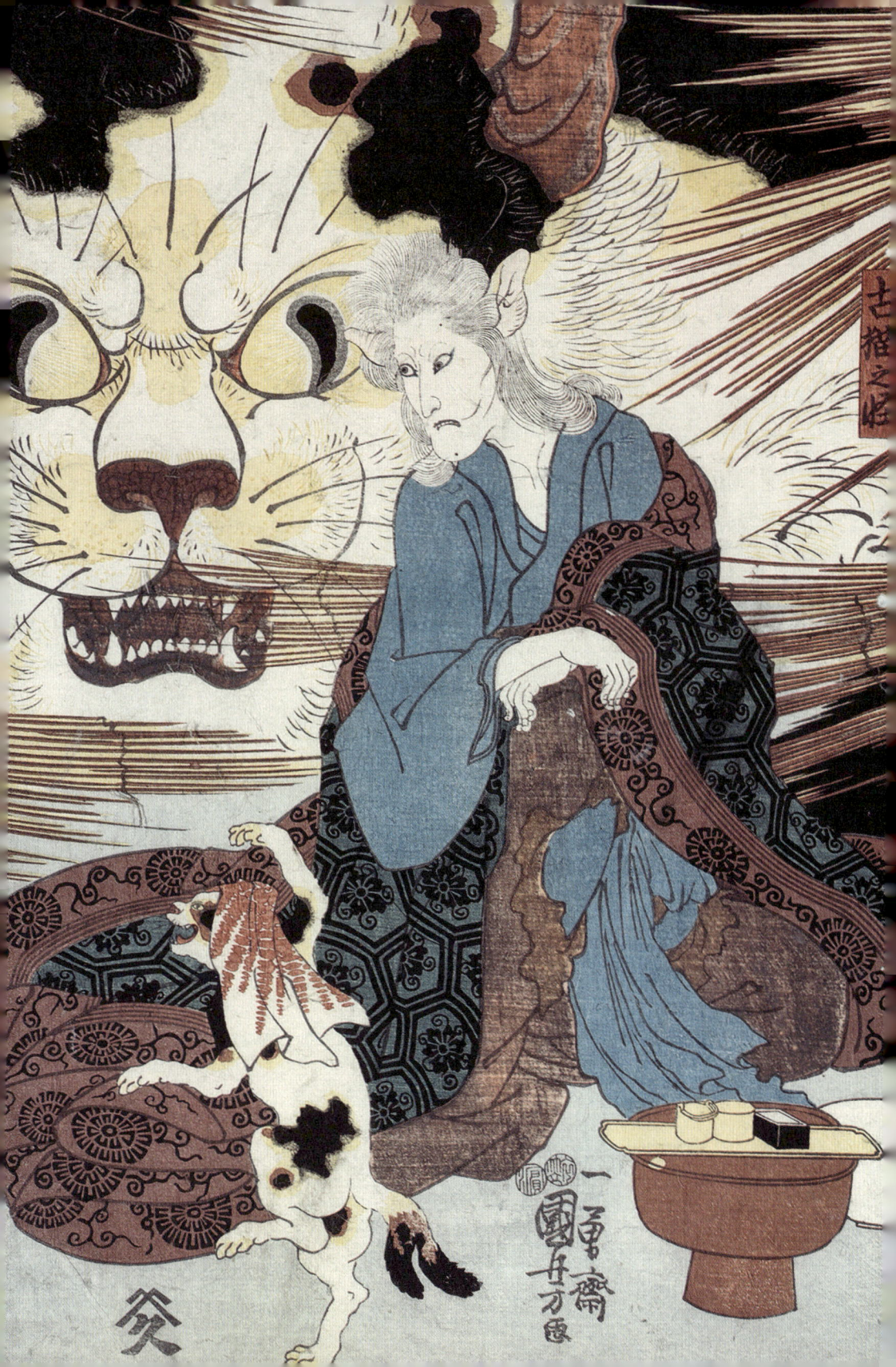

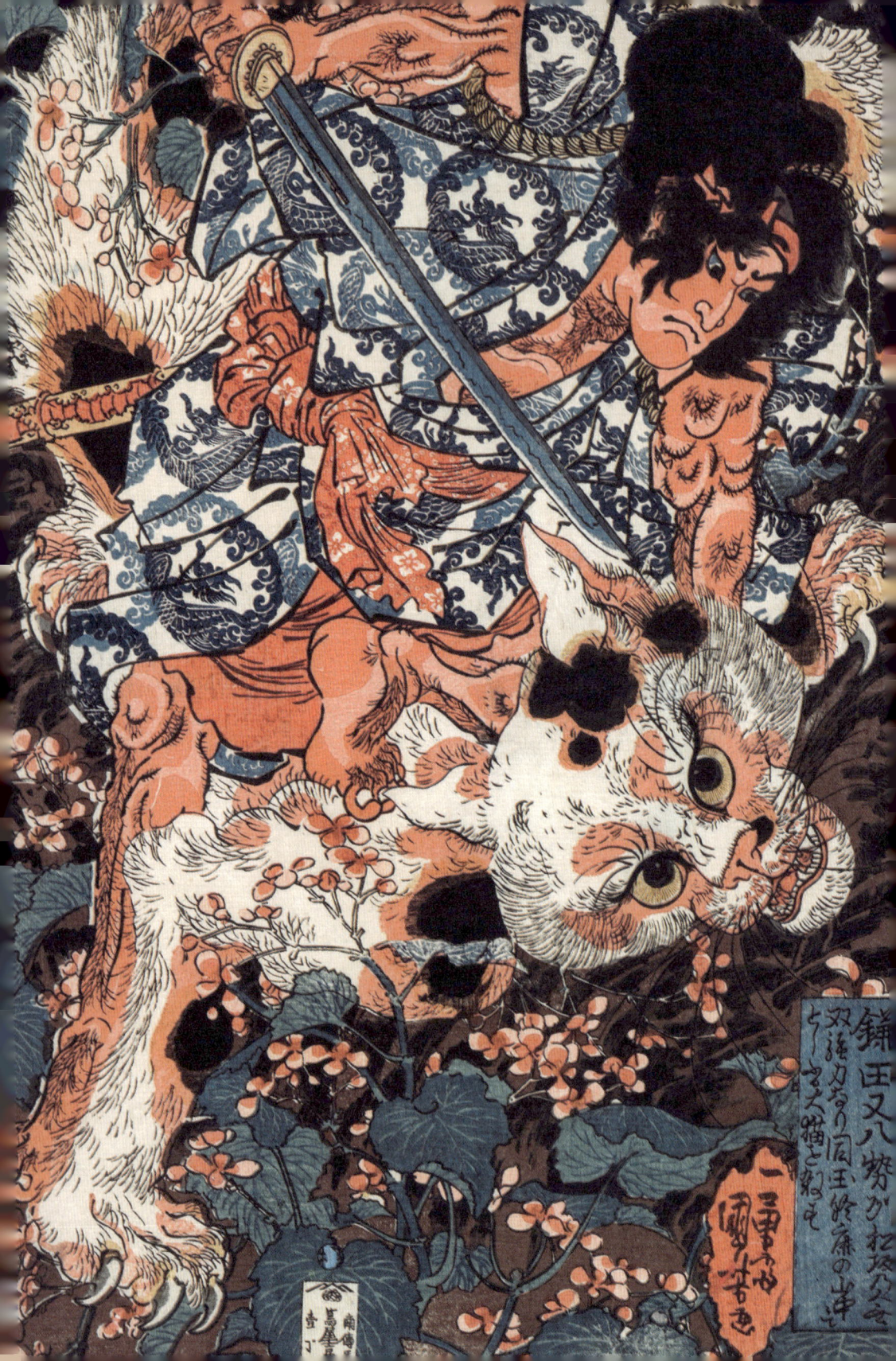

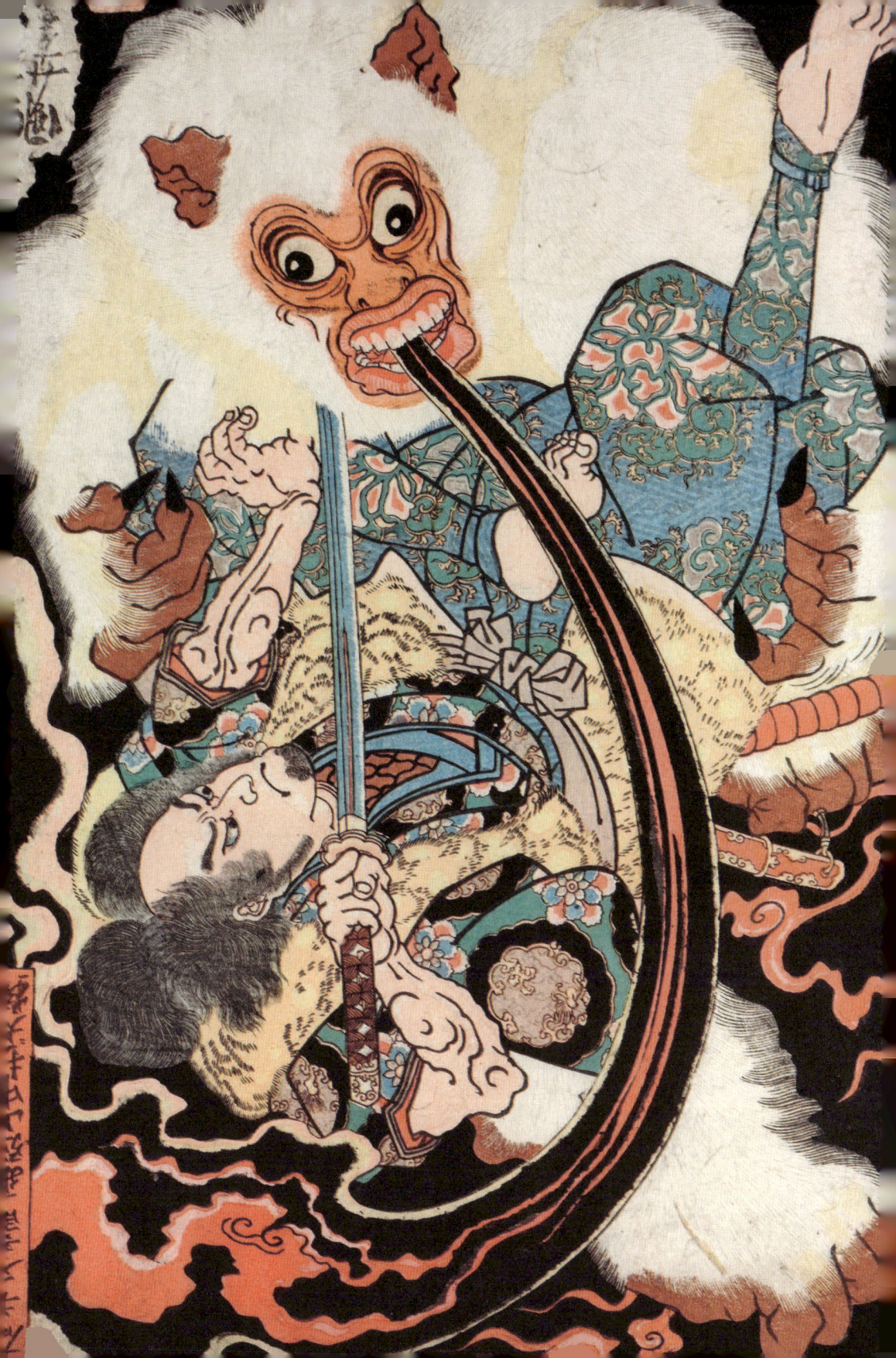

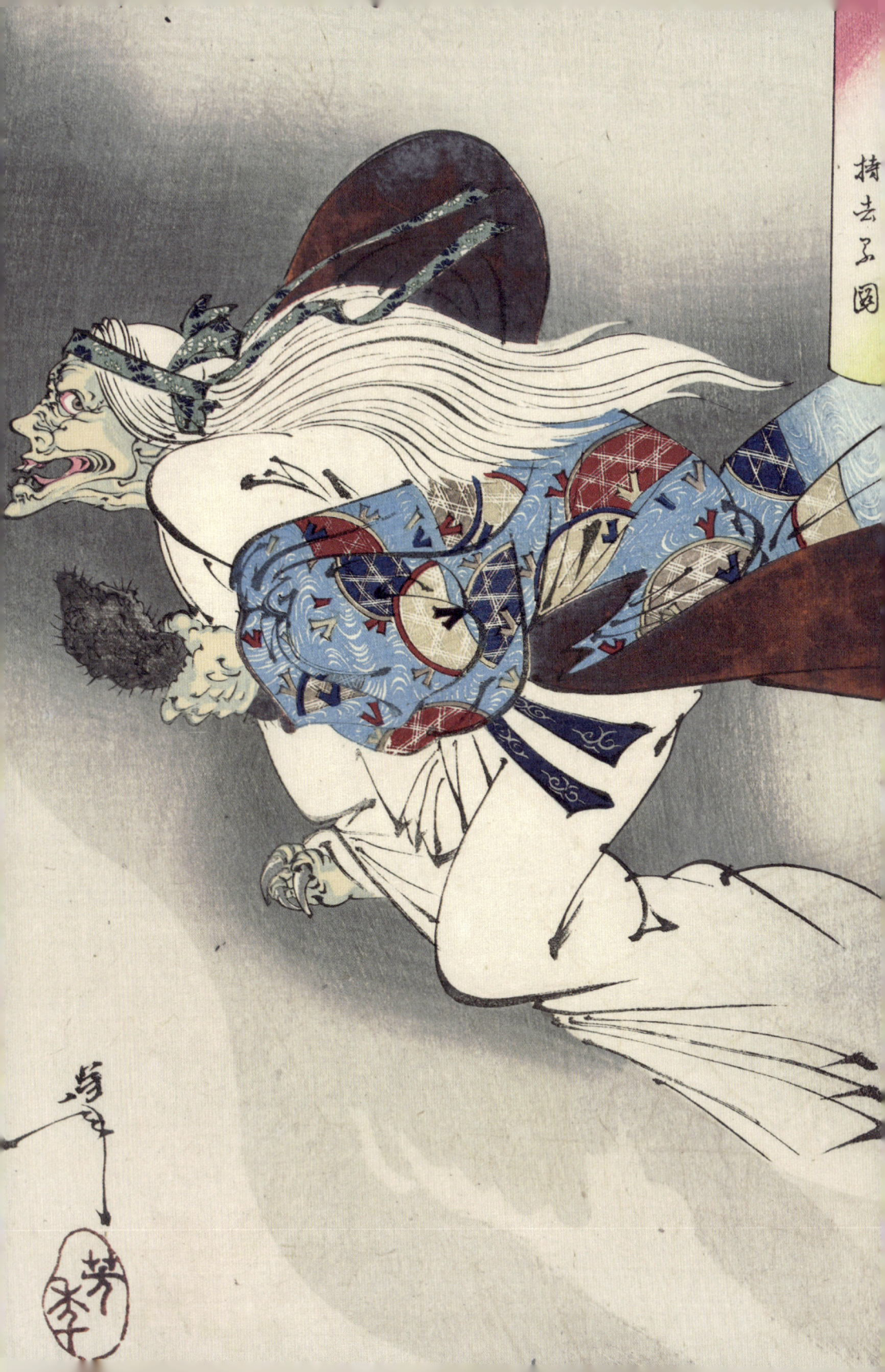

GATHERING THE DIS- PERSED

•

There are as many *yōkai* as there are earthly fears. Wherever death, dread or despair have left their mark, there linger traces of these supernatural beings. Whether at sea, within temple walls, in abandoned houses, or on remote paths; whether night or day, no place is spared from these materialisations of our anxieties and sorrows. The brief sketches below give a glimpse of this world.

Out on the open ocean, a fisherman from Kuwana comes face to face with Umi-bōzu, a kind of aquatic monster that appears as a black ghost and is known as the bald *yōkai* of the seas. When the fisherman reveals that living among men is far more frightening, the creature disappears. — A woman walking by night falls victim to a hair-cutting monster's cruel bite. — In Fukudamachi, in the Kanda district of Tokyo, a grey cloud in the form of a priest enters the house of a carpenter to rape his wife as she is about to go to sleep on her tatami. — The ogress *Ibaraki*, whose arm was cut off by the warrior Watanabe no Tsuna, succeeds in recovering it by disguising herself as an old woman in order to gain entry into the Shinto shrine where the arm was kept. — Travellers who have taken refuge in a deserted temple are attacked by *bakeneko*, cat demons who dance on their hind legs and are led by a giant feline that breaks through walls and bamboo awnings. — *Fukuromujina*, badger demons with long black hair who wear women's kimonos and straw sandals, parade through the streets holding lanterns in their paws. — Lake *yōkai* called *kappa* take the form of half-human, half-turtle water spirits

167

possessing a beak and three anuses, as well as a cup on top of their heads that must be kept full of water to sustain their life force. They devour cucumbers, rape women, entice children to the bottom of ponds to kill them, attack horses and cattle and engage in sumo wrestling. — A giant spider entrusts magic scrolls to the princess Wakana to avenge the death of her father, Ōtomo Sōrin. — A gigantic white monkey, a colossal wild boar, an oversized toad and clouds of magical frogs battle on the slopes of a sacred mountain or against a human army. — A giant snake attacks a courtesan, then abducts the dancer Kakehashi on the orders of the hunter Gamakurō. — A creature with a monkey's head, a snake's tail and tiger's paws attacks a lost traveller. — *Kawauso*, river otter demons, transform into beautiful young women who seduce and kidnap a traveller, taking him to the bottom of a river to drown him, then partly eat him and leave his half-devoured corpse in a ditch. — A faceless monk (*nopperabō*) runs a roadside stall catering to travelling salesmen and pilgrims. — *Hitotsume-kozō*, a boy-sized spirit with a single large eye in the center of his face, eats tofu in an abandoned shop. — Two *yōkai* marry, the bride wearing white (the colour of death) because she is about to leave her father and mother for ever.

As with foxes, one must beware of cats. Are they really animals or are they *yōkai* transformed into inoffensive household pets? Some of these cat demons (*bakeneko*) are believed to have the ability to bring the dead back to life and compel them to serve the *bakeneko*'s will, often for dark or vengeful purposes. The following anecdote recounts how some of these feline *yōkai* came into being. Nabeshima Mitsushige (1632–1700), lord of Saga Province, once drove a rival to suicide after being defeated by him in a game. Overcome with grief, the poor man's mother took her own life, and her cat, licking her blood, transformed into a *bakeneko*. From then on, the vengeful creature haunted Nabeshima Mitsushige relentlessly until one of his servants killed it to break the curse.

Cats that transform into *yōkai* are believed to have lived for many years – typically at least

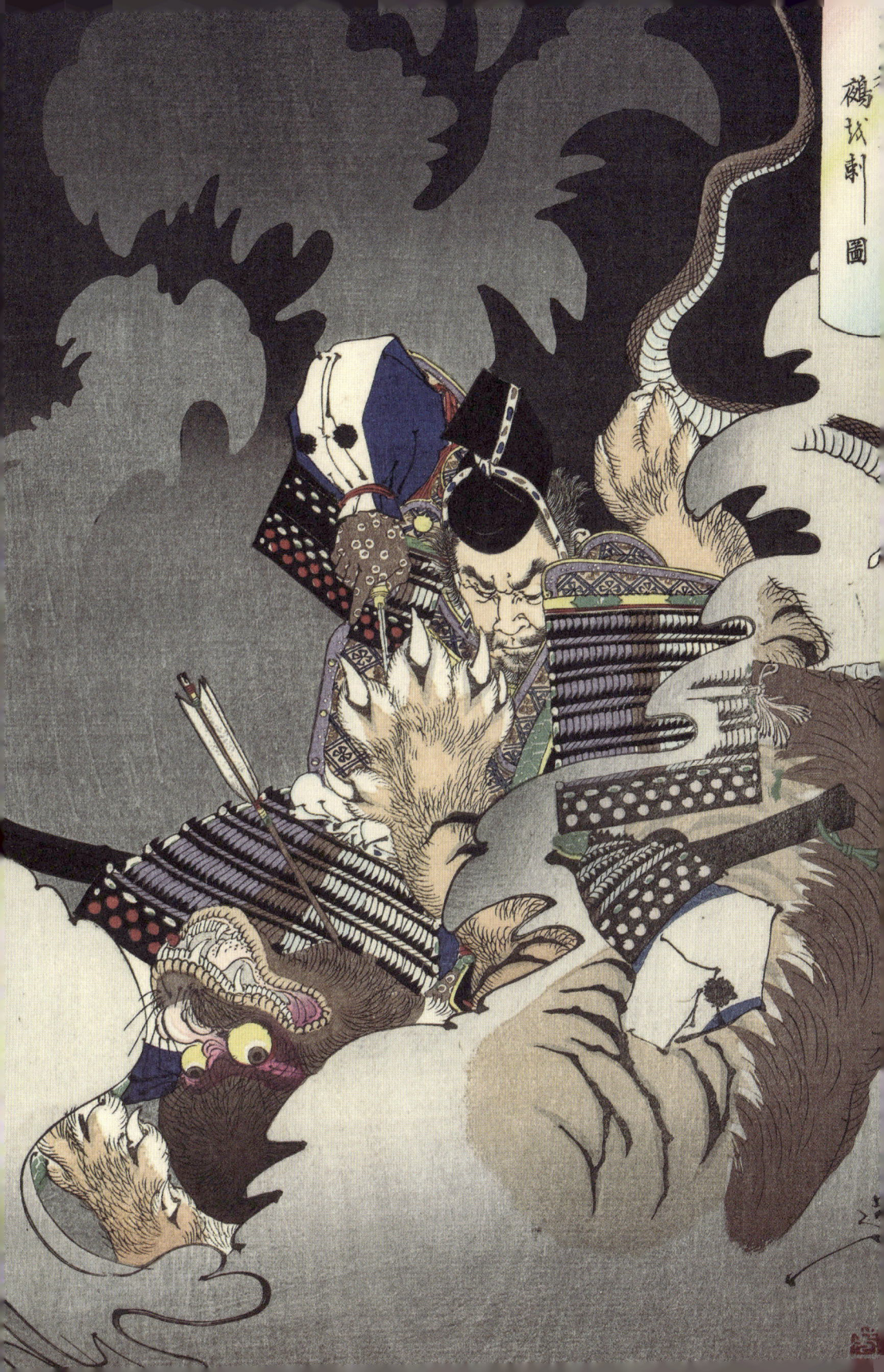

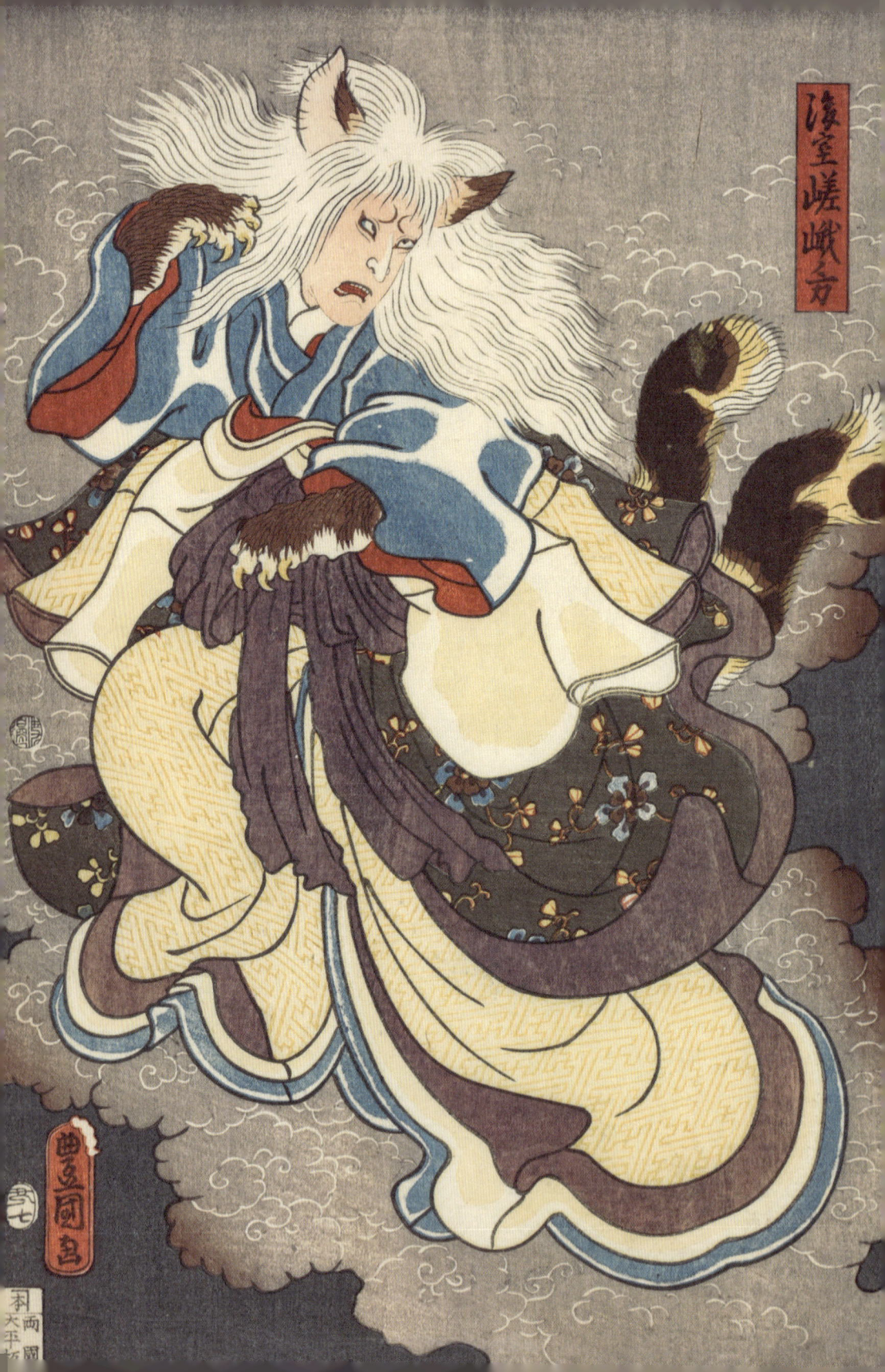

thirteen – and to be particularly heavy. As their wisdom grows, so too does the length of their tails, and they are even said to possess the ability to start fires simply by touch. Tradition has it that a cat's tail should be clipped at a young age, to prevent them from later becoming *yōkai* but also to avoid accidental fires.

Carps also have this power of metamorphosis. A story of the ascetic monk Oniwakamaru recounts that one day, when his mother did not return home after going to gather wood, he found a giant carp (*bakekoi*) near a waterfall. He killed it and when he cut it open, he found shreds of his mother's kimono in its entrails.

In the late nineteenth century, belief in *yōkai* was so widespread that articles were published each week in the press reporting sightings of them across various regions of the Japanese archipelago. Sometimes the apparitions were said to occur following earthquakes that had stirred or awakened them, forcing them to come out of their hiding places. Other articles circulated rumours or offered valuable advice – such as the official prohibition against seamen leaving the port of Kuwana at the end of each month, a time favoured by the *umi-bōzu*, who appeared at sea to terrify fishermen and capsize boats.

With the passage of time and the advent of electric lighting in streets and houses, *yōkai* became less and less frightening and increasingly a source of entertainment and amusement. Although during the Edo (1603–1867) and Meiji (1868–1912) periods they functioned as a form of social criticism, targeting successive governments and the licentious behaviour of certain supposedly exemplary monks, they have come now to serve a commemorative purpose, preserving the legends of the past and becoming associated with specific places or historic figures.

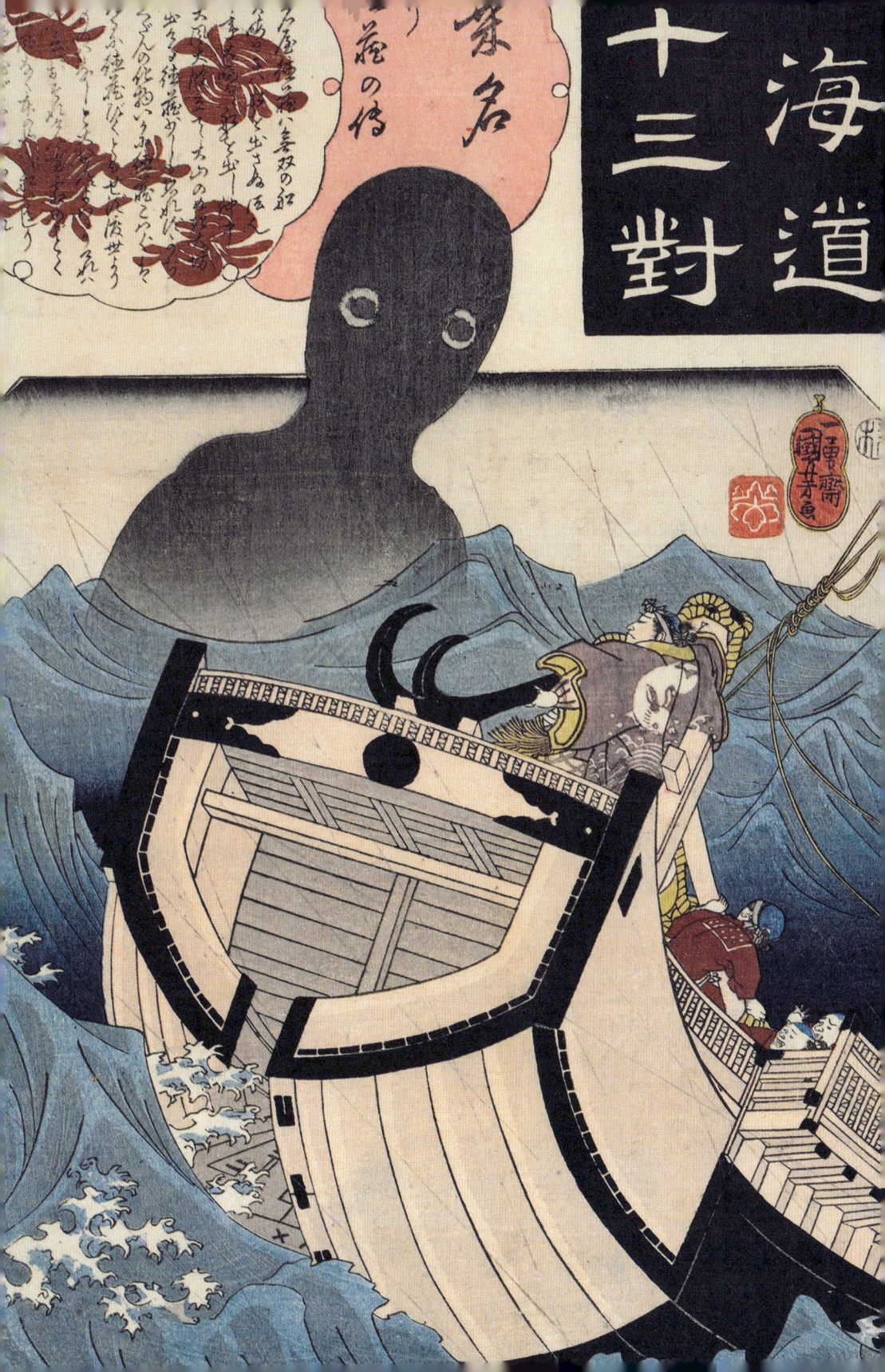

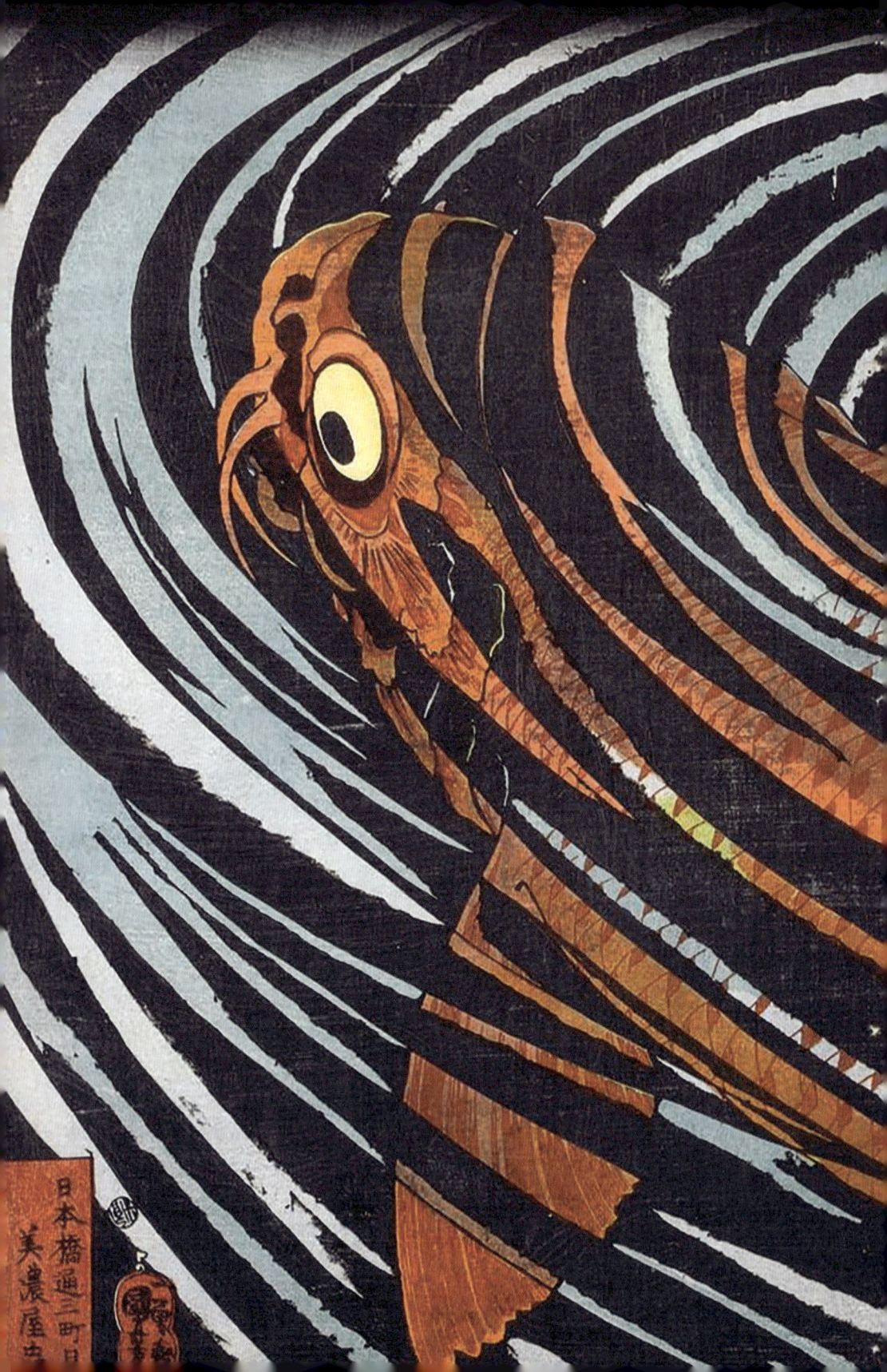

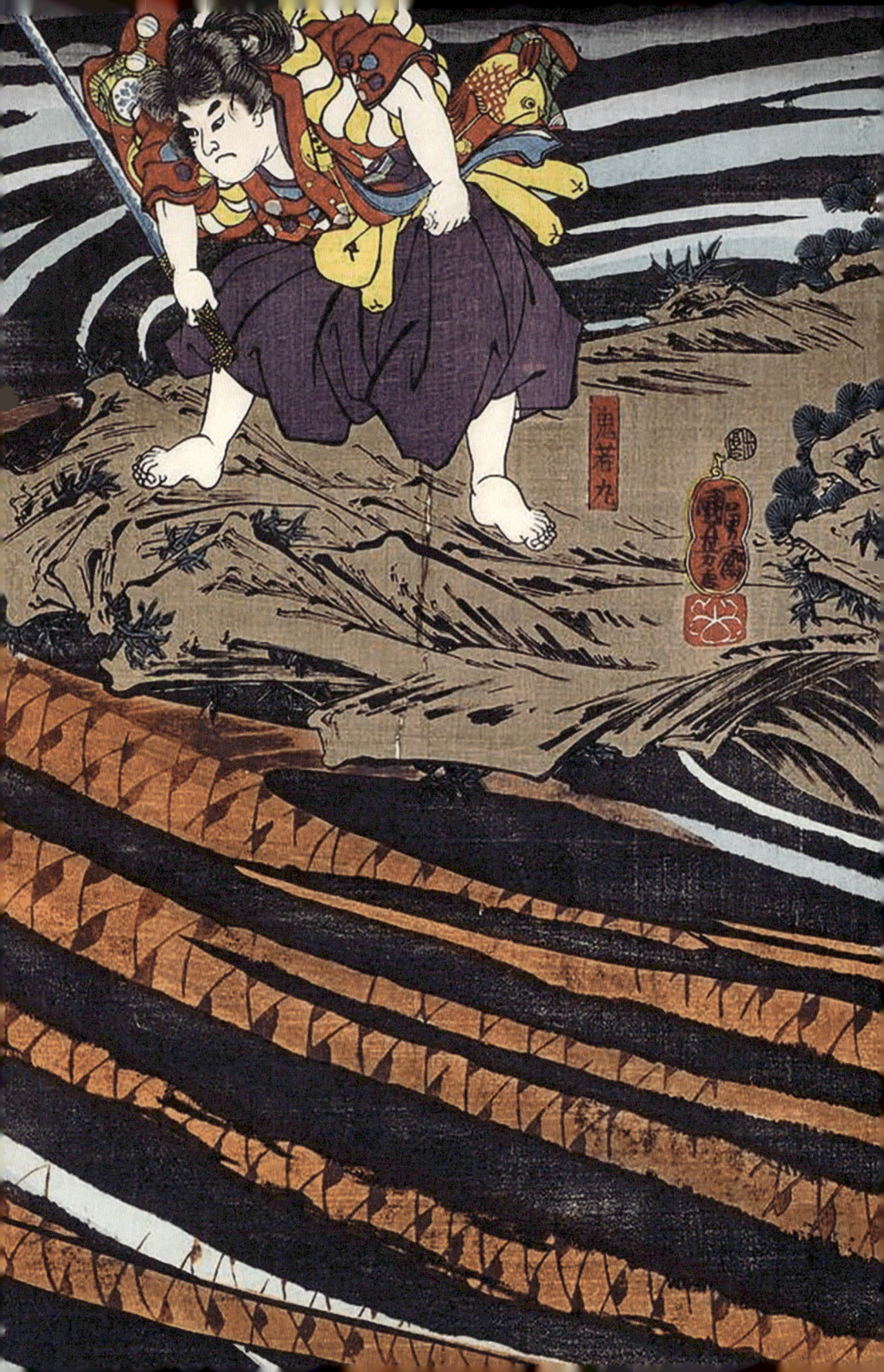

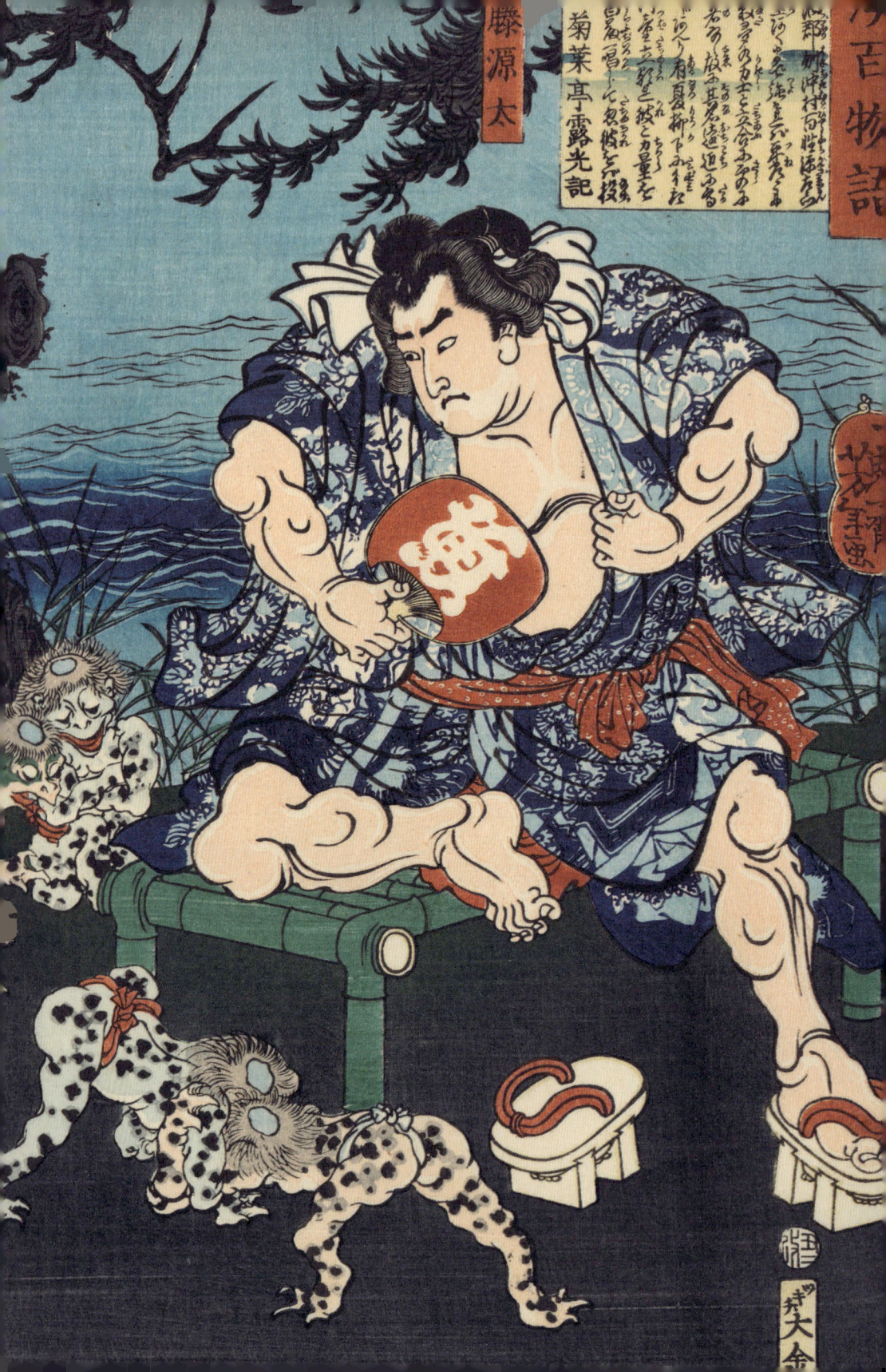

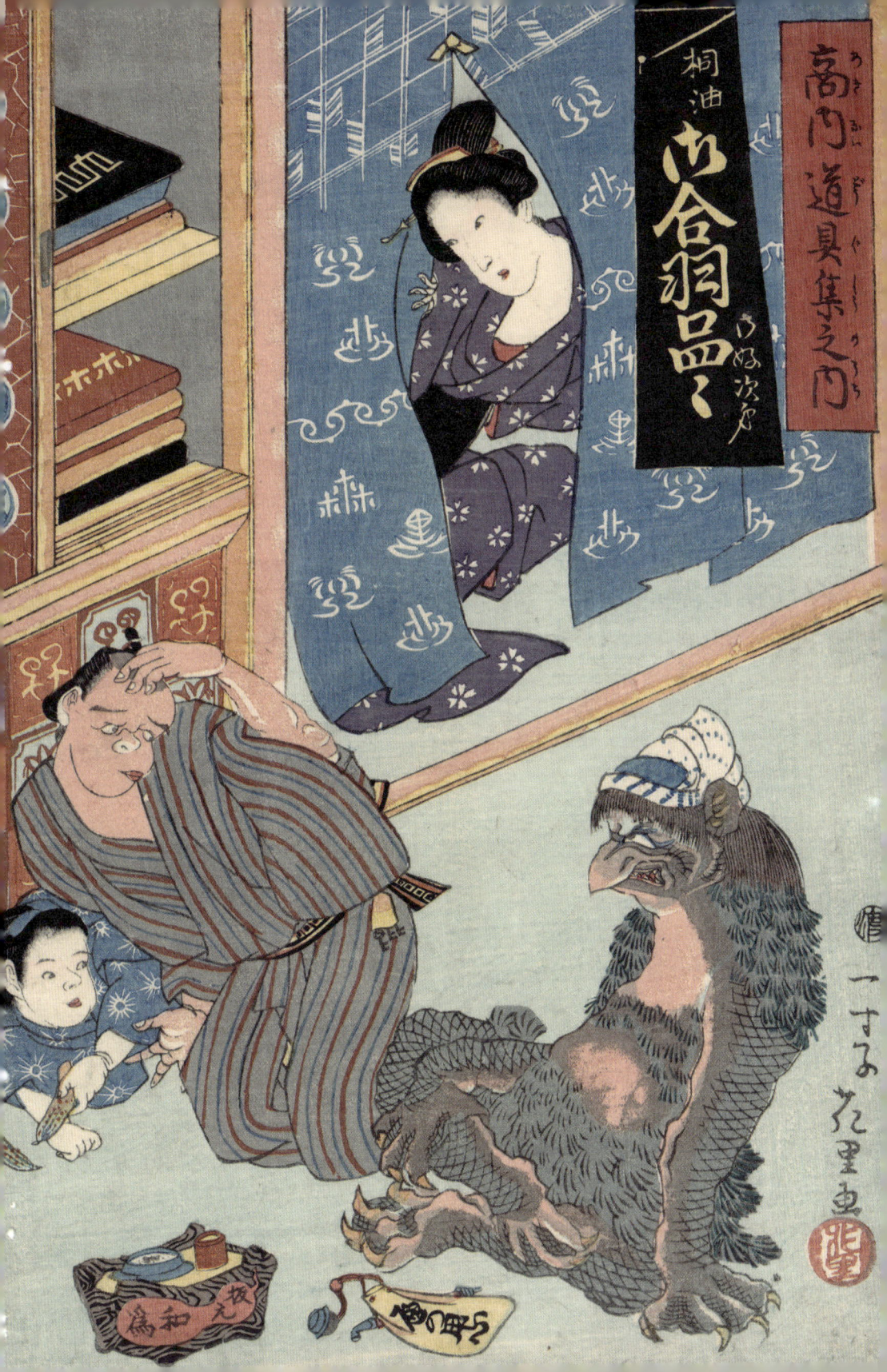

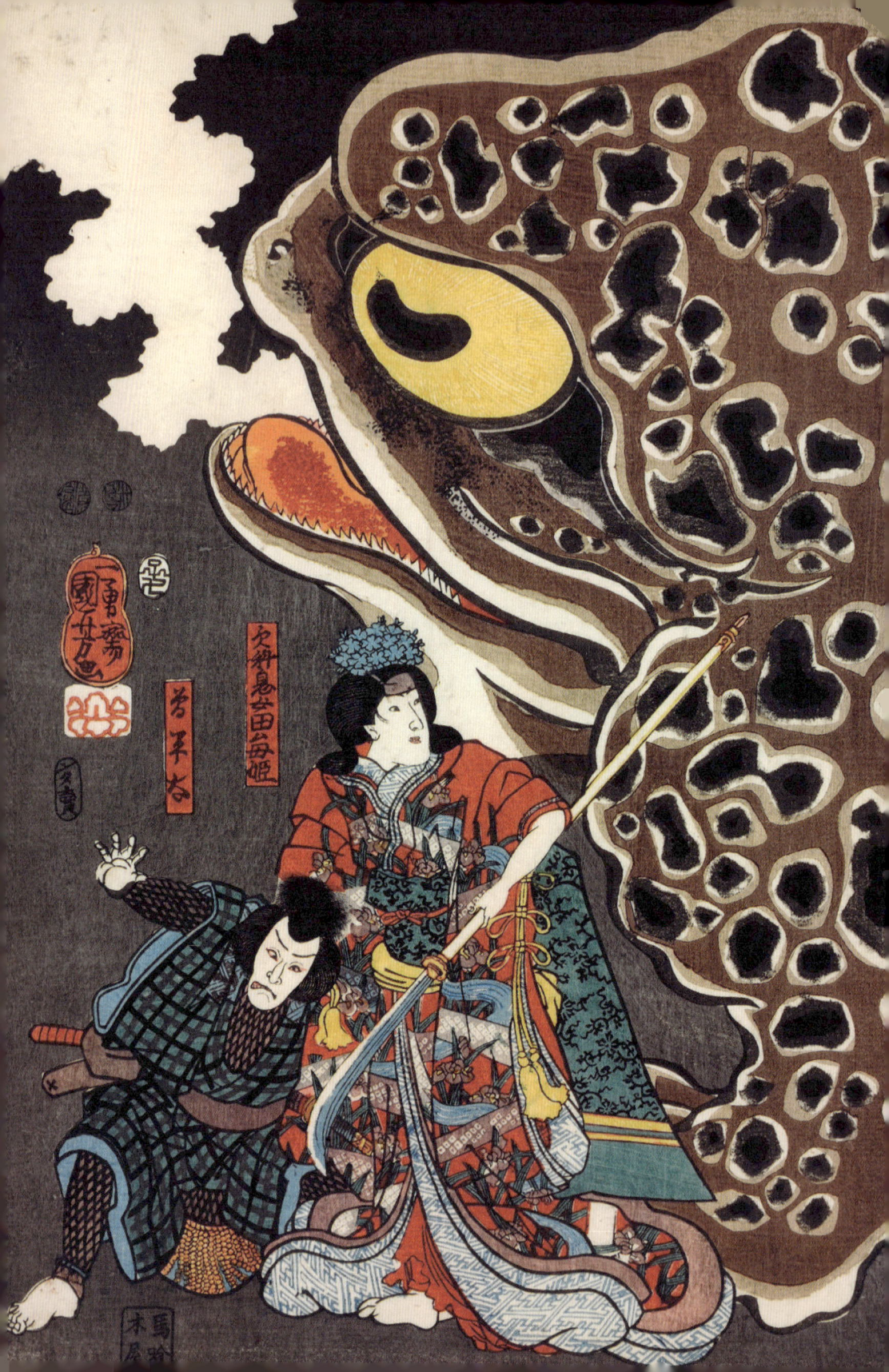

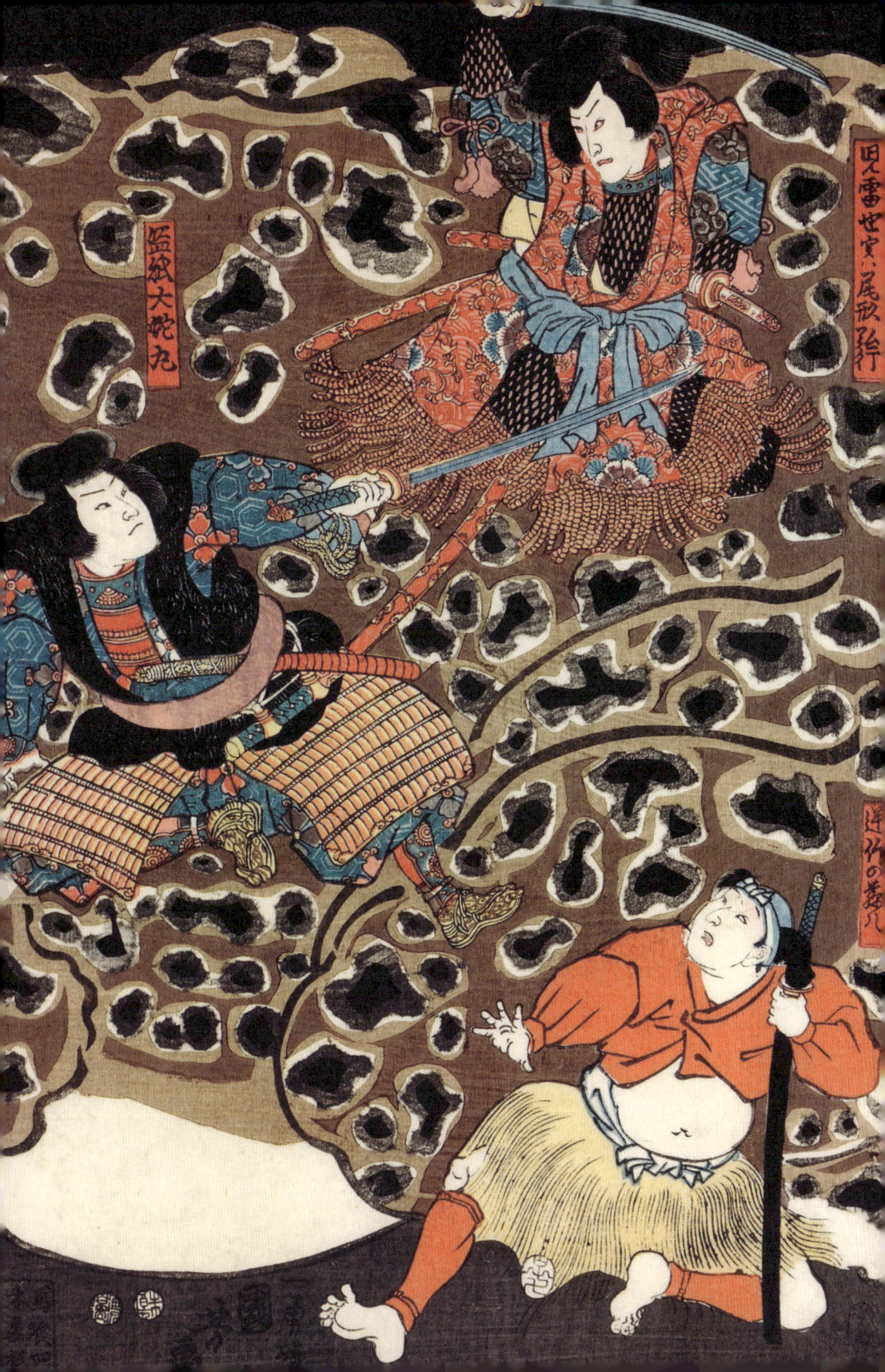

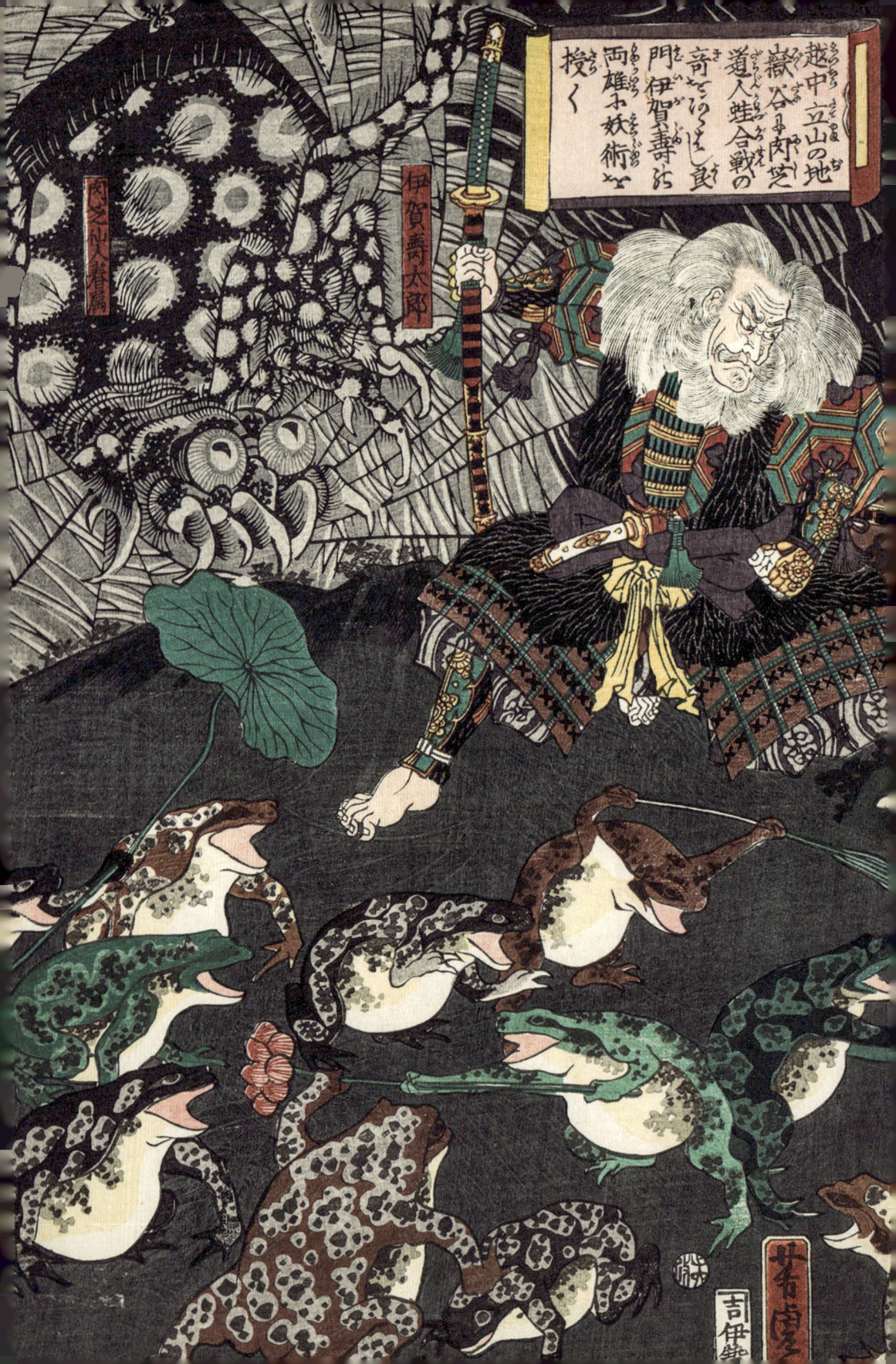

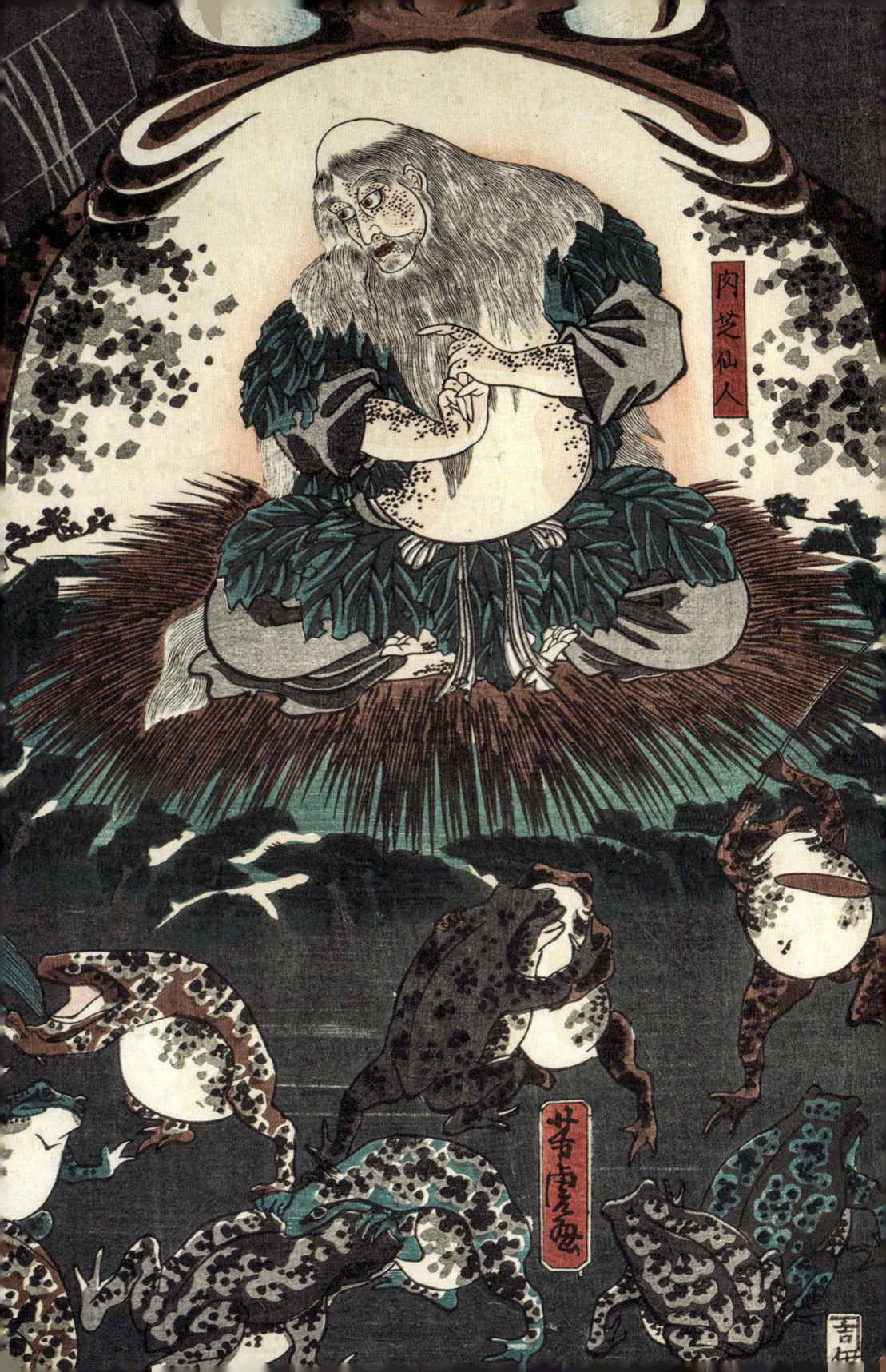

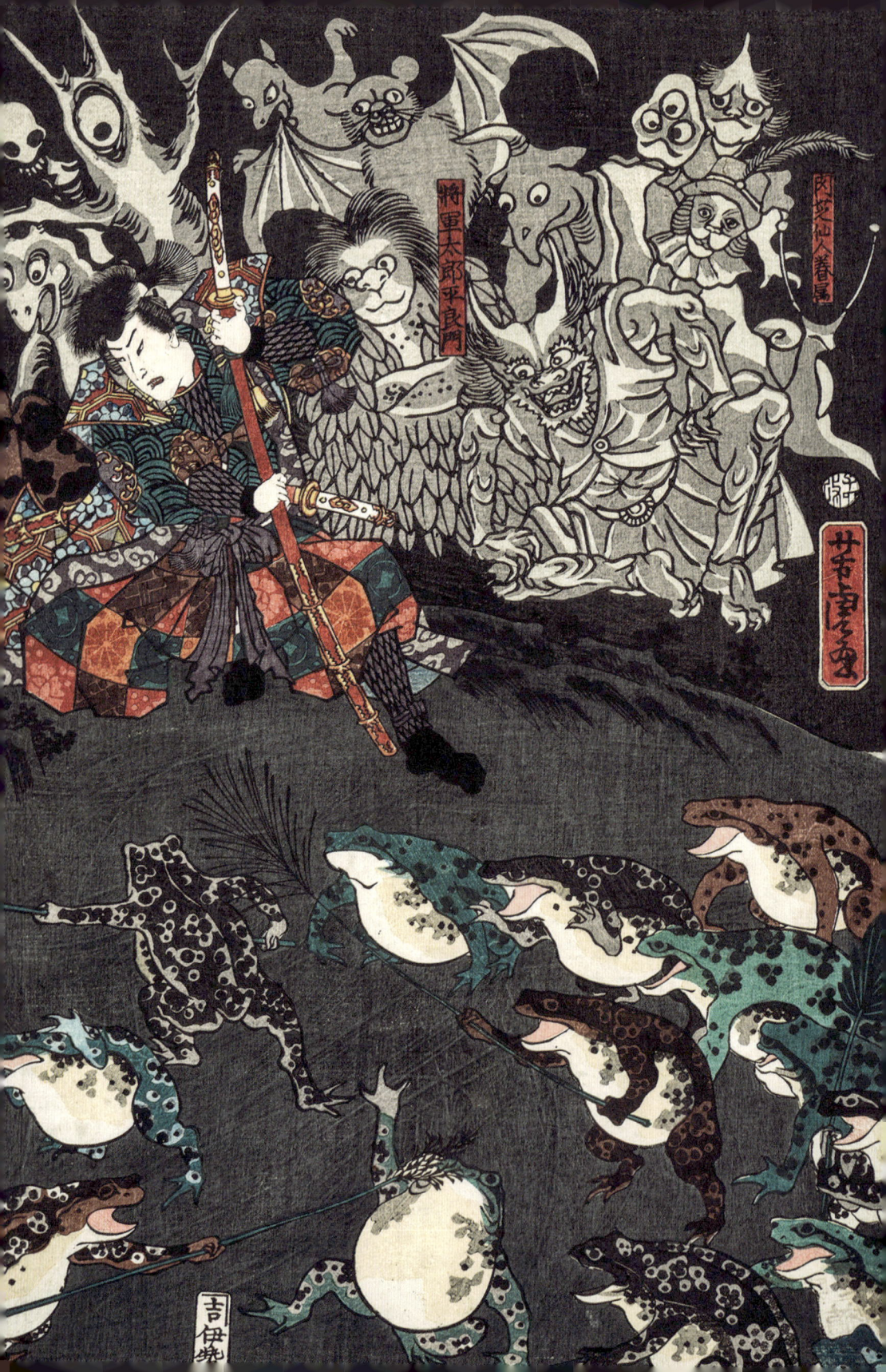

LIST OF ILLUSTRATIONS

Japan: Susanoo no Mikoto Kills the Eight-Headed Serpent at Hirokawa in Izumo Province, details, 1887, woodblock print (nishiki-e), triptych, 39.4 × 80 cm Philadelphia Museum of Art, acquired with funds from the Rhodes and Leona B. Carpenter Foundation, 1989, inv. 1989-47-582a–c

pp. 46–47
Yōshū (Hashimoto) Chikanobu (1838–1912), Susanoo no Mikoto Kills the Eight-Headed Serpent-Dragon from the Hino River in Izumi Province, detail, ca 1880, woodblock print (nishiki-e), triptych Kyoto, Nishiharu

pp. 48–49
Utagawa Kuniyoshi (1797–1861), Jiraiya, from the series Mirror of Warriors of Our Country (Honchō musha kagami), detail, 1855, woodblock print, 36.2 × 25.2 cm Boston, Museum of Fine Arts, William Sturgis Bigelow Collection, inv. 11.38113

BEANS FOR DEMONS

pp. 50–51 and 52
Tsukioka Yoshitoshi (1839–1892), Momotarō Scattering Beans for Setsubun, details, 1859, woodblock print (nishiki-e), triptych, 36 × 76.1 cm Boston, Museum of Fine Arts, William Sturgis Bigelow Collection, inv. 11.37577a-c

p. 55
Toriyama Sekien (1712–1788), One Hundred Monsters Ancient and Modern (Hyakki shūi), detail, 1781, book, woodblock print, 22.5 × 16 cm New York, The Metropolitan Museum of Art, acquired with a donation from the Mary and James G. Wallach Family Foundation, in honour of John T. Carpenter, 2013, inv. 2013.803

pp. 56–57 and 58–59
Unknown artist, Bakemono no e, details, late 17th–18th century, painted scroll, 44 × 525 cm Provo, Brigham Young University Library, inv. 895.63 B17 1863

pp. 60–61
Utagawa Hiroshige (1797–1858), Chronicle of Great Peace and Happiness: the Battle of Rice and Sake, Buy More and More! detail, 1843–1847, woodblock print (nishiki-e), triptych, 36 × 76.3 cm Boston, Museum of Fine Arts, William Sturgis Bigelow Collection, inv. 11.19651-3

pp. 62–63
Toriyama Sekien (1712–1788), The Illustrated Bag of One Hundred Random Demons or A Horde of Haunted Housewares (Gazu hyakki tsurezure bukuro) (1781), detail, 1805, book, woodblock print Tokyo, National Diet Library Digital Collections, https://dl.ndl.go.jp/pid/2551542

WHEN OBJECTS COME TO LIFE

p. 64
Gosōtei Hirosada (dates unknown), One-Legged Umbrella Monster (Kasa obake), detail, 1857, woodblock print (nishiki-e), 24.1 × 18.1 cm New York, The Metropolitan Museum of Art, acquired with donations from the Friends of Asian Art, in honour of James C. Y. Watt, 2011, inv. 2011.147

p. 67
Tsukioka Yoshitoshi (1839–1892), A Tanuki Transformed into the Lucky Tea Kettle of Morin-ji Temple (1890), from the series New Forms of Thirty-Six Ghosts (Shingata sanjūrokkaisen), 1902, woodblock print (nishiki-e), 39.4 × 26.7 cm Philadelphia Museum of Art, acquired with funds from the E. Rhodes and Leona B. Carpenter Foundation, 1989, inv. 1989-47-631

pp. 68–69
Sumiyoshi Hirotsura (1793–1863), Nocturnal Procession of the Hundred Demons (Hyakki yagyō), detail, painted scroll, 37 × 1482 cm Paris, Bibliothèque nationale de France, département des Manuscrits, Smith-Lesouëf K 21 Japonais

p. 70
Katsukawa Shun'ei (1762–1819), Once Upon a Time (A Book of Ghost Stories) (Imawa mukashi), detail, 1790, printed book, woodblock print, 22.4 × 15.8 cm New York, The Metropolitan Museum of Art, acquired with a donation by the Mary and James G. Wallach Foundation, 2013, inv. 2013.819

pp. 72–79
Unknown artist, Nocturnal Procession of the Hundred Demons (Hyakki yagyō), details, painted scroll Tokyo, National Diet Library Digital Collections, https://dl.ndl.go.jp/pid/2540972/1/21

DEFYING THE UNKNOWN

p. 80
Tsukioka Yoshitoshi (1839–1892), Taira no Koremochi Subjugates the Evil Devil at Mount Togakushi (1890), from the series New Forms of Thirty-Six Ghosts (Shingata sanjūrokkaisen), detail, 1902, woodblock print (nishiki-e), 36.8 × 25.2 cm Los Angeles County Museum of Art, Herbert R. Cole Collection, inv. M.84.31.230

p. 83
Katsushika Hokusai (1760–1849), One Hundred Ghost Stories in a Haunted House (Shinpan uki-e bakemono yashiki Hyaku monogatari no zu), detail, 1780, woodblock print (nishiki-e), 23.7 × 35.4 cm Boston, Museum of Fine Arts, gift of C. Adrian Rubel, inv. 46.1417

pp. 84–85
Utagawa Kuniyoshi (1797–1861), Three of Minamoto no Raiko's Retainers, Sakata no Kintoki, Usui Sadamitsu, and Watanabe no Tsuna, Playing Go, with Attempted Interruptions by the Earth Spider's Demons, detail, woodblock print (nishiki-e), triptych, 35.8 × 24 cm, 35.9 × 23.9 cm, 35.9 × 24 cm, mid-19th century London, The British Museum, gift of the American Friends of The British Museum, inv. 2008,3037.20903

pp. 86–87
Katsukawa Shuntei (1770–1820), The Warrior Fujiwara Hidesato Battling the Giant Centipede, detail, between 1815 and 1820, woodblock print (nishiki-e), triptych, 37.2 × 25.2 cm, 37.1 × 25.1 cm, 36.9 × 24.9 cm Washington, Library of Congress, inv. FP 2-JPD, no. 1452 a, b, c

THE EARTH SPIDER

pp. 88–89 and 90
Utagawa Kuniyoshi (1797–1861), The Earth Spider Conjures Up Demons at the Mansion of Minamoto Yorimitsu, details, 1843, woodblock print (nishiki-e), triptych, 37.2 × 25.5 cm (each sheet) Washington, National Museum of Asian Art, Smithsonian Institution, The Pearl and Seymour Moskowitz Collection, inv. S2021.5.591a-c

p. 92
Tsukioka Yoshitoshi (1839–1892), Sakata no Kintoki (Kintaro) and the Earth Spider, detail, 1886, woodblock print (nishiki-e), diptych, 37.3 × 48.9 cm Amsterdam, Rijksmuseum, inv. RP-P-2001-19

pp. 94–95
Utagawa Kunisada I (known as Toyokuni III, 1786–1864), Actor Arashi Rikaku II as Hananomura no Chigusa, actually Toriyama Shūsaku (left); Bandō Shūka I as Shiranui Daijin, actuallly Wakana

hime (right), detail, 1853, woodblock print (*nishiki-e*), diptych, 35.3 × 47.5 cm
Boston, Museum of Fine Arts, William Sturgis Bigelow Collection, inv. 11.43702a-b

pp. 96–97
Utagawa Kuniyoshi (1797–1861), *The Earth Spider Slain by Minamoto no Yorimitsu's Retainers*, detail, ca 1838, woodblock print (*nishiki-e*), *ōban* format triptych

pp. 98–99
Keisai Eisen (1790–1848), *Pictorial History of Heroes* (*Eiyū gashi*), detail, 1836, printed book, woodblock print
Minneapolis Institute of Art, Louis W. Hill Jr. bequest, inv. 96.146.161

pp. 100–101
Utagawa Kuniyoshi (1797–1861), *The Earth Spider*, detail, 1842–1846, woodblock print (*nishiki-e*), 37 × 25.4 cm
Amsterdam, Rijksmuseum, inv. RP-P-2019-204

SPITEFUL MONK, YOU KILLED ME
p. 102
Tsukioka Yoshitoshi (1839–1892), *Priest Raigo of Mii Temple Transformed by Wicked Thoughts into a Rat* (1890), from the series *New Forms of Thirty-Six Ghosts* (*Shingata sanjū-rokkaisen*), detail, 1902, woodblock print (*nishiki-e*), 39.4 × 26.7 cm
Philadelphia Museum of Art, acquired with funds from the E. Rhodes and Leona B. Carpenter Foundation, 1989, inv. 1989-47-621

p. 105
Utagawa Kuniyoshi (1797–1861), *The Kabuki Actors Onoe Kikujiro II as Okinoi and Ichimura Uzaemon XII as Ashikaga Yorikane* (left); *Onoe Kikugoro III as Tenjiku Kaja Conjuring Up Rats* (middle); *Sawamura Tossho I as Fuwa Banzaemon* (right), detail, 1836, woodblock print

(*nishiki-e*), triptych, 37.4 × 25.5 cm, 37.4 × 26 cm, 37.4 × 25.7 cm
London, The British Museum, gift of the American Friends of The British Museum, inv. 2008,3037.19609

pp. 106–107
Tsukioka Yoshitoshi (1839–1892), *Kusunoki Tamonmaru Conquering the Old Badger*, detail, 1860, woodblock print (*nishiki-e*), triptych, 36.2 × 73.8 cm
Minneapolis Institute of Art, Mary Griggs Burke Endowment Fund established by the Mary Livingston Griggs and Mary Griggs Burke Foundation, gifts of various donors, by exchange, and gift of Edmond Freis in memory of his parents, Rose and Leon Freis, inv. 2017.106.9a-c

pp. 108 and 109
Unknown artist, *Bakemono no e*, details, late 17th–18th century, painted scroll, 44 × 525 cm
Provo, Brigham Young University Library, inv. 895.63 B17 1863

pp. 110–111
Utagawa Kunisada I (known as Toyokuni III, 1786–1864), *Watanabe no Tsuna Meets the Ibaraki Demon at Modoribashi Bridge*, detail, ca 1815, woodblock print (*nishiki-e*), diptych, 36.4 × 50 cm
Boston, Museum of Fine Arts, Maxim Karolik bequest, inv 64.824-5

p. 112
Utagawa Kuniyoshi (1797–1861), *Minamoto Yoshitsune Fights Benkei on Gojō Bridge*, detail, between 1847 and 1850, woodblock print (*nishiki-e*), triptych, 36.4 × 24.4 cm (each sheet)
Oxford, Ashmolean Museum, offered by George Grigs, Miss Elisabeth Grigs and Miss Susan Messer, in memory of Derick Grigs, 1971, inv. EA1971.160

p. 113
Toriyama Sekien (1712–1788), *Nocturnal Procession of the Hundred*

Demons (*Hyakki yagyō Shūi*) (1776), detail, 1805, printed book, woodblock print, 22.5 × 15.6 cm
Tokyo, National Diet Library Digital Collections, https//dl.ndl.go.jp/pid/2553975

TENGU
p. 114
Tsukioka Yoshitoshi (1839–1892), *Iga no Tsubone*, detail, 1886, woodblock print (*nishiki-e*), 33 × 22.4 cm
Amsterdam, Rijksmuseum, inv. RP-P-2008-145

p. 117
Tsukioka Yoshitoshi (1839–1892), *Hōjō Takatoki, Lord of Sagami Warding Off Tengu with His Fan*, from the series *Yoshitoshi's Heroes Trembling with Courage* (*Yoshitoshi mushaburui*), detail, 1883, woodblock print (*nishiki-e*), 39.4 × 26.7 cm
Philadelphia Museum of Art, acquired with funds from the E. Rhodes and Leona B. Carpenter Foundation, 1989, 1978, inv. 1989-47-349

p. 118
Kitagawa Utamaro (ca 1750–1806), *Woman Playing with a Child with a Tengu Mask*, detail, 1795–1802, woodblock print (*nishiki-e*), 36.7 × 24.2 cm
Minneapolis Institute of Art, gift of Louis W. Hill, Jr., inv. P.75.51.132

p. 119
Tsukioka Yoshitoshi (1839–1892), *Kobayakawa Takakage Debating with the Tengu on Mount Hiko*, from the series *New Forms of Thirty-Six Ghosts* (*Shingata sanjūrokkaisen*), detail, 1892, woodblock print (*nishiki-e*), 35.8 × 24.1 cm
Los Angeles County Museum of Art, Herbert R. Cole Collection, inv. M.84.31.115

pp. 120–121
Utagawa Kuniyoshi (1797–1861), *Yoshitsune (Ushiwakamaru) Being Taught Swordsmanship with the Tengu King Sōjōbō*, detail, woodblock print (*nishiki-e*), triptych,

36 × 25 cm (each sheet)
London, British Library

pp. 122–123
Utagawa Hiroshige (1797–1858), *Ushiwakamaru Learns Swordplay from the Tengu at Sojogatani on Mount Kurama*, from the series *The Life of Yoshitsune* (*Yoshitsune ichidai zue*), detail, 1827–1839, woodblock print (*nishiki-e*), 24 × 35.9 cm
Chicago, The Art Institute, Clarence Buckingham Collection, inv. 1925.3795

NOBUSUMA
p. 124
Tsukioka Yoshitoshi (1839–1892), *Miyamoto no Musashi Kills a Nobusuma*, from the series *Beauty and Valour in the Novel Suikoden* (*Biyū Suikoden*), detail, 1867, woodblock print (*nishiki-e*), 24.9 × 17.8 cm
Philadelphia Museum of Art, gift of Sidney A. Tannenbaum, 1978, inv. 1978-129-92

pp. 126–127
Utagawa Kuniyoshi (1797–1861), *Miyamoto no Musashi Killing a Nobusuma*, detail, circa 1827, woodblock print (*nishiki-e*), *ōban* format

pp. 128–129
Yashima Gakutei (1786?–1868), *The Warrior Miura no Suke Confronting the Court Lady Tamamo no Mae as She Turns into an Evil Fox with Nine Tails*, detail, circa 1820, *surimono* print, 21.1 × 18.7 cm
New York, The Metropolitan Museum of Art, H. O. Havemeyer Collection, Bequest of Mrs. H. O. Havemeyer, 1929, inv. JP2049

pp. 130–131
Utagawa Hirokage (dates unknown), *Fox Fires at Ōji* (*Ōji kitsunebi*), from the series *Comical Views of Famous Places in Edo* (*Edo meisho dōke zukushi*), detail, 1859, woodblock print (*nishiki-e*), 37.2 × 24.9 cm
Boston, Museum of Fine Arts, William Sturgis Bigelow Collection, inv. 11.16964

pp. 132–133
Utagawa Kunisada I (known as Toyokuni III, 1786–1864), *Abe no Yasunari exorcises the phantoms* (*Abe no Yasunari yōkai o chōbuku no zu*): *Doctor of Astrology (Tenmon hakase) Abe no Yasunari* (right); *Tamomo no Mae, actually a Nine-tailed Fox* (*Jitsu wa kyūbi no kitsune*, middle); and *Miuranosuke Yoshizumi* (left), detail, 1847, woodblock print (*nishiki-e*), triptych, 36 × 71.9 cm (ensemble)
Boston, Museum of Fine Arts, gift of Anne Gordon Keidel Trust, June 2016, inv. 2016.1298a-c

KITSUNE

p. 134
Ippitsusai Bunchō (active ca 1765–1792), *An Actor in the Fox Dance from the Play 'The Thousand Cherry Trees'* (*Yoshitsune Senbon Sakura*), detail, woodblock print (*nishiki-e*), 32.4 × 149 cm
New York, The Metropolitan Museum of Art, Henry L. Phillips Collection, Henry L. Phillips Bequest, 1939, inv. JP2793

p. 137
Tsukioka Yoshitoshi (1839–1892), *The Fox-Woman Kuzunoha Leaving Her Child* (1890), from the series *New Forms of Thirty-Six Ghosts* (*Shingata sanjūrokkaisen*), detail, 1902, woodblock print (*nishiki-e*), 39.4 × 26.7 cm
Philadelphia Museum of Art, acquired with funds from the E. Rhodes and Leona B. Carpenter Foundation, 1989, inv. 1989-47-616

p. 138
Tsukioka Yoshitoshi (1839–1892), *The Fox Trap*, from the series *One Hundred Aspects of the Moon* (*Tsuki hyakushi*), detail, 1886, woodblock print (*nishiki-e*), 24.9 × 19 cm
Washington, Library of Congress, inv. FP 2-JPD, no. 1392

p. 140
Utagawa Kuniyoshi (1797–1861), *Princess Yaegaki*, detail, woodblock print (*nishiki-e*), 36.8 × 25.4 cm, 19th century
New York, The Metropolitan Museum of Art, bequest of Grace M. Pugh, 1985, inv. JP3706

p. 141
Utagawa Kuniyoshi (1797–1861), *Tsumagome: Abe no Yasunari and the Fox Kuzunoha*, from the series *Sixty-Nine Stations of the Kisokaidō Road* (*Kisokaidō rokujūkyū tsugi no uchi*), detail, 1852, woodblock print (*nishiki-e*), 35.2 × 24.5 cm
Boston, Museum of Fine Arts, William Sturgis Bigelow Collection, inv. 11.41803

pp. 142–143
Utagawa Kunisada I (known as Toyokuni III, 1786–1864), *Nakamura Jakunosuke as Arakoma Kotarō* (left); *Sawamura Tanosuke III as Ryōshi Onami and Ichimura Uzaemon XIII as Neko no Chunori the Cat Demon* (middle and right); *Nakamura Shikan IV as Suwa Kazuemon* (right), in the Kabuki Play *Tōkaidō Iroha Nikki*, detail, 1861, woodblock print (*nishiki-e*), triptych, 36 × 73 cm (ensemble)
Tokyo, National Diet Library Digital Collections, https://dl.ndl.go.jp/pid/1301358

p. 144
Kikugawa Eizan (1787–1867), *Geisha Playing the Kitsune-ken Game*, from the series *Three Beauties Playing a Sake Drinking Game* (*Fūryū sake no towamure san bijin*), detail, 1802, woodblock print (*nishiki-e*)
Newark Museum of Art

p. 145
Unknown artist, *Bakemono no e*, detail, late 17th–18th century, painted scroll, 44 × 525 cm
Provo, Brigham Young University Library, inv. 895.63 B17 1863

DEMON MAIDENS

p. 147
Tsukioka Yoshitoshi (1839–1892), *Heron Maiden*, from the series *New Forms of Thirty-Six Ghosts* (*Shingata sanjūrokkaisen*), detail, 1889, woodblock print (*nishiki-e*), ōban format
Chicago, The Art Institute, Bruce Goff Archive, gift of Shin'enkan, Inc., inv. 1990.607.188

p. 148
Tsukioka Yoshitoshi (1839–1892), *The Innkeeper's Daughter Kiyohime Crossing the Hidaka River as a Snake in Passionate Pursuit of a Celibate Monk*, from the series *One Hundred Ghost Tales from China and Japan* (*Wakan hyaku monogatari*), detail, 1865, woodblock print (*nishiki-e*), 39.4 × 26.7 cm
Philadelphia Museum of Art, gift of Sidney A. Tannenbaum, 1978, inv. 1978-129-34

pp. 150–151
Tsukioka Yoshitoshi (1839–1892), *Taira no Koremochi Conquering the Devil Woman on Mount Togakushi*, detail, 1887, woodblock print (*nishiki-e*), diptych, 75 × 26 cm (ensemble)
Chicago, The Art Institute, Frederick W. Gookin Collection, inv. RX22839/03

pp. 152–153
Yōshū (Hashimoto) Chikanobu (1838–1912), *Scene of Fox Fire* (*Kitsunebi*), from the Play 'Honchō Nijūshikō', detail, 1898, woodblock print (*nishiki-e*), triptych, approx. 37 × 25 cm (each sheet)
New York, The Metropolitan Museum of Art, acquired with funds from the Friends of Asian Art, 2005, inv. 2005.352a–c

pp. 154–155
Unknown artist, *Bakemono no e*, detail, late 17th–18th century, painted scroll, 44 × 525 cm
Provo, Brigham Young University Library, inv. 895.63 B17 1863

p. 156
Tsukioka Yoshitoshi (1839–1892), *Enlightenment of the Courtesan Jigokudayū*, 1890, from the series *New Forms of Thirty-Six Ghosts* (*Shingata sanjūrokkaisen*), detail, 1902, woodblock print (*nishiki-e*), 39.4 × 26.7 cm
Philadelphia Museum of Art, acquired with funds from the E. Rhodes and Leona B. Carpenter Foundation, 1989, inv. 1989-47-610

p. 157
Tsukioka Yoshitoshi (1839–1892), *Princess Yaegaki following the Fox Fires in a Scene from the Play 'Nijūshikō* (*Nijūshikō kitsunebi no zu*)', from the series *New Forms of Thirty-Six Ghosts* (*Shingata sanjūrokkaisen*), detail, 1892, woodblock print (*nishiki-e*), 39.4 × 26.7 cm
Philadelphia Museum of Art, acquired with funds from the E. Rhodes and Leona B. Carpenter Foundation, 1989, inv. 1989-47-627

GARBED IN HIS OWN TESTICLES

p. 158
Tsukioka Yoshitoshi (1839–1892), *Travellers Startled by a Tanuki's Giant Scrotum at Hiroonohara*, 'Kyōga Images of Famous Places near Tokyo' (*Tōkyō kaika kyōga meisho*), detail, 1881, woodblock print (*nishiki-e*), 17.8 × 24.8 cm
Philadelphia Museum of Art, acquired with funds from the E. Rhodes and Leona B. Carpenter Foundation, 1989, inv. 1989-47-196

p. 161
Tsukioka Yoshitoshi (1839–1892), *Takeda Katsuchiyo Killing an Old Tanuki*, from the series *New Forms of Thirty-Six Ghosts* (*Shingata sanjūrokkaisen*), detail, 1889, woodblock print (*nishiki-e*), ōban format, Chicago, The Art Institute, Bruce Goff Archive, gift of Shin'enkan, Inc., inv. 1990.607.189

pp. 162–163
Utagawa Kuniyoshi
(1797–1861), *The Story of
Nippondaemon and the
Cat: Sawamura Sōjūrō V
as Nippondaemon* (left);
*Onoe Kikugorō III as the
Spirit of the Cat Stone*
(middle); *Onoe Kikugorō III
as Kotoura* (right), detail,
1847, woodblock print
(*nishiki-e*), triptych, 35.7 ×
73.5 cm (ensemble)
Boston, Museum of Fine
Arts, William Sturgis
Bigelow Collection, inv.
11.27023-5

p. 164
Utagawa Kuniyoshi (1797–
1861), *Kamada Matahachi*,
detail, ca 1840, woodblock
print (*nishiki-e*), 38 × 26 cm
Washington, Freer Gallery
of Art and Arthur M.
Sackler Gallery Collection,
Smithsonian Institution,
Anne van Biema Collec-
tion, inv. S2004.3.167

p. 165
Utagawa Kuniyoshi (1797–
1861), *Usui Matagoro Slays
a Giant White Monkey in
the Mountains of Hida*,
detail, woodblock print
(*nishiki-e*), 37.2 × 25.2 cm
London, The British Mu-
seum, gift of the American
Friends of The British Museum, inv. 2008,3037.21205

GATHERING THE
DISPERSED

p. 166
Tsukioka Yoshitoshi (1839–
1892), *Demon Disguised as
an Old Woman Retrieving
Her Arm*, from the series
*New Forms of Thirty-Six
Ghosts* (*Shingata san-
jūrokkaisen*), detail, 1889,
woodblock print (*nishiki-e*),
35.9 × 24.5 cm
Amsterdam, Rijksmuseum,
inv. RP-P-1983-393

p. 169
Tsukioka Yoshitoshi
(1839–1892), *Ii no Hayata
Kills the Nue at the Imperial Palace*, from the series
*New Forms of Thirty-Six
Ghosts* (*Shingata sanjūrokkaisen*), detail, 1890,
woodblock print (*nishiki-e*),
36.9 × 25 cm,
Amsterdam, Rijksmuseum,
inv. RP-P-1983-394

p. 170
Utagawa Kunisada I
(known as Toyokuni III,
1786–1864), *The Vampire
Cat of Nabeshima*, detail,
1853, woodblock print (*nishiki-e*), 35.9 × 24.8 cm
Amsterdam, Rijksmuseum,
inv. RP-P-2017-6148

p. 173
Utagawa Kuniyoshi
(1797–1861), *Kuwana: The
Sailor Tokuzo and the Sea
Monster*, from the series
*Fifty-Three Parallels of
Tokaido* (*Tōkaidō gojusan
Tsui*), detail, ca 1845,
woodblock print (*nishiki-e*),
ōban format

pp. 174–175
Utagawa Kuniyoshi
(1797–1861), *Oniwakamaru
and the Giant Carp*, detail,
ca 1845, woodblock print
(*nishiki-e*), triptych, *ōban*
format
Edinburgh, National
Museums Scotland, inv.
A.1887.745.68.1.7

p. 176
Tsukioka Yoshitoshi (1839–
1892), *Shirafuji Genta
Watching Kappa Wrestle*,
from the series *One Hun-
dred Ghost Stories from
China and Japan* (*Wakan
hyaku monogatari*), detail,
1865, woodblock print
(*nishiki-e*), 37.6 × 25.7 cm
Los Angeles County Muse-
um of Art, Herbert R. Cole
Collection, inv. M.84.31.59

p. 177
Issunshi Hanasato (dates
unknown), *Kappa in a
Shop of Stencil-Dyed
Goods*, from the series
*Collection of Equipment
of Merchants* (*Akinai
dōgu shū no uchi*), detail,
1843–1847, woodblock print
(*nishiki-e*), 35.5 × 24.5 cm
Boston, Museum of Fine
Arts, William Sturgis Bigelow Collection, inv. 11.37960

pp. 178–179
Utagawa Kuniyoshi
(1797–1861), *Actor Ichikawa
Danjuro VIII as Jiraiya
Atop a Giant Toad in
Combat with Orochimaru,
played by Arashi Rikan
III*, detail, 1852, woodblock
print (*nishiki-e*), triptych,

37 × 25.9 cm, 36.9 × 24.8
cm, 37.1 × 25.5 cm
London, The British Mu-
seum, gift of the American
Friends of The British Museum, inv. 2008,3037.19504

pp. 180–181 and 182
Utagawa Yoshitora (dates
unknown), *At Hell Valley
on Mount Tate, in Etchū
Province, Nikushi Dōjin
Demonstrates a Battle of
Frogs and Teaches Magic
to the Two Comrades
Yoshikado and Iga Jutarō*,
details, 1864, woodblock
print (*nishiki-e*), 35.7 × 74.8
cm (ensemble)
Boston, Museum of Fine
Arts, William Sturgis
Bigelow Collection, inv.
11.41382a-c

p. 188
Toriyama Sekien (1712–1788),
*Illustrated Night Parade
of the Demon Horde* (*Gazu
hyakki tsurezure bukuro*)
(1781), detail, 1805, book,
woodblock print
Tokyo, National Diet
Library Digital Collec-
tions, https://dl.ndl.go.jp/
pid/2551542

pp. 190–191
Unknown artist, *Yōkai and
Personifications of Gen-
ital Organs*, detail of the
opening image of a series
of *shunga* prints inspired
by the story Raikō and the
Earth Spider, woodblock
print (*nishiki-e*), 19.4 × 26.8
cm
Amsterdam, Rijksmuseum,
inv. RP-P-1991-687

187

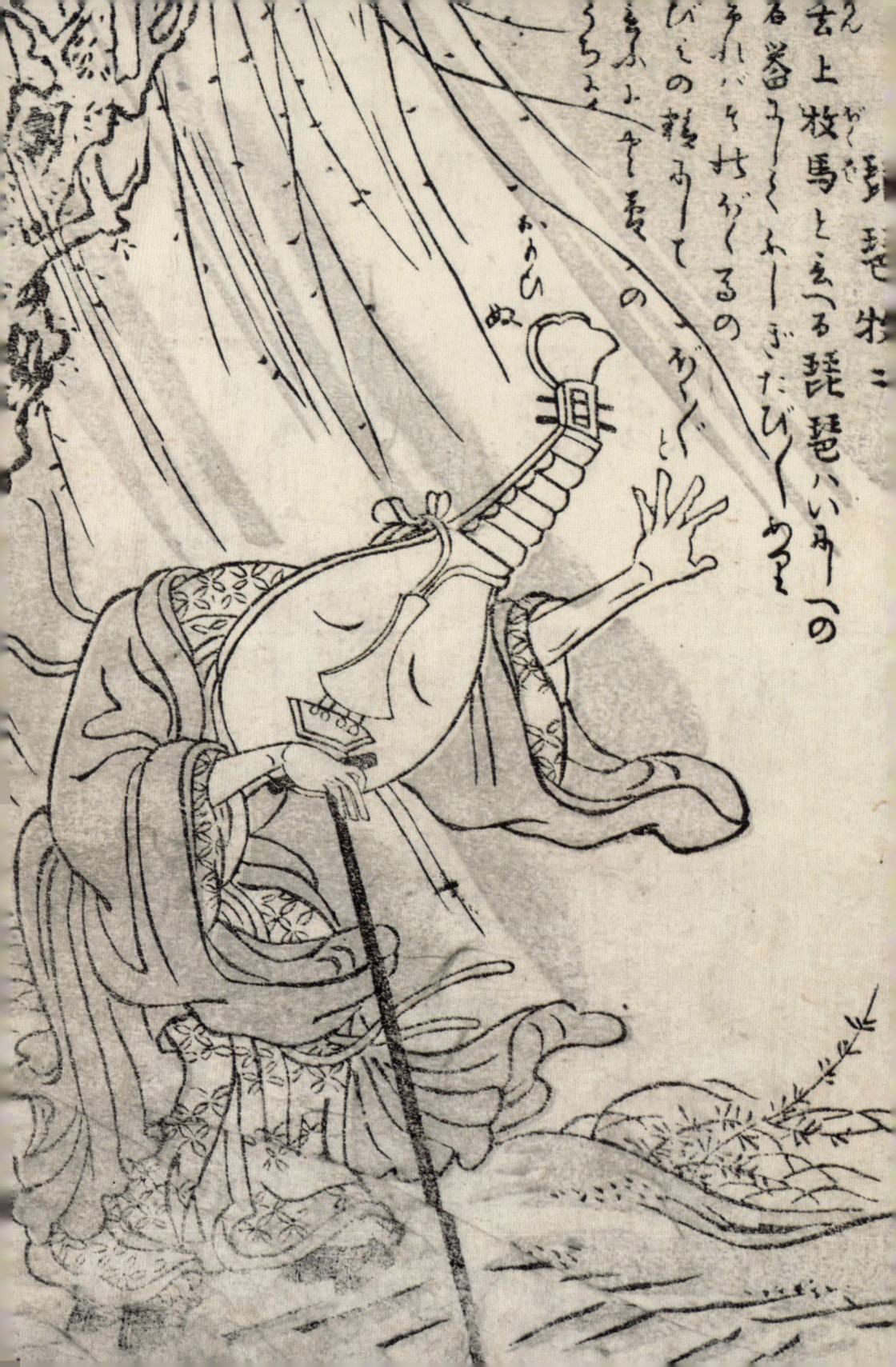

琵琶牧ニ

玄上牧馬と玄（へ）る琵琶ハ内（うち）の
御器（うつは）うつくしくふーぶたびくめで
 それバを持（もち）がくるの
びのの籠（こもり）て
びふて愛（あい）の
るふやで愛（あい）の
ぐくと
ろらよ

がく

あかひ
ぬ

SELECT BIBLIOGRAPHY

Henri-Alexis Baatsch, *Hokusai: Le fou de dessin*, Paris, Hazan, 2014

Philippe Charlier, *Fantômes Yōkai: Yūrei. Histoires d'amour et de mort dans le Japon traditionnel*, Paris, Hazan, 2024

Philippe Charlier, *Les Monstres humains dans l'Antiquité: Analyse paléopathologique*, Paris, Fayard, 2008

Saudamini Deo and Philippe Charlier, 'Local teratogenic factors and high frequency of Japanese folklore cyclops (yōkai)', *Ethics, Medicine and Public Health*, vol. 19, 2021, article 100718

Stéphane Du Mesnildot and Julien Rousseau (eds.), *Enfers et fantômes d'Asie* (exhib. cat.), Paris, Musée du Quai-Branly–Jacques-Chirac and Flammarion, 2018

Michael Dylan Foster, *The Book of Yōkai: Mysterious Creatures of Japanese Folklore*, Oakland, University of California Press, 2015

Bernard Frank (translation, introduction and annotations, original author unknown), *Histoires qui sont maintenant du passé*, Connaissance de l'Orient, Paris, Gallimard, 1968, new edition 2008

Christine Guth, *Le Japon de la période Edo*, Paris, Flammarion, 1996

Lafcadio Hearn, *Fantômes du Japon*, preface by Francis Lacassin, Monaco, Éditions du Rocher (Motifs Poche), transl. Marc Logé, 2007

Henri L. Joly, *Legend in Japanese Art: A Description of Historical Episodes, Legendary Characters, Folklore, Myths, Religious Symbolism, Illustrated in the Arts of Old Japan*, London, John Lane, 1908

Matthi Forrer, *Keisai, le Maître du dessin abrégé: Tous les albums de style Ryakuga*, Paris, Hazan, transl. Dominique Coupé, 2013

Brigitte Koyama-Richard, *Yōkai: Fantastique art japonais*, Paris, Nouvelles Éditions Scala, 2017

Matthew Meyer, *Yōkai: La parade nocturne des 100 démons*, Chermignon, Nuinui, 2020

Shigeru Mizuki, *Dictionnaire des Yōkai*, Paris, Pika, 2015

Adele Schlombs, *Hiroshige (1797–1858): Le maître japonais des estampes ukiyo-e*, new edition, Cologne, Taschen, 2021

Sarah E. Thompson, *Images du monde flotant: Estampes japonaises dans la collection du musée des Beaux-Arts de Boston*, Chermignon, Nuinui, 2023

Kōichi Yumoto, *Le Musée des Yōkai: L'art japonais des êtres surnaturels de la collection Yumoto Kōichi*, Paris, Éditions Sully, transl. Amandine Martel, 2020

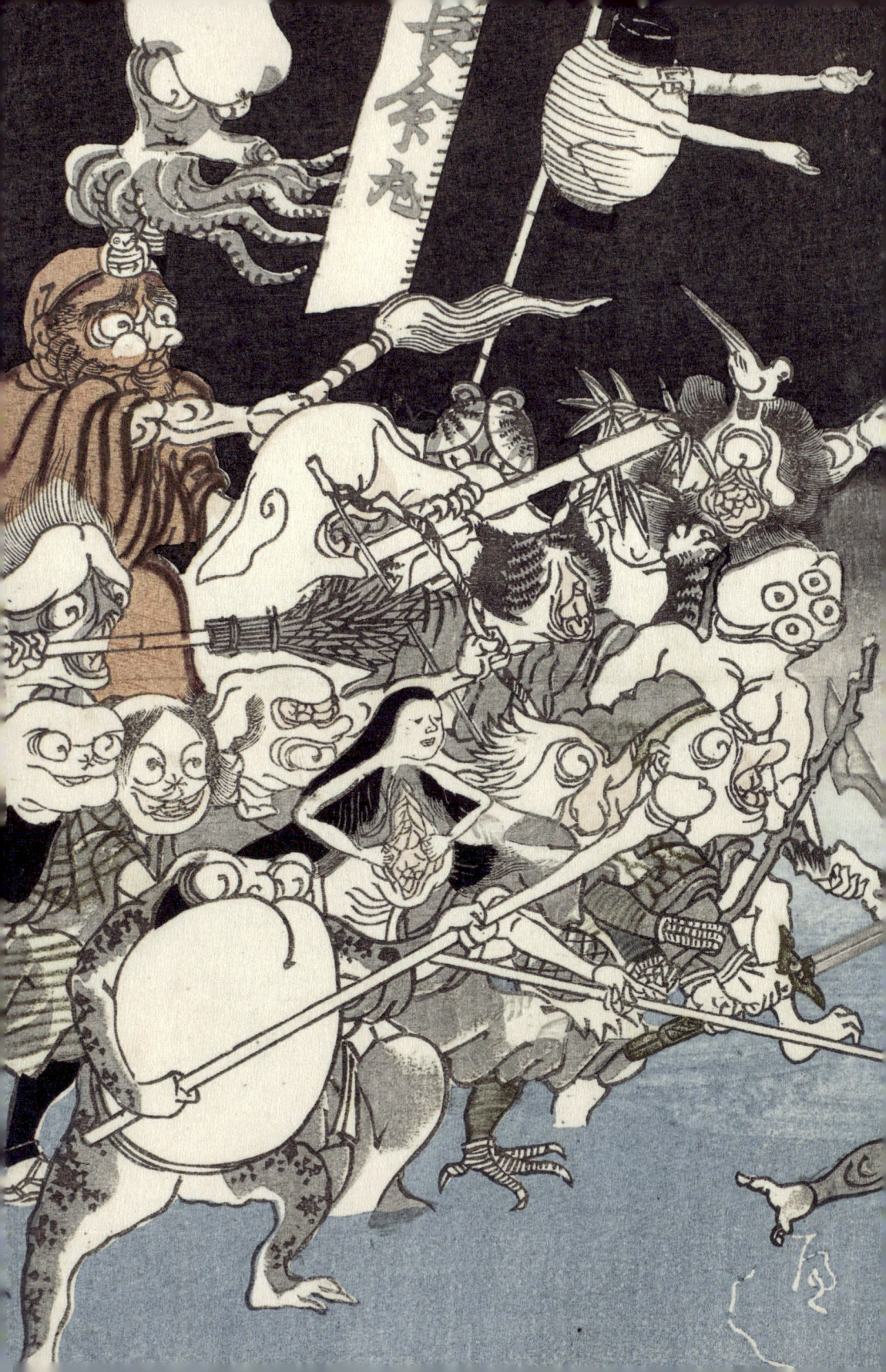

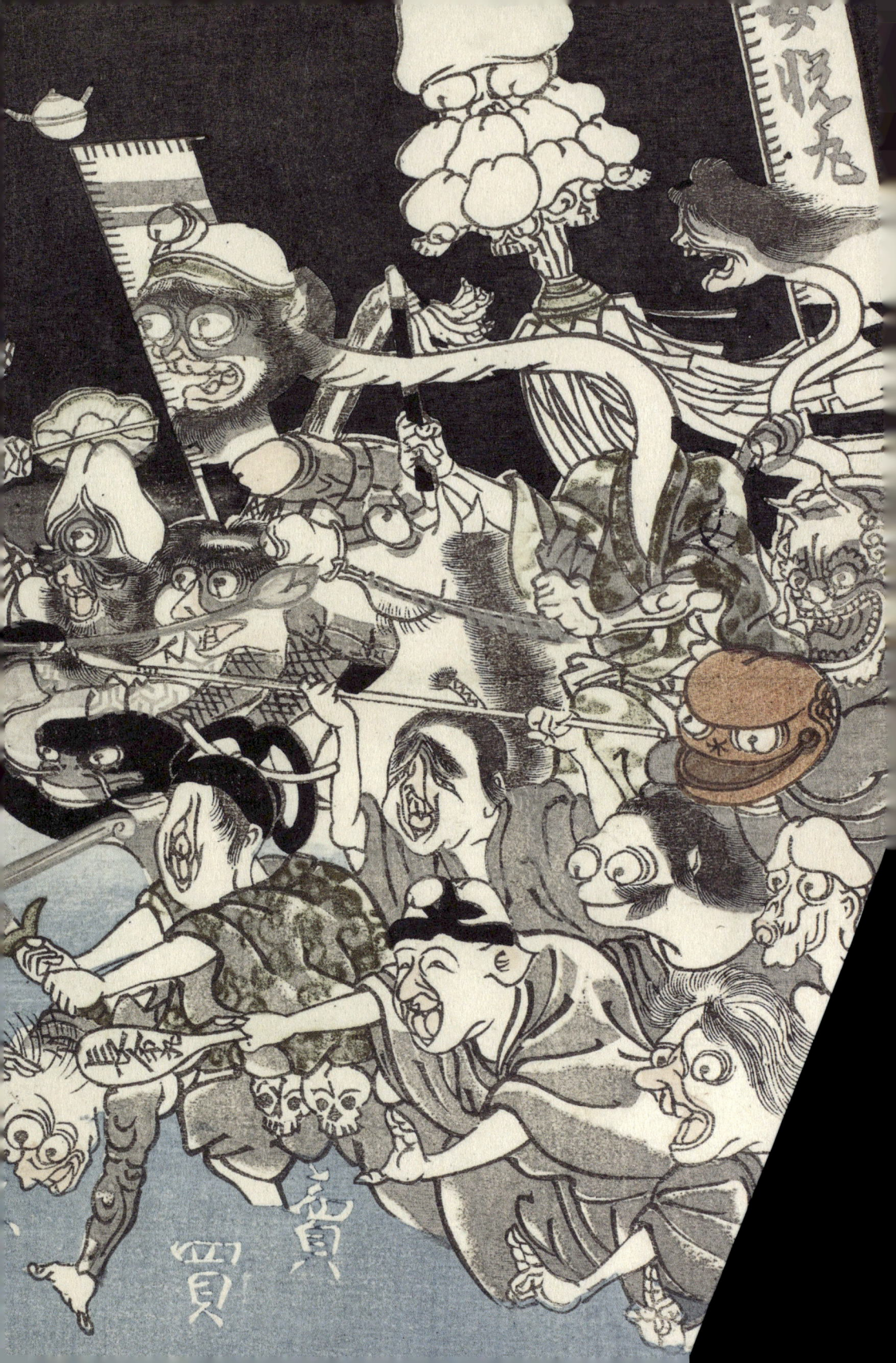

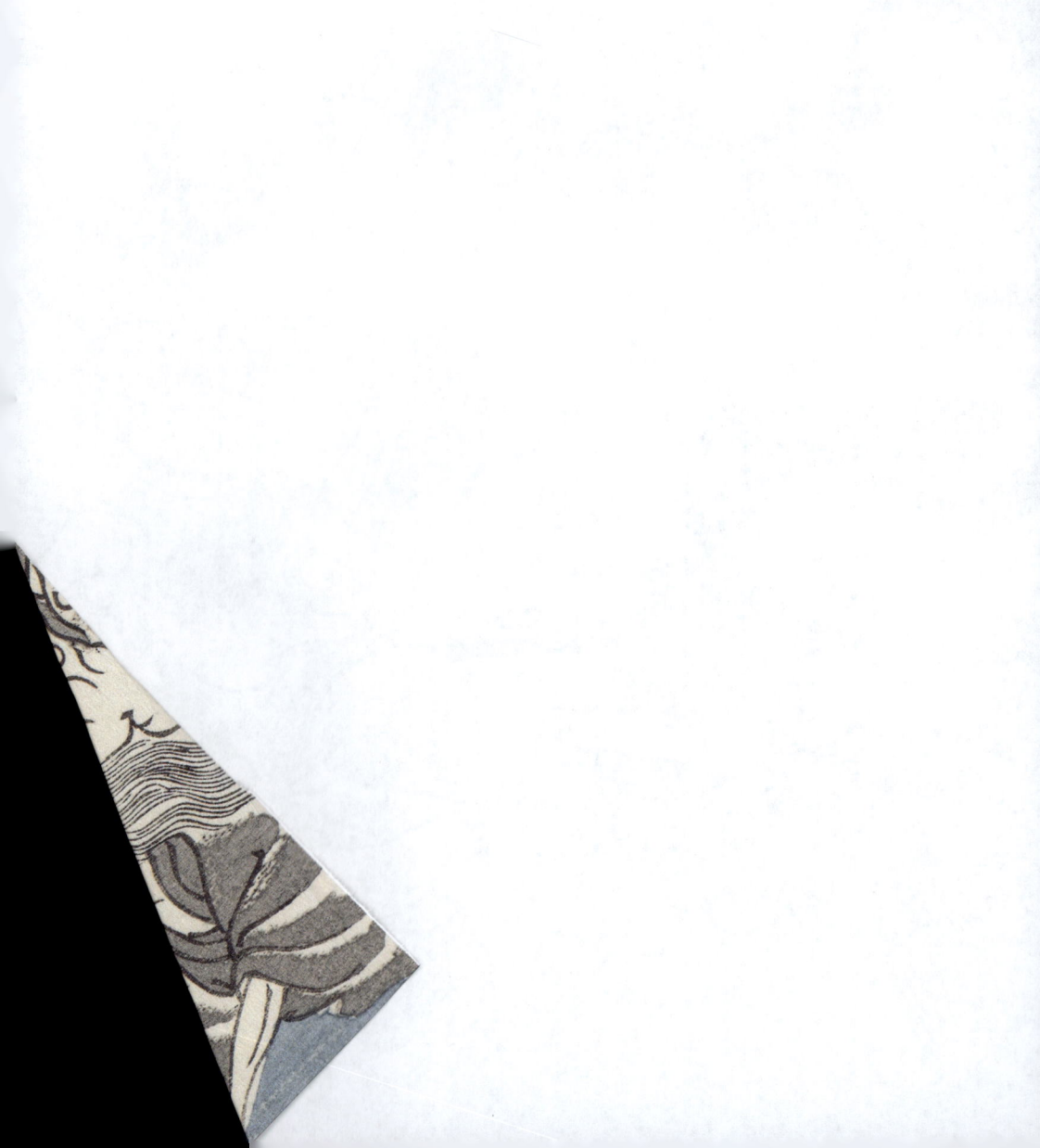

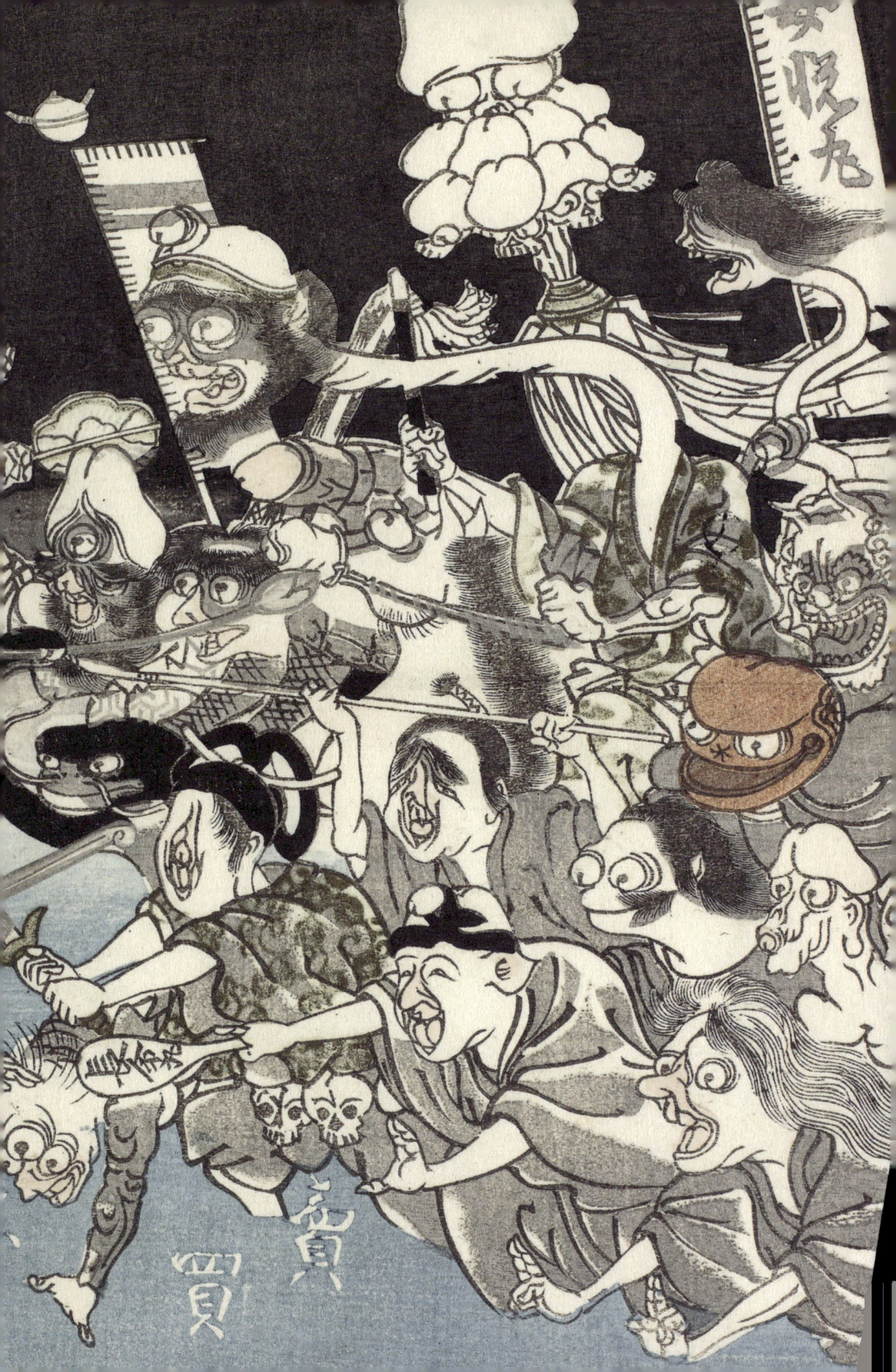

© Prestel Verlag, Munich · London · New York 2026
A member of Penguin Random House Verlagsgruppe GmbH
Neumarkter Strasse 28 · 81673 Munich

First edition 2026

produktsicherheit@penguinrandomhouse.de
(The above information is mandatory information according to GPSR and should be used for all queries relating to the safety of our books.)

Library of Congress Control Number: 2025944213
A CIP catalogue record for this book is available from the British Library.

First published in French as
Monstres Yokai
© Éditions Hazan, 2025

Editorial director Éditions Hazan: Jérôme Gille
Copy editor, image editor Éditions Hazan: Cloé de Lustrac
Graphic design: Paper! Tiger! (Aurélien Farina)
Editing and Proofreading Éditions Hazan: Katia de Azevedo
Production Éditions Hazan: Francis Verdelet, Justine Veillon

Translation from the French: David Wharry, Burzet
Copyediting: Patricia Newman, Berlin
Editorial direction: Barbara Delius, Berlin
Production management Prestel: Martina Effaga
Typesetting: Barbara Delius, Berlin
Separations: Hyphen-Group, Italy
Printing and binding: Toppan Leefung, China

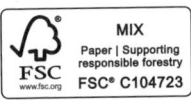

Penguin Random House Verlagsgruppe FSC® N001967

Printed in China

ISBN 978-3-7913-9422-0

www.prestel.com